INDIVIDUALIZING EDUCATIONAL MATERIALS FOR SPECIAL CHILDREN IN THE MAINSTREAM

INDIVIDUALIZING EDUCATIONAL MATERIALS FOR SPECIAL CHILDREN IN THE MAINSTREAM

Compiled and Edited by

Robert M. Anderson, Ed.D.

Professor
Special Education and Rehabilitation
Memphis State University
Memphis, Tennessee

John G. Greer, Ph.D.

Associate Professor
Special Education and Rehabilitation
Memphis State University
Memphis, Tennessee

and

Sara J. Odle, Ed.D.

Assistant Professor
Special Education and Rehabilitation
Memphis State University
Memphis, Tennessee

University Park Press
Baltimore

UNIVERSITY PARK PRESS
International Publishers in Science and Medicine
233 East Redwood Street
Baltimore, Maryland 21202

Typeset by American Graphic Arts Corporation
Manufactured in the United States of America by
The Maple Press Company.

Library of Congress Cataloging in Publication Data
Main entry under title:

Individualizing educational materials for special
children in the mainstream.

Bibliography: p.
Includes index.
1. Teaching—Kids and devices—Addresses, essays,
lectures.   2. Handicapped children—Education—
Addresses, essays, lectures.   I. Anderson, Robert M.
II. Greer, John G.   III. Odle, Sara J.

LB1043.152   371.9′043   78-4147
ISBN 0-8391-1253-X

25/2/79 Becker + Tyler   14.50

Contents

Contributors

Jo Allsop, M.Ed.
Curriculum Coordinator
Shrine School
Memphis City Schools

Janet W. Anderson, M.Ed.
Teacher
Farmington Elementary School
Germantown, Tennessee

Robert M. Anderson, Ed.D.
Professor
Special Education &
  Rehabilitation
Memphis State University
Memphis, Tennessee

Larry L. Chapman
Doctoral Student
Special Education &
  Rehabilitation
Memphis State University
Memphis, Tennessee

Irise M. Friedman
Instructor
Special Education &
  Rehabilitation
Memphis State University
Memphis, Tennessee

Bonnie B. Greer, Ph.D.
Associate Professor
Special Education &
  Rehabilitation
Memphis State University
Memphis, Tennessee

John G. Greer, Ph.D.
Associate Professor
Special Education &
  Rehabilitation
Memphis State University
Memphis, Tennessee

Virginia K. Laycock, Ed.D.
Assistant Professor
Elementary & Secondary
  Education
Clemson University
Clemson, South Carolina

Sara J. Odle, Ed.D.
Assistant Professor
Special Education &
  Rehabilitation
Memphis State University
Memphis, Tennessee

Krista S. Oglesby
Doctoral Student
Special Education &
  Rehabilitation
Memphis State University
Memphis, Tennessee

Dana P. Quertermous
Doctoral Student
Special Education &
  Rehabilitation
Memphis State University
Memphis, Tennessee

H. Lyndall Rich, Ph.D.
Associate Professor
Special Education &
  Rehabilitation
Memphis State University
Memphis, Tennessee

John W. Schifani, Ed.D.
Associate Professor
Special Education &
  Rehabilitation
Memphis State University
Memphis, Tennessee

Randall W. Spinney
Doctoral Student
Special Education &
  Rehabilitation
Memphis State University
Memphis, Tennessee

H. Lynn Springfield, Ed.D.
Associate Professor
Mid-America Nazarene College
Olathe, Kansas

Robert Sterrett, M.Ed.
Director, Mid-South Regional
  Resource Center
Department of Special Education
University of Kentucky
Lexington, Kentucky

Patricia L. Walls
Doctoral Student
Special Education &
   Rehabilitation
Memphis State University
Memphis, Tennessee

Barbara Zia
Doctoral Student
Special Education &
   Rehabilitation
Memphis State University
Memphis, Tennessee

Preface

Individualized instruction is no longer a catch-word among public school teachers. It is now an educational necessity. Vast changes have swept the American school system in recent years, and the age old patterns of instruction are now gravely inadequate. Faced with increasingly heterogeneous student populations, regular class teachers can no longer depend on the programs for large group instruction that have traditionally been employed. Rather, they are now required to accommodate students with instructional needs not contained in the narrow confines of "average" performance. In the wake of numerous legal mandates, most classroom teachers are now involved in "mainstreaming," a term used to conceptualize the trend toward educating children with mild learning and behavioral problems in the regular curriculum. Already, large numbers of these youngsters have been relocated in regular classes and a well informed and demanding public is determined to see more effective and accountable instruction for every child.

To meet this challenge, teachers from every educational level must exploit all of the most recent advances in modern educational technology. There will be no simple solution, and a variety of innovative ideas, such as behavioral objectives, competency based instruction, nongraded schools, and paraprofessional involvement must be employed. To assist in this process, this book focuses in depth on one area of instructional technology that promises to play a key role in providing individual programs for each child: instructional materials. Based on the needs and demands of special education teachers, an impressive array of instructional materials has already been developed and extensively used. The critical need for individualized instruction has long been recognized by those responsible for meeting the divergent needs of handicapped learners, and the selection and use of effective materials has been central to programming efforts with this population.

Although the rationale for this book is predicted on the assumption that the technology for utilization of instructional materials currently exists, it seems clear that too often the delivery of service and sophistication in the use of the technology has not kept pace. It would be interesting, for example, to speculate about the number of undergraduate seniors now completing their degrees in teacher preparation programs who could demonstrate competency with the tasks suggested in this book. It might be even more enlightening, and perhaps disconcerting, to evaluate advanced graduate students with respect to these competencies. With the exception of students and teachers in close proximity to the university programs that are associated with the national network of Special Education Instructional Materials Centers and their satellites, our guess would be that only a small percentage of educators would be able to demonstrate competence in this area. We base this prediction on our previous experiences with college students and beginning teachers in a variety of settings. We suspect that even the most *experienced* teachers would also encounter some problems with this assignment.

This book, therefore, presents a framework for incorporating into education, both regular and special, a sequential program for the acquisition of a set of competencies related to the utilization of instructional materials. Emphasis is placed on providing increased knowledge and greater understanding of the rationale and procedures for selecting, retrieving, adapting, constructing, assessing, and evaluating materials. Practitioners should be familiar with terms such as "descriptors" and "individual prescription" and knowledgeable about techniques for matching instructional materials with specialized strategies and teaching units. Teachers should be skilled in the ability to relate instructional materials to behavioral objectives.

Most of the literature on instructional materials has been aimed at either a special education market or a regular education market. To our knowledge, no existing book on instructional materials has attempted to interrelate general and special education. In regular education, the focus of teacher preparation has been on training the teacher to work with groups of children. In contrast, the approach outlined in this book will assist all teachers in the utilization of instructional materials to meet the needs of individual children who have learning or behavioral problems. In our opinion, all children manifest school-relevant strengths and deficits. When the schools become more cognizant of and responsive to these differences in children, the artificial boundaries that sometimes separate "special" and "regular" education may begin to disappear.

This book has been organized as a textbook or reference for 1) advanced undergraduate and graduate students in regular and special education teacher preparation programs, and 2) supervisors and administrators responsible for designing programs that meet children's individual needs.

The book is divided into three major sections. The first, entitled "Using Educational Materials: A Systematic Approach," contains six chapters that examine the basic steps each educator must follow to ensure effective programming. Chapter 1 provides background information and a rationale for more innovative and effective utilization of instructional materials. Chapters 2 and 3 identify the important characteristics of the learner and of the materials that must be considered in the educational plan. Chapter 4 delineates the critical process of making an optimum match between the unique profile of each learner and appropriate instructional materials. Once this decision is made, the materials selected must be obtained, and Chapter 5 examines the numerous retrieval options that can be utilized by the teacher. Finally, Chapter 6 offers a practical approach to the evaluation of the materials ultimately used. Reliance on ongoing feedback is considered the only sure way to determine whether the instructional materials employed were resulting in desired student performance.

The second section, entitled "Using Educational Materials: Practical Considerations," contains numerous ideas and suggestions designed to further enhance the overall effectiveness of the model described in the first part of the book. Chapter 7, for example, describes and illustrates the various ways in which a teacher can adapt commercially available materials or, when necessary, construct materials to better suit the needs and interests of a youngster. Going one step further, Chapter 8 looks at the wide range of adaptations that have been or can be made to allow sensorially or physically handicapped children to benefit from available instructional materials. Chapter 9 summarizes the supplementary media resources now available to assist the teacher in individualizing instruction. The often overlooked relationships between instructional materials and the affective development of the students is the subject of Chapter 10, and suggestions for improvement in this area are included. Finally, Chapter 11 describes several approaches a teacher can use to encourage the active and eager involvement of the learner with the selected instructional materials programs. The use of educational games, peer assisted learning techniques, and increased participation of parents are highlighted.

The final section of the book is called "Using Educational Materials: Resources and References." Divided into three chapters, it examines other sources to which a teacher may turn for assistance in providing individualized instructional programming for special children in the mainstream. Chapter 12 describes the major information resources currently in existence and explains how they can be used. These include the Council for Exceptional Children (CEC) Information Service, Educational Resources Information Center (ERIC), and the National Center on Education Media and Materials for the Handicapped (NCEMMH). In Chapter 13, a bibliography of references that can serve as models for mainstreaming is provided. Although not an exhaustive list, those studies cited are replete with alternative strategies and innovative ideas developed by educators involved in this endeavor. Finally, after reviewing some of the most significant approaches to the development of prototypes of instructional materials for the handicapped learner, Chapter 14 presents an up-to-date bibliography of materials identified as valuable and effective by teachers who have used them in the classroom.

We would like to acknowledge, with special gratitude, the tolerant and dependable typing provided by Debbie Walker, Gail Davis, Linda Jones, and Robin Kennedy.

INDIVIDUALIZING EDUCATIONAL MATERIALS FOR SPECIAL CHILDREN IN THE MAINSTREAM

PART I
USING EDUCATIONAL MATERIALS
A Systematic Approach

Editorial Introduction

The first section of this book presents a comprehensive model for the selection, utilization, and evaluation of instructional materials. Recognizing the constraints and limitations within which most classroom teachers must operate, emphasis has been placed on procedures that are realistic in terms of required time and effort. Devoid of confusing terminology or complicated formulas, they assist the teacher in the careful yet practical examination of those factors that are critical to the effective utilization of materials.

The first of the following chapters included in this section provides a rationale for the model and, in fact, for the entire book. Because of recent developments in American education—including the practice of mainstreaming, increasing demands for accountability, and legislative action, teachers must identify better ways to provide the individualized instruction so desperately needed by handicapped youngsters. As this chapter points out, tremendous progress made over the past two decades in the area of educational materials has produced a rich new educational resource that will be a major factor in meeting the current challenge.

The next three chapters focus on the all-important process of identifying materials that are appropriate for each individual child. Chapter 3 examines the important characteristics of the learner that the teacher must consider. Likewise, Chapter 4 studies the critical dimensions of materials that must be taken into account. Making an optimum match between the two is the subject of Chapter 5. All of the required steps in this phase are clearly delineated and illustrated with examples.

Once this decision is made, the materials selected must be obtained, and Chapter 6 examines the numerous retrieval options that can be utilized by the teacher. A comprehensive, nationwide instructional materials network is currently being developed with the support of federal funding. Through both this and improved local sources, teachers can today locate and obtain more quality materials than ever before.

Finally, Chapter 7 presents a method for evaluating the effectiveness of the instructional materials ultimately used. The *Instructional Materials Profile* included in the chapter analyzes three important areas: physical characteristics, teacher concerns, and student achievement. The latter, i.e., whether or not the material facilitated student learning and resulted in demonstrable achievement, is considered the most critical in the final judgment.

2

Perspectives and Overview

Robert M. Anderson, Ed.D., John G. Greer, Ph.D., and Barbara Zia

Throughout the history of education in the United States, instructional materials have been employed by teachers to facilitate the learning on the part of students. Whether the materials consisted of a slate board and chalk, a book with printed words, or a chart displaying the alphabet, the function was basically the same—to more effectively enable students to achieve specific educational objectives. Although these early historical materials were supplemental to the direct instruction by the teacher, they did little to increase the effectiveness of instruction or learning. According to Cubberley (1919), "most of the time (in school) was wasted as a result of an almost complete lack of teaching equipment, books, and supplies, and of poor methods of teaching" (p. 35).

Cubberley's remarks were stimulated by several conditions that existed within education before the twentieth century. First, educational budgets were minimal and the excessive cost of materials prohibited their purchase for classroom use. Consequently, materials, except for a few textbooks, were limited to those that were basic to the educational program and that could be constructed within the classroom. Second, because of the time and expense involved, only those materials that could be shared and utilized by the entire classroom group were constructed. These group oriented materials typically consisted of printed information that promoted basic educational objectives pertaining to the "three R's." Third, the traditional didactic procedures did not permit students to use the material independent of the teacher. "Children came forward to the teacher's desk and recited individually to the master or dame, and so wasteful was the process that children might attend school for years and get only a mere start in reading and writing" (Cubberley, 1919, p. 37). Thus, the earlier historical use of materials presents a picture of infrequent and ineffective utilization, group orientation, and teaching limitations.

The first half of this century evidenced rudimentary changes in psychology, education, and technology that encouraged the development and use of individualized methods and materials. Evidence was collected and conceptualized, by such men as Binet, Thorndike, and Dewey, that clearly supported the fact that human organisms behaved and learned according to patterns unique to the individual. Consistent with this new ideological concept, specialized teacher colleges were founded throughout the country that advocated more progressive educational procedures. Technologically, the publication industry developed less expensive procedures for producing materials, particularly books and printed materials. However, corresponding with this rapid attitudinal and technological change toward individualization, greater numbers of students were beginning to pursue the route of formal education. Educators were inundated with masses of students with diverse characteristics, which delayed the needed implementation of individualized programs.

Today's educational programs contain remnants of the problems and conditions experienced throughout this historical movement toward the individualization of methods and materials. The failure to totally individualize programs for today's students is obviously attributable to innumerable causes, some of which remain unknown. However, there are a number of causes that seem to contribute significantly to the delayed implementation of full individualization: the lack of teacher knowledge regarding the availability, construction, and/or use of materials, the broad diversity of student needs and characteristics contained within each classroom, and the limited resources available to the teacher and students. In total, these three deterrents to the individualization of materials constitute a threat to the full educational advantages that should be expected for each student in the classroom.

FACTORS IN CHOOSING
OR ADAPTING INSTRUCTIONAL MATERIALS

Teacher Knowledge of Instructional Materials

The limited materials available during the educational experience of our parents and grandparents can no longer be used to justify the unavailability of materials today. Because of the needs and demands of special education teachers, an impressive array of instructional materials has already been produced and extensively used. Numerous commercial programs are currently available, designed to meet nearly every conceivable student need. Although some have major practical or conceptual weaknesses and others are virtually worthless, there are many that are truly outstanding. "For a few dollars per student, any one of several publishers will place in your hands a thoroughly impressive array of plans, procedures, materials, record forms, and most anything else you need for individualizing instruction in your classroom" (Charles, 1976, p. 179).

The current proliferation of instructional materials can be a great aid to the regular classroom teacher. When the quality of commercial materials is high and the design is appropriate, much valuable teacher time ordinarily spent in material preparation can be directed to other productive areas. However, the teacher's role in evaluation, selection, and application of materials is a difficult one, and if programming and instruction are to be effective, competencies in this area must be developed.

Often, however, the materials available do not meet the specific needs of a student. Therefore, it is necessary for the teacher to adjust instructional approaches or to adapt instructional materials. The skill to do so depends on being familiar with a variety of materials from many sources. Moran (1975) describes the procedure this way: "Just as an automobile mechanic might 'cannibalize' several cars to find parts to repair one automobile, so the teacher must take apart published materials to find appropriate parts to repair skills deficits" (p. 12).

The opportunities afforded the teacher in recent years by the advances of education research and technology are enormous. These advances have created a need among teachers for increased knowledge and greater understanding of the rationale and procedures for selecting, retrieving, adapting, constructing, and assessing the materials being marketed. This book presents a framework for incorporating into both regular and special education a sequential program for the acquisition of a set of competencies related to the utilization of instructional materials. This cluster of competencies is sometimes included in curricula to prepare teachers of the handicapped, but is seldom made available to regular classroom teachers in general education.

Diversity of Students

Because today's education programs are encountering a wide variety of student skills, attitudes, and characteristics, educators can no longer rely on the traditional selection and implementation of materials. Whereas large group instruction, covering the same textbook and at the same rate, may have been commonplace in the past, today's diversity among students must be reflected in the selection and use of materials.

The introduction of special children to the regular classroom has accentuated this diversity among students. Children with different problems, functioning on different levels, and using different learning styles are being placed into classrooms that already represent a variety of individual student needs and characteristics. Special children may have problems with visual perception, auditory discrimination, or auditory memory that typically go unnoticed by the teacher, or, children may be confused by the small print, their comprehension may be poor, and they may be unable to work independently. In the midst of confusion and frustration, these children are labeled as failures very early in their education career. An innovative teacher holds the key to preventing this failure, and must find ways to supplement instruction with worksheets, games, puzzles, group activities, enrichment books, etc. that are individualized to the particular interest, style, modality, and objective of each child. In short, the teacher must be able to assess the needs and characteristics of each student and, based on knowledge of instructional materials, provide an appropriate match between the two—student and materials.

Dunn (1968) noted that the educator is becoming increasingly better prepared to deal with individual differences in children because of advances in instructional methodology and materials and the increased availability of hardware innovations, such as ETV and computerized teaching. Today's teacher who wants to individualize instruction for a particular child is assaulted from all directions by a plethora of commercially prepared instructional materials. The critical need for individualized instruction has long been recognized by those responsible for meeting the divergent needs of handicapped learners, and the selection and use of effective materials has been central to programming efforts with this population.

Resources Available to the Classroom Teacher

Obviously, classroom teachers require an array of physical, professional, and personal resources if the classroom program is to be effectively individualized. Without the necessary training, money, consultation, and time, the typical classroom will result in yet another class in which the "book" becomes the fountainhead from which instruction flows impartially to all students, regardless of individual differences. The responsibilities for providing the necessary resources are primarily shared by the teacher training institutions, the school and school system, and the teachers themselves.

Teacher training programs, which have the responsibility for developing instructional skills among prospective teachers, have placed a low priority on competencies in the areas of special needs, individualization, and the utilization of materials. Although most college and university faculty verbally espouse such competencies, they continue to teach using the traditional lecture-book approach, which does not provide graduates with the skills necessary to implement individualized instruction, diagnostic/prescriptive teaching, behavior management techniques, and other innovative practices. Fortunately, growing criticism of this contradiction in practice has caused a movement toward improving the quality of teacher training programs. Preparation programs, like the personnel they train, are beginning to be held accountable for the methods and the products they produce—hence, the trend toward competency based teacher education and certification.

Within the school and school system, teachers frequently do not receive the necessary materials and services from administrative and professional personnel. Although some schools are providing reasonable assistance in the form of consulting teachers, supplemental materials and equipment, and planning time, the lack of such assistance is more typically the case. Consulting and supervisory services are infinitely delayed, money for supplies and materials is limited, routine and noneducational responsiblities are numerous, and time to develop individualized programs is nonexistent. However, because of the increasing public awareness of the special child, the federal government and many states have passed legislation that provides for the training of specialized personnel, additional training for regular class teachers, and the purchase of specialized materials and equipment, and "excessive costs" that are to be used to provide the resources for the special child in the regular classroom. State and federal funds have already been used to develop and implement a comprehensive, nationwide materials network. Thus, it is becoming far easier and more feasible to obtain existing materials. For the past several years, the Area Learning Resource Centers, Specialized Offices, and the National Center on Educational Media and Materials for the Handicapped (NCEMMH) have provided a wide range of services designed to assist teachers in the evaluation, selection, retrieval, and utilization of high quality materials for the handicapped. Although these agencies have now terminated their contracts with the Bureau of Education for the Handicapped, some of their programs will be continued through new contracts.

The Necessity for Individualized Instruction

Just a few years ago, the approach outlined in this book might have been considered premature or impractical. Faced with large classes and little assistance, most teachers would have been quick to point out how costly, both in time and in money, it is to actually individualize instruction through a wide variety of instructional materials. Although some of the deterrents to individualization remain, much has transpired in the last few years. Vast changes have swept the American school system so that today, the effective use of instructional materials is both more necessary and more possible than ever before.

Individualized instruction is no longer a catch-word among teachers, but an educational necessity. Faced with increasingly heterogeneous student populations, regular class teachers can no longer depend on the approaches to large group instruction that have traditionally been employed. Rather, they are now required to accommodate students with instructional needs outside of the narrow confines of "average" performance. In the wake of numerous legal mandates, most classroom teachers are now involved in "mainstreaming," a term used to conceptualize the trend toward educating children with mild learning and behavioral problems in the regular curriculum. As early as 1971, the acting Associate Commissioner for Educational Personnel Development, U.S. Office of Education, stated that "the regular classroom teacher must assume a new role; this new role will require that the regular class teacher become, with appropriate supportive services, a diagnostician and an educational strategist rather than a mass remediator" (Smith, 1971). Large numbers of handicapped youngsters have already been relocated in regular classes, and a well-informed and demanding public is determined to see more effective and accountable instruction for every child.

These factors represent, in essence, the rationale for this book. Each, therefore, is discussed in detail below. Taken together, they offer a persuasive argument for change.

MORE EFFECTIVE USE
OF INSTRUCTIONAL MATERIALS: A NECESSITY

The obvious need for more sophisticated teacher utilization of instructional materials for children with educational handicaps has been dramatized by two recent trends, mainstreaming and educational accountability. Both of these trends have been reinforced by the passage of Public Law 94-142, which underlines the importance of individualized instruction.

Although this section deals specifically with legal and policy mandates that require greater individualization, the primary concern of teachers, parents, and citizens in a democracy is to maximize human potential. Certainly we are aware of the great waste of human resources that accompanies failure, truancy, disruptions, and general nonlearning classroom situations. Therefore, it is assumed that the need for individualization is basic to the American educational system and that the necessities identified in this section will simply provide the impetus to better fulfill that basic educational philosophy.

Mainstreaming

Mainstreaming is a programming development that has been widely implemented in public schools in the 1970s. As the term implies, it refers to the placement of handicapped children into regular education, or the "mainstream" of public school programs. It is a radical departure from the historical pattern of special education in the United States, and by its definition alone it has profound implications for regular as well as special education. Already, a high proportion of handicapped children from the disability areas of the educable retarded, emotionally disturbed, learning disabled, learning impaired, visually handicapped, and physically handicapped are educated in the regular classroom.

The reasons for mainstreaming are varied and complex. One of the most important factors, which has been repeatedly cited, involves the questionable efficacy of conventional services for handicapped learners. Special education came into existence to serve the child who deviated from the regular class population—whose needs were not adquately met in the regular class, who could not achieve maximum development under ordinary class procedures, or whose inclusion in the regular school program required an alteration of the learning environment. Special self-contained classes were organized in school systems throughout the country. A number of developments in recent years caused the provision of services to the handicapped to come under attack, however. It was asserted that special education had become the "depository" for the problem students with whom education generalists did not want to bother. The results of efficacy studies conducted in the 1960s brought homogeneous grouping of mildly handicapped children into question. General results indicate that the advantages of placing mildly handicapped students in special classes are indeterminate. In fact, some studies show that higher functioning mentally retarded children (75–85 IQ) who are placed in regular classes are equal to or superior in educational achievement to similar children placed in special classes (Goldstein, Moss, and Jordan, 1975).

Considerable criticism has also focused on the labeling of special education students as disabled, mentally retarded, disturbed, slow, etc. A consequence of traditional diagnostic procedures, it has been assailed because it often creates a self-fulfilling prophecy of failure for those so labeled. It lowers the "special" students in the esteem of their peers, and it reduces teacher expectations for these students. The effects of teacher expectations on student performance have been studied, and the results suggest a detrimental effect when students are labeled "slow" (Beez, 1968; Rosenthal and Jacobson, 1968). Lowered self-perceptions for the students can also result. It is believed that mainstreaming will serve to minimize this problem. Welch (1967) studied the effects of placing mentally retarded children in part-time special classes (one-half day in regular classes) and self-contained special classes. She compared the self-derogation and academic achievement of both groups and found that the children in the integrated setting made higher achievement scores and decreased in self-derogation.

A third factor contributing to the breakup of self-contained classrooms in recent years has been the volume and quality of legal action. Parents and others concerned with more adequate programming for handicapped youngsters have gone to court, challenging traditional approaches on numerous counts. For example, the fairness and accuracy of assessment procedures have been questioned. Cruickshank (1972) reported that 73% of the students in one elementary school in a large city were classified as learning disabled after being administered group tests. Such tests are subject to error, are too general for meaningful educational planning, and are known to systematically discriminate against children from culturally different backgrounds. Other issues examined in the courts include the quality of special education programs and their appropriateness for the needs of certain children, the frequent inability of children to return to the regular classroom once placed in the special education "track," the failure to give parents the opportunity to participate in placement decisions, and the overbalance of minority group children in special classes.

A change in conventional programming for handicapped learners was obviously necessary, and the concept of mainstreaming has been widely recognized as a promising alternative. Nevertheless, it will require patient planning and cooperation by all public educators. The National Education Association asserted that it would support mainstreaming handicapped children only when:

> It provides a favorable learning experience both for handicapped and
> regular students.

Regular and special educators and administrators share equally in its planning and implementation.

Regular and special teachers are prepared for these roles.

Appropriate instructional materials, supportive services, and pupil personnel services are provided for the teacher and the handicapped student.

Modifications are made in class size, scheduling, and curriculum design to accommodate the shifting demands that mainstreaming demands.

There is a systematic evaluation and reporting of program developments.

Adequate additional funding and resources are provided for mainstreaming and are used exclusively for that purpose (*Today's Education*, 1976, p. 19).

As a result of the practice of mainstreaming, teachers who have not had professional training and experience in dealing with children who have learning problems are being asked more frequently to work with these children. Clearly, they will need a wide variety of supporting services and much assistance from other professionals. Whatever the educational alternative selected in the mainstreaming situation, the regular and special educators must be in close communication, working together to provide effective individualized programs for all children.

Accountability

Accountability refers to the current trend in education to hold teachers, administrators, and school boards responsible for producing demonstrable learning in students. The practice of being held accountable for results or the lack thereof has long been common in the private business sector of our society; promotions, salary increases, and terminations are characteristically based on the "bottom line" feature of one's performance. However, as noted by Ryan and Cooper:

The whole notion of accountability is a radical reversal of the traditional view of education. Education has tended to be concerned with the "inputs" of the system—instructional materials, teachers' training, new buildings—while accountability is concerned with the "output"—student learning. No matter how good the inputs, if there is no output of student learning the schools have failed. In other words, it's not how you play the game but whether you win or lose (1972, p. 458).

Accountability was first formally associated with education by Leon Lessinger (1971), Deputy Commissioner of the Office of Education, when he communicated to Congress that systematic evaluation of the cost effectiveness of federal programs would be made. Since then, accountability has become one of the most easily identified features of education in the 1970s.

One widely used implementation of the accountability concept is performance contracting. A commercial company is paid to raise achievement levels of students, usually in easily assessed skill areas such as reading or math. The amount paid to the contracting company is determined on the basis of student achievement as measured by standardized tests. The success of this strategy is to this date equivocal, becuase achievement test scores do not necessarily indicate long-term learning, and some reported successes actually involved fraud on the part of the contracting companies who pretaught answers to test items.

Another strategy being employed is the *voucher system,* recommended by Jencks (1970) to encourage private initiative in educating the poor. He proposed the provison of tuition grants or vouchers to parents who then decide which of several educational alternatives they prefer. The voucher is presented to a participating school—public, private, or parochial—that in turn redeems the voucher in cash from the local government. Parents are thus enabled to "shop around" for the best services for their children and to transfer them to another school if they are dissatisfied. Schools are made directly accountable to the parents of the children who attend them.

Although accountability is an intellectually agreeable concept, it is difficult to implement. Agreement must be reached on the objectives—cognitive, affective, motor—for which schools are accountable (Cook, 1972). Learnings such as belief in the democratic system, honesty, ability to interact socially, and opposition to drug use are all responsibilities of the schools. However, not much progress has been made in development of measures in the affective domain. Also, there is a dearth of valid and reliable psychometric instruments with which to measure other aspects of student achievement. Many accountability programs are conventional norm-referenced (standardized) tests and measures in which each student is evaluated according to what others are doing. This approach makes individual prediction difficult. In addition, many students do poorly on standardized tests because of the students' lack of test "sophistication" or the tests' difficult formats. It has been strongly argued that the use of criterion-referenced measures (communicating just what the student can or cannot do) is preferable to standardized tests in accountability plans.

Accountability poses a challenge from the paying public to the educational professionals at whom it is directed. When correctly implemented, it can be an effective means for improving student learning by providing inpetus to discard outmoded instructional methods and adopt new input approaches.

Public Law 94-142

The Education for All Handicapped Children Act (PL 94-142) has been acclaimed as "one of the most significant milestones in the history of American education" (Torres, 1977, p. 1). In essence, Public Law 94-142 states that all handicapped children will be provided a free and appropriate education. Although the law is a complex assortment of labels and definitions because of process procedures and cost reimbursement formulas, the critical features that have direct implications for regular class teachers are the provisons for "individual educational programs" within "the least restrictive environment."

Historically, handicapped children have been assigned to special classes, committed to institutions, or excluded from all educational services. Within the decade of the 1970s, education delivery models such as the "resource room" and "itinerant teacher" emerged as programmatic options to the exclusion of handicapped students from the mainstream of education. It should be noted that "mainstreaming" and "least restrictive environment" are not synonymous concepts. Whereas mainstreaming does involve the placement of handicapped children in the regular classroom, least restrictive environment includes an array of possible assignments, ranging from the regular class through institutional placement. Although mildly handicapped students may be placed in the regular classroom (mainstreamed), the least restrictive environment for students with more severe problems may be a special class or even an institutional placement.

A more direct relationship between Public Law 94-142 and individualized materials is included in the legal specifications for an "individual educational program" (IEP). Specifically, the Act states that:

> A written statement for each handicapped child developed in any meeting by a representative of the local educational agency or an intermediate educational unit who shall be qualified to provide, or supervise the provision of, specially designed instruction to meet the unique needs of handicapped children, the teacher, the parents or guardians of such child, and, whenever appropriate, such child, which statement shall include (A) a statement of the present levels of educational performance of such child, (B) a statement of annual goals, including short-term instructional objectives, (C) a statement of the specific educational services to be provided to such child, and the extent to which such child will be able to participate in regular educational programs, (D) the

projected date for initiation and anticipated duration of such services, and appropriate objective criteria and evaluation procedures and schedules for determining, on at least an annual basis, whether instructional objectives are being achieved (Public Law 94-142, 1975, Section 4, a, 19).

Thus, an IEP has specific conditions that are applicable to instructional materials. Because the educational services must be individualized to the unique needs of the special student, it therefore follows that materials and methods must be individualized to the extent necessary to accommodate the students' level of educational performance and achievement of educational objectives. In short, instructional procedures, including methods and materials, that are uniformly and unilaterally applied to the classroom group, will not be acceptable in terms of the legal requirements. However, the entire educational experience need not be individualized; only the behaviors and/or skills in which the student has identified deficits are included within the context of IEPs.

The programmatic provisions of Public Law 94-142 have been presented in order to dramatize the increasing urgency for the development and implementation of individualized materials for the special student in the regular classroom.

MORE EFFECTIVE USE OF INSTRUCTIONAL MATERIALS: A POSSIBILITY

The need for this book is predicated on the assumption that the technology for the utilization of instructional materials currently exists. Fortunately, for educators, the present demand for more effective teaching strategies is matched by a much higher level of educational sophistication. Developments in various areas of American education are having a ripple effect that is being felt in virtually every classroom. In and of themselves, advances in individually prescribed instruction, criterion-referenced measurement, open education, learning center concepts, paraprofessional utilization, and instructional media and technology have resulted in more beneficial and efficient instruction. At the same time, as can be seen in the following description of these developments, they provide an educational environment that is, more than ever before, conducive to an innovative and imaginative use of instructional materials.

Individually Prescribed Instruction (IPI)

Among the strategies being implemented today to meet the unique needs of students is Individually Prescribed Instruction (IPI). This approach was developed by educational technologists at the Learning Research and Development Center, University of Pittsburgh, as a model seeking to operationalize the goal of individualized education to meet the needs of each student. In 1970, it was estimated that IPI was being used in programs involving 47,000 students (*Phi Delta Kappan,* 1970), and by 1973 the number being served would increase to approximately 100,000 (Scanlon, 1972).

In an IPI setting, the educational environment is structured to accomodate differences among individuals. Several features are always present. Instructional goals are expressed in terms of behavioral objectives that provide measureable products. Assessment is conducted on each child entering the instructional situation to determine where the child is on the learning continuum of each skill area, aptitudes, perceptual-motor capabilities, and the learning styles most appropriate. When this detailed diagnosis is completed, instructional procedures are selected for the child. (Often the child is allowed some decision in selecting his preferences among alternative procedures.)

A plethora of sequentially-ordered materials, varied to accommodate interindividual differences among students, has been developed by IPI. These include tape and disc recordings, programmed materials, individualized reading materials, manipulative devices, and computer assisted instruction. The IPI program contains materials to cover the curriculum areas of math, reading, spelling, science, and social education. The last area is designed to develop a healthy self-image, self-realization, independence, successful interpersonal relations, and skills in dealing with the environment.

It is possible to implement IPI in a self-contained classroom situation or in less formal arrangement, where the students move from one learning center to another. Most materials are self-instructional. The teacher spends very little time in group instruction, and instead gives much attention to diagnosing where the child is on the learning continuum in relation to where he needs to be, and prepares prescriptions to move the child toward the mastery goal. Paraprofessionals are an integral part of the IPI program; they are charged with record keeping, test scoring, and organizing materials.

Evaluation is ongoing. After the placement tests, pretests are conducted at the beginning of each unit to determine at which point in the unit the child should start. Posttests at the completion of units indicate whether the child has mastered the instruction that was prescribed. Curriculum-embedded tests, in the form of short daily checks, are included within the materials to monitor the child's progress.

An important component of IPI is the retraining of administrators and teachers involved in IPI programs in order to ensure: 1) their commitment to and understanding of the system, 2) that they can assume the roles required of them (for example, more flexible scheduling, intrastaff communication), and 3) their participation in the data network and feedback system that monitor the program nationwide and permit IPI to continuously improve its services (Scanlon, 1972).

In research studies comparing the performances of IPI schools with those of control schools, the results have been impressive. IPI students do as well or better on standardized achievement tests than non-IPI students (*Progress Report II: IPI*, 1971). The program produces best results when it is used with disadvantaged, rural, Chicano, Indian, and special education students (Scanlon and Brown, 1971). IPI pupils and teachers are very enthusiastic about school. IPI data reports the students to be more highly motivated, self-directed, and independent than their non-IPI counterparts (Rookey and Valdes, 1972).

Project PLAN A number of similar programs have been developed, and are scattered around the country. One of these is Project PLAN (Flanagan, 1967), which departs from the IPI model in that it is a computer-managed instructional approach, with the computer serving an administrative function—keeping scores and performance files and making recommendations for future unit assignments. It was developed by the American Institute for Research and the Westinghouse Learning Corporation. Under Project PLAN, the student, with teacher's counsel, selects his own educational objectives from a programmed set of behavioral objectives at the beginning of the school year. The objectives are grouped into modules that require about two weeks to complete. The student is also permitted to select the instructional method he feels is suited to his own particular learning style. Thus far, studies indicate that the PLAN system has been quite successful.

IGE Approach Individually Guided Education (IGE) is another widely used approach to individualizing instruction. Developed at the University of Wisconsin, IGE departs from IPI and Project PLAN in that it requires the school organization to be restructured to create units of teachers who instruct different aged pools of students. The multi-unit organizational structure includes the principal, unit leader (lead teacher), other teachers, teacher aides, secretary, and interns. Individualized programs are devised for each student. The program accommodates each pupil's educational needs, motivation level, best learning style, and learning rate. Pupil characteristics are taken into consideration when instructional models and materials are selected. Measurement and evaluation are ongoing. Parental support is considered important for reinforcing the students and, for this reason, close home-school communication is maintained. Instructional materials have been developed at the elementary level in the areas of reading, math, and motivational procedures. Schools can utilize as many areas of IGE curricula as suit their needs and resources. Field tests of IGE curricula have indicated they result in high achievement and are adopted enthusiastically by both students and teachers (Ironside, 1972).

Proliferation and expansion of programs like IPI, PLAN, and IGE will be common in the years ahead. Among the features of these systems will be instructional methods, criterion-referenced testing, self-instructional materials, provisions for self-direction, and self-evaluation.

Criterion-Referenced Measurement

The procedure of criterion-referenced testing has recently become widely discussed and utilized in the field of education. Criterion-referenced measurement provides the teacher with information concerning what specific skills a student has or does not have. If each skill consists of a continuum of subskills, the teacher can easily determine where the student is on the learning continuum by evaluating him to see which of the subskills are actually in the student's repertoire. Criterion-referenced measures answer such questions as: "Can Tom spell 'separate'?" or "Can Sue compute addition problems when she has to carry to the ten's place?" For example, if the task for the child is to learn to read and he is unable to associate sound to the symbols used in reading, the teacher knows he has to first teach symbol-sound relationships (and probably other subskills as well) before the child is able to decide "Nat sat on a mat."

According to Glaser (1971):

> Underlying the concept of achievement measurement is the notion of a continuum of knowledge acquisition ranging from no proficiency at all to perfect performance . . . The degree to which his (the individual's) achievement resembles desired performance at any level is assessed by criterion-referenced measures of achievement or proficiency (p. 7).

Criterion-referenced measurement thus evaluates the individual's performance while providing the teacher with a diagnosis and perscription for subsequent instruction. It also provides the teacher with an evaluation of the effectiveness of his instruction. The student and/or the teacher receive immediate feedback regarding perform-ance on a particular learning task (Block, 1971).

Criterion-referenced measurement is usually contrasted with norm-referenced measurement, which provides information concern-ing the learner's performance as compared with the performance of other students on the same measure. The most commonly employed norm-referenced measurement is the standardized achievement test. One of the weaknesses of the latter is that it communicates little about an individual's actual skills and performance levels (Jones, 1973). It answers the questions: "How much has Joe's reading improved since September?" or "Is Mary's math achievement at, above, or below that of a representative sampling of students her age, grade, sex, state, or region?"

The concept of criterion-referenced measurement has received both criticism and praise. Critics assert that good criterion-referenced measures are not available, and others reject the basic hypothesis of criterion-referenced testing on the basis that mastery is a reasonable criterion for all learning. There is also the contention that some of the learnings teachers wish to impart to their students are not definable in terms of instructional objectives (Ebel, 1971). Nevertheless, criterion-referenced measurement has been praised by many because it offers the educator a valuable tool with which to obtain meaningful and reliable information so critically needed in the process of implementing individualized instruction.

Open Education

Traditionally, the classroom teacher has had the exclusive responsi-bility for individualizing instructional materials. Such a responsi-bility implies that teachers possess a considerable amount of instructional decision-making power, and that the decisions are reasonably accurate and appropriate for each student. Unques-tionably, teachers have been ascribed the power to make instruc-tional decisions within curricular and policy guidelines but the accuracy and appropriateness of such decisions have met with less than total success. The success limitations of this traditional approach revolve around the absolute teacher control of group oriented materials, which do not consider individual student charac-teristics nor permit the pursuit of student objectives independent of the teacher.

Certainly, for many exceptional children in the regular class-room, these teacher role expectations for determining the use of materials are not only required, but are also desirable. However, in many cases, the responsibility for individualizing materials should not be limited to the teacher; it is a responsibility that should be shared with the students. This shared teacher-learner responsibility typically occurs within educational environments that have curricular and physical flexibility (Gump, 1974). This flexible teacher-learner arrangement is called "open education."

Although definitions of open education may vary, three general principles provide the basic foundation for this learning concept: 1) children learn at different rates and in different ways, 2) children should have direct experience with a rich and stimulating environment, and 3) children learn best in a self-directed environment that fosters interaction (Weber, 1971). In practice, the open education classroom abandons the traditional rows of desks in favor of furniture that can be arranged into a variety of individual and small group arrangements. Learning resources, including materials and equipment, are distributed throughout the open classroom, providing challenging opportunities for students to engage in learning activities. Although total group instruction is rare, small group interaction among peers and between teacher and students provides valuable group learning experiences. The atmosphere in the open classroom is positive and informal, with teacher and students freely choosing activities that will enable them to achieve their individual objectives.

The concept of open education as a possibility for individualizing materials should be considered in light of the teacher's responsibility and role behavior, which are highly critical and demanding. The teacher must provide numerous materials suitable for a wide variety of interests and abilities. The availability of materials is central to the effective operation of the open classroom. Individualization of materials occurs as a function of student initiative, rather than teacher prescription. In short, teachers "function as organizers of the learning resources (materials, adults, and other children), making such resources known and available to the children" (Knoblock, 1973, p. 361). The open classroom teachers must be facilitators who enable students to learn what they are interested in learning, rather than what they are expected to learn (Kohl, 1969).

As a precautionary note, not all teachers nor all students will function equally well in an open classroom. Personal needs for structure, order, or consistency may require that the open education philosophy be introduced gradually, or limited to specified time periods, activities, or students. Regardless of the scheduling sequence, open education does provide an option to the individualization of materials for special children in the regular classroom. "Students don't just fool around—not when very interesting activities and materials sit before them. In fact, many teachers find their students work harder, with more interest and less disruption, than ever before" (Charles, 1976, p. 126).

Learning Centers

A learning center is a designated area of the classroom that contains activities and materials pertaining to a specific skill or an area of study. The concept of a learning center is certainly not new, and has been incorporated within many regular classrooms for years. Learning centers vary from elaborate designs containing numerous materials, equipment, and activities, to simplistic centers with a table and a limited number of books.

Within special education, Hewett (1968) developed a classroom model with specialized learning centers that individually focused on educational tasks such as order, communication, and sensory exploration. Adaptations of Hewett's approach have been implemented within special education for a variety of educational objectives, including perceptual task, auditory discrimination, and motor manipulation (Kokaska and Kokaska, 1971).

Movement to centers by children varies from class to class—some are scheduled by the teachers because of skill deficits or student interests, some are used on a rotating or time allocation basis, and some are used on an open and spontaneous basis determined by the individual student.

Learning centers should not be considered a classroom "extra," but should be developed in detail as an integral part of the classroom learning experience. Obviously, the objective and function of a learning center are determined by the type of materials and activities that are contained within the center. Although "free time" areas are an important part of the classroom, learning centers should be designed to assist students in the development of specific skills and/or academic competence.

The significance of a well planned learning center is emphasized by Charles (1976), who has identified 14 components of a center:

1. Introduction (. . . tells what can be done in the center).
2. Specific objectives.
3. Directions for using the center.
4. Reminders (. . . to help students keep different possibilities in mind).
5. Slide viewing area.
6. Photographs.
7. Resouce books.
8. Student reports (. . . a sampling of work done by previous students).

9. Informative papers (. . . short, concise material that explains a particular topic).
10. Scheduling device.
11. Record keeping device (. . . who did what, along with indications of success, failure . . .).
12. Task cards (. . . assigned work).
13. Receptacle for student work.
14. Odds and ends (. . . ideas, suggestions, and pointers . . .) (pp. 135-139).

The range of possible learning centers is indeterminate; space restriction is the most limiting factor. Some schools with decreasing enrollments have converted entire classrooms into specialized math, reading, or science centers. School libraries have similarly developed centers that emphasize aspects of reading and literature. Regardless of the area or objective, learning centers are a vehicle for individualizing materials for the special student in the regular classroom.

Paraprofessionals

The use of paraprofessionals or teacher aides has been a commonly accepted practice in special education programs for several decades (Cruickshank and Haring, 1957). More recently, there has been a trend toward the use of paraprofessionals (e.g., teacher aides, teaching assistants, and volunteer workers) within the regular classroom. The paraprofessional concept has been generally adopted because of the instructional and economic advantages evidenced as a result of the accountability and mainstreaming movements.

Willems et al. (1975) delineated several advantages that explain the current increased utilization of teacher aides. First, the use of aides helps reduce the number of nonprofessional tasks required of teachers. Second, paraprofessionals can lead to greater individualization of instruction by providing teachers with more time and students with more attention. Third, the implementation of instructional techniques such as ungraded classrooms, multimedia instruction and team teaching will be facilitated. Fourth, students will be provided with additional appropriate adult models.

It is generally agreed that because the teacher is a trained, skilled professional, instructional time is too valuable to be spent performing tasks that might as well be handled by noncertificated personnel. Typical demands for the teacher's time include record keeping, preparing materials, supervising the children at rest and play, and monitoring student work. Esbensen (1966) states that the prime role of the effective teacher is to make decisions regarding what is to be taught, instructional methods to be utilized, and the structuring of the learning environment. Aside from the responsibilities that require professional teacher training, an aide can function as an adjunct to the teaching process. An aide can listen to the children read, guide the children in working with assignments, help locate materials, and in general take a more active role in the instructional process. Blessing (1967) refers to the function of an aide as being that of a parent surrogate. The aide functions as the parent does at home—listening, reading, explaining, clarifying, encouraging.

Schools without sufficient economic resources to employ paraprofessionals can initiate a campaign to enlist the assistance of volunteers. Parents, homemakers, semi-retired individuals, and concerned citizens can serve effectively under the direction of the teacher. Some school systems have additionally adopted a cross-age tutoring program with high school honors and pre-teacher students serving in the capacity of elementary teaching assistants.

Obviously, one teacher in a classroom with 30 children is limited in the amount of individualization that can be accomplished. The possibilities suggested in this section and in the remainder of the book will certainly provide assistance and direction toward individualization. However, the more resources available to the classroom teacher, including paraprofessionals, the greater the opportunity for providing individualized instruction.

Advances in Educational Media and Technology

In recent years, the progress made in the area of educational media and technology has been tremendous. The effective utilization of these now abundant resources is, in fact, the purpose of this book. Therefore, there is in this chapter no need to describe in detail the many advances that have taken place. They will be discussed extensionally in subsequent chapters, with numerous practical strategies designed to help teachers and students enjoy the benefits they promise to provide. The following brief summary, however, clearly illustrates the magnitude of this new and modern instructional technology that is now within the practical reach of every classroom teacher.

Instructional materials for virtually every student need are now available. Everything from traditional texts and workbooks to comprehensive multimedia systems is commercially produced. At the same time, the role of educational television and computer assisted instruction has rapidly expanded. Compared to the early 1950s, when between 19,000 and 26,000 pieces of instructional materials were marketed, 1974 boasted an increase equalling more than 10 times that amount. According to the ERIC/AUCR Annual Report

(Komoski, 1974), there were more than 300,000 pieces available by that time.

With the rapid proliferation of these materials, it is not surprising that confusion and guesswork have more often than not characterized the efforts of those who must select and daily employ them with handicapped children. A communication problem has often existed between the educator who wanted to know and the researcher/developer who possessed the knowledge and means for facilitating the learning and teaching process. Recently, therefore, more emphasis has been placed on the evaluation and widespread dissemination of newly developed instructional materials. Federal funds in excess of 40 million dollars have been provided in the last decade to support the development of a comprehensive, nationwide instructional materials network. This network, currently undergoing extensive revision, included 13 Area Learning Resource Centers, four Specialized Offices, and the National Center on Educational Media and Materials for the Handicapped (NCEMMH). Although the future of this network is unclear at this time, it is likely that new contractors will continue to provide invaluable assistance to state and local educational agencies, as well as individual classroom teachers.

This rapid growth in educational technology, both in terms of the quantity and quality of media and materials and the increasingly efficient delivery system, offers opportunities for individualized instruction never dreamed of before. As Withrow (1976) points out, "we must have the insight and courage to provide all of the technological and human resources required to bring handicapped people into the mainstream of American life" (p. 257).

SUMMARY

The effective use of instructional materials is more needed than ever before. With the placement of handicapped learners in the mainstream of education and the resulting diversity in performance levels, learning styles, and problem areas, the need for individualized instruction will be paramount. A more sophisticated and aware public, supported by recent court cases and legislative action, is demanding an appropriate and accountable education for every child. By definition, this requires the maximum utilization of modern educational materials.

Fortunately, this challenge comes during a time that has witnessed tremendous growth in the area of educational technology. Vast increases over the past two decades in the quantity, quality, and availability of instructional materials and media have resulted in an incredibly rich educational resource. Combined with innovative and more flexible approaches to instructional programming, such as Individually Prescribed Instruction (IPI), open education, and the increased use of learning centers and paraprofessionals, these materials can provide the key to efficient and effective classroom instruction.

The remainder of this book is designed to assist each teacher in the selection, implementation, adaptation, and evaluation of this critical educational resource—modern instructional materials.

REFERENCES

Beez, W. V. 1968. Influence of biased psychological reports on teacher behavior and pupil performance. Unpublished doctoral dissertation, Indiana University, Indianapolis.

Blessing, K. R. 1967. Use of teacher aides in special education: A review and possible implications. Except. Child. 34: 107–113.

Block, J. H. 1971. Criterion-referenced measures: Potential. School Rev. 79: 289–298.

Charles, C. M. 1976. Individualizing Instruction. The C. V. Mosby Company, St. Louis.

Cook, J. J. 1972. Accountability in special education. Foc. Except. Child. 3: 1–14.

Cruickshank, W. M. 1972. Some issues facing the field of learning disabilities. J. Learn. Dis. 5: 5–13.

Cruickshank, W. M., and Haring, M. G. 1957. A demonstration: Assistants for Teachers of Exceptional Children. Syracuse University Press, Syracuse, New York.

Cubberley, E. P. 1919. Public Education in the United States. Houghton Mifflin Company, New York.

Dunn, L. M. 1968. Special education for the mildly retarded: Is much of it justifiable? Except. Child. 35: 5–24.

Ebel, R. L. 1971. Criterion-referenced measurements: Limitations. School Rev. 79: 282–288.

Education for All Handicapped Children Act of 1975. 94th Congress, Public Law 94-142.

Esbensen, T. 1966. Should teacher aides be more than clerks? Phi Delta Kappan 44: 237.

Flanagan, J. C. 1967. Project PLAN: A program of individualized planning, and individualized instruction. National Security Industrial Association Project ARISTOTLE Symposium, Washington, D.C.

Glaser, R. 1971. Instructional technology and the measurement of learning outcomes: Some questions. In Popham, W. J. (ed.), Criterion-Referenced Measurement. Educational Technology Publications, Englewood Cliffs, N.J.

Goldstein, H., Moss, J., and Jordan, L. J. 1975. The efficacy of special class training on the development of mentally retarded children. Cooperative Research Project No. 619. U.S. Office of Education, Washington, D.C.

Gump, P. V. 1974. Operating environments in schools of open and traditional design. School Rev. 82: 575–594.

Hewett, F. M. 1968. The Emotionally Disturbed Child in the Classroom. Allyn and Bacon, Boston.

Ironside, R. A. 1972. The 1971–1972 Nationwide Installation of the Multiunit/IGE Model for Elementary Schools: A Process Evaluation. Educational Testing Services, Princeton, N.J.

Jencks, C. 1970. Educational vouchers: Giving parents money to pay for schooling. New Republ. 163: 19–21.

Jones, R. L. 1973. Accountability in special education: Some problems. Except. Child. 39: 631–642.

Knoblock, P. 1973. Open education for emotionally disturbed children. Except. Child. 39: 358–365.

Kohl, H. R. 1969. The open classroom. The New York Review, New York.

Kokaska, S. M., and Kokaska, C. J. 1971. Individualized work centers: An approach for the elementary retarded child. Educ. Train. Ment. Retard. 6: 25–27.

Komoski, P. K. 1974. An imbalance of product quantity and instructional quality: The imperative of empricism. Audiovis. Commun. Rev. 22(4): 357–386.

Lessinger, L. M. 1971. Historical note on accountability in education. J. Res. Dev. Educ. 5: 15–18.

Mainstreaming—What's it all about? 1976. Tod. Educ. 65: 18–19.

Moran, M. R. 1975. Nine steps to the diagnostic prescriptive process in the classroom. Foc. Except. Child. 6:1–14.

Phi Delta Kappan. 1970, 51(10): 539.

Progress Report II: Individually Prescribed Instruction. 1971. Research for Better Schools, Philadelphia.

Rookey, T. J., and Valdes, A. L. 1972. A Study of IPI and the Affective Domain, May. Research for Better Schools, Philadelphia.

Rosenthal, R., and Jacobson, L. 1968. Pygmalion in the Classroom. Holt, Rinehart and Winston, New York.

Ryan, K., and Cooper, J. M. Those Who Can, Teach. Houghton Mifflin Company, Boston.

Scanlon, R. G. 1972. Progress Report, May. Research for Better Schools, Philadelphia.

Scanlon, R. G., and Brown, M. V. 1971. Individualizing instruction. In D. S. Bushnell and D. Rappaport (eds.), Planned Change in Education. Harcourt Brace & Jovanovich, New York.

Smith, W. L. 1971. Special education: The new perspective. Paper presented before the Council of Great Cities Conference, May 5, San Francisco, California.

Torres, S. (ed.). 1977. A Primer on Individualized Education Programs for Handicapped Children. The Foundation for Exceptional Children, Reston, Va.

Welch, E. A. 1967. The effects of segregated and partially integrated school programs on self concept and academic achievement of educable mentally retarded children. Except. Child. 34: 93–100.

Weber, L. 1971. The English Infant School and Informal Education. Prentice-Hall, Englewood Cliffs, N.J.

Willems, A. L., and others. 1975. How should classroom elementary aides be chosen? Education 96: 85–88.

Withrow, F. B. 1976. Educational technology for the handicapped learner. In F. B. Withrow and C. J. Nygren (eds.), Language, Materials and Curriculum Management for the Handicapped Learner. Charles E. Merrill Books, Columbus, Ohio.

3

Assessing Learner Characteristics

Virginia K. Laycock, Ed.D.

The concept of individualized instruction has been highly publicized since the early 1960s. Although most educators espouse the goal of tailoring instruction to unique learning needs, individualizing instruction has not become a universal classroom practice. The issue has come into sharper focus with the advent of mainstreaming. Classroom teachers are being asked to accommodate a wider range of individual differences than ever before. By definition, exceptional children do not profit sufficiently from the regular classroom program. Adaptations in curriculum, methods, and materials are required to serve special children in the mainstream. Individualized instruction for these children can no longer be viewed as an option; it is clearly a necessity.

At the same time that the rights of the handicapped are being recognized, sophisticated educational technology and research are making it apparent that there are no simple or universal solutions for instructional problems. Attempts to identify the "best" instructional methods and materials have proved futile, and understandably so. Education remains a richly human endeavor. No one instructional method or material can possibly satisfy the diverse needs of all. Many of the differences noted among individuals are educationally significant, and do affect responsiveness to instructional experiences. The "best" instructional tools, therefore, are those techniques and materials most appropriate for a particular student and his teacher in a given classroom setting. Designing an educational program is thus a matter of selecting instructional methods and materials that correspond closely to individual learner needs and that can be feasibly implemented by the teacher.

The effectiveness of the entire process of instructional planning hinges upon the accurate identification of learner characteristics. Unless a teacher can pinpoint exactly *what* a child needs to learn and *how* he learns most successfully, any attempt at individualized programming is like a shot in the dark. Chances of being on target in instructional decision-making are dramatically increased when reliable information about the learner is available. Educational assessment or diagnosis is, therefore, a necessary first step in individualized programming.

Diagnosis refers to the process of gathering and interpreting educationally relevant information about a particular learner. As Salvia and Ysseldyke (1978) point out, there are at least five reasons for conducting assessment: screening, placement, program planning, program evaluation, and evaluation of individual progress. Issues surrounding the many functions of educational assessment are both complex and controversial. The present chapter, therefore, considers diagnostic assessment only as it relates to individualized instructional programming. The "educationally relevant information" to be collected, analyzed, and synthesized will provide the basis for the determination of instructional objectives and teaching strategies. Successive chapters will extend the process of individualized education programming to the selection of instructional materials. The approach suggested in this chapter for assessing pupil characteristics and the method proposed in Chapter 4 for assessing material characteristics will be integrated in Chapter 5 into a system for matching material attributes to instructional needs.

THE DIAGNOSTIC PROCESS

Misconceptions and misuses of educational diagnosis abound in practice. Too often, evaluation is viewed as simply a necessary step in getting a child placed in special education. Finding out whether he "qualifies" becomes an end in itself. It is not uncommon for students to be administered the same pre-established battery of test regardless of presenting problems or reasons for referral. Testing is usually administered in a single session by an evaluator who is unfamiliar to the child. The written report sent to the teacher may contain little information that was not already known. Even if it is determined that the student should receive special services, it is probable that he will remain in his regular classroom for at least a portion of the day. When the teacher has received no practical guidance for providing for this child, diagnosis has served no real purpose.

Meaningful educational assessment is far different from the situations just described. It is, first of all, goal directed. Diagnosis is conducted for the express purpose of describing an individual's learning behavior in terms that imply instructional interventions. Complete assessment should focus on gathering and organizing information about three major learning characteristics: 1) present levels of performance, 2) specific skills and behaviors of concern, and 3) learning style. These represent the desired outcomes of assessment. The exact diagnostic techniques to be used for arriving at these determinations may differ in each case, depending on the presenting problem and the information already available. The accurate description of learning behaviors with respect to performance levels, specific skills, and learning style leads directly to the selection of individualized objectives, teaching strategies, and instructional materials.

A second characteristic of good educational diagnosis is that it incorporates a variety of sources for information. Testing is indeed useful, but it is not the sole method of obtaining data. A number of other assessment techniques may also be employed. A medical examination is usually in order to identify health and acuity problems. Interviews may be conducted with the child and his parents to determine their perceptions of the situation. Permanent records and case histories may contribute to the understanding of a child's development and adjustment over time. Valuable information may be gathered by observing the student in his everyday interactions. Finally, formal, standardized tests, as well as informal, teacher-made tests are important assessment tools. The most complete educational diagnoses draw upon many relevant sources of information.

A third requirement for meaningful educational diagnosis is that the classroom teacher must play a central role in gathering and interpreting information. Assessment should be conducted within the child's everyday learning environment to the greatest extent possible, because it is under these conditions that he is asked to perform. The classroom teacher must be actively involved in the assessment process, because it is this individual who is in closest contact with the child and in the position to obtain the richest diagnostic data. In addition, it is the classroom teacher who will be ultimately responsible for implementing many aspects of the instructional program developed from the diagnosis.

The needs of the majority of students in the regular classroom can be adequately assessed by the teacher. When serious learning or behavior problems become apparent, however, the teacher may request assistance in a more intensive evaluation. Different states and school districts have defined their own referral procedures. The titles assigned to the different individuals who assist in educational diagnosis also vary. In many areas, the resource teacher, diagnostic prescriptive teacher, or psychoeducational evaluator is available within each school to work with the classroom teacher. Typically, these individuals will coordinate and conduct whatever necessary assessment cannot reasonably be accomplished in the regular classroom. School psychologists are also available within each district to confer with teachers and evaluators and to administer tests requiring specialized training and certification, such as IQ tests. A multidisciplinary approach is most helpful when a student's problems are particularly complex. Any number of specialists may be involved as needed. Pediatricians, neurologists, ophthalmologists, optometrists, speech and language clinicians, physical therapists, psychiatrists, psychologists, and guidance counselors are but a few of the professionals who might contribute to the complete diagnosis. Although there is no need to prolong the assessment process or to involve any more individuals than necessary, multifaceted problems do require the expertise of other professions whenever these might have direct bearing on the child's performance in the classroom. Educational diagnosis, then, begins in the classroom, and its end product, an individualized instructional program, must also be classroom oriented. Along the way, the teacher may consult any number of individuals who can directly contribute to the understanding of a child's learning behavior.

A final characteristic of meaningful educational assessment is that it is an ongoing process. Certainly, there must be a limit to initial diagnostic efforts. If one simply tested and observed until all desired information was known about a child, one would never reach the stage of designing an instructional program. Assessment is not an end in itself; it is, rather, the means to delivering the appropriate educational services. Initial diagnosis should be conducted until educators have achieved a working knowledge of a child's present levels of performance, related behaviors and skills, and learning style. An individualized program can then be developed. Results of the diagnosis are not infallible. Furthermore, the student's performance is subject to change over time. For these reasons, diagnosis is continually amended in light of current evidence. The teacher's daily interactions with the learner provide the best indications of his abilities. Assessment, therefore, should be inseparable from instruction, characterizing teaching in a diagnostic prescriptive way.

In summary, meaningful educational diagnosis differs from its less effective counterparts in several important respects. It is goal-directed, conducted specifically to describe three aspects of student performance: functional levels, skills and behaviors of concern, and learning style. The most valuable diagnostic information is drawn from a variety of sources and does not result solely from testing. Diagnosis is likely to be most relevant for instruction when the classroom teacher plays a key role in the process. Other school personnel and professionals should assist in diagnosis to whatever extent is indicated. Preliminary assessment is necessarily finite. The process of diagnosis, however, is never-ending, because it continues to pervade all teaching interactions. Assessment information is updated and revised based on daily observations of the child's performance.

In the sections that follow, each of the three areas of investigation are discussed in greater detail. It is beyond the scope of the present chapter to deal with the specific applications of the various measurement techniques. The construction, administration, and interpretation of assessment devices constitute a major study in their own rights. This chapter attempts only to describe the *types* of diagnostic information to be gathered and the *organization* of these data into a form that facilitates instructional planning.

MEASURING PRESENT PERFORMANCE LEVELS

A teacher may have only a global definition of a student's problem as assessment is begun. Because assessment progresses from the general to the highly specific, it is sometimes viewed as a process of pinpointing or "zeroing-in" on the exact difficulties. An early step in the process is the determination of performance levels. Within any area of development—motor, perceptual, language, cognitive, social, academic, etc.—there exists an orderly progression of skills. The age at which the majority of learners demonstrate specific skills is determined empirically and referred to as the norm. In reality, individual children pass through a sequence of skills at different rates. For this reason, it is helpful to measure performance levels to indicate at what stage the child is presently functioning in developmental sequences in the areas of concern.

The terms performance level, functional level, and developmental level are often used interchangeably. Age or grade equivalents are the customary means of reporting these levels. To obtain such normative data, educators must rely for the most part on formal, standardized testing. These tests have been norm-referenced so that a child's obtained score can be compared with the scores of his chronological peers in the standardization sample to yield an age or grade equivalent. Thus, a student who earns a developmental age of 14-2 performed comparably to children in the standardization sample who were 14 years, 2 months of age. Similarly, a derived score of 2.5 on an achievement test would indicate that the child in question performed as those in the standardized sample who were in mid-second grade.

Caution must be exercised to avoid overinterpretation of age or grade equivalents. The same derived age or grade may mean different things for different chronological ages. One should not expect a 12-year-old child with a developmental age of 6, for instance, to behave the same as a 5-year-old with a developmental age of 6. Furthermore, identical abilities are not implied even for children of the same chronological and performance ages. Age or grade equivalents merely provide an index of the child's functional level. They serve a valuable role in narrowing the range of abilities under consideration and in guiding further investigation.

Intelligence Testing

When learning problems exist, it is generally helpful to obtain an estimate of the child's overall cognitive capabilities. Information from an intelligence test that has been correctly administered, scored, and interpreted can be useful in clarifying the nature of a child's problem and in predicting school performance in the near future. In many states, an IQ test is required as one basis for judging a student's need for special services. Never should an IQ score be the sole criterion for labeling a child or assigning him to special education. Such abuses of intelligence testing have been opposed on educational, ethical, and legal grounds.

It is important for the teacher to understand what intelligence testing can and cannot do. Based on a comprehensive review of literature, Sattler has summarized the limitations of intelligence testing as follows:

1. The IQ is limited in predicting occupational success.
2. The IQ is limited in predicting nonacademic skills.
3. Intelligence tests do not provide measures of innate capacity.
4. Intelligence tests provide limited information about the domain of cognitive functions.
5. Intelligence tests do not measure the processes underlying the test responses.
6. Intelligence tests penalize nonconventional responses.
7. Intelligence tests may be unreliable for long range predictions (1974, p. 24).

Additional complex issues must be considered when IQ tests are used with children from minority groups, whose sociocultural experiences often differ significantly from the conventional and from the backgrounds of the children comprising the standardization sample. Until the matter of nondiscriminatory testing is resolved, extreme caution must govern any decision-making based on the results of standardized testing of minority group children.

Despite the shortcomings of intelligence testing, it remains the best available means of measuring an individuals's general level of functioning. It has been found to correlate highly with scholastic achievement, and it is one of the most useful predictors of the ability to profit from the types of educational experiences customarily provided in the schools. When IQ tests are used responsibly, they serve as one valuable source of information about a child's learning behavior.

Many tests are currently available that purport to assess intelligence. In most school districts, group intelligence tests are administered in designated grades, usually in conjunction with achievement tests. Although group tests may prove useful as screening devices, they are usually inadequate intelligence measures for children with learning and behavior problems. Disorders of attention, perception, reading, and handwriting can interfere with performance and produce inaccurate IQ scores. Individually administered intelligence tests are, therefore, preferred for in depth educational diagnosis.

The two individually administered tests of intelligence most commonly used are the Wechsler Intelligence Scales (1955, 1967, 1974) and the Stanford-Binet Intelligence Scale (Terman and Merrill, 1973). The administration of these tests is restricted to psychologists or evaluators who have received specialized training and licensing. Teachers in both regular and special education, however, should become sufficiently familiar with the construction, administration, and interpretation of these tests that they can utilize the information provided in reports of psychological evaluations to student advantage.

Performance Levels in Other Areas

Getting an estimate of overall cognitive functioning may be a common starting point in the assessment of children with learning problems, but it is also important to determine performance levels in specific areas of concern. According to the nature of a student's problems, any of the following might warrant investigation: gross and fine motor development, visual processing, auditory processing, language development, social-emotional development, and the basic academic skills of reading, writing, spelling, and mathematics.

Numerous assessment devices are available to assist in the measurement of performance levels. For the most part, the necessary information may be collected using either of two techniques—tests or developmental checklists.

In testing, stimuli are presented to an individual under controlled conditions to sample from the domain of behavior under consideration. The situation is structured to evoke behavior in a form that can be measured and quantified. A test is valid to the extent that responses sampled truly reflect a person's performance in the intended area.

Behavior samples also provide the basis for assessment when developmental checklists or rating scales are employed. With developmental checklists, however, it is not necessary for the child to demonstrate target behaviors under actual testing conditions. Instead, a parent, teacher, or other responsible individual reports whether the child has performed each behavior at some time in the past in his everyday environment.

Developmental checklists or rating scales have proved most useful in the assessment of abilities that do not readily lend themselves to testing. It is often difficult, for example, to sample the richness of an individual's language behavior under controlled testing conditions. Aspects of social and emotional adjustment may also need to be evaluated in the natural environment. Rating scales are particularly helpful in the assessment of very young children when testing is not always appropriate. Many of the tasks considered landmarks in early childhood development would be difficult to elicit under testing conditions.

An example of a developmental checklist for preschool children is provided in Figure 1. This section of the *MEMPHIS Comprehensive Developmental Scale* (Quick, Little, and Campbell, 1974) is designed for assessing personal-social abilities. The 60 skills to be sampled are arranged in developmental order from simple to complex. One month's credit is assigned for each task the child successfully performs. A developmental age can then be calculated.

For most of the items listed, an observant parent, teacher, or guardian would be able to indicate whether a child has mastered the task in question. In instances where the adult is not certain of the child's capabilities, the situation may be structured in the attempt to elicit the desired response. In application then, the *MEMPHIS Scale* incorporates both the reporting by significant adults and the informal testing of specific skills as necessary.

The usefulness of rating scales depends directly on the reliability of the sources consulted. Those reporting may be subtly biased or simply unaware of a child's actual abilities. To reduce chances of error in diagnosis, developmental checklists are generally employed in conjunction with formal or informal testing and systematic observation. When tenuous data are verified by using these other

Raw Score	Years	Months	P	F	PERSONAL–SOCIAL SKILLS
60	5.00	60	P	F	Plays competitive exercise games.
59			P	F	Dresses self with attempts at tying shoes.
58			P	F	Spreads with knife, partial success.
57	4.75	57	P	F	Uses play materials constructively; builds, does not tear down.
56			P	F	Dresses self except tying shoes.
55			P	F	"Picks up" some after playing with no coaxing.
54	4.50	54	P	F	Attends well for short stories.
53			P	F	Uses paper straw appropriately without damaging.
52			P	F	Washes face well.
51	4.25	51	P	F	Separates from mother easily.
50			P	F	Distinguishes front from back of clothes.
49			P	F	Completely cares for self at toilet, including cleaning and dressing.
48	4.00	48	P	F	Plays with others with minimal friction.
47			P	F	Buttons medium-sized buttons.
46			P	F	Goes on very short distance errands outside the home.
45	3.75	45	P	F	Performs for others; i.e. performs a simple rhyme or song.
44			P	F	Washes hands well.
43			P	F	Brushes teeth adequately.
42	3.50	42	P	F	Attempts help at little household tasks; i.e. sweeping, dusting.
41			P	F	Completely undresses for bedtime.
40			P	F	Removes clothing for toileting.
39	3.25	39	P	F	Buttons large buttons.
38			P	F	Performs toilet activities by self (not dressing, cleaning).
37			P	F	Plays cooperatively, interacts with others.
36	3.00	36	P	F	Puts on shoes and socks (tying not required).
35			P	F	Feeds self with little spilling, both fork and spoon.
34			P	F	Shares upon request.
33	2.75	33	P	F	Avoids simple hazards (hot stove, etc.)
32			P	F	Puts on a coat (buttoning not required).
31			P	F	Dries hands well.
30	2.50	30	P	F	Is not overly destructive with household goods, toys, etc.
29			P	F	Gets a drink unassisted from fountain or sink.
28			P	F	Sucks from a plastic straw.
27	2.25	27	P	F	Eats with fork but spills some.
26			P	F	Recognizes self in mirror.
25			P	F	Uses single words or likenesses to show wants.
24	2.00	24	P	F	Minds—does as told generally.
23			P	F	Removes coat or dress (unbuttoning not required).
22			P	F	At least asks to go to toilet—day and night.
21	1.75	21	P	F	Does not place objects on floor in mouth.
20			P	F	Eats with spoon, spilling little.
19			P	F	Voluntarily "slows down" to take naps or rest.
18	1.50	18	P	F	Plays around other children effectively.
17			P	F	Drinks from cup or glass unassisted.
16			P	F	Pulls off socks, but not necessarily shoes.
15	1.25	15	P	F	Follows simple commands or instructions.
14			P	F	Feeds self with a spoon—some spilling allowed.
13			P	F	Holds out arms to assist with clothing.
12	1.00	12	P	F	Temporarily responds to "no," "stop."
11			P	F	Cooperates with dressing—does not resist.
10			P	F	Chews food.
9	.75	9	P	F	Places food in mouth with hands.
8			P	F	Grasps small objects with thumb and index finger.
7			P	F	Desires personal attention and contact beyond just holding.
6	.50	6	P	F	Drinks from a cup or glass with assistance.
5			P	F	Occupies self with a toy for a short period of time.
4			P	F	Grasps foot or brings hand to mouth.
3	.25	3	P	F	Pulls at clothing with hands.
2			P	F	Sucking and swallowing are present.
1			P	F	Reaches for and wants to be held by familiar persons.

Left margin labels: Chronological Age · Developmental Age · Raw Score · Date of Evaluation · Name · Date of Birth

This scale reprinted by permission of the Author and the Publisher, Fearon Publishers, Inc., 6'Davis Drive, Belmont, Calif. 94002.

Figure 1.   An example of a developmental checklist for preschool children.

measures, rating scales can be helpful tools in determining developmental levels.

For academic subjects, grade equivalents are usually considered more instructionally relevant than performance ages. Although developmental checklists can be used effectively, testing may be a more efficient means of determining grade equivalents. Several different subject matter areas may be sampled within a relatively short period of time by means of achievement tests. Group achievement tests are often administered to all students within a school district at established intervals. Results of such testing should be considered in educational diagnosis, but interpretation of achievement scores should take into account the possible confounding effects of a child's specific disabilities. A serious reading problem, for example, may contaminate scores on all other subtests, even those purporting to measure skills in other areas such as science or mathematics. Individually administered achievement tests are therefore advised for the more accurate identification of the performance levels of students with learning and behavior problems.

In addition to achievement tests, diagnostic tests may also be used to obtain grade equivalents. Whereas achievement tests briefly sample from several different areas at a time, diagnostic tests focus in greater detail upon a single subject. Although the major function of diagnostic tests involves the determination of specific skill deficits, the majority of diagnostic tests are also norm-referenced to provide grade equivalents as well.

Thus far, discussion has centered on assessment of a child's performance in comparison to the performance of his chronological peers to identify his level of functioning. Measuring an individual's abilities with reference to his age-mates represents a concern for *interindividual differences.* Of equal importance is the consideration of *intraindividual differences.* Intraindividual differences refer to the discrepancies that exist among the child's own levels of functioning across the various developmental areas. A certain amount of unevenness in development is to be expected, because all individuals are more advanced in some areas than in others. Individual profiles must be interpreted with care and with a knowledge of what constitutes significant differences. When approached in this way, analysis of intraindividual differences may reveal whether a child's deficiencies are generalized or limited to specific areas. It may also indicate relative strengths that might be used to the student's advantage.

A case study is now introduced to illustrate the application of the assessment process described. Background information about the student is first presented. Data contributing to the identification of performance levels are then summarized. This same case study is later extended within this chapter to provide examples of the organization of diagnostic data into the remaining categories—skills and behaviors of concern and learning style.

Case Example

Jason, age 13 years, 9 months, is an eighth grader experiencing many problems in the regular classroom. His teacher has become greatly concerned over his disruptive behavior and his sporadic academic performance.

Jason is a fair-skinned boy with expressive blue eyes. He is shorter than average for his age and considerably overweight.

Jason's family resides in a small community where his father is a practicing attorney. Jason's mother has a master's degree in education and teaches in a nearby elementary school. Jason has two older sisters, one of whom is away at college. The parents feel that Jason learns slowly because he lacks the necessary motivation. They would like for the school to help Jason improve his work habits.

Jason's general health is good, with no indications of vision or hearing difficulties. The pediatrician has recommended several weight reduction diets in the past, but Jason has been reluctant to cooperate. At times he complains of upset stomach and trouble with sleeping. His mother tends to attribute these problems to "nerves."

An investigation of Jason's school history revealed that no serious problems were reported in the primary grades. Jason attained B's and C's in his schoolwork. In the fourth grade, Jason's parents first became aware of his difficulties—he received unsatisfactory grades in several subjects and was also labeled as a discipline problem. Jason was promoted into fifth grade on the condition that he receive special help. A private tutor was hired to work with Jason until his grades rose to A's and B's the second semester. In sixth and seventh grades, however, he began failing in math and science. Jason was also suspended from school on three separate occasions for fighting, yelling obscenities at the teacher, and refusing to participate in class.

The results of Jason's educational assessment are summarized and presented for each area of investigation. First summarized are results from present levels of performance assessment.

On the Wechsler Intelligence Scale for Children—Revised (WISC-R), Jason obtained a Full Scale IQ of 77 ± 3. The chances that the range of scores from 74 to 80 includes his true IQ are about 68 out of 100. This indicates that, overall, Jason is functioning in the borderline range of intelligence, and at the 6th percentile with respect to children of his age in the standardization sample. Jason achieved an IQ of 91 ± 4 on the Verbal Scale, showing average ability. A Performance Scale IQ of 65 ± 5 reveals deficient performance of tasks requiring nonverbal, primarily visual-motor capabilities. The 26 point difference between Jason's Verbal and Performance IQs is significant. Although he is able to deal adequately with situations requiring language skills, his performance deteriorates when he is forced to rely on his less developed perceptual skills.

Results of the Bender Visual Motor Gestalt Test confirm Jason's difficulties in the performance areas. Jason was unable to reproduce designs adequately and attained a developmental age of 7 years, 10 months, a functional level approximately 6 years below his chronological age.

On the Wide Range Achievement Test, the following grade equivalents were obtained: Reading—7.2, Spelling—6.4, and Arithmetic—4.3. Jason's performance in all three academic areas was lower than his actual grade placement of 8.2. Jason received his lowest score in arithmetic, which is also one of the subjects he is failing in the classroom.

On an individual reading inventory used as a placement test for the school's basal reading program, Jason's instructional level was high seventh grade. His independent level was high sixth grade, and his frustrational reading level was mid-eighth grade.

IDENTIFYING SKILLS AND BEHAVIORS OF CONCERN

The measurement of functional levels was presented as a necessary first step in assessing learner characteristics. A developmental age or grade equivalent helps to narrow the range of skills under consideration. Once a child is described as having a language age of 2-6, for example, one has a general idea of his receptive and expressive capabilities. Likewise, a sixth grade reading level implies a certain subset of competencies. As helpful as performance levels might be, however, they cannot provide the direct bases for academic or behavioral programming. Typically, children with learning problems have acquired skills in somewhat piecemeal, nonsequential fashion. Simply knowing *where* a student is functioning in a developmental sequence does not guarantee accurate knowledge of *what* he can and cannot do. One has to measure specific skills.

If affective and social difficulties are evident, these too must be specifically assessed. Frequently used terms such as dependency, hyperactivity, poor self-concept, withdrawal, and aggression suggest only general behavior patterns and fail to imply what can be done for a particular child. The problem must be behaviorally defined before appropriate intervention strategies can be planned. A teacher needs to know exactly what a child *is doing* or what he *is not doing* that fails to meet expectations. Rather than saying that a child is aggressive, for example, the problem could be operationally defined as hitting classmates and addressing the teacher as "old lady." Instead of labeling a student withdrawn, a more useful assessment would point out that the child walks off by himself on the playground, does not volunteer to participate in class activities, and does not initiate conversation with the teacher.

Once target behaviors are specified, related diagnostic information can be gathered. One can determine the extent of the problem by measuring how frequently the behavior is occurring and comparing this with the desired level. It is also helpful to identify the conditions under which the behavior is typically demonstrated.

The task at this stage of the diagnostic process is to describe problem skills and behaviors as specifically as possible, so that goals can be easily derived for instruction and intervention. The assessment tools most useful for this purpose are criterion-referenced testing and direct observation.

Criterion-Referenced Testing

Although norm-referenced devices were most useful for ascertaining performance levels, criterion-referenced devices are best suited for pinpointing exact strengths and weaknesses. In criterion-referenced testing, an individual's performance is evaluated against a pre-established criterion or standard for mastery rather than against the performance of his peers. Criterion-referenced measurement allows a teacher to describe a child's competency in absolute instead of relative terms. A result of such testing might be, for example, the determination that a second grade student can print 23 lower case letters correctly but misforms the letters *e, g,* and *y.* From a criterion-referenced reading inventory, a teacher might learn that a pupil is able to read 80% of the 220 Dolch Sight Words correctly. On the scoresheet, individual words would be marked to indicate correct or incorrect responses.

There are many criterion-referenced tests published commercially. Some are entitled "diagnostic," to emphasize the detailed analysis of skills. Formal diagnostic tests are often constructed to yield both norm- and criterion-referenced results. In selecting a particular test for use, a teacher should want the necessary skills to be thoroughly sampled through instructionally relevant tasks. Ease and efficiency in administration and scoring are also desirable attributes.

When published tests are unavailable or inappropriate, an informal, teacher-made test may be constucted to assess a child's specific abilities. Effective informal assessment for any developmental or subject matter area involves essentially the same steps. These are:

1. Locating or developing a skill sequence for the area of concern
2. Defining each skill as an observable, measurable behavior
3. Specifying the conditions for performance of each skill in terms of materials and mode of presentation
4. Establishing criteria for mastery of each skill in terms of number correct, percentage, rate, or other standard
5. Preparing stimulus materials and scoring sheets
6. Presenting designated tasks to the child
7. Recording responses
8. Evaluating performance in reference to criteria

Informal testing conducted in this manner can be a highly valuable source of diagnostic information. A test can be designed to tap the exact skills of interest, and the assessment tasks devised can be closely related to teaching tasks. In this way, results of testing can be generalized to the instructional setting with greater confidence.

Formal or informal diagnostic tests usually require more time to administer than achievement tests, because they involve a more in-depth sampling of skills. Interpretation is also done in detail. In addition to the basic determination of whether or not a student has achieved mastery of each skill, the teacher is also concerned with the nature of learning difficulties demonstrated.

By analyzing a pupil's errors, one can often detect a pattern. In some cases, a child gives the same type of wrong response consistently, suggesting that he has learned the skill or concept incorrectly. At other times, a student may make numerous errors with no apparent pattern, leading one to conclude that he has not yet learned any consistent association. Although the two overall scores might be similar, the response patterns have different instructional implications.

Diagnostic Observation

Although testing is a powerful tool for educational assessment, one must not underestimate the usefulness of observation. Testing and observation actually complement each other in the assessment process. When a parent or teacher has carefully observed a child in home or classroom activities, the adult can often provide accurate descriptions of his behavior. In many instances, good observation reduces the amount of testing that is necessary. It can also serve as an informal reliability check after testing is done by providing evidence to confirm or contradict the results of testing.

Observation can take many different forms. It is usually characterized in terms of the degree of structure imposed in the perceiving and recording of behaviors. The simplest, unstructured observation consists of watching behavior with no attempt to systematize or quantify the information. The chances of overlooking or forgetting important diagnostic information can be reduced by applying more methodical approaches.

Many teachers keep daily journals and record brief notes about a child's performance. Other teachers prefer to use checklists on which they simply mark or date the skills a child has demonstrated.

To avoid the loss of precision and objectivity that often results from recording in retrospect, direct observation can be conducted for chosen times and situations. Narrative recording or naturalistic observation involves writing down a behavior sequence as it is actually taking place. This type of observation is most helpful when a teacher is first defining a problem, because it provides a record of the total situation in sequence. Once specific behaviors have been targeted, other systems may prove more efficient for measuring the extent to which behaviors are demonstrated.

When behaviors of concern are discrete—that is, they have a definite beginning and end—either frequency counting or duration recording may be appropriate. Frequency counting should be used when a teacher wants to know how often a behavior is occurring. This technique is sometimes called "event recording," because one simply counts the number of times the behavioral event takes place. When a teacher is interested in finding out how much time a student spends engaged in a particular behavior, duration recording is in order. A stop watch or regular clock is used to keep a running account of the time elapsing while a student is performing the target behavior.

When behaviors are not discrete, or when several behaviors are to be measured at once, time sampling may be the preferred technique. Time sampling involves "recording the presence or absence of the behavior within short, uniform time intervals" (Sulzer and Mayer, 1972, p. 264). After these or similar systems are employed to collect baseline data for several days, the teacher has obtained a more precise description of the problem.

Case Example

The sample assessment summary is now continued with a description of Jason's specific academic skills and classroom behaviors.

It is apparent from both testing and observation that Jason demonstrates strong language abilities. His Verbal IQ on the WISC-R was significantly higher than his Performance IQ. Within the verbal areas, Jason displayed a good background of general information and could give socially acceptable solutions for practical problems. He was able to solve oral arithmetic problems adequately and could define vocabulary words well. He showed average ability in recalling a series of digits. Observations by both parents and teachers emphasize Jason's strengths in comprehending and producing oral language.

Overall, Jason's perceptual motor skills are weak. His low Performance IQ resulted from significant difficulties in completing puzzles of familiar objects, reproducing abstract block designs, and attending to details in pictures.

Visual-motor problems were evident in Jason's drawings on the Bender Gestalt. In copying the nine geometric designs, Jason tended to distort shapes and to position them incorrectly in reference to each other.

Jason's visual-motor deficits are further apparent in his handwriting. Jason continues to print rather than to write in cursive. Letters are sometimes left incomplete, and capital and lower case letters are not correctly proportioned. Inconsistent sizing and spacing render Jason's printing nearly illegible at times.

Reading is one of Jason's stronger subject areas. His ability to read and comprehend paragraphs is close to grade level, as evidenced by his score on the reading inventory. Jason often chooses to read in his free time and particularly enjoys comic books and mystery stories. When reading words in isolation, such as on the Wide Range Achievement Test, Jason tends to guess at unknown words rather than decode them systematically. His higher grade level attained on the paragraph inventory may reflect his ability to use context clues to his advantage in attacking unfamiliar words.

Jason's comprehension skills are adequate on the literal level. He has difficulty with certain more advanced skills, such as drawing conclusions and detecting cause and effect.

An informal phonics inventory supported the teacher's observations that Jason can adequately recognize and identify basic consonant and vowel patterns. He becomes confused when one sound may be represented by more than one symbol, as c and s or ou and *ow.* In such instances where one must rely on visual memory to recall which symbol appears in a particular word, Jason does not do well.

His visual memory difficulties also affect his spelling. Most of Jason's errors occur on phonetically irregular words where he has tried to apply phonic generalizations inappropriately. On the Wide Range Achievement Test, for example, he misspelled "nature" as "nacher." Jason also omitted some letters in longer spelling words. In testing as well as in his everyday work, Jason refused to attempt long words (over five letters) that he could not readily spell.

Math is Jason's weakest subject area. According to an informal math assessment and teacher observations, he has mastered basic addition and subtraction combinations, but occasionally reverts to counting on his fingers. Jason can demonstrate the processes involved in addition and subtraction computations, but makes many seemingly careless mistakes when asked to complete a set of these problems independently.

Jason does not know all of his multiplication facts automatically. In performing computations, he sometimes goes back to recite a table from the beginning in order to figure out a particular combination. In multiplication problems with two or more digits per term, Jason frequently errs in carrying or in aligning the partial products.

Jason demonstrates an understanding of the process of division and can complete examples with single digit divisors adequately. He tends to have trouble grouping digits correctly in the dividend. Common errors also include leaving remainders larger than divisors.

Jason's skills in applying basic money, measurement, and time concepts are satisfactory. The only Roman numerals that he recognizes consistently are I, V, and X.

Jason can add and subtract fractions with like denominators but cannot reduce fractions to lowest terms or find least common denominators.

Jason's teacher described his behavior in the classroom as "disruptive." Her anecdotal records revealed the following behavioral incidents occurring over a four-week period:

> Came to class without paper or pencil; talked constantly and refused to do his work; put his head down on his desk; walked around the room; made faces at others; tried to cut another child's hair; glued pages of his reading book together; handcuffed his own hands behind his back; went up on the roof to get a ball and would not come down; balanced a book on his finger during reading; and tried to leave school grounds.

The following items were checked on an adaptive behavior scale as characteristic of Jason: often wastes time, moves sluggishly, does not persist with assignments even though he has the ability, and talks back to adults.

Narrative recording conducted during three 20-minute work periods suggested that disturbing behaviors, such as talking loudly to himself or rolling a pencil across the desk, tended to occur when the teacher was at the far side of the room. Peers typically responded to Jason's behavior with giggling and tattling.

A five-day check showed that Jason completed 20% of his written assignments in math. In other subject areas, he completed approximately 55%.

Time sampling was conducted for three days to assess two specific off-task behaviors during independent work periods. Target behaviors were talking aloud without permission and handling objects other than assigned instructional materials. Behaviors were recorded at 30-second intervals for 15 minutes each day. It was found that Jason was talking aloud during 35% of the intervals sampled. In 15% of the intervals, he was handling inappropriate objects.

DESCRIBING INDIVIDUAL LEARNING STYLE

The determination of functional levels and specific deficits provides the essential information for deciding *what* a child should be taught. Deciding *how* to teach him effectively requires a different data base. The aspect of student performance having the greatest implications for teaching method is learning style. Learning style refers to an individual's characteristic way of responding to certain variables in the instructional environment. Stated more simply, a student's learning style is the way that he learns best. All individuals have developed personalized techniques for acquiring and remembering information. More appropriate instructional strategies and materials can be selected for a particular child when the teacher is aware of his learning style.

There are few standardized tests that contribute meaningfully to the assessment of learning style. Educators must rely, for the most part, on their observational skills. The determination of learning style requires time. Only a few characteristics may be apparent upon completion of preliminary diagnosis. As a teacher continues to interact with a child and to observe him at work, the understanding of learning style becomes more complete. A teacher is apt to notice patterns emerging in student performance. The way that a learner tends to organize himself for work, to study assigned material, to solve problems, and to make decisions all reveal something about his unique style.

Observations during individual testing may be particularly fruitful. Although the tests themselves may be measuring other abilities, the child's behavior during testing provides many clues about his learning style. In addition to observing a student's general approach to problems, the examiner is often able to detect the individual's bases for decision-making from the types of errors that he makes.

Another useful application of observation occurs in diagnostic prescriptive teaching. By manipulating specific variables in the instructional program and observing the effects on student performance, the teacher can determine how he learns most effectively.

In describing learning style, therefore, the many forms of observation play a primary role. The nature of learning style and the lack of appropriate standardized devices make it necessary to assess this aspect of student performance in the actual instructional setting.

Dimensions of Learning Style

An individual's learning style might be characterized in numerous ways. Only six of the more common aspects of learning style are considered here. Not all of these will be relevant in a single assessment, because not all children exhibit distinctive differences in every dimension.

The first four factors listed are essentially derived from information processing theory. Within this general orientation, several different conceptual models have been proposed (Bown, 1972; Friedus, 1964; Kirk, McCarthy, and Kirk, 1968; Osgood, 1957). Although the models vary in many respects, they are all based on the assumption that there exists a sequentially ordered set of subprocesses involved in receiving and responding to stimuli from the environment. Such processes as attention, perception, cognition, memory, integration, and response formation intervene between sensory input and behavioral output.

Many types of learning difficulties have been attributed to weaknesses in specific processing skills. If these deficits can be accurately identified, instructional programs might be planned either to remediate the weaknesses or to compensate for them. The four dimensions of learning style related to information processing are now introduced.

Modality Preference   The aspect of learning style that has generated the most study and also the most controversy is modality preference. This refers to an ability to learn and retain information more efficiently when certain channels of communication are employed. Some students learn best visually, others aurally, and still others through tactual-kinesthetic means. Students who are achieving adequately may experience little difficulty in learning through less-preferred perceptual pathways. They may acquire information more easily through their stronger channel, but they are not actually deficient in any channel. Many children with learning problems, however, do have significant weaknesses in perceptual skills, to the extent that they are unable to profit from instruction directed primarily to that channel. In these instances, the identification of students' open or intact modalities becomes more critical.

Certain standardized tests designed to measure perceptual and psycholinguistic skills have been widely used for the determination of modality preference. The empirical support for this practice has proved less than satisfactory, however. It has been found that the most commonly used instruments fail to differentiate adequately between normal children and those diagnosed as learning disabled (Larsen, Rogers, and Sowell, 1976; O'Grady, 1974). Unsuccessful attempts to enhance achievement by matching instructional treatments to perceptual learning styles have been attributed to the lack of adequate assessment devices (Sabatino, Ysseldyke, and Woolston, 1973; Ysseldyke, 1973).

A more promising means of identifying learning style may be the trial lessons approach. Specific informal tests incorporating trial lessons have been proposed by Mills (1956) and Roswell and Natchez (1971) for assessing modality preferences in learning to read. In successive lessons, new words are taught using four major reading approaches: visual, phonic (auditory), combination, and multi-sensory (visual-auditory-tactual-kinesthetic). The student is tested for immediate and delayed recall of the words taught. By keeping the difficulty of the words, the duration of the lessons, and the time intervals between testing constant, one is able to parcel out modality effects and identify a child's learning style. Similar trial lessons have been recommended for assessing modality strengths in spelling (Westerman, 1971).

The trial lessons paradigm is highly similar to diagnostic prescriptive teaching. As such, it can be applied in any subject matter area. Trial lessons and diagnostic prescriptive teaching permit the investigation of modality preference in the actual content area of concern without having to generalize from tests that were not specifically designed for this purpose.

In consideration of the nature and degree of a child's perceptual deficits, the teacher must decide if it is necessary to emphasize the open channel for instruction. In most learning situations, the visual and auditory systems play primary roles. It is possible to adjust the relative demands on these channels to capitalize on a child's learning strengths. When a student demonstrates severe deficiencies in both visual and auditory processing, the teacher can enlist tactual-kinesthetic cues to provide an additional association. Knowledge of a student's modality preferences thus aids in the formulation of teaching strategies and in the selection of appropriate instructional materials.

Attention Control   Students differ considerably in their ability to focus and sustain attention on a given task. Children with learning difficulties are generally more distractible than their peers. These children exhibit problems in filtering out extraneous stimuli in order to attend to the significant information. Because attention occurs very early in the information processing sequence, faulty attention skills can seriously impede learning.

There is no way of knowing for certain when an individual is "paying attention." Therefore, one can assess attention skills only by measuring the behavioral evidence available. One possible route is to investigate the products of attention, because it can be assumed that a person must attend in order to perform an assigned task adequately. It is the student who seldom completes assignments or who makes many errors along the way that raises concern about attention skills.

A word of caution is in order. Assessment of attention abilities can easily be confounded by other factors. A teacher should carefully examine task demands to ensure that the amount of work and the skills required are reasonable and appropriate for a given child. Once this has been checked, baseline observational data may be collected to determine the actual number of assignments or the percentage of assigned work completed acceptably.

In addition to measuring the products of attention, one can also investigate the process. Certain behaviors suggest whether or not an individual is attending. Eye contact and body orientation are two common indicators. Specific signs of task involvement, such as writing in a workbook or focusing on an open book and turning pages, may also serve as evidence of attending. Obviously, such behavioral indicators are fallible. It is possible for an individual to demonstrate eye contact or to turn pages in a book without really attending to the task. For this reason, multiple measures of attentive behaviors usually provide a more reliable indication. Most of the behaviors associated with the process of attending are continuous rather than discrete and would, therefore, lend themselves better to duration recording, interval recording, or time sampling than frequency counting.

The teacher who is aware of the extent of a child's attention difficulties is better prepared to deal with them in educational programming. In most cases, a teaching strategy that reduces distraction and directs attention to the significant aspects of instruction is most helpful. The format of instructional materials should be chosen with care to include an appropriate medium and an uncluttered presentation. Some materials may be found to use color coding or other means of highlighting the important information. Pacing of materials is also a concern. Any lessons that drag in tempo may encourage distractibility. Aid in attracting and sustaining attention may come from the motivating attributes of the material. A colorful and attractive design may capture a child's attention, and interesting thematic content may sustain it.

Reflection-Impulsivity   Through the work of Kagan and his associates, a generalized tendency has been recognized for a child to display fast or slow decision times across various kinds of tasks that contain response uncertainty (Kagan and Kogan, 1970). In problem-solving situations, reflective individuals pause and evaluate the quality of a decision before responding. Impulsive children, on the other hand, are less cautious, respond more quickly, and make a greater number of errors. Bruner observed similar tendencies in children, but labeled them differently. His "conservative focusers" perform reflectively, and the "gambling focusers" are more impulsive (Bruner, Goodnow, and Austin, 1956).

A visual discrimination task devised by Kagan, "Matching Familiar Figures," has been used to identify an individual's characteristic response style. The consistency noted across different kinds of tasks suggest that an observant teacher could detect evidence of extreme reflection or impulsivity from a child's classwork by focusing on the time it takes a student to formulate a response and the number of errors made.

The student's style on this dimension should be taken into account when decisions are made regarding the pacing of lessons. Impulsive children respond more favorably to instruction when speed of responding is de-emphasized and accuracy only is stressed. If the slow tempo of the reflective child is interfering with his performance, materials that encourage more rapid responding may be helpful.

Levels of Processing   The fourth aspect of learning style related to information processing concerns the levels of complexity or abstraction that can be successfully employed. Most of the theoretical models have postulated levels to represent the range of human information processing (Bown, 1972; Kirk, McCarthy, and Kirk, 1968; Meyers and Hammill, 1969; Osgood, 1957). The most basic level deals with sensory data. Successive levels correspond to perceptual motor and habitual automatic functions. The most organized levels require highly symbolic cognitive integration.

At present, the concept of processing levels requires further clarification and empirical support. Neither assessment nor treatment procedures has been adequately developed for classroom application. The practice of characterizing a child's competence in manipulating symbols is not new, however. The traditional distinction between concrete and abstract functioning captures the essence of the current, more elaborate constructs.

A child who is very concrete in his thought processes depends heavily on sensory and perceptual information. To understand a concept, he must experience it. Slightly less concrete learners can profit from pictorial representations. At the advanced end of the continuum are students functioning at the abstract level. These learners are able to deal successfully with symbols in verbal and graphic form.

Observation and diagnostic prescriptive teaching are the major tools for assessing a child's differential ability to manipulate concrete things or abstract symbols. The instructional materials chosen for a particular child should utilize a format that is appropriate for his level of processing.

The two remaining dimensions of learning style are not derived from the information processing approach. A child's responsiveness to reinforcement and grouping arrangements are additional factors that affect the choice of teaching strategies and materials. Each of these aspects of learning style is now considered.

Reinforcement   Reinforcement can be defined only by its effect on behavior. What serves to strengthen or maintain behavior of one individual may have far different effects on another. For this reason, it is necessary to determine the types of reinforcers that work with a particular child.

The majority of students respond favorably to certain generalized or common reinforcers, such as attention, praise, knowledge of results, and grades. These are some of the customary means of maintaining desired school behaviors. Many children with learning and behavior problems, however, do not work sufficiently for these rewards. They often need more personalized and powerful reinforcers. Tokens, such as gold stars, check marks, or chips, may be effective with some pupils. Others will work hard to earn special privileges. There are children who require tangible rewards, and some who will respond only to food, a primary reinforcer.

A teacher may identify effective reinforcers in a number of ways. The most direct means of finding out reward preferences is to ask the child. Interest inventories may also be used for this purpose. More reliable information, however, is obtained through observation. The way a student chooses to spend his free time is usually indicative of his real interests. Other clues from a child's behavior suggest things he might respond to. Prospective reinforcers must always be tested empirically. Observing and recording data are the only means of determining for certain whether the application of a particular contingency is truly reinforcing.

The schedule, as well as the type of reinforcement, is important. Most students perform adequately under conditions of partial or intermittent reinforcement. Continuous reinforcement is necessary only when new behaviors are being acquired. Exceptional children, however, often have difficulty in learning to defer reinforcement.

Understanding the needs of a particular child regarding type and schedule of reinforcement allows the teacher to choose suitable teaching strategies and materials.

Grouping Preferences   In most classrooms, a number of different grouping arrangements are employed to facilitate teaching and learning. Many children function productively whether they are working in a large group, small group, a student dyad, one-to-one with the teacher, or independently. There are other pupils, however, who do not work as effectively in one or more of these modes. Describing a child's learning style on this dimension involves identifying his productive grouping patterns.

It is not unusual to find that special children need a greater degree of structure and supervision. They often learn best in teacher-directed, small group, or one-to-one situations. Peer tutoring may also be effective with many students. Children with learning and behavior problems have seldom developed the necessary skills to work independently for more than a brief period of time. A diagnostic prescriptive approach will help a teacher to identify the specific arrangements that are successful with an individual child.

The child's grouping preferences should be taken into consideration when the teacher is planning instructional modes and examining the formats of instructional materials.

Case Example

Jason's levels of functioning and specific difficulties have been described earlier in this chapter. This final section of the assessment summary deals with Jason's learning style.

Modality Preference   Test results, observation, and prescriptive teaching all concur that Jason has strong auditory-verbal skills. He is able to profit more from a teacher's oral explanations than from reading and studying about a concept on his own. He seems to learn best when he is allowed frequent opportunities to verbalize his understandings.

Attention Control   Jason has trouble maintaining his attention on task. At present, he is completing only about 40% of his assignments. He is highly distracted by other events in the room and can work more productively in a private study office. Jason often refuses to use the carrels, however.

Reflection-Impulsivity Jason displays many impulsive tendencies. His patterns of guessing at reading words, making numerous careless errors in math, and erasing and crossing out in handwriting support this interpretation. Jason's impulsivity becomes more pronounced in testing or in other situations where he feels on the spot. When confronted with evidence of behavioral infractions, for example, his outrageous explanations reflect his style of grabbing quickly for answers.

Levels of Processing Jason seems able to deal adequately with the abstract, particularly verbal concepts.

Reinforcement Jason is highly responsive to social reinforcers. His disruptive behaviors in the classroom seem to be maintained by attention from his peers. Attention from the teacher, even in the form of a correction, has the effect of increasing behavior. Praise from the teacher for appropriate behavior works only if it is given at frequent intervals.

Jason's preferred reward is food. He has responded favorably to the contingency that he must complete his assignments before he can have his snack, which consist of fruit and a diet drink he brings from home. Because of Jason's weight problem, the teacher would rather not use food as a reward.

Jason does respond to activity reinforcers. Talking aloud without permission decreased 40% when Jason was allowed to choose a special privilege each day that his behavior improved. His preferred activities were reading comics and using the cassette recorder. Jason tires easily of the same reinforcers, however, and needs novelty.

Grouping Preferences Jason has difficulty working constructively in a large group. His disruptive behaviors occur most frequently in this setting. Jason also performs poorly when asked to do written work on his own, but he can read or use manipulative materials independently for as long as 20 minutes, at times. Jason tends to make abusive comments when he must work in a small group with girls. He does participate adequately in teacher-directed lessons for small groups of boys, but responds most consistently to one-to-one instruction.

SUMMARY

Diagnosis has been defined as an ongoing process of gathering and interpreting educationally relevant information about a particular learner. Meaningful educational diagnosis should result in the accurate specification of functional levels, skills and behaviors of concern, and learning style. These three aspects of student performance have important implications for instructional decision-making.

A number of different techniques may be employed in assessment. Norm-referenced, standardized tests contribute primarily to the determination of performance levels. Formal and informal criterion-referenced testing, direct observation, and diagnostic prescriptive teaching are the most useful tools for defining problems behaviorally and for analyzing learning style. Specific dimensions of learning style discussed in this chapter included modality preference, attention control, reflection-impulsivity, levels of processing, reinforcement, and grouping preferences.

The role of the classroom teacher is emphasized, because it is this individual who is ultimately responsible for translating assessment results into a workable instructional program. Other school personnel and professionals from related fields may be called upon to assist in the diagnostic process as needed. Preliminary diagnosis is completed when there is a sufficient data base for planning an individualized program.

Knowledge of a student's functional levels, specific skills, and behaviors of concern should enable the teacher to pinpoint instructional goals and objectives. Awareness of the child's learning style permits the more systematic selection of teaching strategies. In turn, the chosen objectives and teaching strategies provide the bases for the selection of instructional materials. Once preliminary diagnosis has contributed to the development of the initial individualized program, the system should become self-perpetuating. The program is continually refined and updated in light of current student performance.

REFERENCES

Bown, J. C. 1972. A communication model for evaluation and remediation. Except. Child. 38: 385–394.

Bruner, J., Goodnow, J., and Austin, A. 1956. A Study in Thinking. John Wiley and Sons, New York.

Friedus, E. 1964. Methodology for the classroom teacher. In J. Hellmuth (ed.), The Special Child in Century 21, pp. 303–321. Special Child Publications, Seattle.

Kagan, J., and Kogan, N. 1970. Individuality and cognitive performance. In P. H. Mussen (ed.), Carmichael's Manual of Child Psychology. Vol. 1, pp. 1273–1365. John Wiley and Sons, New York.

Kirk, S. A., McCarthy, J. P., and Kirk, W. D. 1968. The Illinois Test of Psycholinguistic Abilities. Rev. ed. University of Illinois Press, Urbana, Ill.

Larsen, S. C., Rogers, D., and Sowell, V. 1976. The use of selected perceptual tests in differentiating between normal and learning disabled children. J. Learn. Dis. 9: 85–90.

Meyers, P. I., and Hammill, D. D. 1969. Methods for Learning Disorders. John Wiley and Sons, New York.

Mills, R. E. 1956. Learning Methods Test. 1612 E. Broward Blvd., Fort Lauderdale, Fl.

O'Grady, D. V. 1974. Psycholinguistic abilities in learning disabled, emotionally disturbed, and normal children. J. Spec. Educ. 8: 157–165.

Osgood C. E. 1957. A behavioristic analysis of perception and language as cognitive phenomena.   In J. S. Bruner (ed.), Contemporary Approaches to Cognition, pp. 75–118. Harvard University Press, Cambridge, Ma.

Quick, A. D., Little T. L., and Campbell, A. A. 1974. Project MEMPHIS: Instruments for Individual Program Planning and Evaluation. Fearon Publishers, Belmont, Ca.

Roswell, F., and Natchez, G. 1971. Reading Disability: Diagnosis and Treatment. Rev. ed. Basic Books, New York.

Sabatino, D. A., Ysseldyke, J. E., and Woolston, J. 1973. Diagnostic-prescriptive perceptual training with mentally retarded children. Am. J. Ment. Def. 78: 27–36.

Salvia, J., and Ysseldyke, J. E. 1978. Assessment in Special and Regular Education. Houghton Mifflin Company, Boston.

Sattler, J. M. 1974. Assessment of Children's Intelligence. Rev. ed. W. B. Saunders Company, Philadelphia.

Sulzer, B., and Mayer, G. R. 1972. Behavior Modification Procedures for School Personnel. Holt, Rinehart and Winston, New York.

Terman, L. M., and Merrill, M. A. 1973. Standford-Binet Intelligence Scale: Manual for the Third Revision. Houghton Mifflin Company, Boston.

Wechsler, D. 1955. Manual for the Wechsler Adult Intelligence Scale. Psychological Corporation, New York.

Wechsler, D. 1967. Manual for the Wechsler Preschool and Primary Scale of Intelligence. Psychological Corporation, New York.

Wechsler, D. 1974. Manual for the Wechsler Intelligence Scale for Children—Revised. Psychological Corporation, New York.

Westerman, G. 1971. Spelling and Writing. Dimensions, San Rafael, Ca.

Ysseldyke, J. E. 1973. Diagnostic-prescriptive teaching: The search for aptitude-treatment interactions. In L. Mann and D. L. Sabatino (eds.), The First Review of Special Education. Grune and Stratton, Philadelphia.

4

Critical Dimensions of Instructional Materials

Virginia K. Laycock, Ed.D.

NEED FOR MODELS FOR ANALYZING
AND SELECTING INSTRUCTIONAL MATERIALS

A visit to a local or regional Materials Center, a survey of current publishers' catalogs, or a browse through materials displays at a professional conference should convince anyone that the production of instructional materials has become a multimillion dollar industry. Instructional materials and equipment of all types now offer numerous options for instructional programming. More teaching aids are available to draw upon than ever before. Although it might seem that the wealth of instructional materials would ease the burden of the classroom teacher, it has instead created new difficulties. When keeping abreast of recent developments is challenging in itself, the task of selecting particular products over alternatives often seems overwhelming.

Many teachers have not been adequately prepared to critically examine instructional materials in order to make informed choices. Because the use of materials plays a major role in individualizing instruction, one would expect this topic to be addressed in textbooks employed in the preservice training of teachers. A survey of current methods textbooks in special education revealed that this is not the case. Out of 20 textbooks on teaching exceptional children published between 1972 and 1977, only three dealt specifically with the analysis and selection of instructional materials (Haring and Schiefelbusch, 1976; Meyen, Gault, and Howard, 1976; Smith, 1974). Despite the seriousness of the problem, teachers have been given little guidance in the decision-making process.

When teachers do attempt to choose their own instructional materials, certain prominent features of the materials tend to overshadow other important considerations. Attractive design and packaging, for example, can produce biasing effects if the consumer is not aware of the many other factors that contribute to the effectiveness of a material. Choices are often influenced solely by budgetary limitations, when a more careful investigation might reveal that the least expensive material is not necessarily the best educational bargain. Without more definite guidelines, judgments easily become based on subjective impressions rather than on objective assessment of material characteristics. Recognizing the dilemma, many teachers simply shy away from selecting new and different materials and resort to using those already on hand. Clearly, what is needed is a practical and systematic model for analyzing and selecting instructional materials.

Model for Materials Analysis

Few systems have been proposed that adequately guide the process of materials selection. As Adamson and Van Etten (1970) have pointed out, a useful approach must be based on the analysis of differences in instructional materials that are directly related to information in the diagnostic profiles of individual learners. It is generally agreed that the strengths and weaknesses of the student should be the primary consideration in selecting materials. Other factors, however, such as teaching style and cost efficiency, necessarily affect the choices to be made. Unless a model systematically deals with these concerns as well as the variables related to learner needs and learning style, it cannot be applied to the selection of instructional materials in a realistic or meaningful way.

The Brown Instructional Analysis System (1974) is an example of an approach that is extremely elaborate with respect to the learning task, but that fails to take the more practical issues into account. Brown's system is based on Guilford's three-dimensional Structure of Intellect Model. Materials are characterized in terms of stimulus, operation, and response properties. Additional variables defined as subject matter area, difficulty level, time consumption, independence-dependence, and durability are also assessed. The process proposed requires working knowledge of Guilford's Model and Meeker's Flow Charts of Guilford's Structure of Intellect. The adoption of this framework leads to an intricate analysis of instructional materials in terms that do not readily correspond with the language customarily used in educational diagnosis and programming. Although Brown's model offers a thorough analysis of the instructional task, it ignores many other material characteristics that are relevant to teaching.

Weinthaler and Rotberg (1970) have developed a model for materials selection that is based on an inventory of learning abilities and skills. The authors recommend that material characteristics be assessed in the same terms that are used in the diagnostic descriptions of learners' assets and deficits. Six specific variables that provide the basis for matching materials to learner needs include level of the task, modality of reception, modality of expression, types of psycholinguistic processes, the number of modalities, and the content of the task. Although the Weinthaler and Rotberg system attempts to clarify the role of materials in individualized programming, its practical value is limited by its scope. The model focuses exclusively on processing requirements and fails to address the broader range of concerns in materials selection.

One of the most balanced and comprehensive approaches for analyzing instructional materials is employed by the Prescriptive Materials Retrieval System (1970). Eight basic types of descriptors are used to characterize materials in terms of major areas, specific content, format and special characteristics, grade level, reading level, mental age, input-output requirements, and psycholinguistic processes. Within these categories, over 400 different descriptors are used to classify instructional materials. Thousands of materials have been analyzed and coded into the retrieval system. Use of the Prescriptive Materials Retrieval system greatly facilitates the investigation of specific material attributes and the selection of appropriate teaching aids. Unfortunately, few teachers have access to this commercially produced system. This approach has nonetheless served as a model for the systematic analysis and selection of materials.

Recognizing that most educators do not have access to well-developed systems, the National Center on Educational Media and Materials for the Handicapped (NCEMMH) sponsored the development of a test of "Standard Criteria for the Selection and Evaluation of Instructional Materials" (1976). These guidelines explicitly direct the teacher through a four-stage process, outlined in Table 1. Stage I, Identification of Needs, requires a description of the target learner and the learning environment before any consideration of instructional materials. Initial Selection occurs in Stage II. In searching for potential materials, the teacher is encouraged to consult many different sources for information, including colleagues, journals, materials bibliographies, curriculum centers, professional organizations, governmental agencies, and retrieval systems. The teacher screens available information to identify at least two instructional materials that seem appropriate and warrant further investigation. The third stage, Review, necessitates actual examination of prospective materials in an in depth analysis. The teacher attempts to match

Table 1.   Standard criteria for the selection and evaluation of instructional material[a]

Teacher level

   I. Identification of Needs
    A.   Learner characteristics
    B.   Program characteristics

  II. Initial Selection
    A.   Search
    B.   Screen

 III. Review
    A.   Analyses of material
    B.   Matching material to learner

 IV. Decision Making

[a] Prepared by the ALRC/SO/NCEMMH Program, 1976, The Ohio State University, Columbus, Ohio. Copies of actual document available from: Council for Exceptional Children, 1920 Association Drive, Reston, Va. 22091.

specific material characteristics to previously defined learner requirements. To direct the teacher through analysis and matching, 23 questions pertaining to different qualities of the material and 11 questions relating to compatibility of the material for instructional needs are provided. Decision-making is then possible in Stage IV. Choices should be further individualized by the teacher on the basis of particular priority concerns.

The sequence of steps recommended in the "Standard Criteria" table provide realistic guidelines for the selection process. Characteristics of the learner and the educational program must be defined before any consideration of instructional materials. The range of alternatives is then narrowed as the teacher attempts to locate materials that seem appropriate. These materials are investigated in detail to identify critical attributes. Only after such analysis can materials be accurately matched to learning needs. The remainder of this chapter describes one method for assessing material characteristics that can facilitate this selection process.

Guidelines for the Analysis of Instructional Materials

A useful system aids in characterizing instructional materials along those dimensions most relevant for educational purposes. Aspects of materials that directly affect the learner must be thoroughly explored. It is also essential to identify related financial and managerial requirements. In order to deal with major considerations systematically, the model now introduces clusters factors into three areas: instructional specifications, teaching concerns, and cost effectiveness.

Some of the information required for this materials assessment may be gathered from publishers' catalogs or brochures. In most cases, however, complete analysis requires actual examination of materials and accompanying manuals. This approach enables a teacher to review materials in a simple yet thorough manner, because each material is analyzed and briefly described in terms of 18 specific factors.

Instructional Specifications   Factors included in the set of instructional specifications denote the primary instructional qualities of materials. As a piece of material is investigated in terms of these variables, a teacher learns what the material purports to teach, for whom it is intended, and how it attempts to accomplish its purposes. The eight separate factors involved in delineating these instructional specifications are described in detail below.

Objectives   A first concern in approaching a piece of instructional material should be to identify the specific skills or concepts to be taught. This information is typically presented in catalog descriptions and in prominent sections of teachers manuals or guides. Although statements of purpose may be easy to locate, they are often written in vague and general terms. For example, a workbook may be marketed "to strengthen vocabulary skills," or a filmstrip designed "to increase awareness of ecological problems." Such statements do nothing more than identify the subject area or topic.

More meaningful statements of purpose focus on the actual skills to be developed. Objectives should be described in terms of measurable learning outcomes or skills that a student should be able to perform after using the material as directed. A math material, for instance, may assist the learner "to compute sums of two one-digit numbers." After using a readiness game, the student will be expected "to name the colors red, blue, and yellow." Many publishers are now providing behavioral objectives of this nature for their materials.

More complex materials usually involve an entire series of objectives. In such cases, the teacher must be concerned not only with content, but also with the scope and sequence of objectives. Scope is examined to determine if all the desired skills are included. To assist students in developing study skills, for example, the material may be sufficiently broad in scope to deal with uses of the dictionary, table of contents, index, glossary, encyclopedia, and card catalog. The sequence, or the order in which skills are introduced, should be logical and developmental, building from the simpler to the more complex. To facilitate the analysis of materials, many publishers are providing complete scope and sequence charts to accompany their programs.

When objectives have already been stated in specific, behavioral terms, this initial task in materials assessment is an easy one. It becomes more difficult and time consuming when such objectives are not available, because then one must examine a material in considerable detail in order to identify the specific skills that can be taught.

Target Population Every piece of instructional material is directed toward a particular group of learners. The authors focus on students with certain characteristics and capabilities when developing the materials. Some materials have been designed for specific types of learners, and others have broader ranges of applicability. In assessing instructional materials, it is important to note significant characteristics of the target population.

Chronological age is the most frequently used descriptor. Authors and publishers usually identify the age range for which the material is intended. This suggests that the material has been geared toward the interests, abilities, and learning needs typically displayed by students at that age. Because exceptional children, by definition, have not developed at the same rate as their chronological peers in all areas, age itself may not be the most meaningful descriptor when one is concerned about materials for the handicapped. Mental age range is often preferred, because it more accurately reflects the developmental level of intended learners. Mental age alone is insufficient, nonetheless. An adult retardate may have the mental age of a young child, but their interests and needs may be worlds apart. Descriptive data are, therefore, most complete when both chronological and mental age ranges are specified.

Additional developmental descriptors may be necessary, depending on the nature of the material. Materials dealing with language skills may cite a language age, whereas materials devoted to visual-motor training may state perceptual age equivalents. Grade level equivalents are often employed to limit the focus of materials for academic subjects. The reading level of printed material is an essential consideration. When such information is not provided by the publishers, a teacher may need to calculate this by employing one of the many readability formulas available (Fry, 1969; McLaughlin, 1969; Spache, 1953). In all basic skill areas, grade level descriptors can contribute to the identification of the learners most likely to benefit from use of a material.

When materials are designed specifically for handicapped children, it is helpful to locate as many relevant descriptors of the target population as possible. Because developmental discrepancies are often noted in levels of functioning across different areas, single normative descriptors are seldom adequate. It is highly possible that a child's chronological age, mental age, and reading age are all different. Certain qualitative descriptors are often specified in addition to the age and grade equivalents. In some cases, the nature of the handicapping condition is an important consideration. A particular material may be designed for the blind or visually impaired. Another material may be directed toward primary age trainable mentally retarded children. Background experiences are of concern in some instances. Many materials are now geared toward students living in urban or inner city areas because their interests, problems, and daily activities may differ considerably from their rural or suburban counterparts. Materials intended for learners with special needs, therefore, may need to employ a variety of descriptors to adequately characterize the target population.

Prerequisite Skills   Although both the quantitative and qualitative descriptors discussed above are helpful in limiting the focus of a material, they are broad referents and do no indicate specific abilities of the learner that are necessary for successful use of the material. For this reason, many authors list entry behaviors or prerequisite skills required for achieving maximum results with a material. For a supplementary material dealing with basic addition facts, it may be recommended that a child identify and write numerals 0-9 and count objects to 9 before attempting to use the addition exercises. A set of typing drills may be designed for use after a student is able to demonstrate correct posture for typing, insertion of paper, and positioning of fingers on the home keys.

Such specific information is valuable in determining how a material fits into the general developmental sequence for the designated skill area. It also contributes to more accurate identification of prospective users. Once again, if the desired information is not provided by authors and publishers, the necessary prerequisite skills must be pinpointed by the teacher while assessing the material.

Learning Modalities   The review of material characteristics must include an analysis of the way in which the learner interacts with the material. By considering the way information is presented, one can identify primary input or receptive modalities. Many materials rely heavily on one receptive channel. Textbooks, worksheets, flashcards, and charts are familiar examples of visually-oriented materials; records and tapes typify materials with primary auditory emphasis. Many other materials are designed to involve more than one receptive modality. Multisensory materials may be audiovisual. Movies, television, videotapes, and filmstrips are common audiovisual materials in which sight and sound are presented simultaneously. Many individualized programs employ cassette tape presentations to assist students in reading or to direct them through written exercises. In instances where the learner is required to handle or manipulate materials, tactual and kinesthetic modalities are activated. Puzzles, tracing templates, and concrete aids for counting are typical multisensory materials that incorporate tactual and kinesthetic involvement.

Response or output modalities must also be considered. Although all responses are actually motoric in nature, it is often useful to differentiate certain major classes of motor behavior. Verbal and graphic responses are typically distinguished from other gross and fine motor responses. In addition, it is helpful to identify the complexity of the response required. Some materials may call for a simple verbal response such as "yes or no," or another answer of only a few words. Other materials may involve more complex verbal responding, such as telling a story, defining a term, or explaining a concept. Likewise, graphic responses vary in complexity from the simple marking of choices to the writing of complete sentences or paragraphs. Gross and fine motor responses also range from simple head nodding and pointing to more complex motor patterns, such as pantomiming, reproducing parquetry designs, or operating equipment.

Materials should be classified by listing major channels involved in both receiving and responding to information conveyed by the material. A domino game, for example, may be characterized as requiring visual input and simple motor output. A set of story-starter cards for creative writing may involve visual input and complex graphic output. A taped phonics program may present information using both visual and auditory channels and may require simple verbal and graphic responses. These are but a few examples of the many possible combinations of input and output modalities found in instructional materials.

Format Learning modalities are closely linked with instructional format. It is necessary, nonetheless, to specify the format, because two instructional materials may involve the same input-output requirements but may organize and present information in different ways. A first concern regarding format is to identify the medium of communication employed. Major types of educational media include real objects, models, pictures, print, audiotapes, overhead transparencies, slides, filmstrips, motion pictures, and videotapes (Thiagarajan, Semmel, and Semmel, 1974). A teacher may further categorize certain formats according to mode of presentation. Printed media, for instance, may be subclassified into textbooks, workbooks, charts, duplicated sheets, reading kits, flash-cards, etc. Audiotapes are more specifically described as cassette or reel-to-reel tapes.

Beyond identifying the medium employed, certain judgments are required to complete the assessment of instructional format. The quality or clarity of presentation should be appraised. Questions such as the following should be considered. Are audiotapes intelligible and free from distortion? Are the voice quality and the pacing of speech effective? Is a chart readily visible from an appropriate distance? Are illustrations that accompany the printed text of sufficient quality to portray the intended information?

Additionally, spatial features of the format should be examined whenever the material relies on visual methods of presentation. The teacher must determine whether items are suitably sized and spaced for the designated population of learners. If a material is designed for young or developmentally immature children, then large stimuli should be presented in an uncluttered manner. More advanced learners are able to deal with a greater number of items and details per page or frame.

A final consideration regarding format for presentation pertains to safety features. Materials should be designed to minimize hazards when in use by the target audience. Materials intended for young children, therefore, should be examined for potential dangers, such as sharp points, rough edges, and small pieces that might be easily swallowed. General sturdiness should be tested to avoid injuries that may result from breakage. It is apparent, then, that thorough assessment of instructional format requires that the reviewer not only identify the medium employed but also make certain judgments concerning the appropriateness of the chosen format for the intended learners.

Pacing   Pacing refers to the speed at which the student progresses through the material. Both rate and flexibility of pacing should be taken into account when characterizing materials of this dimension. Two factors that affect rate of presentation are the size of the steps in the skill sequence and the amount of practice provided at each level. When a complex skill is broken down into only a few sub-skills and reinforcement activities are limited, a material should be considered fast-paced. In contrast, a material should be described as slowly paced if it offers extensive practice for each small step involved in the attainment of the desired goal.

For many materials, pacing is not pre-established, and the learner is allowed to proceed at his own rate. Such self-pacing permits a material to be tailored closely to student needs. For this reason, self-paced materials are often labeled "individualized." Adequate determination of pacing, then, involves rating allowances made for individual differences as well as rating the pace along a slow-to-fast continuum.

Feedback Mechanisms   As a material is reviewed, the teacher must also determine how feedback or knowledge of results are provided following student responses. This is an essential consideration, because learning theory supports the principle that practice enhances learning only when it is reinforced. Typically, the communication of feedback is left to the discretion of the teacher when materials are meant to be used under direct supervision. Some teachers manuals do suggest general guidelines for this process, and a few prescribe the exact procedures to be used following both correct and error responses.

The provision of knowledge of results is most critical when materials are intended for independent student use. If the learner is to proceed on his own through individualized or programmed lessons, then feedback mechanisms must be directly incorporated into the materials. There should be provisions for reinforcing desired responses as well as for correcting errors. Programmed materials typically provide knowledge of results following every response by the learner. In most cases, the student is instructed to correct any frame in which his answer does not match the answer provided. Individualized materials usually direct the student to check his work for each lesson by consulting the appropriate key. In addition to rating whether or not knowledge of results is provided, the teacher should also consider the number of responses required of the learner before feedback information is given. In general, learning occurs most efficiently when students are frequently informed concerning the accuracy of their performance. In any media, materials designed for independent use should allow frequent checking of responses and permit advancement only by the performance of correct responses.

Motivating Factors   A final instructional specification involves those aspects of the material that attract learner interest. Any piece of instructional material should be designed to appeal to the particular population addressed. Despite the adage against judging a book by its cover, students often base their opinions of materials on first impressions. Materials need not be flashy in appearance, but they should be sufficiently colorful and attractive to stimulate attention.

Thematic relevancy is a motivating factor along with aesthetic appeal. Students respond more eagerly to instructional materials that capitalize on their interest. Educational games, for example, often incorporate sports themes. Materials for young children may involve cartoon characters in presenting information. Such materials draw upon students' interest and experiences to make learning more meaningful and also more fun.

The issue of relevancy assumes great importance with respect to reading materials. Although readers often include an assortment of classics selections, historical sketches, folktales, and features on people from other lands, they should also deal with contemporary life in a realistic way. Few students are motivated by bland or outdated content. Illustrations have a similar effect. If the material is meant to be compatible with the background and needs of the target learners, then both the text and accompanying pictures must reflect current life styles. In reviewing materials, therefore, the teacher must examine the ways in which publishers utilize elements of content as well as external design to attract and sustain student interest.

Teaching Concerns   The first set of factors, Instructional Specifications, centered on meeting the needs of the learner, but the set of material characteristics now under consideration focuses on needs of the teacher. Attributes of instructional materials clustered in this group refer to teaching style and instructional setting. One investigates those features of a material that facilitate its use by a particular teacher within a given classroom situation. Factors included in this group relate to teacher competencies, teaching environment, teaching aids, evaluative procedures, and teacher time.

Teacher Competencies   Most instructional materials are designed to be used under the direction of a teacher who has had formal training in educational theory and methodology. Basic competencies for working with children are assumed. Given the vast array of educational materials now available, however, it is perhaps presumptuous to believe that all teachers already possess the skills necessary for effective implementation. In some instances, specialized skills or training may be necessary to use a material as prescribed. Certain affective education materials, for example, are recommended for use only by teachers or counselors who have training and experience in communication and group process skills. Publishers of many other instructional programs, particularly those that are innovative in nature, suggest that inservice training be provided before teachers attempt to apply the materials. Consultants from the publishing companies are usually available to assist educators who are using their materials.

Although sophisticated materials and equipment may require specialized skills of professional educators, other materials have been intentionally designed for use by paraprofessionals or student tutors with no formal training. Because materials are produced for such diverse purposes, it becomes important for the reviewer to note the types and levels of expertise required for directing the use of a particular material effectively.

Teaching Environment The management of physical and human resources within a classroom directly affects the impact of instructional materials. For this reason, it is necessary to identify favorable conditions for use of a material. Grouping arrangement is a first consideration. Some materials are meant to be employed with large groups, but others are meant for small groups, one-to-one instruction, or independent work. Classroom structure or organization is another variable to consider. Many materials are designed to be incorporated into teacher-directed lessons, but other materials are more suited to an individualized or learning center approach.

Physical space is also a factor. One must consider how much room is required for proper use and storage of a material. Finally, it must be noted whether any special equipment or facilities are necessary. A set of cassette tapes would be useless without a cassette tape player. A listening station with head phones might also be advised. Laboratory facilities should be available in order to benefit fully from many science materials. These are but a few of the situations in which environmental conditions critically affect the usefulness of a material. It is essential, therefore, to describe relevant aspects of the learning environment in which a material is to be used.

Teaching Aids In examining instructional materials, teachers are usually interested in the supportive resources provided. Most materials are accompanied by teachers guides, which vary from simple pamphlets to elaborate handbooks. Information should be presented to explain the rationale and design of the material and direct its implementation. Whatever the size of the teachers manual, it is essential that instructions for use of the material are clearly written and complete.

Beyond these basic guidelines, manuals can offer teachers additional assistance in tailoring the material to specific needs. Many times, preparatory and follow-up activities are suggested. In some cases, alternative activities are included in each lesson to facilitate individualization. Techniques are often recommended for adapting lessons for learners with special problems or for enriching experiences for advanced pupils. It is often helpful for the manual to provide a list of related references and professional resources. Some supplementary materials even provide charts showing how their lessons are correlated with those in major developmental programs.

The format of the teachers manual may also be of concern. Information is easier to locate when an index is provided for more lengthy manuals. Subheadings in bold face type serve the same purpose when guidelines are presented in more concise form for less complex materials. If the manual must be used as a reference during the actual lesson, instructions for the teacher must be legible. Many teachers guides use color coding to distinguish the teacher's script from the surrounding text. Whatever format is employed should ensure that all information is readily accessible and lesson plans are easily followed. Characterizing teaching aids thus involves assessing both the quality and the quantity of the information provided.

Evaluative Criteria   Another concern from the teacher's perspective is the inclusion of evaluative procedures. When criterion checks or tests are directly incorporated into the material, the teacher is freed from the difficult and time consuming task of constructing appropriate measures of student performance. When materials are self-paced and individualized, it becomes critical that evaluative components are provided. Without such criterion checks built into the materials, it is extremely difficult to monitor student progress accurately.

Determination of whether or not evaluative measures are included in a program is only a first step. One must also appraise the adequacy of the evaluative procedures. Student performance should be tested at appropriate intervals. Check-tests that are widely spaced may fail to reveal learning problems in the early stages. Individual progress is managed most efficiently when performance is frequently assessed. Not only is timing important, but so is the nature of the evaluative tasks. Skills evaluated should relate directly to stated objectives. A sufficient number of responses should be sampled to gather reliable data and to avoid excessive bias from chance responding. When criterion checks are constructed in light of these considerations, one obtains a representative measure of student performance.

A final point related to evaluation involves the standard or criterion specified for mastery. The authors of many programs suggest levels of proficiency to be attained before students should advance to successive skills. Results of field testing have often contributed to the selection of criteria. When criteria for mastery are provided, along with evaluative procedures, the teacher gains valuable assistance in instructional decision-making. For this reason, a teacher should investigate evaluative components of instructional materials.

Teacher Time   A very real concern of teachers is time—time to perform the myriad responsibilities necessary to maximize learning opportunities for children. A critical aspect of instruction materials, therefore, is the amount of teacher time consumed in preparation, supervision, and evaluation. Materials vary greatly in this respect.

Preparation may demand a great deal of time if activities must be planned, equipment gathered, and materials arranged. On the other hand, preparation time is minimized when teachers guides are complete and explicit, and materials for each activity are easily accessible. The amount of time devoted to supervising use of a material may also vary from negligible to excessive amounts. Although many materials require direct adult participation, others are designed to be used independently by students. Time spent evaluating student performance must also be taken into account. If a teacher must construct, administer, and correct all criterion tests, then large amounts of time must be reserved for these tasks. Much less time is devoured by evaluation and record keeping when students can take tests on their own, correct their work, and record their results.

There are no value judgments implied concerning this time dimension. Not all materials can or should be designed for independent student use. The teaching of certain skills in certain ways necessitates direct teacher involvement, which may be time consuming. The reason this factor should be considered in materials assessment is that the teacher must estimate time demands of a material in order to judge whether use of that material is feasible in terms of managing priorities in his daily schedule.

Cost Effectiveness   Needs of the learner and concerns of the teacher were paramount in reviewing the two preceeding clusters of material characteristics. The remaining set of factors pertains to practical considerations that often dictate, to a great extent, which instructional materials are finally selected for use. The determination of cost effectiveness involves weighing the purchase price of a material against the benefits likely to be derived from its use. One is not only concerned with matters of cost, durability, and the number of students served, but also with other evidence of worthiness such as research data and the avoidance of discriminatory representation. By gathering this information, one is able to determine whether a particular piece of instructional material represents a sound educational investment.

Cost   When one is reviewing instructional materials for possible purchase, the price of products cannot be overlooked. Depending on the nature and design of materials, costs may range from just a few dollars to thousands of dollars. There is more to consider, however, than list price of the material. Often, individual components of programs or kits may be purchased separately. Although the complete unit price is typically lower than the cost involved in buying each piece separately, it makes sense to purchase only certain items when the entire kit is either financially or instructionally inappropriate.

The teacher should also determine the costs of replacement parts. Many materials contain some pieces that are consumable. Students write on the materials or otherwise use them up in some way. At other times, pieces may be lost or destroyed. It is important to find out whether these parts can be purchased separately and how expensive it is to replace them. One should then estimate the projected cost over time. A particular kit, for example, may originally cost $80.00. After the first year of use, student workbooks must be replaced for $25.00 per set. Over five years, the kit actually costs $180.00. In order to avoid unexpected financial burdens, one must look beyond the initial purchase price of the material.

Durability In conjunction with cost, one must also assess the durability of the material by estimating its life expectancy if used in the manner prescribed. Unless materials are meant to be consumed in some way, they should be sufficiently sturdy in construction to resist wear and to withstand classroom accidents that commonly occur. A game constructed in a plastic frame, for instance, should not only tolerate expected manipulation by children, but also be break-resistant in case it is accidentally knocked off a desk. Materials designed specifically for handicapped students must be especially durable. Paper products should be laminated or otherwise treated so that they are easy to wipe and difficult to tear. Tough plastic, rubber, metal, and wood are likely to survive the test of time. When an instructional program involves many pieces, they should be arranged in a sturdy container to preserve their quality.

The durability of mechanical equipment intended for student use is a frequent concern. Generally, the simpler the design of the equipment, the less the chance of breakdown. The basic push-button cassette recorder, for example, has fewer parts to go wrong than a complex recorder with many dials and regulatory devices. Certain seemingly minor details, such as heavy rubber feet on a table-top machine, may reduce mishaps and contribute to the longevity of equipment. Although it would be impossible to come up with a precise figure, the teacher must gauge the length of time one could reasonably expect a piece of instructional material or equipment to hold up under normal classroom conditions.

Number Served Cost effectiveness is also determined by the number of learners who will be able to benefit from use of a material. A very expensive program suitable for only a few students may not be a good investment. In contrast, a material that can be used by many different children over time may be considered cost-effective. Filmstrips and movies are examples of materials in the latter category. Although these may involve rather large initial expenditures, they can reach sizable audiences at a time. Similarly, many other instructional materials can be used with a large group. In instances where a material can be used only by small groups or individual children, the material may still prove to be cost-effective if the turnover time is relatively brief. A Language Master, for example, is typically used by only one child at a time. Ordinarily, a student does not work with the Language Master for extended periods of time, however, and many different children are able to use the device in the average day. The number of learners involved with a particular material is therefore an important variable to consider in assessing cost effectiveness.

Research Data The ultimate test of a good educational investment is the acutal effectiveness of the material as a teaching aid. Regardless of economic advantages, unless a material does what it purports to do, it is of questionable value. Empirical results of field testing should be presented for instructional materials to demonstrate evidence of their effectiveness. Because extensive field testing before marketing is costly to publishers in terms of both time and money, this important step has often been omitted in the production of instructional materials. Certain publishing companies have been more dedicated than others to gathering such a data base. Educators themselves have often overlooked the necessity of this research.

The mere fact that field testing is conducted is not sufficient, however; one must also consider the quality of the studies reported. Sound educational research depends on many aspects of experimental design, including the size and representativeness of the sample, the duration of the study, the appropriateness of evaluative measures, and the ability to control for extraneous influences such as novelty effects.

Costly developmental or remedial materials that lack empirical support represent a serious educational gamble. The importance of demanding adequate field testing of materials cannot, therefore, be overemphasized. Teachers must seek out this information in order to assess instructional materials meaningfully.

Nondiscriminatory Representation A final factor in cost effectiveness involves the worth of the material from a human rights perspective. Given the impact of instructional materials on attitudes and beliefs as well as on cognitive skills, concern has arisen in recent years over the nonbiased portrayal of all segments of the population. Attempts are being made to correct the obvious white middle-class leanings of previous instructional materials. In response to the demands of pressure groups both within and outside the field of professional education, authors and publishers are trying to achieve greater equality in instructional content. Racial and ethnic minorities should be represented in the instructional materials. The emphasis on suburbia should be replaced by a blending of urban, suburban, and rural influences. Women should be included in instructional presentations as frequently as men.

Not only should a teacher be concerned with adequacy of representation in terms of numbers, but also in terms of roles portrayed. Stereotyping of all kinds should be avoided. Positions of prestige and honor should be shared by members of all ethnic groups. Likewise, antagonists in situations presented should be drawn from diverse backgrounds. The participation of women in the home and career world must be expanded beyond the traditional roles. Men must also be portrayed with greater sensitivity, avoiding stereotyping notions of what is "masculine" or "feminine" behavior. Instructional materials must reflect a realistic and impartial cross-section of human life.

This final characteristic of instructional materials may be difficult to assess. Discrimination is often subtle and can take many forms. Teachers must be alert to discern biasing information in instructional materials in order to avoid perpetrating prejudice. A material that distorts the uniqueness of each individual cannot be considered a good educational investment. Cost effectiveness is thus influenced by the adequacy of racial and sexual representation in instructional content.

Sample Analyses

The following is an example of a worksheet for the analysis of an instructional material:

Title of Instructional Material
Publisher

Briefly describe relevant characteristics of the material in each of the following areas.

INSTRUCTIONAL SPECIFICATIONS
1. *Objectives*   (behavioral statements, scope, sequence)
2. *Target Population*   (C.A., M.A., grade equivalents, descriptors)
3. *Prerequisite Skills*   (entry behaviors)
4. *Learning Modalities*   (input-output channels)
5. *Format*   (medium, quality, spatial, and safety features)
6. *Pacing*   (rate, flexibility)
7. *Feedback Mechanisms*   (provision and schedule of knowledge of results)
8. *Motivating Factors*   (aesthetic and thematic appeal)

TEACHING CONCERNS
1. *Teacher Competencies*   (level of training and expertise)
2. *Teaching Environment*   (classroom organization, physical requirements)
3. *Teaching Aids*   (complete teachers guide, supplementary resources)
4. *Evaluative Criteria*   (provision and adequacy of criterion measures)
5. *Teacher Time*   (preparation, supervision, evaluation)

COST EFFECTIVENESS
1. *Cost*   (total, components, replacement parts)
2. *Durability*   (years of service)
3. *Number Served*   (number of learners participating)
4. *Research Data*   (provision and adequacy of field testing)
5. *Nondiscriminatory Representation*   (racial, sexual)

When a teacher, using the analysis system described above, examines an instructional material in detail, the worksheet could be used. Recording brief notations in each of the 18 categories, a relatively simple material may be assessed in 15 to 20 minutes. More complex instructional materials may require 30 minutes to 1 hour for complete analysis.

Results of materials assessment conducted according to the proposed model are now presented. Two very different materials, a math teaching machine and an affective education kit, were chosen as examples to illustrate the flexibility of the system.

Title of Instructional Material: Digitor

Publisher: Centurion Industries, Inc.
             Redwood City, Ca. 94063

INSTRUCTIONAL SPECIFICATIONS
1. *Objectives*   To assist students in mastery of basic computation skills in addition, substraction, multiplication, and division. Digitor can be programmed to present equations in any one of the four operations. Difficulty of the factors (0-3, 4-6, 7-9, 0-9) and the number of problems may be selected as needed.
2. *Target Population*   No age or developmental levels are specified. It seems that Digitor could be used by children as young as 5 and would also be appropriate for adults. The authors recommend it for physically and educationally handicapped in special education.
3. *Prerequisite Skills*   None are specified by publisher. To operate Digitor as prescribed, a learner must be able to recognize numerals and to demonstrate understanding of $+$, $-$, $\times$, $\div$, and $=$ signs. Sufficient manual dexterity is required to depress keys approximately one-quarter inch square.
4. *Learning Modalities*   Visual input—simple motor response. Learner reads an equation displayed and depresses numbered keys to indicate his answer.

5. *Format*   Digitor is a small electric machine resembling a calculator. Keys are clearly numbered and easily accessible. Operation, reset, and advance keys are color coded. Numbers lit up on the display are large and plainly visible. Digitor is compact, light, and portable.
6. *Pacing*   Self-paced. Amount of practice at each skill level can be controlled.
7. *Feedback Mechanisms*   "When the student responds to a problem, Digitor immediately displays the word 'Right' with a green Happy Face or 'Wrong' with a red Sad Face. In either case, only the correct answer is displayed for each equation. If the student's response is incorrect, the same problem is presented again when the 'Go' button is pressed. At the end of the problem series, the number of correct responses is displayed, and if the student scored 100%, the Happy Face flashes" (Manual, p. 7).
8. *Motivating Factors*   Machine is round and situated upon four legs like a lunar module. Keyboard resembles a real calculator. Digitor would be highly motivating for most students.

TEACHING CONCERNS
1. *Teacher Competencies*   No specialized skills are required. Digitor use could be supervised by peer tutor or paraprofessional.
2. *Teaching Environment*   Digitor can be adapted to any classroom structure. Manual suggests how Digitor might be used independently, in teams, or in small groups. It lends itself to use in a resource center, open space school, or home setting, as well as in a regular classroom. Very little space is required for storage, and Digitor can be operated on any desk or table with access to an electric outlet.
3. *Teaching Aids*   Teachers manual is brief but provides clear instructions for operating Digitor. Guide also suggests ways in which Digitor may be used for diagnosis and individualized instruction. Sample math contracts, individual and group record sheets are included.
4. *Evaluative Criteria*   Every response is immediately reinforced. A total score is provided upon completion of each set of problems. Teacher must set individual criteria for mastery and advancement.
5. *Teacher Time*   Negligible.

COST EFFECTIVENESS
1. *Cost* $289.50
2. *Durability*   Digitor has a metal base. Mechanisms are encased in heavy plastic. Control buttons and two selector dials are simple to operate and seem difficult to jam. Usage is estimated to be 3 to 5 years.
3. *Number Served*   Although only one student may press keys at a time, small groups may take turns solving problems within a set. Many different children might use the machine in a given day. Because it is compact and portable, Digitor could be shared among classes or kept in a central location, such as a media center.
4. *Research Data*   None cited.
5. *Nondiscriminatory Representation*   Not applicable.

Title of Instructional Material: Developing Understanding of Self and Others (DUSO), D-2 Kit
Publisher: American Guidance Services, Inc., Circle Pines, Minnesota 55014

INSTRUCTIONAL SPECIFICATIONS
1. *Objectives*
    1. "To develop understanding and positive valuing of one's unique self; to be aware of and feel positive about one's identity.
    2. To develop understanding of interpersonal relationships.
    3. To develop understanding of the purposive nature of human behavior in both cognitive and affective areas.
    4. To develop understanding of dynamic interrelationships among ideas, feelings, beliefs, and behavior so that one can express feelings accurately.
    5. To develop understanding of competence and components of accomplishments; to develop awareness of one's resources and talents" (Manual, p. XV).

    Manual also lists social-psychological developmental tasks as eight unit themes.
2. *Target Population*   DUSO D-2 is designed for upper primary and grade four levels, ages 7–10.
3. *Prerequisite Skills*   None specified.
4. *Learning Modalities*   A variety of input-output channels are employed, but there is a strong emphasis on the auditory-verbal mode. Responses range from simple to complex.
5. *Format*   Different media are included in the kit—cassette tapes, posters and pictures, activity cards, and hand puppets. Voice quality and narrative pace of the tapes are pleasant and intelligible. Illustrations are large, colorful, and well-spaced.
6. *Pacing*   The program suggests more than enough lesson activities for one school year. As presented, individual lessons are fast moving and contain a variety of activities. Developmental themes are reinforced in successive lessons. As an alternative, the teacher may select particular activities from the total program to fit specific group needs. Pacing is flexible, because teachers are encouraged to follow up personal concerns revealed by the children during their activities.
7. *Feedback Mechanisms*   The emphasis of right or wrong answers is discouraged in favor of open and honest expression of individual attitudes and feelings. The leader provides reinforcement through positive verbal and nonverbal communication. Misunderstandings and disagreements are handled through discussion and role playing within the group.
8. *Motivating Factors*   Children's materials are colorful and attractive. "Duso," "Coho," and the six other puppets are particularly appealing. The pictures and situations used to stimulate discussion seem relevant to concerns of elementary children.

TEACHING CONCERNS
1. *Teacher Competencies*   No specialized training or skills are required for use of DUSO D-2. Manual encourages the leader to establish a warm and open atmosphere with genuine verbal and nonverbal communication.

Introductory sections of the manual provide background and guidelines for accomplishing this.

2. *Teaching Environment*   Lessons are best conducted in a small group, although no specific recommendations are made as to the number of participants. DUSO D-2 can be used in any classroom setting. The only requirement is an open, nonthreatening atmosphere. All lessons are led by the teacher. Aside from the materials included in the kit, only a cassette tape player is needed for complete implementation. All items are stored in a metal case.

3. *Teaching Aids*   The Teachers Manual presents clear and complete instructions. Lesson plans are well developed and simple to follow. Manual encourages adaptations and alternative activities to meet the needs of the group. Supplementary activities and reading are suggested for each unit.

4. *Evaluative Criteria*   No method is proposed for evaluating affective growth. Teacher could set individual criteria for evaluating the quantity and quality of student's participation.

5. *Teacher Time*   A moderate amount of time is required to prepare for the lesson and to set up materials. A teacher would be involved in leading each lesson for 30 minutes to 1 hour. Evaluation is conducted during actual sessions.

COST EFFECTIVENESS

1. *Cost*   Complete DUSO D-2 Kit with 5 cassettes is $110.00 All component parts may be ordered separately.

2. *Durability*   There are no consumable parts. Materials are well made. It is estimated that the kit could be used for at least 5 years.

3. *Number Served*   Groups of children participate in DUSO activities. Teachers could easily share one kit, enabling many students to benefit from DUSO D-2 over time.

4. *Research Data*   Field testing was carried out in 175 classrooms in 17 states involving over 5,100 students. Specific procedures and results are not cited. Results of field testing contributed to modification and refinement of materials.

5. *Nondiscriminatory Representation*   Both sexes and many different ethnic groups are portrayed in a variety of roles.

SUMMARY

The proliferation of instructional materials in recent years has created a wealth of teaching resources. By employing the appropriate materials, a classroom teacher can tailor the instructional program to individual learning needs. In order to make informed choices from the many diverse options available, the teacher needs simple yet thorough criteria for assessing characteristics of instructional materials. Such a system has been proposed in this chapter. Eighteen separate factors for analysis are grouped into three clusters focusing on instructional specifications, teaching concerns, and cost effectiveness. The information obtained by studying materials in terms of these specific factors will enable the teacher to choose the most suitable materials for specific instructional needs.

REFERENCES

Adamson, H., and Van Etten, C. 1970. Prescribing via analysis and retrieval of instructional materials in the Education Modulation Center. Except. Child. 36: 531–533.

Brown, L. F. 1974. The analyses of instructional materials. Ment. Retard. 21–25.

Developing Understanding of Self and Others (DUSO), D-2 Kit. Manual. 1973. American Guidance Services, Circle Pines, Mn.

Digitor. Manual. Centurion Industries, Redwood City, Ca.

Fry, E. B. 1969. The readability graph validated at primary levels. Read. Teach. 22: 534–538.

Haring, N. G., and Schiefelbusch, R. L. 1976. Teaching Special Children. McGraw-Hill Book Company, New York.

McLaughlin, G. H. 1969. SMOG Grading—A new readability formula. J. Read. 12: 639.

Meyen, E. L., Gault, S., and Howard, C. 1976. Instructional Based Appraisal System: A Basic Planning and Management Tool. Edmark Associates, Bellevue, Washington.

Prescriptive Materials Retrieval System. 1970. B. L. Winch and Associates, Rolling Hills Estates, Ca.

Smith, R. M. 1974. Clinical Teaching: Methods of Instruction for the Retarded. McGraw-Hill Book Company, New York.

Spache, G. 1953. A new readability formula for primary grade reading materials. Elem. School J. 53: 410–413.

Thiagarajan, S., Semmel, G. S., and Semmel, M. J. 1974. Instructional Development for Training Teachers of Exceptional Children: A Sourcebook. Leadership Training Institute/Special Education, University of Minnesota, Minneapolis.

Weinthaler, J., and Rotberg, J. M. 1970. The systematic selection of instructional materials based on an inventory of learning abilities and skills. Except. Child. 36: 615–619.

5

Making the Match: Rationale for Selection

Virginia K. Laycock, Ed.D.

The point of origin for all instructional decision-making is the thorough assessment of learner characteristics. Once a child's present level of performance, specific strengths and weaknesses, learning styles, and behavioral and affective needs have been identified, the teacher is then prepared to plan his educational program. Based on the diagnostic information, the teacher is able to define goals and objectives and to select appropriate teaching strategies. For many skill areas, the student's program may be developmental in nature. He is placed at his instructional level in the ongoing curriculum and continues to advance through the developmental sequence. In areas of weakness, however, the child may require remedial instruction in an attempt to correct specific deficiencies before resuming developmental programming. The choice of instructional materials is critical in either case. Material characteristics must be strategically matched to identified learning needs.

Although the present chapter is primarily concerned with the selection of materials, this represents but one task in the entire process of instructional planning. The application of instructional materials can be discussed meaningfully only in this context. The initial sections of this chapter, therefore, describe two methods for individualizing instruction. First, the annual education program is reviewed, because this is now required in written form for all handicapped students receiving special services. The second portion of the chapter is devoted to diagnostic prescriptive teaching as a means of translating the annual plan into daily lessons with the student. Once these two approaches have been considered, the final section presents a model of choosing suitable instructional materials for either long- or short-term purposes.

INDIVIDUALIZED EDUCATION PROGRAMS

Where exceptional children are concerned, the process of individualized programming has recently been structured by the Education for all Handicapped Children Act of 1975 (Public Law 94-142). Not only does this federal law mandate that all children, regardless of handicapping condition, have the right to a free public education, but it further defines what "appropriate" special education must entail. Before any child can receive special services, a written educational plan must be developed to provide for his unique needs. The individualized educational plan (IEP) is the basic management tool for ensuring that a personalized, comprehensive program is developed, maintained, and evaluated for each handicapped child.

Designing the education program is not viewed entirely as the teacher's responsibility. Instead, the law stipulates that the IEP be devised at a meeting with the following individuals participating:

1. A representative of the local educational agency, other than the child's teachers, who is qualified to provide, or supervise the provision of, special education
2. The child's teacher or teachers, special or regular, or both, who have a direct responsibility for implementing the child's individualized educational program
3. One or both of the child's parents
4. Where appropriate, the child
5. Other individuals, at the discretion of the parent or agency (Section 121a 223).

In interpreting these participation requirements, Abeson and Weintraub point out that "the individualized education program is an agreement between all parties and that, while it is not a contract, it is clearly a statement setting forth what will be provided to the child" (1977, p. 6).

Public Law 94-142 further specified the content of the individualized educational program. The individualized education program for each child must include:

a) A statement of the child's present levels of educational performance, including academic achievement, social adaptation, prevocational and vocational skills, psychomotor skills, and self-help skills;
b) A statement of annual goals which describes the educational performance to be achieved by the end of the school year under the child's IEP;
c) A statement of short term instructional objectives, which must be measurable intermediate steps between the present level of educational performance and the annual goals;
d) A statement of specific educational services needed by the child (determined without regard to the availability of those services) including a description of:

(1) All special education and related services which are needed to meet the unique needs of the child, including the type of physical education program in which the child will participate, and

(2) Any special instructional media and materials which are needed;

e) The date when those services will begin and length of time the services will be given;

f) A description of the extent to which the child will participate in the regular educational programs;

g) A justification for the type of educational placement which the child will have;

h) A list of the individuals who are responsible for implementation of the IEP; and

i) Objective criteria, evaluation procedures, and schedules for determining on at least an annual basis, whether the short term instructional objectives are being achieved (Section 121a, 225).

No uniform format is required for writing in IEP, but all of the above components must be present in whatever form is employed.

The law never actually uses the term "mainstreaming," although it does refer to the "least restrictive environment," assuring that:

to the maximum extent appropriate, handicapped children, including children in public or private institutions or other care facilities, are educated with children who are not handicapped, and that special classes, separate schooling, or other removal of handicapped children from the regular educational environment occurs only when the nature or severity of the handicap is such that education in regular classes with the use of supplementary aids and services cannot be achieved satisfactorily (Section 121a, 442).

Clearly, the intent of the law is to educate handicapped children in as normal a situation as possible.

The impact of Public Law 94-142 on our educational system promises to be profound and far-reaching. Many have referred to this law as a Bill of Rights for the Handicapped. A greater number of handicapped children will be served in the public schools, and the majority of these children will participate in the regular classroom program for at least a portion of the day. The matter of providing the most appropriate instructional materials as vehicles for learning has assumed greater significance than ever before.

Goals and Objectives

Of central importance in the individual educational program is the listing of annual goals and major short-term objectives. These represent the first instructional decisions to be made, and provide the basis for further judgments regarding placement, methodology, and materials. The determination of appropriate long-range goals can be a tedious task. Goals follow logically for assessment data, however, if those data are sufficiently specific and compiled in terms of basic skill areas. Meaningful educational diagnosis results in the identification of a child's present levels of performance in the areas of concern. This information is usually stated as age or grade equivalents that help to narrow the focus within each of the areas of functioning to particular subsets of skills. Adequate diagnostic reports also specify exactly which skills the learner can and cannot perform. Given these observations, the educator is equipped to formulate goals and objectives.

Instructional goals should emerge directly from diagnostic data. Assessment results indicate what a child is able to do successfully at the present time; educational goals stipulate what he will be expected to do at a designated time in the future. Goals simply clarify what skills will come next. They serve as landmarks in an educational program.

When writing an educational plan, it is often helpful to consult various references in order to ensure that goals and objectives adhere to developmental sequence. Curriculum guides from both regular and special education may prove useful. Textbooks in professional education may also provide skill sequences for the particular subject areas under study. Finally, diagnostic tests themselves can be considered resources, because they are based on the orderly progression of skills. The Key Math Diagnostic Arithmetic Test (Connolly, Nachtman, and Pretchett, 1971) is one example of a test accompanied by its own sequence of objectives. The teacher need only refer to the appendix to locate specific objectives corresponding to test items failed by the student. Within each area, published skill sequences are likely to vary somewhat in content as well as in progression. For this reason, planners may want to have several different references available to assist in the identification of appropriate objectives for a particular learner.

Goals and objectives are usually distinguished in terms of the time anticipated for mastery. Goals pertain to relatively long-range accomplishments for a school year, semester, or perhaps a grading period. Objectives refer to both intermediate and immediate steps leading to the attainment of the target goal. For an individualized education program, it is only necessary to list the main intermediate objectives. Immediate objectives, those that can be achieved within a few days, are important for daily lesson planning but do not have to be included in the annual program. Both goals and objectives must be stated in specific, measurable terms, identifying the exact behavior the learner is to perform. The criterion or standard established for mastery must also be indicated. A final component must describe the relevant conditions under which the behavior is to be demonstrated and evaluated. Statements formulated in this way provide clear guidelines for the educational program.

Once goals and objectives are defined, the developers of the IEP can make decisions concerning the types of services necessary to assist the learner in their attainment. Regulations governing the writing of the individualized education program have accentuated the importance of behavioral goals and objectives derived from the assessment of learner characteristics. The nature and complexity of these objectives, and not the availability of existing programs, must dictate the choice of a particular service delivery model. The program must be tailored to the child. Likewise, goals and objectives will influence the selection of instructional methods and materials.

DIAGNOSTIC PRESCRIPTIVE TEACHING

The IEP, the basic management and recordkeeping tool for the annual educational program, must have a counterpart for daily planning. The comprehensive, long-range program has to be made operational in the everyday instructional interactions with the child. Of the many alternative systems that have been proposed to accomplish the individualization of instruction, the diagnostic prescriptive approach seems most applicable for the developmental and remedial teaching of handicapped learners. Diagnostic prescriptive teaching has become a somewhat generic term. Several models, differing in specific details, have been entitled "prescriptive" (Charles, 1976; Peter, 1965; Schwartzberg and Smith, 1978). Several other approaches, such as Clinical Teaching (Lerner, 1976; Smith, 1974) and Directive Teaching (Stephens, 1976), are sufficiently similar to be considered among prescriptive programs.

These different versions of diagnostic prescriptive teaching are highly compatible in philosophy. The initial identification of learner attributes is viewed as the basis for the selection of instructional strategies and materials. Diagnosis, however, is not limited to this preliminary assessment, but is defined as a continuous, ongoing process. The daily performance of the child provides the most accurate and current estimates of his ability. Diagnosis is, therefore, an integral part of all teaching tasks. Instructional plans are evaluated and revised in light of the learning demonstrated by the individual student.

Diagnostic prescriptive teaching models are necessarily structured and systematic. All teaching activities are goal-directed, being derived from a sequence of subobjectives leading to the performance of the desired skill. Diagnostic prescriptive teaching is behavioral in its orientation. Learning can only be evidenced by observable and measurable outcomes. The affective and psychomotor domains, as well as the cognitive, may be involved in prescriptive programming. Within this framework, a variety of instructional strategies and materials are employed. Prescriptive teaching thus describes a particular philosophy and organizational system for teaching. It is not bound to any one specific method. In this way, it provides a structured yet flexible approach for programming to meet the diverse needs of handicapped children.

Prescriptive Teaching Cycle

For the implementation of prescriptive teaching, available models differ in the number of steps required and in the terminology used to describe these steps. Essentially, diagnostic prescriptive teaching involves seven tasks as illustrated in Figure 1. The relationship between diagnostic prescriptive teaching and individualized education programming is clearly apparent. Although federal guidelines did not characterize the IEP in these terms, its development, implementation, and evaluation follow essentially the same sequence. Where the IEP is concerned, several months to an entire year might elapse before a cycle is completed. In contrast to this long-term cycle is the recurring cycle of diagnostic prescriptive teaching.

The entire process of individualized programming might best be conceptualized as a spiral composed of a progression of teaching cycles, as diagrammed in Figure 2. In planning, the comprehensive, long-range IEP must be developed first. This serves to organize and direct the course of the child's program. The program cycle is then broken down into a series of cycles of shorter duration corresponding to major intermediate objectives. In turn, intermediate objectives are further analyzed into a sequence of immediate objectives for the daily prescriptive cycles. Planning, then, proceeds from the long-range, through the intermediate, to the immediate level of prescriptive teaching. The long-term and intermediate goals can only be attained by providing the appropriate learning opportunities for the child on a day-to-day basis. Evaluation of the program must, therefore, begin on the immediate level, advancing through the intermediate to the more comprehensive level of total program evaluation. The prescriptive cycles at the different levels must all fit together to result in an integrated instructional program for the learner.

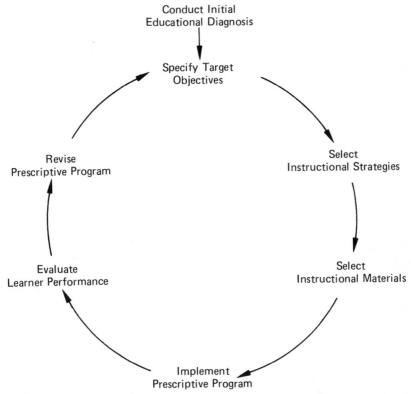

Figure 1.   The diagnostic prescriptive teaching cycle.

For any level of prescriptive planning, decisions must be made regarding instructional materials. Material selection is the fourth step in each diagnostic prescriptive cycle. The initial assessment of relevant learner attributes (Step 1), as described in Chapter 3, culminates in the specification of target objectives (Step 2). To assist the student in mastering these objectives, basic instructional strategies or methods are devised (Step 3). Not until this point is the teacher prepared to locate appropriate instructional materials. The choice of instructional material is, therefore, governed by the outcomes of three prior diagnostic prescriptive tasks: defined learner needs, established objectives, and designed teaching approach. With these tasks clearly determined, suitable materials can be chosen for each level of prescriptive planning. Some materials are needed for the comprehensive program level. Basic developmental or remedial programs are often available that correspond to the learner's long-range needs and can serve as the core of his instructional system. Other materials may be required to facilitate the attainment of inter-

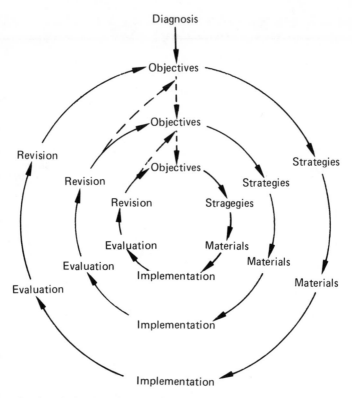

Figure 2. A spiral of teaching cycles representing the diagnostic prescriptive programming on the long-range, intermediate, and immediate levels.

mediate objectives. Such materials would not be as broad in scope as the major instructional programs, but would provide learning experiences in several skill areas. Finally, it is usually necessary to have many materials relating to the highly specific, immediate objectives. These materials are very limited in scope, but play a vital role in teaching and reinforcing daily objectives.

The selection of materials for all levels of prescriptive teaching may be clarified by an actual example. In an individualized education program for a 9-year-old student, one of the long-range goals was stated as follows: "By the end of the school year, Pamela will read on the 3.0 level with at least 95% accuracy in word recognition and 75% accuracy in comprehension." In the prescriptive cycle at the program level, the decision was made to use a developmental series for basic reading instruction. Intermediate subobjectives also listed in the IEP focused on specific reading competencies. One of these objectives specified, "Pamela will decode phonetically regular words of one syllable with 85% accuracy." Although the basal reading program included a phonics component, the teacher wanted to emphasize word attack skills to a greater extent. For this reason, a phonics skills kit was also employed for the intermediate prescriptive cycles. Where daily prescriptive cycles were concerned, supplementary teaching aids were necessary to provide additional reinforcement of specific skills. Several materials were located to allow practice of consonant blends and consonant digraphs. Two phonics games and a set of dittoed worksheets were chosen to reinforce vowel combinations. All of the materials selected for Pamela related to her individual learning characteristics, to instructional strategies tailored to her needs, and to designated goals and objectives in reading.

Not all decisions regarding instructional materials are made at once. As regulations for Public Law 94-142 stipulate, major instructional materials should be identified in the written IEP. This means that basic developmental or remedial programs for the long-term cycle should be selected at that time. As each intermediate objective is approached, appropriate materials must then be located. In these intermediate prescriptive teaching cycles, children may use the same set of materials for several months. Materials are changed most frequently on the immediate level in daily prescriptive teaching. On this level, decisions are made on a day-to-day basis according to the student's present performance. Fortunately, selection of materials for this short-term cycle is not the complex task that it may be at the more comprehensive levels. Materials that are useful for teaching highly specific and immediate objectives are typically more simple to assess. Decisions, therefore, can and must be made more quickly for daily prescriptive teaching.

SELECTING INSTRUCTIONAL MATERIALS

The ideal instructional material for any teaching situation would be one that presents what needs to be taught (objectives) in the best possible way (teaching strategy) for a particular learner. This would represent the optimal match between material characteristics and instructional needs. In reality, this perfect correspondence is difficult to achieve; however, it is possible for the teacher to approximate this ideal more closely by using a systematic model to aid in decision-making. A useful model will expedite the process of selecting suitable instructional materials by helping the teacher to focus on aspects of greatest importance for each educational problem. Such a model has been emerging in the preceding chapters. Chapter 3 described an approach to educational assessment that facilitates understanding of a child's unique characteristics and needs. Chapter 4 discussed the analyses of instructional materials in terms of three clusters of important attributes. Previous sections of this chapter have proposed a diagnostic prescriptive approach applicable for both long- and short-range programming. All of these efforts now interlace in the selection of instructional materials.

At this stage of prescriptive programming, the teacher should have the following records available: the summary of learner assessment, the individualized education program, and worksheets for the analyses of instructional materials. With this information, the teacher is ready to begin the process of narrowing down the alternatives by matching material characteristics with instructional requirements until the most appropriate materials are identified.

The first criterion for determining suitable materials is that they meet Instructional Specifications. The results of material analysis for this set of factors related to pupil characteristics and needs must correspond closely to the objectives and teaching strategies that have been defined for the particular learner. Materials that do not meet established needs regarding Instructional Specifications would not be adequate teaching tools in that situation. The selection of appropriate instructional materials for a particular learner thus involves a process of elimination: only materials that are found to fulfill initial Instructional Specifications are retained for further investigation. The material actually used with the learner should be the one whose characteristics coincide most closely with priority needs.

Meeting Instructional Specifications

To assist in the process of matching materials to instructional needs, a Rating Scale is introduced in Table 1. This Rating Scale includes the same factors that are itemized on the Worksheet for the Analysis of Instructional Materials. A completed Worksheet summarizing important material attributes can be kept as a reference and used many times. The teacher should have analyses worksheets completed for several different prospective materials so that comparative judgments can be made. A separate Rating Scale is used for each instructional decision, however, because material characteristics are evaluated each time in light of one student's unique learning needs. A material that receives a low rating for one pupil may be appropriate for another.

The Rating Scale allows the teacher to indicate the suitability of an instructional material for a given learner along critical dimensions. When material characteristics correspond *exactly* to established needs, a score of 3 is assigned. A rating of 2 indicates an

Table 1.   Matching materials to instructional needs: A Rating Scale

Learner:
Title of Instructional Material:
Publisher:

For each of the following factors, indicate to what degree material characteristics correspond to identified instructional needs by circling the appropriate number. If certain variables are not applicable, write NA in the right-hand column. Where low correspondence is observed, comment briefly on the potential for adaptation or modification in the area.

| | Degree of Correspondence | | | |
	High	Adequate	Low	Notes
INSTRUCTIONAL SPECIFICATIONS				
Objectives				
Scope	3	2	1	
Sequence	3	2	1	
Target Population				
Chronological Age	3	2	1	
Mental Age	3	2	1	
Age/Grade Equivalent	3	2	1	
Other Descriptors	3	2	1	
Prerequisite Skills	3	2	1	
Learning Modalities				
Input	3	2	1	
Output	3	2	1	
Format				
Medium	3	2	1	
Quality	3	2	1	
Spatial arrangement	3	2		
Safety features	3	2	1	
Pacing				
Rate	3	2	1	
Flexibility	3	2	1	
Feedback Mechanisms				
Type of Reinforcement	3	2	1	
Schedule	3	2	1	
Motivating Factors				
Aesthetic appeal	3	2	1	
Thematic appeal	3	2	1	

Total _____
Number of factors rated _____
Mean rating _____

adequate or acceptable degree of correspondence. When material characteristics do not meet instructional needs, a score of 1 is given, designating low correspondence. Not all factors will be applicable for every material. When a certain factor does not apply, the letters "NA" (not applicable) should be written in the column reserved for notes. In this column, the teacher may also comment on those dimensions where low correspondence was reported. It is often helpful to note whether or not a material could be adapted in order to conform to specific needs in that respect. The remainder of this section discusses scoring considerations for each of the factors included in Instructional Specifications.

Objectives   The first test for suitability involves instructional objectives, because a material can only qualify as appropriate if it teaches what the student needs to learn. When comparing material objectives to program objectives, it is essential to focus on specific, observable skills rather than general content. The child's individual educational program serves as the guide for the selection of major developmental and remedial materials. The objectives stated for the material should correspond to long-range goals and intermediate objectives written in the IEP. Comprehensive instructional materials must be compatible with program objectives not only in terms of what skills are being taught (scope), but also the order in which they are introduced (sequence). Selecting materials for daily prescriptive teaching is less complicated, because materials need only correspond to one or two immediate objectives. When this is the case, scope must still be rated, but sequence may not be applicable.

Target Population   Once it has been determined that a material teaches the desired skills, the teacher must decide to what extent the material is addressed to students like the child in question. Do described characteristics of the material's target population match the characteristics of the individual learner? A teacher can readily tell if the child's age and grade fall within the suggested ranges. In addition, age and grade equivalents obtained through standardized testing in the areas of concern should be reported in the assessment summary. The teacher is then able to judge whether the material is appropriate for the child's functional level as well. If any additional descriptors are used to characterize the target population of a material, such as reference to handicapping condition, the teacher should also rate these as they apply to the particular learner.

Prerequisite Skills   Certain competencies are usually required of the student in order to interact successfully with an instructional material. It is important, therefore, to establish whether or not the individual student possesses the necessary prerequisite skills. To make the judgment, the teacher compares the assessment summary with the Worksheet for the Analyses of Instructional Materials. The results of educational diagnosis should reveal specific strengths and weaknesses as well as level of functioning. Knowing what the child can and cannot do, the teacher is able to rate the appropriateness of entry requirements.

Learning Modalities   Learning modalities and the next four factors relate specifically to teaching strategy. These variables can be adjusted in the attempt to tailor instruction to individual needs. The understanding of a child's learning style obtained through educational assessment provides the basis for making these decisions regarding teaching approach or strategy.

Instructional materials may involve any combination of input-output modalities. The teacher must determine the suitability of particular processing requirements for an individual learner. In introducing new concepts and skills, the teacher may want to capitalize on a child's processing strengths to teach the child in the way that he learns best. With a student who demonstates a preference for the visual modality, for example, a teacher may enlist a variety of visual representations to accompany a verbal explanation. Many children benefit from a multisensory approach. Students with visual and auditory weaknesses can often use tactual-kinesthetic cues to their advantage. On the other hand, too much stimulation can overload the processing capabilities of some learners. The complexity of input and output requirements is also an issue. The teacher does not want to complicate learning or confound its evaluation by requiring more complex processing than the child is able to perform. The teacher must be aware of the student's learning style with respect to modality preference and level of abstraction in order to judge whether a given instructional material will make appropriate processing demands.

In some instances, the teacher is specifically programming to remediate processing deficiencies. The material characteristics required in this case are somewhat different. The weaker modality is intentionally the focus of instruction, but additional modalities may be involved for support as necessary.

Format   A number of different types of materials can be found to teach the same skills. It is up to the teacher to select an effective vehicle for conveying the information to the particular learner. The choice of media should be made first. Preferred learning modalities help to narrow the range of alternatives somewhat. A child with auditory strengths, for instance, may require teacher-directed presentations or mechanized audio materials. The teacher must still decide among tapes, slides, filmstrips, motion pictures, and videotapes with sound if he intends to teach through the child's strengths in his independent work. When printed media are conducive to learning, the teacher may choose from a number of different types, including textbooks, workbooks, charts, duplicated sheets, activity cards, and flashcards. A determining factor in this decision is the child's ability to work independently. Given the student's learning style and established objectives, the teacher must judge whether a particular format offers an effective means of learning.

The quality of the format can also be rated at this time. In any medium, the information should be presented in a clear and intelligible manner. Any aspects of the format that might be distracting to a learner detract from the quality of the material.

Spatial arrangement warrants consideration whenever content is presented visually. A young or low-functioning child, or a child with visual perception deficits, needs an uncluttered presentation. Stimulus items should be large and generously spaced. More advanced learners are able to cope with a greater number of items and details per presentation.

Safety factors must also be evaluated in reference to learner characteristics. Materials for a young or developmentally immature child should avoid potentially dangerous features such as rough edges, sharp points, and pieces small enough to be swallowed. Students with physical handicaps or serious coordination difficulties may need special safeguards. Any machinery or equipment to be operated by students should meet maximum safety requirements.

Pacing   Students differ tremendously in the rate of learning acquisition. Through initial assessment of learning style and subsequent diagnostic prescriptive teaching, a teacher is able to identify a child's characteristic rate of learning. Whereas some students need a skill to be broken down into minute subskills, others are able to grasp it more globally. Some pupils require more repetition than others in order to master a concept. It is necessary, therefore, for the teacher to determine whether the pacing of the material is compatible with the child's learning rate. If the material contains provisions for self-pacing, it is more easily tailored to individual learning style.

Feedback Mechanisms   Knowledge of the child's reinforcement preferences is helpful in judging the suitability of a material in terms of feedback provisions. Materials that have built-in reinforcing properties typically are limited to giving knowledge of results. This type of feedback is a powerful way to induce learning for most students. Some children are not functioning at this level, however, and are not sufficiently reinforced by knowledge of results. Many children need social reinforcers or more tangible evidence of success, such as tokens.

The schedule for reinforcement is also a concern. Even students who are able to work effectively for knowledge of results differ in their ability to delay feedback. Some learners require reinforcement for every response in order to maintain their level of performance. Other learners can complete an entire unit before seeking knowledge of results. Anticipating a child's needs in this area is the result of thorough educational assessment and diagnostic prescriptive teaching. For each material under consideration, the teacher must rate the adequacy of feedback provisions for the particular learner.

Motivating Factors   The final variable in Instructional Specifications, motivating factors, requires a somewhat subjective judgment. The teacher asks himself, in effect, "Will this material appeal to my student?" The teacher does have information to draw upon for this decision. Knowledge of general tastes and interests of children of the particular age and background provides an initial criterion. This is refined in light of diagnostic observations. The greater the teacher's awareness of an individual's likes and dislikes, the better the chance that the chosen material will appeal to him. The teacher must rate both aesthetic and thematic appeal. Aesthetic appeal pertains to the physical attractiveness of design and packaging, and thematic appeal involves the relevancy of the content given the learner's interests and background experiences.

This factor assumes greater importance when the student of concern has a history of failure and frustration. Although a sound instructional material must have much more to offer than just fancy packaging, the flashy colors and catchy gimmicks are sometimes necessary to attract the seemingly unmotivated student. These superficial features may not be able to sustain attention, but they can often get the child sufficiently involved for the other instructional attributes to exert their effect. The reluctant participant may show renewed interest when a carefully chosen material begins to convince him that he *is* able to learn successfully.

Once several different materials have been matched to Instructional Specifications, a mean rating score should be calculated for each by dividing the total rating by the number of factors scored. The average is a better indicator of suitability than the total score, because not all factors are rated for every material. Materials receiving a mean rating of 2 or above correspond adequately to Instructional Specifications and should be retained for further investigation. If a number of materials were rated and found suitable in this initial test, the teacher may wish to choose only the higher scoring materials for additional evaluation. Materials with mean ratings less than 2 correspond poorly with instructional needs. Because they do not seem to be appropriate for the learner in question, there is no need to rate them on remaining variables.

Materials meeting Instructional Specifications qualify for further consideration. These materials seem to be appropriate for learner needs, but there are other factors that also contribute to the desirability of instructional materials. Certain aspects of materials pertain more to the management of instruction than the learning itself. These variables related to teaching style and classroom organization have been labeled Teaching Concerns. Another set of factors reflect the practical realization that instructional materials represent both education and economic investments. These factors have been grouped under the heading Cost Effectiveness.

Although both sets of variables affect materials selection, their relative degree of influence may vary with the situation. Teaching concerns, although always important, assume even greater weight in decision-making when a material is to be employed by a very inexperienced teacher, paraprofessional, parent, or peer tutor. Similarly, Cost Effectiveness may become a more powerful influence when budgetary restrictions are such that it is senseless to consider items beyond a given price range. Instructional Specifications, centered on the needs of the learner, must remain the first priority in materials selection. Once materials are found to meet these criteria, however, the teacher has some flexibility in establishing subsequent priorities between Teaching Concerns and Cost Effectiveness. Whichever set of factors has the greater effect on the final decision should be considered next.

Teaching Concerns

The rating of the five Teaching Concerns is now described, although in actual practice, the teacher is free to designate either Teaching Concerns or Cost Effectiveness as the second set of variables. Materials being considered at this stage have already been matched to learner needs. The teacher is now looking for materials that correspond to his own needs. The section of the Rating Scale shown in Table 2 is completed in the same manner as the first section involving Instructional Specifications. Worksheets for the Analyses of Instructional Materials are the only references necessary for rating on these dimensions. The teacher simply marks 1, 2, or 3 to indicate how particular features apply to him and his teaching situation.

Table 2.   Matching materials to instructional needs: A Rating Scale (cont.)

| | Degree of Correspondence | | | |
	High	Adequate	Low	Notes
TEACHING CONCERNS				
Teacher Competencies				
Training	3	2	1	
Specialized skills	3	2	1	
Teaching Environment				
Classroom organization	3	2	1	
Physical requirements	3	2	1	
Teaching Aids				
Teachers guide	3	2	1	
Supplementary resources	3	2	1	
Evaluative Criteria				
Test items	3	2	1	
Scheduling	3	2	1	
Teacher Time				
Preparation	3	2	1	
Supervision	3	2	1	
Evaluation	3	2	1	

Total _____
Number of factors rated _____
Mean rating _____

Teacher Competencies Certain levels of training and expertise are usually stated or implied for effective use of a material. Considering personal preparation and skills, the teacher assigns ratings in these categories to reflect the degree of correspondence between recommended and demonstrated competencies.

Teaching Environment The teacher must also consider how the prospective material would fit into the existing classroom structure. Each class operates in its characteristic way. The basic approach may be teacher-directed, student-centered, or some blending of the two. Certain grouping arrangements may predominate over others. Materials should first be judged as to suitability for use within familiar patterns of classroom organization.

Physical environment must also be taken into account. Some materials require an unusual amount of space for proper use or storage. Other materials need specialized equipment or facilities for full implementation. In scoring, the teacher must indicate how well the material lends itself to use within the given physical setting.

Teaching Aids The teaching aids category calls for teacher evaluation of supportive resources that accompany the material.

Because individuals differ considerably in their use of manuals and guides, teachers may apply personal criteria in judging their adequacy. Even when a teacher does not anticipate relying heavily on a manual, complete accessible instructions for using the material should be a minimum requirement. For the teacher who does intend to refer to the manual while teaching, the format and the flexibility of lesson plans should be considered in the rating.

Many teachers like to have supplementary resources provided as well. Additional background information, teaching activities, correlated materials, and professional references may be suggested. The teacher should evaluate available teaching aids in light of his own needs, with higher scores indicating that the teachers guides and supplementary resources meet individual expectations.

Evaluation Criteria   The difficult task of evaluating progress can be alleviated by the provision of effective measures within instructional materials. Many materials, particularly those that are teacher-directed, do not have evaluation components. These become more necessary with individualized materials. When evaluative procedures are incorporated into a material, the teacher should rate their adequacy in terms of the nature and number of responses sampled, and the frequency of testing within the instructional program.

Teacher Time   Within the classroom setting, the teacher must be free to manage his time effectively. With a basic schedule in mind, the teacher knows approximately how much time can realistically be allotted to specific instructional tasks. Materials differ considerably in the amount of teacher involvement required. As each material is being considered, therefore, the teacher should decide how reasonable are the time demands for preparation, supervision, and evaluation.

Cost Effectiveness

Remaining factors affecting suitability of materials are involved in Cost Effectiveness. Based on information contained in Completed Worksheets for the Analyses of Instructional Materials, the teacher weighs the advantages of each material against the expense incurred. When several materials, all fulfilling Instructional Specifications, are compared on this set of factors, the teacher is able to choose the material that should offer the greatest educational returns for the money.

The section of the Rating Scale dealing with Cost Effectiveness is provided in Table 3. The same system that was introduced above continues to be used for scoring. The first three factors may not be

Table 3.   Matching materials to instructional needs: A Rating Scale (cont.)

| | Degree of Correspondence | | | |
	High	Adequate	Low	Notes
COST EFFECTIVENESS				
Cost				
Total price	3	2	1	
Component prices	3	2	1	
Replacement parts	3	2	1	
Durability	3	2	1	
Number Served	3	2	1	
Research Data	3	2	1	
Nondiscriminatory	3	2	1	
Representation				

Total _____
Number of factors rated _____
Mean rating _____

applicable when materials are already onhand in the classroom or available from a local media center. The fourth and fifth factors, however, should be considered any time materials are being selected. Scoring for each of the Cost Effectiveness factors is described.

Cost   When materials are being considered for possible purchase, the teacher cannot disregard the cost factor. The assignment of high, adequate, or low ratings should reflect an awareness of the general price range of comparable materials, as well as an exact knowledge of available funds. If only certain parts of a kit or program are needed, the teacher may choose to purchase these items separately. Whenever parts are consumable or susceptible to loss or damage, the teacher should also rate replacement costs. When any of these prices exceed the budget or the prices quoted for similar products, a score of 1 is in order. Costs within reason should receive a rating of 2. A rating of 3 should be reserved for materials whose prices compare very favorably with both budget allowances and market values.

Durability   Rating the durability of a material requires a relative judgment. Considering the cost of the material and its construction, the teacher must decide whether the material is likely to provide sufficient years of service. A material with a modest price may be used for only a short time and still be a worthwhile investment. Many consumable products, such as workbooks, fit this description. They are used up fairly quickly, but they also cost very little. In weighing the expense against the amount of service, an adequate rating (2) is justified. On the other hand, a very expensive material should not be consumable or easily damaged. When a substantial amount of money is invested in a material, it is expected to be sufficiently durable to withstand normal handling for a reasonable period of time.

Number Served   Once again, rating is influenced by the cost factor. The teacher must decide whether enough children can benefit from the particular material to justify the expense involved. If the material can be used by a large group at one time or can be employed by each child briefly in succession, it warrants a high rating. A very expensive material that would reach only a limited audience should receive a low score in this category.

Research Data   It matters little what the material purports to do or how reasonably it is priced if there is no evidence to show that the material is effective as an instructional aid. The many materials that present no reports of field testing should receive a score of 1 on this factor, because they fail to meet acceptable standards in this respect. When information on field testing is provided, the teacher must still evaluate the quality of the research. A score of 3 should be awarded only to those materials that present data-based results of field testing with samples of adequate number and representation.

Nondiscriminatory Representation   Purchasing or selecting a material for use constitutes, in effect, an endorsement of that material. Before choosing a particular material, therefore, the teacher must evaluate the content carefully. Materials that portray any race or sex is a negative or stereotyped manner are to be avoided. To earn a high rating on this dimension, a material should include individuals from a variety of ethnic backgrounds. Both men and women should be shown in domestic and career roles.

Making Decisions

Materials selection has been described as a process of elimination. First, prospective material were matched to Instructional Specifications. The remaining sets of factors, Teaching Concerns and Cost Effectiveness, were placed in their order of importance in decision-making. These were then designated set 2 and set 3 variables, accordingly. Materials with the higher mean ratings on Instructional Specifications, those corresponding closely to learner needs, were then rated on set 2 factors. Lower scoring materials were eliminated, and higher scoring materials were evaluated on set 3 factors.

Although the prioritied approach allows some flexibility in materials selection, teachers may wish to include other factors on the Rating Scale. Any considerations that affect the choice of instruction materials should be itemized and rated.

The completion of ratings may lead to several possible outcomes. The most fortunate situation exists when several materials have survived the elimination process by receiving acceptable ratings on three sets of variables. When this is the case, the teacher may base her final decision on any distinctive features of the materials. If two programs have comparable composite ratings, for example, the teacher may choose one over the other because he feels more comfortable with the material he has used in the past. In most instances where nearly equivalent ratings are obtained, the teacher simply decides in favor of the material most readily accessible. Obviously, there would be no point in purchasing or even borrowing a new material if one is already available that adequately serves the purpose. The fact that most teachers are programming for many students often adds a determining variable. Whenever the same material is found to be suitable for several students, it becomes especially attractive to the teacher. These are but a few of the special considerations that may help to settle a tie between two or more materials that seem well suited to instructional needs.

It sometimes happens that none of the materials rated at first seem to be appropriate. This leaves the teacher with several options. The search can be resumed in an attempt to locate more promising instructional materials. This new group of material is then analyzed and rated. A second possibility is to choose the material that corresponds most closely to one's needs and also lends itself to adaptation in the areas that are not exactly appropriate. Materials can usually be modified more easily when necessary adjustments involve procedures rather than content. A final alternative is to construct a teacher-made material. The advantage of designing a material to conform precisely to specifications can make the time and effort of construction worthwhile.

SUMMARY

The selection of instructional materials is but one essential task in the total process of individualized programming. Many approaches have been proposed for bridging the gap between assessing learner needs and providing for them. The recent federal mandate, Public Law 94-142, has standardized basic procedures for developing individualized education programs for handicapped students. With the impact of this law, the written IEP is becoming the major force in the planning, implementation, and evaluation of instruction for children with special learning needs.

Among other required components, the IEP must contain long-range goals and subobjectives derived from assessment of the student's present levels of performance. Whatever special services or instructional materials are needed to attain these objectives must be specified. Finally, the IEP must provide for systematic evaluation of learner progress toward the accomplishment of target goals.

Basic similarities between programming requirements of Public Law 94-142 and diagnostic prescriptive teaching approaches were pointed out. In this way, the IEP may be thought of as long-range prescriptive programming. Essentially the same steps are involved in long-term, intermediate, and daily educational programming: defining objectives, selecting strategies, selecting materials, implementing, evaluating, and revising the program. To conceptualize the relationship of programming for different time frames, a spiral of diagnostic prescriptive teaching cycles was proposed.

The recommended approach for materials selection applies whether materials are to be used once or for an entire year. Actual materials selection was described as a process of matching material characteristics to established objectives and teaching strategies. A Rating Scale was presented to assist in determining the degree of correspondence. Meeting Instructional Specifications was the first priority. Beyond this, teachers are free to designate Teaching Concerns and Cost Effectiveness as second and third priorities, according to their particular importance in decision-making. Materials receiving acceptable ratings on Instructional Specifications are then rated on set 2 and set 3 factors. The most suitable materials emerge with the highest mean scores. These materials correspond closely to learner needs, teacher needs, and financial needs, and thus seem most appropriate for the given instructional program.

CASE EXAMPLE

In Chapter 3, diagnostic data were presented on a student named Jason to illustrate the approach for educational assessment. In Chapter 4, one of the instructional materials analyzed as an example was Digitor, a computational device. The assessment summary and completed worksheet for material analysis provide the necessary information for determining whether Digitor is an appropriate teaching aid for Jason.

Although Jason's main problems were behavioral, he was experiencing learning difficulties in math. One of the intermediate objectives written for his IEP stated that "Jason will compute basic multiplication facts 0-9 with at least 90% accuracy." It was felt that Digitor might serve Jason's needs in this area.

SAMPLE RATING SCALE

Learner:
Title of Instructional Material:
Publisher:

For each of the following factors, indicate to what degree material characteristics correspond to identified instructional needs by circling the appropriate number. If certain variables are not applicable, write NA in the right-hand column. Where low correspondence is observed, comment briefly on the potential for adaptation or modification in the area.

	Degree of Correspondence			
	High	Adequate	Low	Notes
INSTRUCTIONAL SPECIFICATION				
Objectives				
Scope	③	2	1	
Sequence	③	2	1	*Programmed as needed*
Target Population				
Chronological age	3	②	1	
Mental age	3	②	1	
Age/Grade equivalent	3	2	1	
Other descriptors	3	2	1	*N/A*
Prerequisite Skills	③	2	1	*N/A*
Learning Modalities				
Input	3	②	1	
Output	③	2	1	
Format				
Medium	③	2	1	*He loves machines*
Quality	③	2	1	
Spatial arrangement	3	②	1	
Safety features	③	2	1	
Pacing				
Rate	③	2	1	*completely self-paced*
Flexibility	③	2	1	
Feedback Mechanisms				
Type of reinforcement	3	②	1	
Schedule	③	2	1	
Motivating Factors				
Aesthetic appeal	③	2	1	
Thematic appeal	3	2	1	*N/A*

Total ___43___
Number of factors rated ___16___
Mean rating ___2.7___

TEACHING CONCERNS

	High	Adequate	Low
Teacher Competencies			
Training	③	2	1
Specialized skills	③	2	1

	Degree of correspondence			
	High	Adequate	Low	Notes
Teaching Environment				
Classroom organization	③	2	1	
Physical requirements	③	2	1	
Teaching Aids				
Teachers guide	3	②	1	
Supplementary resources	3	2	1	N/A
Evaluative Criteria				
Test items	③	2	1	Every response is
Scheduling	③	2	1	evaluated — continual
Teacher Time				diagnosis
Preparation	③	2	1	
Supervision	③	2	1	
Evaluation	③	2	1	

Total __29__
Number of factors rated __10__
Mean rating __2.1__

COST EFFECTIVENESS

Cost				
Total price	3	②	1	
Component prices	3	2	1	N/A
Replacement parts	3	2	1	N/A
Durability	3	②	1	
Number Served	3	②	1	
Research Data	3	2	①	none
Nondiscriminatory	3	2	1	N/A
representation				

Total __7__
Number of factors rated __4__
Mean rating __1.75__

The Rating Scale is shown as it was completed in this case. Because Digitor deals with 0–9 combinations in all four operations, its scope is more than adequate. A rating of 3 was also given for sequencing of subobjectives, because this can be programmed to adjust to individual needs. No specific descriptors were used by the publishers to define a target population for Digitor, but according to the teacher's analysis, the device would be appropriate for a learner of Jason's chronological and mental age. Remaining descriptors were not considered applicable. Because Jason was able to demonstrate all identified prerequisite skills, a high degree of correspondence was noted for this factor.

In terms of learning modalities, the teacher judged the visual input provided by Digitor to be adequate. A rating of 3 was not assigned because an optimal instructional task for Jason would also incorporate his strong auditory skills. The simple motor output required allows for efficient responding and was, therefore, given the maximum score. Digitor's mechanized format was considered a highly appropriate means for providing individual drill of multiplication factors. The quality of instructional presentation and the safety features of the machine were also judged very favorably. Spatial arrangement, although adequate, could not be given the maximum rating. The teacher would have preferred a larger keyboard with more generous spacing between keys.

The pacing of Digitor was considered a strong point. Individual equations could be processed quickly, allowing a high rate of responding. The programmed device was also seen as providing a desirable degree of flexibility in pacing. The learner can advance to the next problem as soon as he makes a correct response. The amount of practice presented at each level of difficulty can also be controlled.

Although Jason responded best to social reinforcers, the teacher felt that Digitor's provision of knowledge of results would be adequate. The fact that every response is immediately corrected or reinforced was perceived as a strength. Overall, the teacher expected Jason to be highly motivated by Digitor. Because he was interested in machines, computers, and science, the module design would be especially appealing.

Digitor conformed well to Instructional Specifications; it was therefore rated on Teaching Concerns, which had been established as a second priority. No special training or skills are required to supervise the use of Digitor; therefore, scores of 3 were assigned to these factors related to teacher competencies. The maximum rating was also given for the two aspects of teaching environment, because Digitor lends itself well to various patterns of classroom organization and needs only an electric outlet for full operation. The teacher felt the device could easily be employed in the resource room or regular classroom.

The teachers manual was considered brief but adequate. The teacher did not think additional supplementary resources were necessary. The evaluative capabilities of Digitor were impressive features. A total score is provided after each set of problems, so the child's performance can be continually monitored. The teacher was seeking a material that could be used independently by the student, and he considered the minimal time demands of Digitor an important asset in an individualized program.

The material was then rated on Cost Effectiveness. Although expensive, Digitor was found to be priced in the range of other electronic teaching devices. Because it could feasibly be purchased out of the resource budget, it was rated as an acceptable cost. No component or replacement parts were involved; hence, the notations "not applicable" were recorded for these categories. The teacher estimated an expected 3 to 5 years of use from Digitor, and gave a satisfactory rating for Durability. A score of 2 was also assigned for "number served." Although only one child operates Digitor at a time, the teacher reasoned that such a compact teaching aid dealing with basic math facts could be used by a number of different children in a given day. With no evidence of empirical validation, a rating of unsatisfactory had to be given for Research Data. The final variable, "nondiscriminatory representation," did not apply to this math material.

The composite mean score obtained for Digitor was 2.6, indicating high correspondence with instructional needs. Mean ratings for the three separate groupings revealed that characteristics of Digitor more than adequately fulfill Instructional Specifications and Teaching Concerns. The absence of research data contributed to the lower score for Cost Effectiveness, although the resulting mean was still within an acceptable range. Based on these results, Digitor would be a good choice for Jason's instructional material.

When the teacher compared Digitor's rating with those obtained for other computation aids, Digitor seemed most desirable. The decision to purchase the device was reinforced by the discovery that it was also well suited to the needs of several other students in the resource program.

REFERENCES

Abeson, A., and Weintraub, F. 1977. Understanding the individualized education program. In S. Torres (ed.), A Primer on Individualized Education Programs for Handicapped Children. The Foundation for Exceptional Children, Reston, Va.

Charles, C. M. 1976. Individualizing Instruction. The C. V. Mosby Company, St. Louis.

Connolly, A. J., Nachtman, W., and Pretchett, E. M. 1971. Key Math Diagnostic Arithmetic Test. American Guidance Service, Circle Pines, Mn.

Federal Register. 1976. Vol. 41, no. 252, p. 56986, Thursday, December 30.

Lerner, J. 1976. Children with Learning Disabilities. 2nd ed. Houghton Mifflin Company, Boston.

Peter, J. L. 1965. Prescriptive Teaching. McGraw-Hill Book Company, New York.

Schwartzberg, I. M., and Smith, M. L. 1978. Prescriptive Teaching. Unpublished manuscript.

Smith, R. M. 1974. Clinical Teaching: Methods of Instruction for the Retarded. McGraw Hill Book Company, New York.

Stephens, T. M. 1976. Directive Teaching of Children with Learning and Behavioral Handicaps. 2nd ed. Charles E. Merrill Publishing Company, Columbus.

6

Retrieving Appropriate Materials

*Krista S. Oglesby, Robert M. Anderson, Ed.D.,
and Robert Sterrett, M.Ed.*

In the last three chapters, a practical model for the selection of instructional materials was carefully described. The model requires the teacher to do three things. First, he must assess the relevant characteristics of the learner. Among other things, the student's present level of functioning, unique profile of strengths and weaknesses in specific skill areas, individual learning style, and affective or behavioral needs must be determined. Second, the teacher must analyze available instructional materials in terms of several critical dimensions. In addition to primary instructional features, such as prerequisite skills, learning modalities, format, and feedback provisions, the teacher must be cognizant of such things as compatibility with teaching style, learner's appeal and motivation, and cost effectiveness. Finally, by matching material characteristics with instructional requirements, the teacher can narrow down alternatives until the materials most appropriate for an individual youngster are identified.

This careful selection procedure will be effective and valuable only if the teacher can obtain the materials that he ultimately selects. Once the matching process is completed, and several appropriate materials are identified, the teacher must be aware of and have access to sources where he can locate them for either loan or purchase. Selection and retrieval go hand in hand. One without the other is of little practical value. This chapter, therefore, examines ways in which teachers can obtain those materials that they have identified as essential in their efforts to provide individualized instruction to their students.

Because of restrictions in terms of both time and money, all retrieval efforts should start close to home. A resourceful teacher can accumulate a tremendous variety of materials in a short time. The classrooms of experienced teachers in almost every school serve testimony to this: shelves, file cabinets, tables, cartons, and cans are overflowing with instructional materials of all kinds. Each teacher should complete a thorough inventory of all the materials he currently has, noting any previously overlooked materials, as well as others that could be modified to meet instructional needs. Organization is essential, and teachers should label materials and storage areas so that everything can be found in and returned to its own particular spot.

Outside the classroom there are numerous other local sources that are usually productive. Fellow teachers have always been a reliable source of needed materials and typically do not mind sharing them if they are not being used at the time. Some school systems place instructional materials and equipment in the school library or audiovisual room. Others house such items in a centrally located building with distribution on a district-wide basis. Nearby colleges may have curriculum libraries or materials centers. Although probably established for preservice teacher training programs, such resources are typically open to teachers who wish to inspect or even borrow the materials. Special schools for exceptional children, if there are any in the area, offer yet another source. Their librarian or curriculum director will be able to supply information on the kinds of materials and media that they employ to meet the specific needs of that particular school population. Finally, the public library may serve as a local source of instructional aids, often providing such things as large-print materials, high-interest low-vocabulary readers, "talking books" and audiotapes.

When local resources prove insufficient, the teacher must depend on the various statewide regional and national retrieval systems that have been developing in recent years. With federal support, the Instructional Materials Centers, Regional Media Centers Network (IMC/RMC), and National Center on Educational Media and Materials for the Handicapped (NCEMMH) were designed and implemented to provide, among other things, practical assistance to classroom teachers. Utilizing a web of regional and associate centers, a large variety of both print and nonprint materials have been made available to teachers on a short-term loan basis. Although funding has run out for these particular programs, similar services are still provided by several other agencies.

Both local and national instructional materials resources will necessarily be tapped by most teachers in their efforts to provide adequate and effective instruction to their students. With patience, resourcefulness, and an awareness of a variety of retrieval strategies, they can obtain most if not all of the materials they need. This chapter provides suggestions and information designed to facilitate this process.

LOCAL SOURCES

Canal Zone Retrieval System

Since the inception of educational services in the Canal Zone (Panama), the relative isolation of the school system has necessitated that teachers and administrators become highly self-sufficient. Therefore, the retrieval system developed in the Canal Zone probably stands as one of the best examples of the results of innovative leadership coupled with a concerted effort by teachers to provide an effective, practical approach to the selection of instructional materials with very little assistance other than their own ingenuity and dedication. Dr. James M. Wolf, Assistant Superintendent and Director of the Department of Prescriptive Education, was far in advance of the times in developing a mainstream program in the Canal Zone, replete with a materials retrieval system, long before this approach was mandated in the United States. Under Wolf's direction, a special education prescriptive retrieval system was developed during the early 1960s. As the program moved philosophically in the direction of mainstreaming, there was an obvious need to make materials accessible to regular classroom teachers so that classroom remediation could follow diagnosis and prescription.

As one part of a solution to this challenge, a retrieval system of instructional items was developed, to be used in correlation with the results obtained from the Cooper-McGuire Diagnostic Word Attack Test. In a cooperative effort, a group of remedial reading teachers analyzed more than 1,400 educational materials and correlated them, page by page, with a series of behavioral objectives. Each behavioral objective was actually correlated with a specific page. This represented a definite improvement over other retrieval systems that the staff had considered at that time inasmuch as most of the existing systems referred the teacher to a workbook, textbook, or a total kit, rather than to the specific page that contained the material related to the behavioral objective.

The system consists of two components. The *Directory for Prescriptive Materials* (Wolf and Makibbin) contains over 1,400 instructional items, which allows for very specific retrieval of instructional materials correlated with the 32 behavioral objectives of the

Cooper-McGuire Diagnostic Word Attack Test. A *Prescriptive Material Kit* is located in each elementary school and is an additional resource available to teachers in obtaining materials to be used with the total class, ad hoc groups, and/or individually to assist students in the development of word attack skills. The following instructions, included in the *Directory for Prescriptive Materials,*[1] describe the utilization of the system. This description has been included to assist school officials in the development of a materials retrieval system, should this model meet local needs.

How to Use the Directory for Prescriptive Materials
The *Directory for Prescriptive Materials* is for the teacher's use in the classroom. Instructional items contained in the Prescriptive Materials Kit have been classified according to specific *target skills* to be taught and have been rated for appropriate *grade level* use. Each instructional item has been given a *code number* for locating the item in the Prescriptive Materials Kit. All instructional items have been correlated to and listed under a specific behavioral objective. The following steps are suggested as a guide for using the *Directory for Prescriptive Materials:*

1. Analyze your Completed Class Record Chart and determine the specific skills that need to be learned by each student.

    Example: As determined by the result of Test P-13, an ad hoc group needs instruction on vowel digraphs *au, aw.* Supplementary materials are needed to teach these vowel digraphs.

2. Consult the Table of Contents for page numbers of instructional items listed under Behavioral Objective P-13. (This objective states that: "The learner will be able to identify the letters representing the vowel digraphs or diphthong he hears when these sounds are dictated.")

3. Turn to Page 36 in the *Directory*. Scan listings under the heading "Target Skill" for vowel digraphs *au, aw.* Determine if it can be used at your grade level by referring to column three. Note item number in column one: P-13-5G. The first code letter will include an R, a P, or an S. The R is for the Readiness Behavioral Objectives in the Cooper-McGuire Work Attack Test, the P is for Phonic Analysis Objectives, and the S is for the Structural Analysis Objectives. The second code symbol makes reference to the specific behavioral objectives, and the third code number refers to the number of the items under the behavioral objective.

---

[1] Reprinted with permission from the *Directory for Prescriptive Materials* by J. M. Wolf and S. M. Makibbin.

The final code letter refers to an additional page of the specific instructional item.

Example: P—(Phonic Analysis)
13—(13th behavioral objective in Phonic Analysis section)
5—(5th instructional item under objective P-13)
G—(7th page of the specific instructional item under Behavioral Objective P-13-5)

4. The Prescriptive Materials Kit contains a file folder for each behavioral objective listed in the Cooper-McGuire Word Attack Test. Pull File P-13. Locate instructional item P-13-5G, which is a sample copy.
5. After you have made use of the sample copy, replace it in the appropriate folder according to the code number.

How to Use Prescriptive Materials In order to make optimal use of the instructional items in the Prescriptive Materials Kit, the following suggestions are summarized for consideration:

1. *Board Work*
   Certain materials in the Kit are appropriate for board work. It is possible to copy the sample sheet on the chalkboard for the presentation of a specific skill to be taught and/or for a reinforcement or reteaching exercise. Pupils copy or complete the exercise from the board as seatwork.
2. *Creating Novel Material*
   Another effective use would be for the teacher to utilize the sample copy as a point of reference for creating novel materials and methods of presentation. For example, the creation of every pupil's response cards; self-directing, self-correcting materials; tutorial materials for student's use with other students; etc.
3. *Overhead Transparencies*
   A third use of the materials is for the teacher to make overhead transparencies of sample copies that lend themselves to this medium. Transparencies are effective for total class instruction and ad hoc skill groups.
4. *Ditto Masters*
   Last, the teacher may consider making ditto masters from the sample copy, thus enabling him to make a copy for each child for reinforcement after the skill has been taught.

Supplements to the Prescriptive Materials Kit
Supplement A contains Re-tests for P-1 through P-17 and S-1 through S-10. These are teacher-made re-tests and may be used with ad hoc groups after the specific skills have been taught.

Supplement B contains a descriptive analysis sheet for each instructional item included in the Prescriptive Materials Kit. It lists the complete source for the item (author, publisher, address, price, target skill, grade level, and a brief description of the item).

Supplement C includes word attack materials that may be requested from the Audiovisual Center.

Procedure for Adding Materials to the Prescriptive Materials Kit   Teachers may be aware of other materials that correlate with the Cooper-McGuire Diagnostic Word Attack Test. These materials may be commercially prepared or teacher-made. The 1,400 items included in the Kit should be considered a starter set, and new materials need to be added and the Directory updated when indicated. If the reader has an instructional item to include in the Kit, he should submit it to the remedial reading teacher serving his school and correlate it with the appropriate behavioral objective. The remedial reading teacher will forward the instructional item to the Educational Achievement Center, where it will be coded and a sample copy reproduced for each elementary school. When additional items are obtained from the Educational Achievement Center for inclusion in the Kit, the code number will need to be included in the Directory. A master copy will be maintained at the Educational Achievement Center, from which a revised Directory will be produced. Assistance in adding materials to the Kit will be greatly appreciated.

Fundamentals Operations Resources (FORE)

In 1967, the Los Angeles Unified School District, Special Education Division, initiated a system for individualizing instruction. Fundamentals Operations Resources (FORE) is comprised of 11 strands or sequences of skills in the three areas of language, reading, and math. Each of the strands is divided into hierarchies that are stated behaviorally and sequenced developmentally. The skills are arranged in 18 developmental levels. Each level is assigned a Strand-Level-Item (SLI) accession number (Reeder and Bolen, 1976).

An informal inventory has been developed for each item. Criterion-referenced data are obtained on what specific skills a student has or has not mastered. The teacher uses this information to set educational goals and short-term objectives and to effectively monitor the student's performance.

Once the child's instructional needs are diagnosed, the next step is the selection of materials. The resource segment of System FORE is comprised of materials information lists and cards. The lists and cards are designed to correlate both teacher-made and commercial materials to specific objectives in the developmental sequences. Standard catalog information such as publisher, price, information, grade level/age, learning center, modality, and interest level is included. Materials are selected by completing the student assessment, identifying the unmastered SLIs, and finding the corresponding numbers on the materials list. The list can be used without the assessment data by searching the skill categories, or by material type. Materials lists catalogs are duplicated to allow each teacher to have a copy. Circulation policies enable teachers to borrow materials from each other. Materials are often transported from program to program by district courier services.

In addition to the lists, materials are indexed on McBee encoding cards. This enables the teacher to select materials not only by SLI number but by learning center options, materials format, input/output modalities, and material location. Holes in the instructional material information cards are coded from information contained on the card and related to the sequences of instruction. Cards listing appropriate materials are easily separated by insertion of a key sort needle.

The process of correlating instructional materials to the sequences requires the following: instructional materials; developmental sequences in reading, language, and math; McBee cards, notcher, and card saver; sequence indexes for reading, language, and math; and master list of materials encoded in FORE. First the function of the material must be analyzed. Then the SLIs that can be most effectively taught by the material are chosen. The appropriate learning center, material type, modalities, and location are decided and marked on the card. After the cards are notched they can be filed in separate academic-area file boxes. The encoded information on the cards is used to compile the instructional materials lists. Blanks are provided to the right side of the page for additional information. This gives teachers a personalized materials access mode and supplies media personnel with a continual master or update process. School systems that adopt system FORE can tailor the system to reflect the instructional materials available in the local school system.

Fountain Valley Teacher Support System (FVTSS)

The primary goals of the Fountain Valley Teacher Support Systems (FVTSS), available for both reading and arithmetic skills, grades one through six, are to help teachers analyze students' learning difficulties and to identify materials for teaching specific academic skills. The reading system, first to be developed, was originated in response to a need by the teachers in the Fountain Valley, California school system for help in identifying skill weaknesses and selecting appropriate materials to remediate these weaknesses.

The FVTSS comes in kit form. Kits are color coded by grade level. The teachers manual includes behavioral objectives for each of the reading or arithmetic skills appropriate for each grade level. A series of tests on cassette tape and self-scoring worksheets provide for individual or group testing. Test items are correlated to the objectives in the teachers manual, and to the information in the Teaching Alternatives Supplement (TAS), which is also included in the kit. The teacher identifies specific skill deficiencies. A record of what skills were mastered and when reteaching of deficit skills began can be kept on the Pupil Progress Profile. By means of the TAS, appropriate instructional materials for the reteaching of the specific skill can be identified. This Teaching Alternatives Supplement identifies the exact page in various reading or mathematics series on which the particular skill is taught.

Questions about either the reading or arithmetic system should be directed to:

> Richard L. Zweig Associates, Inc.
> 20800 Beach Blvd.
> Huntington Beach, Ca. 92648

Prescriptive Materials Retrieval System (PMRS)

The Prescriptive Materials Retrieval System (PMRS) is a self-contained rapid search and retrieval system for location of instructional materials to meet individual needs. One of the most widely used commercially produced systems, the PMRS uses computer punched Descriptor Cards, Descriptive Analysis Sheets, a Card Reader or light box, and an *Educational Descriptor Dictionary* to cross index, describe, and retrieve information on educational materials. The user can pinpoint materials by grade level, reading level, mental age, input-output, and other educationally relevant descriptors (Adamson and Van Etten, 1970). Operated either manually or in a computerized format, the PMRS provides the teacher with a tool to expedite the process of narrowing down the alternative materials by matching material characteristics with instructional requirements until the most appropriate materials are identified. This procedure for selecting materials, congruent with procedures suggested in Chapter 5, is based on a systematic assessment of the learner and the consequent individualized education program prescribed for the learner. About 10,000 educational materials from some 200 publishers are currently indexed and classified under 418 descriptors (found in the *Educational Descriptor Dictionary*) that cover:

—Specific Skill or Content	—Mental Age Level
—Format	—Input-Output (Stimulus/Response)
—Grade Level	—Process
—Reading Level	—Major Areas

These areas are described as follows:

1. *Specific Content Descriptors* pinpoint the specific skills, concepts, or information offered within the instructional materials analyzed in the PMR System.

2. *Format and Special Characteristic Descriptors* allow the user to stipulate the particular format or special characteristics desired in the material to be selected.

3. *Grade Level Descriptors* allow the user to designate the grade level for which material is needed.

4. *Reading Level Descriptors* allow the user to stipulate exactly the reading level of the material to be selected.

5. *Mental Age Descriptors* allow the user to retrieve material to match the mental age of the students. There are a limited number of materials available that are described by mental age. This descriptor is coded into the system when instructional material indicates an appropriate mental age suitability.

6. *Input-Output Descriptors* allow the user of the system to state the stimulus and response characteristics of the material to be selected.

7. *Process Descriptors* are included for those who are concerned with the process by which students learn. Remediation personnel planning programs around the Illinois Test of Psycholinguistic Ability will find the Process Descriptors of great value. They allow for direct programming from noted deficits on the ITPA. For example: if the educational programmer wants to select materials to strengthen visual sequential memory skills, he is immediately directed to names and descriptions of such materials through the use of only one Descriptor Card.

8. *Major Area Descriptors* allow users to select descriptions of all materials in any major area. For example: if one wishes to obtain descriptions of all perceptual motor materials in the system, one can do so through the use of one Descriptor Card. This provides an objective preview of educational materials before acquisition. Also, the Major Area Descriptors can be used as an immediate basis for classifying materials as they are purchased.

Case Example The following case example, which uses a seven-step procedure, illustrates how the system may be used manually.

Step One Describe the pupil's educational diagnosis and suggested prescriptive programming in your own terms, and translate your terms into *descriptors* that correspond to those found in the *Educational Descriptor Dictionary*. Suppose that your pupil has a *chronological age of 9* and a *mental age of 7*. Among his diagnosed problems is difficulty with *initial consonants*. Based on his unique profile of strengths and deficits, a *workbook* format has been suggested as a part of his intervention program. Therefore, you will need to match these descriptors (chronological age 9, mental age 7, initial consonants, workbook format) as closely as possible with the descriptors found in the *Educational Descriptor Dictionary*. In this case, the precise descriptors are contained in the dictionary.

Step Two Each of your descriptors in the *Educational Descriptor Dictionary* is numbered and color coded. For initial consonants the code is Y-67. Each descriptor has a corresponding descriptor card. List the descriptor numbers and locate the cards by number in the descriptor file box.

Step Three Each descriptor card has a number of computer drilled holes, each of which is a key to a published material. In this example, card Y-67 and the cards for the other three relevant descriptors are extracted from the file for placement on the illuminated Card Reader (light box).

Step Four The four descriptor cards are placed in a stack on the card reader. Where the holes coded into the four cards coincide, the light will show through. Each illuminated code hole represents an educational material. Inappropriate materials are, therefore, eliminated.

Step Five Record the number assigned each code hole. These numbers refer to numerically listed descriptive analysis sheets.

Step Six Examine the Descriptive Analysis Sheets. Each sheet provides a one and one-half page physical description of an applicable product (author, title, publisher, price, and description, including teacher involvement required).

Step Seven Using the information obtained in Step Six, select your material and plan a prescriptive program. Space is provided on each Descriptive Analysis Sheet for your own shelf number to facilitate the step from sheet to material.

By pinpointing materials that fit the needs of a given student population, the PMRS can also serve as a buying guide for a school system.

According to the publisher, an update is available. Materials to be included in each update are determined by recommendations from field users of the system. Additional information may be obtained from:

> B.L. Winch and Associates
> 45 Hitching Post Drive, Building 2
> Rolling Hills Estates, Ca. 90274

STATEWIDE SOURCES

The majority of resource programs established on the state level actually function on a regional basis. Typically, a state is divided into geographic regions, with a learning resource center located within each region. The purpose of the center is to meet the instructional materials needs of educators within its boundaries. This may be accomplished by the regional center alone or through smaller district centers that are supported by the regional center.

Most state instructional materials programs are managed by the state education agency. The primary function of the program at the state level is administrative, supporting and coordinating the activities of the regional centers. Two model statewide resources systems, one in Texas, the other in Iowa, are described in this section.

Texas Resource System

The goal of the Texas resource center is to supply a wide variety of materials, services, and resources to teachers of exceptional children. The system is made up of three levels: local, regional, and state. The Special Education Resource System (SERS) is organized by a local school district or by a Special Education Cooperative (two or more districts joined together). Its primary function is to lend instructional materials for use by teachers of the handicapped. Specific services include: 1) the circulation of child-use instructional materials requested by teachers to meet the educational needs of the students; policies regarding eligible users, length of loan, and criteria for materials purchase are determined by the SERS; 2) the provision of an information retrieval system that matches instructional materials to the specific needs of learners; 3) the dissemination of information concerning services offered, materials available, and training opportunities; 4) training and giving technical assistance to teachers and support personnel in the areas of educational materials and selection criteria; 5) conducting or participating in needs assessments and future projections regarding instructional materials services, results of which are incorporated in a five-year plan for special education, which is submitted to the Texas Education Agency by each district or cooperative (Townsend, 1976).

The next level of the resource continuum is the Education Service Center. The centers are located in 20 geographically defined regions throughout Texas. They give needed assistance to the SERS in the areas of instructional, administrative, and informational services. To aid the SERS within a region, each center directs a Special Education Instructional Materials Center (SEIMC). Materials located at the SEIMC are used primarily for evaluation on a preview-for-purchase basis. Teachers check out materials, use them with students, analyze their effectiveness, and decide if they should be purchased at the local level. The SEIMC also supplies: 1) assistance in establishing and improving SERS, 2) training in the use of instructional materials, and 3) direct support services, such as lists of available materials or minicatalogs of materials listed by context area or grade level. The SEIMC helps in conducting needs inventories, dispersing information about materials training, and acting as a go-between for the Texas Education Agency and the local district or cooperative. The SEIMC provides an information retrieval system to match its inventory to the instructional needs of handicapped students.

The Texas Education Agency (TEA) is the third level of authority in the resource system. The TEA assists the Special Education Instructional Materials Centers to aid the SERS. Its primary goal is "to establish and make operational a statewide special education instructional materials delivery system to provide services to exceptional children" (Townsend, 1976). TEA provides leadership to ensure the implementation and continued development of the materials delivery service. Teachers and administrative and supportive personnel are given inservice and preservice training by the TEA. Information concerning instructional materials and related services is provided in *Notes,* a bimonthly newsletter of the State Learning Resource Center.

Supporting all these services is the Regional Resource Center (RRC), located at the University of Texas. RRC supplies instructional and professional support to the SEIMC personnel and to college or university faculty involved in special education training.

Iowa Resource System

In 1966, 16 regional educational materials centers were established by the Iowa State Board of Public Education under Title II of the

Elementary-Secondary Education Act. A county Board of Education in each of the 16 areas was designated as a sub-agency for Title II purposes. The county superintendent and his board were responsible for coordinating efforts of educators and school boards to supply the leadership and financial support for the development of the regional media centers. These centers serve 399 school districts, 228 nonpublic schools, and over 670,000 students (Iowa State Department of Public Instruction, 1973).

Each of the regional centers functions independently. Circulation policies, methods for funding, staffing, specific services offered, and mode of delivery are determined by the individual centers. Although the programs vary in the details of their operation, they share many basic characteristics. All new materials are purchased using Title II grant monies. The majority of the programs assess each participating county a set amount per census child to fund the operating budget. Each media center provides both print and nonprint materials. Books, 16-mm films, multimedia kits, tapes, transparencies, slides, art, and study prints, in addition to special education materials, comprise the collection found in most of the centers. Delivery varies from a monthly basis in some regions to twice a week in others. Materials are sent by mail or delivered by vans operated by the centers. All centers allow teachers to obtain materials from the center in person. Information concerning the activities and services provided by each center is disseminated through newsletters, bulletins, or announcements on local radio and television programs. Listings of materials in the centers are made available to the teachers either in the form of a catalog or card file. In addition to distributing instructional materials, the centers provide inservice workshops, support local and statewide pilot programs, develop multimedia instructional packets, and participate in various special education and special needs projects. Each center works cooperatively with county and local agencies for the improvement of instruction in Iowa's elementary and secondary public and nonpublic schools.

REGIONAL AND NATIONAL SOURCES

The Instructional Materials Center Network

The beginnings of a comprehensive, nationwide instructional materials network, unlike most other events of the 1960s, were undramatic, but nevertheless contained the seeds of the system currently in existence (Anderson, Zia, Springfield, and Greer, 1977).

Two prototype Instructional Materials Centers were established by the US Office of Education in 1964 under authority of Public Law 88-164, Title III. These pilot programs were conceived to provide needed services in special education. They did this by collecting existing instructional materials appropriate for special education; by cataloging, storing, and loaning these materials; by publishing acquisition lists; by conducting workshops; by consulting educators; by giving assistance to others starting their own centers; and by publishing materials (McCarthy, 1968). Because of the success of these centers, new regional centers were established. By 1967, 15 Instructional Materials Centers were in operation around the United States, each operating independently, servicing satellite centers established in the region, and coordinating its activities with the other Centers and the Instructional Materials Center Network for Handicapped Children and Youth (IMCNHCY), of which it was a part.

The concomitant proliferation of knowledge and data in the behavioral sciences, particularly the expanding body of information about the handicapped, led to the development of sophisticated systems of information storage and retrieval. First, several computer based information systems became operational within the nationwide network of IMCs. Second, the Educational Resources Information Center Clearinghouses (ERIC) were established to compile and evaluate different resource areas for children with learning problems. The ERIC system has been primarily used as a source of professional information, research studies, and other professional literature (see Chapter 15), whereas the IMC retrieval systems functioned primarily as a resource for classroom teachers seeking educational materials to be used with children.

National Center on Educational Media and Materials for the Handicapped

The creation of the National Center on Educational Media and Materials for the Handicapped (NCEMMH) in 1972, as a result of Public Law 91-61, demonstrated continued public commitment to the need to provide instructional media, materials, and educational technology for exceptional learners. Before the termination of its contract in August, 1977, the NCEMMH broadened the base and scope of activity of the IMC network already in existence. Besides coordination of the accumulated network of instructional materials, the National Center, located at The Ohio State University in Columbus, was engaged in the development and delivery of these materials. It promulgated standards for special education materials, evaluated and field tested new products developed elsewhere, and made determinations concerning the suitability of materials for dissemination throughout the network. In addition, NCEMMH served as the national coordinating office of the four Specialized Offices and 13 Area Learning Resource Centers created by subsequent legislation. NCEMMH assumed a leadership and organizing role for the nationwide system of federally funded area centers and state and locally funded centers. Concerning its leadership role at the national level, Samuel C. Ashcroft, Director of NCEMMH, wrote:

> The leadership role of the National Center in special education might best be described as a cooperative agent, coordinator, and colleague. In the past year, the Center, acting as a national agent, has organized and sponsored several conferences and workshops. It has initiated a national needs assessment on media and materials for special education. It has worked with the model schools for the deaf and other handicapped children on a variety of undertakings. In the immediate future the National Center will continue to support and coordinate research and development dealing with educational technology for the handicapped. At the same time it will work closely with the national network of Area Learning Resource Centers (ALRC) and with the commercial sector. In addition to these functions already undertaken, the National Center would seem to be the natural institution to set up a program for continuing educator, advanced study, and professional renewal for those who work with exceptional children (1974, p. 2).

In 1974, a restructuring of the extant IMC Network was engineered by the Bureau for Education of the Handicapped, US Office of Education. This effort sought to redirect the activities of the numerous projects with varied focuses that had been set up by BEH in the preceding decade. According to Blackhurst (1974), several difficulties had been encountered in attempting to coordinate these projects into a concerted, effective national effort to provide solutions to instructional problems encountered in educating exceptional children. Included among these problems were the lack of coordination of project activities, the fact that funds came from several different sources, the unavailability of the services of some programs nationwide, and the fact that projects were in varying degrees of development. In response to these problems, 13 regions were established covering the United States and its territories, each to have one Regional Resource Center (RRC) and one Area Learning Resource Center (ALRC). The RRC programs were concerned with development of assessment and programming practices for the handicapped, and the ALRC programs encourage development of media, materials, and educational technology.

Instructional products were reviewed and recommended for effectiveness and marketability for commercial and noncommercial publication and distribution. NCEMMH also provided developers with technical assistance on product development and distribution. Information services include the development, production, and dissemination of catalogs, bibliographies, indexes, profile matches, and directories. The National Instructional Materials Information System (described later) was developed and maintained by NCEMMH.

In addition to providing supportive services to the ALRs, the four Special Offices of the ALRC/SO/NCEMMH Network located usable materials to fill unmet needs, adapted materials to meet such needs, developed materials that were not considered marketable by commercial developers, and field tested newly developed materials for target populations. They also identified child-use materials, evaluated them by standard criteria, and described them for entry into NIMIS (Ashcroft, 1976).

"Three of the four Special Offices have common scopes of work differentiated by their unique focus on handicapping conditions" (Ashcroft, 1976). The Specialized Office for the Visually Impaired (SOVI) functioned as a part of the American Printing House for the Blind. It furnished technical assistance in the areas of materials identification, adaptation and development, field testing, and evaluation of instructional products for the visually handicapped. Assistance in the areas of materials identification, adaptation, development, field test, and evaluation for the hearing impaired was provided by the Specialized Office for the Hearing Impaired (SOHI). Materials identification, adaptation, development, field tests, and evaluation for various handicapping conditions were provided by the Specialized Office for Other Handicapping Conditions (SOOH). The function of the Specialized Office for Materials Distribution (SOMD) was "to deliver on a loan or rental basis those materials that are selected and described by the other Special Offices" (Ashcroft, 1976). Each RRC and ALRC joined in a cooperative effort with the state education agencies within its region to provide effective delivery of services for all handicapped populations.

National Instructional
Materials Information System (NIMIS)

The ALRC/SO/NCEMMH system was designed to provide supportive services for state and local media and materials programs. Communication was maintained throughout the network by the National Instructional Materials Information System (NIMIS), the national support system for materials information. NIMIS was a computer-based retrieval system designed to help parents, teachers, and professionals from education-related fields locate materials they needed to work with the handicapped. It was designed and implemented by NCEMMH and operated in conjunction with the ALRCs and SOs.

The objective of NIMIS was to provide a nationwide comprehensive network providing information concerning appropriate special education materials and media. This was the first nationally coordinated attempt to provide such services. When NIMIS was in full operation, descriptive information was provided concerning the following types of materials—child-use, teacher training, measurement and evaluation, and prototype (models for future development). The materials were almost evenly divided between print and nonprint item. In the latter category were items such as instructional kits, films, cassettes, teaching machines, and toys. NIMIS entries provided the user with bibliographical information (author, title, publisher, price) and abstracts/descriptions. This information was available instantaneously through computer terminals at the National Center and in printed NIMIS bibliographies available at the ALRCs, SOs, and local learning resource centers.

A user of NIMIS first contacted his local or state learning resource center, which formulated a request to NIMIS through its ALRC. The request contained specific information concerning the materials desired, so that the user's needs could be matched as closely as possible with available materials. Entries contained in the system were available through local and state centers or on loan from the Specialized Office for Materials Distribution.

Current Status of National Sources

The National Center on Educational Media and Materials for the Handicapped, the Area Learning Resource Centers, and the Specialized Offices ended their contracts with the Bureau of Education for the Handicapped (BEH) during August and September, 1977. Many of the services provided by these centers have been continued through a new series of projects funded by BEH.

Some of the services of the Area Learning Resource Centers will be provided by Regional Resource Center projects. There are 17 Regional Resource Centers that provide services to and through the state education agency located in 57 states and territories. For information regarding services in a particular state, contact the state director of special education in the state education agency.

The work of the National Instructional Materials Information System, as well as the marketing of special education materials formerly handled by NCEMMH, is now being conducted by new contractors. For specific information regarding the availability of services, contact:

Dr. Paul Andereck, Education Specialist
USOE/BEH/LRB
4849 Donahoe Building
6th and D Streets, S.W.
Washington, D.C. 20202
202-472-4650

The four specialized offices are being closed. Two new offices will take over some of their functions.

At the same address as the former Specialized Office 4, but operating as a subcontract to the Conference of Executives of American Schools for the Deaf, materials distribution continues from:

Specialized Office for Materials Distribution
Indiana University
Audio-Visual Center
Bloomington, In. 47401
812-337-0531—Main Office
812-337-1511

In the same location as the former Specialized Office 2, similar services are now contracted to:

Media Development Project for the Hearing Impaired
University of Nebraska—Lincoln
318 Barkley Memorial Center
Lincoln, Ne. 68583
402-472-2141

Computer Based Resource Units (CBRU)

A series of Computer Based Resource Units has been developed at the State University College at Buffalo, New York. Units of study are available for children (K–12) on various topics such as alcohol, career education, and sensory perception. Skill development programs include such units as physical conditioning, movigenics, and visual motor development.

Initially, groups of teachers, working cooperatively, listed all of the major objectives they felt a teacher might select for a class preparing to study a specific topic. Then they listed all of the books, films, filmstrips, and other materials that they found as potential resources. After that, they wrote as many statements of content about the topic as they thought were relevant. Taking into account the many different characteristics of children, they listed activities that they felt were appropriate. These materials, activities, content items, and evaluation devices were then tied to each related objective. All of this was coded along with learner variables and stored in the memory bank of the computer. Classroom teachers who utilize CBRUs may now select up to five specific objectives for their class and two per individual child for each resource unit or skill development program requested. Activities are retrieved according to each child's needs, interests, developmental tasks, sex, reading level, mental and chronological ages, physical handicaps, and learning environment.

A computer printout, called a Resource Guide, specifies suggested large and small group activities, content, materials, and evaluation devices that can be used for the entire class. A second part of the printout includes individualized suggestions and information for each student in the class, based on the objectives selected and the various designated learner characteristics. The advantages of such a system are summarized as follows:

1. The system contains a wealth of knowledge and teaching-learning possibilities stored by computer for rapid retrieval, saving infinite teacher hours of sorting, classifying, and researching.

2. CBRUs allow for the teacher to be creative by providing for a variety of teaching strategies related to each objective selected by the teacher and/or his class.

3. Depending on the particular objectives selected, each Computer-Based Resource Guide is unique and tailored to the needs and interests of the particular class.

4. Each guide (printout) that the teacher receives contains only the information related to the objectives selected by the teacher; no erroneous information.

5. There is the possibility for continuous updating and revision. New materials and suggestions can be programmed into the computer. Obsolete and erroneous data can be deleted.

6. There is greater possibility for individualizing instruction; the use of well-formulated instructional objectives and individual characteristics make it possible for better pupil-teaching planning.

7. The teacher ultimately makes all decisions, because the printout offers many suggestions that can be used or ignored.

Additional information may be obtained by writing:

Computer Assisted Planning
Communications Center
Professional Studies Research and
Development Complex
State University College at Buffalo
1300 Elmwood Avenue
Buffalo, N. Y. 14222

SUMMARY

A great variety of instructional materials is needed in the process of individualizing instruction for handicapped children. The tremendous diversity of their educational needs precludes the use of many of the more traditional, group oriented programs. The educational progress of these youngsters, therefore, depends largely on the teachers' ability to select and obtain materials more appropriate for them. This chapter was designed to assist in this critical endeavor, and it reviews various strategies for the retrieval of instructional materials in detail.

Although much has been accomplished in the area of materials selection and retrieval, there is still much left to be done. "The continuing assessment of needs for instructional materials; for training on media, materials and instructional technology; and for information about media and materials is essential to the effective evolution of the program of learning resource centers" (Ashcroft, 1976). A comprehensive National Needs Assessment (NNA) has been initiated and funded by the Bureau of Education for the Handicapped through its Intramural Research Program. This survey is intended to determine the kinds of media and materials that are needed to provide appropriate instruction programming for handicapped students. It has been designed so that the information gathered will be directly useful, not only at the national level, but for state and local needs also.

The NNA survey questions will deal with instructional materials development; media, materials, and instructional technology training; media and materials information; and materials distribution. For each of these areas, information will be collected and analyzed by handicapping condition, respondent population, and grade interval, and combined at state, regional, and national levels. This will supply a list of needs, arranged according to priority, that will serve the bureau of Education for the Handicapped, state education agencies, regional materials centers, and local school districts, as well as commercial media and materials developers and producers. This and similar efforts will result in an increasingly practical and effective national retrieval system that will make available to virtually every classroom teacher all the materials he will need to provide an appropriately individualized instructional program for all of his handicapped learners.

REFERENCES

Adamson, G., and Van Etten, M. C. 1970. Prescribing via analysis and retrieval of instructional materials in the educational modulation center. Except. Child. 36: 531–533.

Anderson, R. M., Zia, B., Springfield, H. L., and Greer, J. G. 1977. Educational media and materials for the handicapped: A bicentennial review. Educ. Train. Ment. Retard. 12 (3): 226–234.

Ashcroft, S. C. 1974. A significant era in special education. Apropos Spring: 1–3.

Ashcroft, S. C. 1976. NCEMMH: A network of media/material resources. Audiovis. Instruct. 21 (10): 46–47.

Blackhurst, A. E. 1974. The language resource center program—A blueprint for the future. Teach. Except. Child. 6: 216–217.

Iowa State Department of Public Instruction. 1973. A Look at Iowa's 16 Regional Educational Media Centers. Des Moines, Ia.

McCarthy, J. H. 1968. An overview of the IMC network. Except. Child. 35: 263–266.

Reeder, A. F., and Bolen, J. M. 1976. Match the materials to the learner. Audiovis. Instruct. 21 (10): 24–25.

Townsend, D. R. 1976. Build a statewide resources system. Audiovis. Instruct. 21 (10): 50–51.

Wolf, J. M., and Makibbin, S. M. Directory for prescriptive materials. Canal Zone, Division of Schools, Balboa Heights, Canal Zone. Mimeographed.

7

Evaluating Materials

Randall W. Spinney, Bonnie B. Greer, Ph.D.,
and Robert M. Anderson, Ed.D.

During the past two decades, the quantity of instructional materials available to teachers of handicapped learners has vastly increased. In 1974, Komoski estimated that there were more than 300,000 instructional materials available commercially, and there is every reason to believe that even more are being produced today. An examination of a few representative commercial catalogs reflects an overwhelming proliferation of not only textbooks, but films and filmstrips, records, overhead projection transparencies, audiotapes and cassettes, multimedia kits, videotapes and video cassettes, instructional games, and innumerable other programs and/or devices designed to enhance learning. Unfortunately, this remarkable quantity of instructional materials has not been consistently matched by quality. Although some are brilliant in design and will undoubtedly lead to significant successes in the classroom, others are clearly not worth the expenditure required to obtain them. Because of this, teachers are bewildered by what should offer them hope. Knowing full well that instructional materials are critical in education and that they often hold the key to individualized learning, they are nevertheless frequently at a loss as to which material to use. They need help, but actually get very little. As Komoski (1974) concluded, probably less then one percent of the materials have been developed with instructional effectiveness as a primary concern.

In recognition of this problem, this chapter focuses on the evaluation of instructional materials. As was pointed out in earlier chapters, educators are being pressured to document the effectiveness of their teaching. Cost effectiveness is a term familiar to most educators today. However, as McIntyre (1970) notes, we can more easily determine the cost of a material than the benefits that accrue from its use. A systematic form of evaluation is absolutely necessary. Classroom teachers and media specialists, working in cooperation with national instructional media centers throughout the country, must identify materials that have proved effective in the classroom and those that have not. Objective data must be collected, interpreted, and disseminated so that successes can be repeated and future failures avoided.

CONFUSION SURROUNDING
EVALUATION OF INSTRUCTIONAL MATERIALS

As with most human endeavors, evaluation is easier said than done. It is a complex matter that already has received considerable attention (Abt, 1970; Adamson and Van Etten, 1970; Baum, 1972; Bogaty, 1971; Campion and Komoskie, 1969; Drew and Martinson, 1971; Eash, 1969; Junkala, 1970; Lance, 1969; Lilly, 1969; McIntyre, 1970; Moss, 1968; NCEMMH, 1976; Proger, Carfioli, and Kalapos, 1973; Weinthaler, 1970). It remains the subject of considerable confusion and misunderstanding, however.

In a cogent examination of this subject, Proger et al. (1973) identified four myths common among materials evaluators that flaw existing schemes for evaluation. They state that it is erroneously believed that: a) all educators know what an instructional material is and what evaluation means, b) all materials to date can be evaluated, c) the differential effects of various materials used simultaneously to achieve an educational objective can be isolated, and d) teacher opinion of materials is alone sufficient for the evaluation of their effectiveness. Each of these beliefs bears heavily on the subject of this chapter; they are, therefore, discussed in some detail.

A clear definition of terms is a requisite first step in any cooperative effort such as the evaluation of instructional materials. Proger et al. therefore address the confusion surrounding the terms "instructional materials" and "evaluation," and offer needed clarification for both. Notwithstanding the vast range in format that characterizes instructional materials and the various ways and combinations in which they are employed, instructional materials can be defined as "vehicles (pieces of instructional hardware) used by the teacher, along with instructional techniques, to convey the content (software) of instruction to students" (Proger et al., 1973, p. 272). In Proger et al.'s of evaluation, a clear distinction is made between the description of instructional materials (i.e., the characteristics of the learner, the material, the setting, etc.) and time assessment of its effectiveness. Critical of evaluation models that rely primarily on descriptive analysis of materials, Proger et al. define evaluation as "the actual judgements that are made with regard to the quality of the material, its success in use with students, and other strengths and weakness" (p. 272). Both of these definitions help to eliminate the ambiguity in the area of evaluation, and are wholly suitable for the purposes of this chapter.

The second myth, that it is possible to evaluate all the instructional materials currently available, is refuted by Proger and his colleagues on two important points. First of all, despite the far-ranging capabilities of computerized data-banking, the tremendous volume of existing materials would doom any effort to adequately evaluate all of them. Moreover, any generalizable findings would have to be based on replications with different teachers, settings, children, etc. Sufficient time and money are not available for such an undertaking.

It is critical that educators understand the fallaciousness of the third myth discussed by Proger et al. Contrary to the thinking that has been apparent in many materials evaluation programs, past and present, it is impossible to isolate the relative effectiveness of individual materials when they are used at the same time to achieve an educational objective. Beause most instructional programs do, in fact, employ a variety of materials together, the subsequent evaluation of the success or failure of the involved materials is suspect. Although Proger et al. state that a material used alone to accomplish a single instructional objective might produce reliable data, even this situation is clouded by other variables. As McIntyre (1970) points out, evaluation concerns not only the material used but also the pupil, individually or in a group, interacting in some way with the teacher, paraprofessional, peer tutor, or even a mechanical device. Clearly, these aspects of the instructional setting will have a marked effect on the outcome, and must not be overlooked when interpreting any materials evaluation.

The final myth identified by Proger and his colleagues concerns the prevalent belief that teacher opinions are a sufficient basis upon which to judge the effectiveness of an instructional material. Although they recognize the fact that several evaluation models use ratings by teachers, they emphasize the subjectivity inherent in the approach. Teacher ratings are seen as undoubtedly valuable and have proved reliability, but the evaluation of materials should be supplemented by more objective data.

The above discussion serves well to caution the reader against acceptance of any casual approach to the evaluation of instructional materials. It is a difficult task that, if done appropriately, will require a systematic accumulation of data from a wide array of sources. As pointed out, this process at best will provide meaningful judgments on only a fraction of the materials currently employed in

American classrooms. Nevertheless, a distinction must be drawn between the ideal and the practical. This chapter is designed to help the classroom teacher evaluate the materials he has utilized, and to assist him in obtaining data on which to base the important programming decisions that must continually be made. Therefore, the approach suggested herein is adjusted to the realities of the classroom and the constraints within which most teachers operate. It cannot isolate the effects of a particular material or control for the ever present influence of other instructional variables. As designed, it is likewise based on the relatively subjective opinions of classroom teachers. However, as long as these weaknesses are recognized and the resultant evaluators qualified, such a teacher-based approach can play a valuable role.

It must also be remembered that, although experimental control is lacking and subjectivity is inherent in the approach, these two primary sources of error can be limited. If teachers are sensitive to common factors, such as teaching styles and motivational levels of the students, which can significantly affect the ultimate success or failure of an instructional material, they will be far more accurate in their overall judgements. Similarly, when the critical components of a good instructional material have been identified, and consistent procedures and criteria are developed with which to evaluate them, teachers will become increasingly effective and efficient in this difficult but clearly worthwhile endeavor.

Existing Evaluation Techniques

A review of the various evaluation procedures and devices described in the literature over the past decade repeatedly reflects the complexity and confusion, discussed above, that characterize our efforts in the evaluation of instructional materials. Although some of the approaches advocated involve little more than a simple checklist, others consist of intricate and technical system analyses. This diversity in methodology is complicated by an absence of any standard or common terminology. Nevertheless, the various devices reported do provide a beginning. Those briefly described below are representative of the concrete, practical classroom oriented approach that is emphasized in this chapter. None is completely adequate, but taken together, they provide a foundation upon which to build an instructional materials evaluation program that should be easy and effective for teachers to use.

Most of the evaluation devices found in the literature are simply a compilation of questions that assist the teacher in focusing on the key elements of instructional materials in their evaluation. Junkala

(1970), for example, offers such an approach. His framework for teacher evaluation of material consists of a list of questions that require the user to first examine the publisher's rationale and the context in which the materials are to be or have been used. Then, looking at the informational and organizational aspects of the materials, he focuses on such things as the provision for reinforcement of earlier learning, the sequential presentation of skills, and whether or not performance criteria are stated in behavioral terms. Questions are also included to help the teacher/evaluator analyze the procedural requirements of the material. For example, he asks whether or not materials are presented in lesson format, with clear goals for readiness and performance. What is expected of the teacher, in terms of time and involvement? What is expected of the student? Are any special materials needed in addition to what is provided? Finally, Junkala has the user consider additional factors that may affect the use of the materials. For example, can they be modified for use with different populations?

Brown (1975) offers a similar approach. Using a question sheet (Q-sheet) containing a list of 31 questions, he also directs teacher attention to those aspects of instructional materials that he considers critical to their effectiveness. The device is similar in scope to that of Junkala, but differs in format. Each query is accompanied by a brief discussion of the item, designed to help the teacher understand its intent and determine the appropriate answer. Although some of Brown's questions can be answered on a yes/no basis, most involve more detailed and comprehensive replies.

Different items are found on Levine's (1969) rating scale, but by and large the scope of the evaluation is approximately the same as those discussed above. The teacher evaluates the materials on the basis of age of instruction, age level, senses involved, amount of repetition allowed for, probability of successful use, cost, curability, accessibility, type of interaction, and appeal to the child. The role of the teacher in the evaluation process, however, is seen as possibly more extensive than others have suggested. Levine reports that teachers, in a "game-like atmosphere," could develop a meaningful set of criteria and could come to agreement on these standards. Nevertheless, he concedes that there are difficulties inherent in designing rating scales or checklists, no matter who is involved. They are never inclusive and, as noted earlier in this chapter, it is impossible to take into account the impact of varying teaching styles on the value of an instructional material.

The rating instrument developed by Eash (1974) is divided into four sections: a) objectives, b) organization of material (scope and sequence), c) methodology, and d) evaluation procedures. Each section contains a series of items that focuses on the ways these constructs are generally provided for in the instructional material. Some of the questions can be answered in a yes/no format, but space for open-ended responses is provided when the material examined does not measure up to any of the listed contingencies. Teacher/evaluators indicate their judgments of the overall value of a material in each of the four areas on a semantic-differential gradient. The author claims that by systematically drawing attention to the four instructional design constructs included in his instrument, teachers can better judge a material's effectiveness to meet educational needs. Given the somewhat complex nature of Eash's instrument, a short training period is advocated by the author to ensure familiarity with the technical language and design framework used in the instrument.

Bleil (1975), in his approach to the evaluation of instructional materials, identifies three separate stages. In the first, teachers are encouraged to clarify themselves to the objectives they wish to accomplish with their students and then relate them to the basic characteristics of the instructional material they are examining. The second step involves a careful examination of the material to determine whether or not commercial "gimmicks," used to promote the product, result in a misleading or inaccurate conception of what it can do. Finally, an objective evaluation using a short answer format is advocated as the last step in the evaluation process. Here Bleil places emphasis on three broad areas: a) teacher needs, b) student needs, and c) general needs. Questions similar to those of the previously described rating scales are suggested.

For the most part, the different instruments presented above have dealt with what Wiederholt and McNutt (1977) call static evaluation. Static evaluation utilizes a set of predetermined guidelines to obtain information, before a program is implemented, that will be used to determine which material could be employed with particular students. According to Wiederholt and McNutt, this type of evaluation can also provide assistance in identifying needed modifications or adaptations that must be made before they are used.

The role of such rating instruments in the initial selection of instructional materials is not disputed. Several of the devices described were, in fact, designed with this in mind. It is not surprising, therefore, if the reader recognizes substantial similarity with sections of Chapter 3, which looks at the critical characteristics of instructional materials. Nevertheless, although awareness of these factors is certainly necessary in materials selection or purchase, their reconsideration is also important after the materials have been used. Much can be learned from a second look, and these "static" elements will necessarily be included in any form of after-the-fact evaluation. The major thrust of evaluation, however, must focus on what Weiderholt and McNutt call dynamic evaluation.

Dynamic evaluation focuses on whether or not an instructional material has succeeded in facilitating student learning. The ultimate concern of everyone engaged in the process of evaluation should be the pupil and his benefit, and this is best demonstrated in achievement. Did the student achieve the instructional goals for which the use of a particular material was intended? This is the most important question in the entire process of evaluation, and it is central to dynamic evaluation. The remainder of this review, therefore, studies methods of determining reliable answers to it, and lays the groundwork for the "dynamic" emphasis reflected in the instructional materials profile presented later in this chapter.

Although the term dynamic evaluation is not used, an excellent paper by Van Etten and Van Etten (1976) carefully examines the important relationships between instructional materials evaluation and the measurement of student progress. In agreement with the proposition that current reliance on guidelines and checklists is an insufficient basis for materials selection and evaluation, they present a conceptual model designed to focus attention on results. Various measurement procedures employed in instructional materials or by teachers are judged in terms of two critical factors: the frequency and the directness of measurement.

Traditionally, the measurement of student progress has been carried out at periodic intervals throughout the academic year. For example, achievement tests and unit tests, administered every few weeks or at the end of a semester, are common in most educational settings. The Van Ettens call this approach noncontinuous measurement, and note major problems associated with it. It is apparently less expensive in both time and effort, but it can be inefficient and costly in the long run. Because of infrequent assessment, valuable instructional time is lost. Teachers do not become aware of needed adjustments and modifications until the prescribed time has elapsed or the material has been covered. Variable or inconsistent performance also goes unnoticed.

Oftentimes the measurement of progress is also indirect. IQ tests, various diagnostic tests, and standardized achievement tests all employ this approach. "Since all possible responses cannot be measured, critical skills are sampled. Success on the sampled items is interpreted to mean that the person taking the test has mastered most of the behaviors from which the sample is drawn" (Van Etten and Van Etten, 1976, p. 470). The disadvantages with this approach are obvious, especially with handicapped learners. Because all behaviors taught are not measured, teachers may overlook gaps in a child's performance. Critical skills may not have been learned. Also, as the authors point out, the practice of not measuring the exact behaviors that are taught can result in incorrect responses caused by a child's inability to generalize rather than an inability to master what was presented.

Although noncontinuous and indirect forms of measurement are appropriate for certain educational purposes, such as the evaluation of overall school programs or the comparison of group performance levels, they are unable to provide the meaningful data needed by the classroom teacher. The Van Ettens, therefore, encourage the use of strategies that are both more frequent and more direct. The progress test strategy, for example, starts with a pretest to determine correct placement level, and then continues with criterion tests at the end of each short unit. Failure at any point results in the student being recycled or provided with some form of remediation. It is a more sensitive process, in which difficulties are quickly discovered and help provided.

More frequent and direct forms of measurement are an integral component in more effective materials evaluation, but there are other techniques that can also assist the teacher in this process. Wiederholt and McNutt (1977) suggest three: analytic teaching, observation, and interviews. The first refers to methods that enable a teacher to analyze a student's performance in instructional situations and to change or modify programs whenever necessary. Using one of the systems already developed (Hall, 1972; Kunzelman, 1970; Lovitt, 1975), the teacher could closely monitor the students' "(a) understanding of either verbal or written directions prior to undertaking a task, (b) perception of the significance of the lesson, (c) need for additional instruction prior to beginning the program or any section thereof, (d) performance when positive reinforcement is built into each activity, and (e) need for periodic modifications in the format of istructional units in order to keep lessons interesting and appealing over time" (Wiederholt and McNutt, 1977, p. 7).

Observational techniques, both informal and complex, have proved effective in an endless variety of empirical and/or classroom settings. Such procedures can addi valuable information on which to base decisions about instructional materials. By systematically observing a student during instruction, his particular reactions, weaknesses of the specific material, and needed modifications became apparent.

Finally, Wiederholt and McNutt point out that, in some situations, interviews can play a role in the evaluation of instructional materials. While actively working on a material or after completing several lessons, students can be asked to share their opinions of it. Teachers using this approach should probably prepare a list of questions that focus on the type information needed. Candid and nonthreatening discussions with students could provide interesting and relevant information for the materials evaluator.

INSTRUCTIONAL MATERIALS PROFILE

The above review of existing evaluation techniques, although incomplete, reflects the substantial progress that has already been made in the area of instructional materials evaluation. Nevertheless, as of yet there is apparently no definitive model wholly appropriate for use in the classroom. In this section, therefore, the most important strengths of existing evaluation strategies, in the authors' opinions, have been combined into one practical and reliable instructional materials profile. In a unique combination, it incorporates the following four features:

1. *The Profile is designed specifically for teachers.* Teachers, those persons actually employing instructional materials on a day-to-day basis in their classrooms, are the most qualified to evaluate the effectiveness of a material. This belief is shared by teachers. In a recent study, Baum (1972) explored the attitude of special class teachers toward teacher evaluation of instructional materials. He determined from the responses to his questionnaire, sent to 100 teachers of mentally retarded children, that teachers believe that: a) they possess the necessary skills to review and evaluate instructional materials, b) teachers are better evaluators of materials than both principals and school psychologists, c) teacher evaluations of materials are more useful than the claims of the publishers, d) other teachers' evaluations would be of value to them, e) most teachers have the time to complete an evaluation, f) teachers overwhelmingly want to share their evaluation results, and g) previously evaluated materials by teachers should be made available to other teachers who may want to borrow or purchase them.

   Therefore, this profile was designed with the constraints and limitations of the classroom setting in mind. It is devoid of confusing terminology, takes little time to administer, and is easy to score. Although a longer checklist is provided to sensitize the teacher to the various critical dimensions of a material, its use will be unnecessary as soon as the teacher is familiar with its focus and understands the basis on which profile ratings are made.

2. *Emphasis is placed on student achievement.* The general objective of materials evaluation is to determine the global efficiency of the material in question. No dimensions of the evaluation process should be omitted in making this determination. However, although critical physical characteristics and teacher concerns are considered in materials evaluation, the primary focus must be on the progress of the learner. As asked earlier, did the student achieve the instructional goals for which the use of a particular material was intended? In the Instructional Materials Profile the answer to this question is weighed heavily.

3. *Student opinions and reactions are considered.* Far too often, in past attempts to evaluate instructional materials, little or no effort was made to examine student opinions. In some situations of course, constructive criticism may not have been forthcoming, but this is the exception. In most classroom settings it is logical and relevant to solicit pertinent responses from those youngsters using a particular material. The authors have devised a questionnaire that can be used for this purpose, although less formal procedures could also be used by the teacher. In any case, student opinion is included in the Instructional Materials Profiles and will affect the rating that each material receives.

4. *The Profile results are easily interpreted.* There would be little reason for developing an evaluation model if it did not yield meaningful results and provide a sound basis for the frequent decisions concerning instructional materials that must be made by the classroom teacher. The information obtained by using the profile is concrete and practical and can easily be translated into needed instructional changes. It is also sufficiently objective to share with other classroom teachers.

PROCEDURES OF THE
INSTRUCTIONAL MATERIALS PROFILE (IMP)

The actual evaluation of any given material, using the IMP, involves 10 statements that the teacher rates on a scale of 1 to 5. The numbers represent the teacher's opinion of each statement, with 1 being very negative and 5 very positive. There are two parts to the IMP: the IMP Checklist and the IMP Summary. The Checklist is used in rating the material, and the Summary is primarily designed to profile the strengths and weaknesses of the material, to ultimately provide a recommendation about its use.

Within the IMP Checklist, each of the 10 summary statements is accompanied by a list of clarifying statements that are answered either "yes" or "no." The sole purpose of these clarifying statements is to assist the teacher in deciding how to rate the summary statement: 1—Strongly disagree, 2—Disagree, 3—Undecided, 4—Agree, or 5—Strongly agree. After marking the appropriate number on the scale under each of the 10 summary statements in the Checklist, the Comments section should be completed. This section allows the teacher to give input into the evaluation process in his own words.

The final step in using the profile involves completing the Summary. The teacher simply transfers the numbers marked on each of the 10 rating scales in the Checklist to the corresponding 10 rating scales in the Summary. Because the Summary form does not have the clarifying statements, but only the 10 summary statements, it is easier to see the overall ratings. This overview is supplemented with a graph, where the teacher plots each of the 10 ratings he has previously recorded for the statements.

Throughout the Profile, the 10 statements have been classified into three areas: Physical Characteristics, Teacher Concerns, and Student Performance. After plotting the graph, the numerical ratings within each of these three areas are averaged. Thus, the ratings for statements 1–4 are averaged to get one score for Physical Characteristics, the ratings for statements 5–9 are averaged to obtain one score for Teacher Concerns, and the rating for statement 10 is used for Student Performance. These three scores are then added together, resulting in a Materials Quotient (MQ).

By comparing this Materials Quotient to the suggested interpretation, the teacher can obtain a rough estimate of success in using a particular material. Thus, if a material has an MQ of 5 on the following scale, he might reexamine the appropriateness of this material for his class.

MQ	Recommendation
12–15	Effective
8–11	Marginal
5–7	At risk
3–4	Choose another material

Assuming that the teacher has become well acquainted with the IMP, the MQ can also be obtained by omitting the Checklist and completing only the Summary. This would save time by eliminating the duplicate process that is needed by those who are unfamiliar with the content of the IMP. Each of the 10 summary statements would be rated directly in the Summary, without benefit of the clarifying statements. The rest of the IMP Summary would be completed as usual.

A Student Questionnaire (see Table 1) is mentioned under Question 7 in the IMP Checklist. This questionnaire should be administered to the students who use the material being evaluated so that they can have direct input into the evaluation process. Because it is the students for whom the material has been designed, their opinions should be included in the evaluation. Even if the Checklist is omitted, the questionnaire can still be administered and the results included as one variable in the teacher's rating of Question 7 in the Summary.

SUMMARY AND CONCLUSIONS

Instructional materials are an integral part of the educational process. They provide the key to the individualized instruction so necessary in today's classrooms. Nevertheless, their effectiveness is seldom evaluated in any systematic way. Although a wide range of assessment and measurement techniques is employed in all schools, the techniques typically focus solely on the product of instruction, i.e., student achievement. The process of instruction, including such things as teacher skills and instructional materials, is totally excluded. This practice produces two unfortunate results. First, the burden of responsibility is placed primarily on the student. Any failure to achieve is not automatically related to teaching approaches, and usually is considered a result of inability or lack of motivation. Second, whatever curricular changes are made to improve student progress are made without objective data, resulting in haphazard and somewhat whimsical classroom instruction.

Recent events are pressing educators to make serious changes in this area. As discussed in the second chapter, accountability is being demanded by the public. Teachers must now document the effectiveness of their approaches. Modifications in programming must be based on fact. Expenditures for the purchase of materials require sound justification, and will be increasingly scrutinized by cost-conscious principals, superintendents, and school boards. It is more necessary than ever before for teachers to systematically evaluate the practices and materials they employ.

Recognizing this problem, this chapter presents an instrument that can be used by the classroom teacher to evaluate the effectiveness of instructional materials. Incorporating the strengths of several

INSTRUCTIONAL MATERIALS PROFILE

DIRECTIONS:
I. Complete the Instructional Materials Profile Checklist
   A. Read each numbered statement.
   B. Answer the respective yes/no clarifying statements.
   C. Mark the appropriate number on the scale that expresses your opinion of the numbered statements.
      1 — Strongly disagree
      2 — Disagree
      3 — Undecided
      4 — Agree
      5 — Strongly agree
   D. Complete the Comments section.
II. Mark the Instructional Materials Profile Summary
   A. Transfer the numbers marked on each of the 10 rating scales in the Checklist to the corresponding rating scales in the Summary.
   B. Plot each of these 10 numbers on the graph.
   C. Compute the average score for each of the three sections: Physical Characteristics, Teacher Concerns, and Student Performance.
   D. Add the three scores to obtain the Materials Quotient (MQ):
      12 — 15   Effective
      8 — 11   Marginal
      5 — 7   At risk
      3 — 4   Choose another material

INSTRUCTIONAL MATERIALS PROFILE CHECKLIST (IMPC)

A. PHYSICAL CHARACTERISTICS
   1. The format of the material made it easy to use.

1	2	3	4	5
Strongly disagree	Disagree	Undecided	Agree	Strongly agree

                                                                        YES   NO

   a. The directions were specific and easy to follow.   ____   ____
   b. It was unnecessary for the teacher to make changes in
      the directions or material before it could be used.   ____   ____
   c. The sequence of the content was appropriate and
      logical.   ____   ____
   d. Pictures, tapes, graphs, charts, etc. were clear and
      free of distortion or distracting stimuli.   ____   ____
   e. Considering the age group for which it was designed,
      the material was safe even for independent use.   ____   ____

2. Pacing within the material allowed the student time for optimal learning.

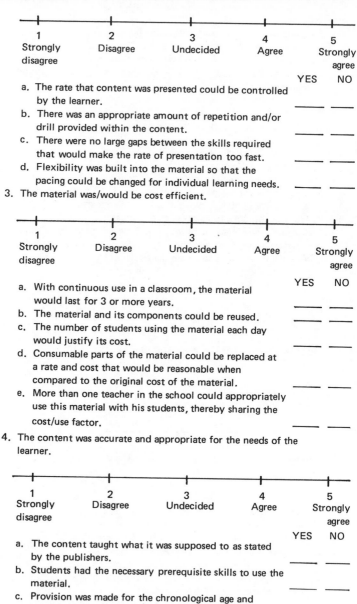

1	2	3	4	5
Strongly disagree	Disagree	Undecided	Agree	Strongly agree

YES   NO

a. The rate that content was presented could be controlled by the learner.   _____ _____

b. There was an appropriate amount of repetition and/or drill provided within the content.   _____ _____

c. There were no large gaps between the skills required that would make the rate of presentation too fast.   _____ _____

d. Flexibility was built into the material so that the pacing could be changed for individual learning needs.   _____ _____

3. The material was/would be cost efficient.

1	2	3	4	5
Strongly disagree	Disagree	Undecided	Agree	Strongly agree

YES   NO

a. With continuous use in a classroom, the material would last for 3 or more years.   _____ _____

b. The material and its components could be reused.   _____ _____

c. The number of students using the material each day would justify its cost.   _____ _____

d. Consumable parts of the material could be replaced at a rate and cost that would be reasonable when compared to the original cost of the material.   _____ _____

e. More than one teacher in the school could appropriately use this material with his students, thereby sharing the cost/use factor.   _____ _____

4. The content was accurate and appropriate for the needs of the learner.

1	2	3	4	5
Strongly disagree	Disagree	Undecided	Agree	Strongly agree

YES   NO

a. The content taught what it was supposed to as stated by the publishers.   _____ _____

b. Students had the necessary prerequisite skills to use the material.   _____ _____

c. Provision was made for the chronological age and intellectual abilities of the student within the content.   _____ _____

d. Irrelevant, distracting information was avoided.   _____ _____

YES   NO

e. There were no prejudicial or discriminatory aspects to
the content presented.   ___ ___

f. Alternative, supplemental tasks were included in the
content.   ___ ___

g. Prompting and cuing techniques were included in the
content.   ___ ___

h. There was ample opportunity provided in the material
for the student to attempt to master the objectives.   ___ ___

i. The learning modality(ies) (auditory, visual, kinesthetic)
and content were appropriately matched to the student's
needs.   ___ ___

B. TEACHER CONCERNS

5. Use of the material in the classroom did not interrupt
teacher efficiency.

1	2	3	4	5
Strongly disagree	Disagree	Undecided	Agree	Strongly agree

YES   NO

a. Students used the material without monitoring or one-to-one
instruction by the teacher.   ___ ___

b. An aide or peer could substitute in the teacher's role when
students were using the material.   ___ ___

c. A minimum amount of preparation time was required by the
teacher to make handouts, preteach skills, etc. before using
the material.   ___ ___

d. The material was used within the existing classroom structure;
room arrangement, space, physical facilities were adequate.   ___ ___

6. A minimal amount of training was needed for the teacher to use
the material.

1	2	3	4	5
Strongly disagree	Disagree	Undecided	Agree	Strongly agree

YES   NO

a. A teachers manual was provided by the publishers and gave
instructions on using the material.   ___ ___

b. The teacher already had the needed skills or competencies
to use the material.   ___ ___

c. A consultant from the school system or publisher was able
to quickly teach the teacher how to use the material.   ___ ___

d. Supplemental suggestions for using the material were
included with the teacher's manual.   ___ ___

e. It was unnecessary to attend a workshop or several training
sessions to gain the skills needed to use the material.   ___ ___

7. Students enjoyed using the material and it motivated them to learn.

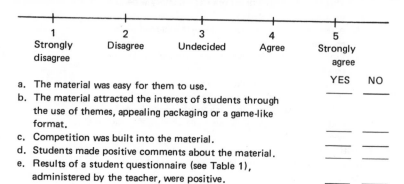

		YES	NO
a.	The material was easy for them to use.		
b.	The material attracted the interest of students through the use of themes, appealing packaging or a game-like format.		
c.	Competition was built into the material.		
d.	Students made positive comments about the material.		
e.	Results of a student questionnaire (see Table 1), administered by the teacher, were positive.		

Table 1.   Student Questionnaire.

Answer each of the questions below. This will let your teacher know what you think of

(name of material)

YES   NO

___ ___ 1. Were the directions easy to follow?

___ ___ 2. Did you know what you were supposed to learn from using the material?

___ ___ 3. Was the material fun to use?

___ ___ 4. Was it easy to use the material without breaking any of the parts?

___ ___ 5. Could you tell how you were doing on the tasks before you finished using the material?

___ ___ 6. Were the tasks clear enough so that you didn't get confused and have to ask the teacher or a friend for help?

___ ___ 7. Could you easily see or hear everything presented in the material?

___ ___ 8. Was the way that you were graded on using the material fair?

___ ___ 9. Do you think you learned what you were supposed to from the material?

___ ___ 10. Could you use the material again without any help?

___ ___ 11. If you were a teacher, would you use this material with your students?

8. The material was adaptable.

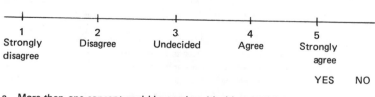

		YES	NO
a.	More than one concept could be taught with this material.		

YES   NO

b. The teacher could designate alternative objectives to
those presented in the material and make the necessary
modifications to use the material in a different context.   _____   _____

c. Individual students as well as large or small groups could
use the material.   _____   _____

d. Modifications could be made to enable different types
of exceptional children to use the material.   _____   _____

9. Evaluation of student progress was built directly into
the material.

1	2	3	4	5
Strongly disagree	Disagree	Undecided	Agree	Strongly agree

YES   NO

a. A pretest: posttest format was included to evaluate
student progress.   _____   _____

b. Immediate feedback allowed the student to check his
own progress while using the material.   _____   _____

c. A culminating final activity was used to evaluate the
student's performance on the behavioral objectives.   _____   _____

d. The material provided for a continuous recording of
student progress, either by the student or the teacher.   _____   _____

e. It was necessary for the teacher to develop his own
evaluation strategy.   _____   _____

C. STUDENT PERFORMANCE

10. The student was able to master the objectives either
stated or implied in the material.

1	2	3	4	5
Strongly disagree	Disagree	Undecided	Agree	Strongly agree

YES   NO

a. The objectives specified in the material incorporated
the most important skills to be mastered with the
material.   _____   _____

b. Objectives were stated (in the material or by the teacher)
in behavioral terms and the student mastered the criterion
level.   _____   _____

c. Tasks and subtasks provided in the content were mastered
in sequential order.   _____   _____

d. When a task was failed by the student, immediate alternative
strategies were incorporated with the material.   _____   _____

COMMENTS

List three major strengths of the material:

1. _____
2. _____
3. _____

List three major weaknesses of the material:

1. _____
2. _____
3. _____

List any modifications or adaptations that you made while using the material:

1. _____
2. _____

If the student (s) did not achieve the objectives of the material, explain any extenuating circumstances that would account for the failure.

INSTRUCTIONAL MATERIALS PROFILE SUMMARY (IMPS)

A. PHYSICAL CHARACTERISTICS

1. *The format of the material made it easy to use.*

1	2	3	4	5
Strongly disagree	Disagree	Undecided	Agree	Strongly agree

2. *Pacing within the material allowed the student time for optimal learning.*

1	2	3	4	5
Strongly disagree	Disagree	Undecided	Agree	Strongly agree

3. *The material was/would be cost efficient.*

1	2	3	4	5
Strongly disagree	Disagree	Undecided	Agree	Strongly agree

4. *The content was accurate and appropriate for the needs of the learner.*

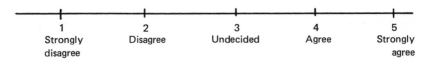

1	2	3	4	5
Strongly disagree	Disagree	Undecided	Agree	Strongly agree

B. TEACHER CONCERNS

5. *Use of the material in the classroom did not interrupt teacher efficiency.*

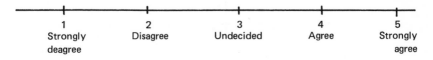

1	2	3	4	5
Strongly disagree	Disagree	Undecided	Agree	Strongly agree

6. *A minimal amount of training was needed for the teacher to use the material.*

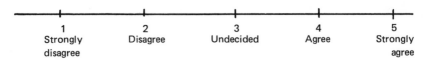

1	2	3	4	5
Strongly deagree	Disagree	Undecided	Agree	Strongly agree

7. *Students enjoyed using the material and it motivated them to learn.*

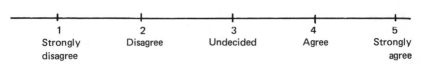

1	2	3	4	5
Strongly disagree	Disagree	Undecided	Agree	Strongly agree

8. *The material was adaptable.*

1	2	3	4	5
Strongly disagree	Disagree	Undecided	Agree	Strongly agree

9. *Evaluation of student progress was built directly into the material.*

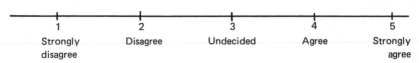

1	2	3	4	5
Strongly disagree	Disagree	Undecided	Agree	Strongly agree

C. STUDENT PERFORMANCE

10. *The student was able to master the objectives either stated or implied in the material.*

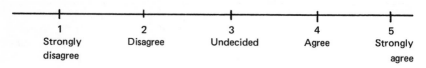

1	2	3	4	5
Strongly disagree	Disagree	Undecided	Agree	Strongly agree

IMP SUMMARY GRAPH

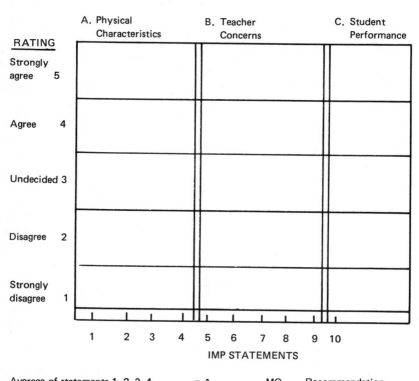

Average of statements 1, 2, 3, 4   = A
Average of statements 5, 6, 7, 8, 9   = B
Rating on statement 10   = C

A + B + C = Materials Quotient (MQ)

MQ	Recommendation
12 − 15	Effective
8 − 11	Marginal
5 − 7	At risk
3 − 4	Chose another material

Table 2. Compilation card

INSTRUCTIONAL MATERIALS PROFILE
Compilation Card

Title of Material: _____ Designed for: _____

Publisher: _____ Age Range: _____

Cost: _____ Grade(s): _____

Objectives:

Name of Evaluator: _____ Grade/Level: _____

School: _____ Dates of use (term): _____

Number of students using materials: _____ Average time/weeks in use: _____

Physical Characteristics: _____

Teacher Concerns: _____

Student Performance: _____

Overall rating — MQ _____

Given the same situation, would you purchase this material again?

previously developed approaches, the Instructional Materials Profile is designed as a practical and easily administered device that can be used in any classroom situation. The information obtained with it should provide a sound basis for the frequent decisions concerning instructional materials that the teacher has to make.

It is hoped that the use of the Instructional Materials Profile will encourage teachers to share information with one another. The ratings are relatively objective and are easily interpreted, and could provide the basis for a schoolwide or districtwide instructional materials evaluation bank. A compilation card designed for this purpose has been included (see Table 2). The design and format of the bank may simply be a cross-categorized filing system stored in the principal's office, or, more elaborately, a computerized systems storage file. The degree of sophistication would depend on the importance that a school district assigns to materials evaluation and on the dollar resources available. However, continuing teacher interest would be the crucial factor in ensuring open and productive communication.

REFERENCES

Abt, C. 1970. An evaluation model: How to compare curriculum materials. Nat. Schools 86: 21–28.

Adamson, G., and Van Etten, C. 1970. Prescribing via analysis and retrieval of instructional materials in the Educational Modulation Center. Except. Child. 36: 531–533.

Baum, D. D. 1972. The attitudes of teachers of the mentally retarded toward teacher evaluation of instructional materials. Educ. Train. Ment. Ret. 7(1): 46–50.

Bleil, G. B. 1975. Evaluating educational materials. J. Learn. Dis. 8: 12–19.

Bogaty, B. E. 1971. An investigation of teacher expectancies of instructional materials. Except. Child. 38: 233–236.

Brown, V. A. 1975. A basic Q-sheet for analyzing curriculum materials and proposals. J. Learn. Dis. 8: 407–416.

Campion, K. E., and Komoskie, K. 1969. Evaluation Practices Used in the Selection of Educational Materials and Equipment. Division of Educational Communications, State Univeristy of New York and State Education Department, Albany, N.Y.

Drew, C. J., and Martinson, M. C. 1971. Educational methodology: An examination of approach. Except. Child. 38: 117–120.

Eash, M. J. 1969. Assessing curriculum materials. A preliminary instrument. Educ. Prod. Rep. 2(5): 18–24.

Eash, M. J. 1974. Instructional materials. In H. J. Walberg (ed.), Evaluating Educational Performances: A Sourcebook of Methods, Instruments, and Examples. McCutchan, Berkeley.

Hall, R. V. 1972. Behavior modification: The measurement of behavior: Part I. In R. V. Hall, (ed.), Managing Behavior. H and H Enterprises, Lawrence, Ks.

Junkala, J. 1970. Teacher evaluation of instructional materials. Teach. Except. Child. 2: 73–76.

Komoski, K. P. 1974. An imbalance of product quantity and instructional quality: The imperative of empiricism. Aud. Vis. Commun. 22(4): 387–407.

Kunzelman, H. P. 1970. Precision Teaching: An Initial Training Sequence. Special Child Publications, Seattle.

Lance, W. D. 1969. Development and evaluation of instructional materials. In J. Arena (ed.), Selected Papers on Learning Disabilities: Progress in Parent Information, Professional Growth, and Public Policy. Association for Children with Learning Disabilities, Pittsburgh, Pa.

Levine, S. J. 1969. Empirical study of instructional materials evaluation in special education. In Selected Convention Papers. Council for Exceptional Children, Washington, D.C.

Lilly, S. 1969. Evaluation of Instructional Materials: A Child-Centered Approach. Northwest Regional Instructional Materials Center for Handicapped Children and Youth, University of Oregon, Eugene.

Lovitt, T. C. 1975. Applied behavior analysis and learning disabilities: Part I. J. Learn. Dis. 8: 432–443.

McIntyre, R. B. 1970. Evaluation of instructional materials and programs: Applications of a systems approach. Except. Child. 37(3): 213–220.

Moss, M. H. 1968. Evaluation as a responsibility of the IMC network. Except. Child. 35: 303–306.

NCEMMH. 1976. Standard criteria for the selection and evaluation of instructional material. National Center on Educational Media and Materials for the Handicapped, Columbus, Oh.

Proger, B. B., Carfioli, J. C., and Kalapos, R. L. 1973. A neglected area of accountability: The failure of instructional materials evaluation and a solution. J. Spec. Educ. 7(3): 269–282.

Van Etten, C., and Van Etten, G. 1976. The measurement of pupil progress and selecting instructional materials. J. Learn. Dis. 9(8): 469–480.

Weinthaler, J. 1970. The systematic selection of instructional materials based on an inventory of learning abilities and skills. Except. Child. 36: 615–619.

Wiederholt, J. L., and McNutt, G. 1977. Evaluating materials for the handicapped adolescent. J. Learn. Dis. 10(3): 11–19.

PART II

USING EDUCATIONAL MATERIALS

Practical Considerations

8

Editorial Introduction

The five chapters included in this section are a source of practical and classroom-tried information that can provide assistance and direction toward individualization of educational experiences. Numerous specific suggestions are given and materials, methods, and adaptations described. These are representative examples of the infinite number of ways in which the classroom teacher can create an appropriate learning environment for the mainstreamed child.

Chapter 9 describes and illustrates various ways to adapt commercially available materials, construct one's own materials, and modify teaching methods. The suggested materials and procedures have been used by the author with children of varying ages, handicaps, and educational achievement, and they have proved versatile and practical.

The common-sense approach in Chapter 10 to the problem of adapting to the presence of the sensorially or physically handicapped child in the classroom should reassure the teacher who has felt inadequate when faced with the possibility of enrolling such a pupil. The role of the itinerant/resource teacher in helping to provide appropriate services is explained. Illustrations of the various simple devices that help the physically handicapped student to more normally participate in classroom activities will prove useful to the parents of such children in providing a more normal home environment.

The classroom teacher often fails to make full or appropriate use of one of the best and most available ways of individualizing instruction—the use of audiovisual media. Chapter 11 summarizes media resources that are commonly available, and gives suggestions for their more effective use. More complex systems, which are seen as having future potential, are also described.

Concern with the educational achievement of pupils often causes teachers to overlook the very important relationship between instructional materials and affective development. The author of Chapter 12 explains the need for teachers to be concerned with selection of materials affectively appropriate to the child's needs, as well as with those educationally suitable. Failure to take this very important aspect of materials selection into consideration may cause the educational program to fail.

Instructional games have an important role in the education of students of all ages, whether handicapped or not. The rationale for their use and examples of appropriate use in the classroom are given in Chapter 11. Other approaches to encourage active and eager involvement of the learner, such as peer assisted learning, are described. Ways in which parent-child participation in game-playing can reinforce classroom learning are pointed out. Suggestions for inexpensive construction of multilevel, multiuse games will be valuable for the classroom teacher concerned with providing motivational instructional activities.

9

Constructing and Adapting Materials

Sara J. Odle, Ed.D.

The present philosophy of mainstreaming requires that the regular classroom teacher assume more responsibility for the exceptional child in his room (Kohfeldt, 1976). Teacher-adapted and teacher-constructed materials have become more important as teachers face the problems involved in individualizing instruction to provide appropriate educational experiences to such children.

The child with learning problems may have been appropriately evaluated and an individualized learning plan developed, but too often the apparent unavailability of suitable educational materials impedes the implementation of the individualized program. The teacher is aware that the child needs experiences that are not being provided, but may see purchase of specialized materials as the only way to provide appropriate remediation. "Special education," to many teachers, connotes the use of esoteric materials and methods unknown to regular education. This erroneous belief sometimes delays delivery of appropriate educational experiences.

"I don't have the right materials" is not a legitimate excuse for failure to implement the child's individual learning program, even though the materials available to the teacher are unsuitable in their present form. When materials appropriate to the student's identified needs do not exist or are not accessible, the teacher must adapt or modify existing materials, or develop original ones.

One of the major educational problems of the slow learner is inability to cope with the traditional curriculum. Whether or not he succeeds in the regular classroom may therefore depend on the ability of the teacher to adapt or construct teaching materials that will be effective in meeting his needs. The purpose of this chapter is to emphasize the need for and the advantages of teacher adaptation, modification, or construction of materials, and to provide practical suggestions and examples to assist the teacher in the task of providing appropriate educational experiences to all children in the classroom.

Listed at the end of this chapter are representative sources of activities and ideas for use of materials. Also included in the listing are books on construction of learning materials, sources of free and inexpensive materials, and other publications relevant to adaptation and construction of materials and methods to provide appropriate learning experiences. The reader is also referred to Part III of this book, which focuses on resources and references.

ADVANTAGES OF
TEACHER ADAPTATION OR CONSTRUCTION

Producers of educational materials have been quick to capitalize on the greatly expanded market for materials for the "exceptional child." Many materials are often sold as tools for special education at high prices, when the same items are available much more cheaply at discount stores (Berman, 1977). Commercial materials developed specifically for the exceptional child have been widely used, even though there has been little or no objective evaluation made of their efficacy. Often the only information available on the material is the promotional brochure distributed by the publishers. There are commercial materials and programs that are acceptable and even desirable, but even for these, little data are available to support the claims of the manufacturers as to effectiveness of the materials in remediation of disabilities. Although commercially produced materials may be effective, there is no program or device that can meet the needs of every child. Exceptional children are a heterogeneous group; some will profit from certain methods and materials and others will not (Minskoff, 1973). Few materials are successfully used with all children. No matter how well equipped the classroom is, there will always be the child with a problem that requires "something else" for remediation. Skill in adaptation or construction of materials is necessary to provide for this child's needs. It also becomes necessary to adapt or construct materials when there is nothing commercially available that adequately and effectively presents a concept, skill, or idea.

Teacher-made materials are often needed to supplement or fill gaps in commercially prepared courses of study (Kohfeldt, 1976). The sequential steps in commercial materials may be too great for the child's understanding and mastery; intermediate levels must be inserted. Often insufficient skill practice is provided. Parallel activities and experiences are needed to allow fuller development of a concept or mastery of a skill, or to reinforce learning. Preparation of multilevel materials, with sequential steps fractioned into smaller units of learning, and with horizontal expansion of experiences and practice, makes "making the match" (described in Chapter 5) easier.

The low cost of adaptation or construction is a very important consideration where little or no money is available for purchase of items. Modification or construction of materials may then be the only way to secure needed equipment. This is also a way through which funds may be released for purchase of suitable commercial materials, thus stretching available money. In some instances, because of budgeting or procedural problems, suitable materials may be unavailable at the time they are needed. The school system may have exhausted its funds for the year. The process of requisition of materials, securing purchase order approval, and placement and filling of the order may be a lengthy one. In some systems, materials must be ordered in the spring for delivery the next fall. Obviously, no match of materials with immediate needs is possible in such cases. Adaptation or construction of materials is then necessary in order to implement needed remediation, because the specific item can in this way be made immediately available.

Blatt and Garfunkel (cited in Anderson, Hemenway, and Anderson, 1969) give an additional reason for the active involvement of the classroom teacher in the development of appropriate materials for the children in his class. This involvement in materials development requires that the children be more carefully studied. The more that is learned about the children, the better the teaching should become. In addition to being able to more precisely match needs and remediation, motivation and a higher interest level can be provided by the teacher's knowledge of the child. The need for selection of materials affectively appropriate (see Chapter 12) can be more easily recognized, and steps can be taken to ensure suitability of materials in this too often overlooked area.

LOCAL AND AREAWIDE PROGRAMS
FOR PROVISION OF APPROPRIATE MATERIALS

A school system or educational institution may hold workshops or implement other projects designed to help teachers become more confident and competent in preparation of appropriate materials. An example of one such project is the Materials Access and Production (Project MAP) program of the Upper Cumberland Instructional Resource System (UCIRS), Tennessee Technological University, Cookeville, Tennessee. Although this is a federally funded program, description of those features that have made it a success is relevant to the individual teacher as well as to the principal or systemwide administrator who is concerned with appropriate individualization of instruction.

Project MAP

Project Materials Access and Production (Project MAP) (Willis and Willis, 1977a) develops custom-made prescriptive educational materials upon request from teachers of children with learning problems in the 14 counties of the Upper Cumberland area of Tennessee. The project is supported jointly by funds awarded under the Comprehensive Employment and Training Act of 1977 and Tennessee Technological University. Fifteen long-term unemployed individuals serving on three Task Forces construct, deliver, demonstrate, and consult with teachers on implementation of individualized prescriptive materials with children in their classrooms.

The procedure utilized by teachers to request custom-made materials is "simplification personified" and has been in use by teachers requesting commercial materials from the UCIRS for several years. Teachers of children with problems in learning throughout the 14 Upper Cumberland Counties telephone the UCIRS collect. The Project MAP secretary accepts the call and completes a request form that includes questions regarding age, grade, sex, specific academic objectives to be taught, receptive and expressive sensory modalities to be used by the child when responding to the material, format of the material if the teacher has a preference, and any specific interests of the child that can be incorporated into the materials as motivations.

The importance of each of the above dimensions in planning and producing a teaching material cannot be overstressed. Thomas (1975) maintains that learning centers should be constructed in terms of: 1) the content and skill to be learned, and 2) the characteristics of the children who will utilize the center in an educational program. Garvey (1972) states that the first step in displaying materials for student use is to establish and define the educational purpose for the material. The first question asked of the teacher who is requesting materials from Project MAP is to pinpoint the *specific* skill to be taught. It is the teacher's responsibility to determine the objective for each material and to decide exactly what it is that he wishes his students to know (Bullough, 1974). Project MAP prepares various types of educational materials (learning centers, individual task sheets, games, etc.), but the educational objective of each must be stated by the teacher.

The desired format is the second item on the Project MAP request form. In this instance, the teacher's task is to select the most appropriate input-output sensory modality of the materials. This, in part, determines the format. In making this decision, the teacher must consider the most appropriate presentation for the pupils (that is, how will the pupil learn best?) and the most appropriate presentation in terms of the initial objective.

The teacher is also requested to relate any specific interest of the pupil who will use the materials. Materials that do not hold the child's interest will cause his attention to wander (Coppen, 1971) and will "turn students off" educationally (Garvey, 1972).

The approximate reading level of the pupil is an important consideration when preparing teaching materials. This factor ensures that the materials will not exceed the present educational attainment and level of sophistication of the students. Project MAP frequently provides an audiotape with instructional materials to explain directions, provide information, etc. for any student who is a nonreader.

Because many teachers are limited in the amount of classroom space for learning centers or for students to do independent work, the space requirement of requested materials is recorded on the request form. The number of students who are expected to use the material at the same time is also noted. The sex and age of the pupils are provided to suggest a possible interest topic if the teacher is unable to specify a known interest area.

When Project MAP was in the planning stages, an important consideration of producing custom-made educational materials was the cost factor. Even though most of the schools in the service area were not well equipped, Project MAP was planned as an exemplary program in production of educational materials. The cost of the materials must conform to the financial limitation of each teacher and the materials must be constructed from readily available supplies. It is anticipated that teachers will begin to prepare materials from inexpensive and locally available supplies after seeing what Project MAP has been able to produce with similar restraints. It is also believed that teachers will realize that teacher-made materials can solve the problem of not having enough money to purchase expensive items as well as fill the instructional gaps within the classroom.

The Project MAP Coordinator reviews the completed request, giving consideration to the subculture of the child's school and community and specific academic objectives to be taught. If the teacher requesting the material is using the System FORE Classroom Management Program (Willis and Willis, 1977b), the holdings of the UCIRS and Project MAP are reviewed to ascertain whether a learning center or other material to teach that academic objective may have already been developed. All material holdings of the UCIRS and Project MAP are encoded into System FORE materials lists to permit rapid materials retrieval. If the material is not available in the present holdings, the Project Coordinator presents the request with academic level, modality, and motivational and cultural specifications to the Materials Construction or Audiovisual Task Forces.

Specifications are restricted to minimum levels to permit as much individual motivation and innovation as possible by Task Force participants as they construct the materials. Material formats may include games, learning centers, audio/visual/video programs, etc. When the material is completed and ready to be used by the teachers, the participants of the Materials and Media Task Force deliver the finished product to the school, demonstrate how it is to be used, and consult with the teachers concerning other material they might request throughout the school year. These travelers, or "circuit riders," complete trips to each of the 14 Upper Cumberland County schools at least three times each month.

The following example of the utilization of Project MAP in the execution of a child's educational program illustrates the implementation of this teacher support system. A request was received from a special education resource teacher, who desired a material that would reinforce and provide practice in addition and subtraction of two-digit numbers. The teacher supplied the following additional information:

Format—manipulative (child has a motor coordination problem)
Input/Output sensory modality—no preference
Reading level—not important (child reads several levels above present grade placement)
Interest area—heavy construction equipment (father's occupation)
Size limitation—none
Age of child—10 years
Grade placement—4th
Sex—male

Using the provided information, a member of the materials construction Task Force created the "Subtractor." The objectives, materials, and method for use are described below.

Objectives of the Activity   The objectives of the Subtractor activity are:

1. To reinforce and practice skills of addition and subtraction of two-digit numbers
2. To illustrate the difference in the processes of addition and subtraction

Materials   Materials required are:

The Subtractor (a toy bulldozer, purchased or constructed)
Styrofoam blocks, representing stones, each having an appropriate number on its side
The work board (see Figure 1)—this should be made large enough to allow the bulldozer to be appropriately maneuvered

Method for Use   Teacher or child places blocks in the corner "cut" areas; the pupil, with the Subtractor, pushes a block to an area with the mountain lines and height number. The number on the block should then be "cut," or subtracted, from the number indicating the height of the mountain. (Grease pencils may be used on the clear Contact paper covering the work board for the child to compute his answers.) With the remainder written in the mountain area, the block is then pushed to the "add" corner. More blocks may be pushed into the mountain area to be subtracted from the previous remainder. Then the blocks in the "add" area are added as the stock pile.

In this Appalachian area, where commercial materials seldom mesh with the cultural or motivational needs of the local child, Project MAP has provided services that are unique to the local

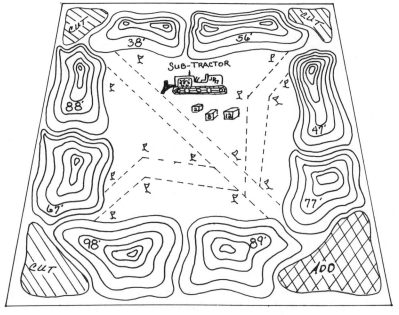

Figure 1.   The subtractor work board. Courtesy B. Willis and S. Willis.

region, Tennessee, and to the nation. One positive side effect of the project has been to demonstrate to teachers that they can construct individualized prescriptive materials that are inexpensive, using raw materials that are readily available in their local area.

Cooperation Provides for Pupil Needs

Individualized work does require many materials. Much teacher time and money can be used in constructing, adapting, or acquiring appropriate materials. However, most classrooms contain materials more suited to other teachers' needs. Such materials lie unused on the classroom shelf, or are inappropriately used merely because they are available. Teacher time and effort can be saved by sharing such materials. Teachers within a school might find it advantageous to set up a materials (and games) pool. Such items as were presently unneeded in each classroom might be marked with teaching objectives, appropriate uses, and age levels, and cataloged and located in a centrally convenient area within the school building, to be checked out when needed and returned when the instructional objective was reached by the pupil. This within-school materials center could save teacher time and funds. The success of such a effort would depend on the cooperation of the faculty both in contributing materials and in returning those checked out for use.

A second important factor in the sharing of materials with others is the use of a common descriptive format through which each teacher can provide information that will help others to determine if the material is suitable for their needs. Explicit directions for the use of materials or execution of procedures are also essential.

Lack of appropriate commercial materials has resulted in the development by teachers of many excellent materials and procedures. Sharing of such procedures with others often proves impossible because the teacher does not know how to describe the procedure in replicable terms. McCormack (1976) suggests a format that will help the teacher in modification or development of materials or procedures, and will at the same time provide a written record for the use of tutors (parents, peers, aides, volunteers) or other teachers who want to use the procedure. Once the instructional objective has been determined, and has, if necessary, been broken down into smaller, intermediate steps, the other elements involved in the instructional task should be indicated. The necessary additional information needed for replication would include prerequisite skills, materials required, means of assessment, reinforcement or reward and reward schedule, criteria for performance, and maintenance activities. Figure 2 illustrates McCormack's format for an instruc-

PHASE	MATERIALS	WHAT YOU DO WITH THE MATERIALS	WHAT YOU DO AND SAY	WHAT THE LEARNER DOES	PRESENT EACH STIMULI	TOTAL TRIALS	WHAT YOU DO IF HE DOES IT RIGHT	WHAT YOU DO IF HE DOES IT WRONG
Pre-Test	Conduct Phase 8 as a Pre-test:							
1	color cued shapes; 3 of each: circle (orange), star (blue), square (red), triangle (black)	△□○☆ △○☆○□☆△	"sort and match the shapes"	sort shapes into appropriate piles	twice	16	token and praise after each correct response	correct immediately and explain
2	As Above	△☆□ □△□○☆○△☆○	"sort the shapes"	As Above	twice	18	As Above	As Above
3	As Above	△☆ ☆○□△☆□○△○□	As Above	As Above	once	10	As Above	As Above
4	As Above	△ □○☆□△☆○□△○☆	As Above	As Above	once	11	As Above	As Above
5	As Above	△○○□☆□○△☆☆○△□	As Above	As Above	once	12	As Above	As Above
6	3 of each; star (blue), triangle (black), circle & square (orange)	□△○□☆☆△□○☆□○	As Above	As Above	once	12	As Above	As Above
7	3 of each; star circle & 9 square (orange), triangle (black)	□○☆△△☆○□○□△☆	As Above	As Above	once	12	As Above	As Above
8	3 of each; star circle, square and triangle (all orange)	☆○□△□△☆☆△○○□	As Above	As Above	once	12	As Above	As Above

Figure 2. Instructional sequence record sheet. Copyright 1976 by Division on Mental Retardation, The Council for Exceptional Children. Reprinted by permission.

INSTRUCTIONAL SEQUENCE COVER SHEET

Sequence Name: __Shape Sorting_____ Draft # _2___

Author(s): __James E. McCormack_____

Date of this Draft: __December 1974_____

Suggested Session Frequency and Length: __4–5__ sessions per week
__5–10__ minutes per session

Sequence Designed for: Individual☒, small groups ☐, class ☐ Instruction.

1. *Instructional Objective:* in a one-to-one instructional situation the learner will be able to physically sort cardboard shapes (triangle, star, circle, square) into appropriate piles upon verbal request and without assistance (see #7 for success criteria).

2. *Statement of need/relation to long term goals:* this pre-academic sequence relates to the development of visual discrimination and hand/eye coordination skills. In addition it provides the basis for the development of various pre-vocational and vocational skills.

3. *Prerequisite skills:* can match cardboard shapes and can maintain attention for five to ten minutes.

4. *Materials required:* various cardboard cutout shapes; each approximately 3″ × 3″.
   star: 3 blue and 3 orange
   triangle: 3 black and 3 orange
   square: 3 red and 3 orange
   circle: 3 orange

5. *Means of initial assessment:* conduct Phase 8 as a pre-test.

6. *Reward/reward schedule:* this sequence is designed to use token or social reinforcement; however other forms of reinforcement can be used and in such cases should be indicated in the Sequence Record column, "What You Do If He Does It *Right*"

7. *Sequence and phase criteria:* sequence criteria—90% or better correct for 3 consecutive sessions completed in less than 4 minutes. Phase criteria—90% or better for 2 consecutive sessions completed in less than 5 minutes.

8. *Maintenance activities:* include task in group activities and other sorting tasks that require more detailed discriminations.

Figure 3.   Instructional sequence cover sheet. Copyright 1976 by Division on Mental Retardation, The Council for Exceptional Children. Reprinted by permission.

tional sequence, giving all necessary information for replication. Figure 3 is a suggested cover sheet for the instructional sequence, containing information that will assist other teachers in deciding whether the sequence or procedure is appropriate for their needs.

CONSIDERATIONS FOR MODIFICATION

Criteria appropriate for selection of commercially prepared materials are also appropriate for teacher adaptation and construction of materials. Consideration of the points made in Chapter 5, therefore, will aid in determining the usefulness of the adaptation under consideration. In addition, answers to the following questions will be of particular importance:

1. What is the instructional objective, and will it meet the previously identified instructional need of the child?
2. Is the material at the student's interest level? Are the format, the vocabulary, and the sensory approach appropriate?
3. How will it be used? Can it be used independently? Will there be a need for supervision? By whom?
4. Does it reinforce learning? Can it be made self-checking? What means will be used for evaluation of learning?
5. Can the material be used with other pupils, other subjects, or other levels?

Adaptation or construction of some materials will require a substantial investment of time and, in some cases, money. Neither should be wasted on materials having no immediate and direct application to learning objectives, or on fragile or one-usage materials. Emphasis should be placed on preparation of materials versatile enough to be used at different levels for different learnings. Materials that the teacher will find most useful are those that can be used with the same student for various tasks or levels, or with various students through alteration of tasks or levels of difficulty. Many problem learners will need repetition and over-learning, so durability or reusability of the material is important. Other important characteristics of teacher-made and teacher-adapted materials, as listed by Kohfeldt (1976), include motivation, high-interest level, and self-correction. The element of self-correction provides immediate feedback and reinforcement for the child, and allows him to proceed at his own rate, which frees the teacher for other interaction with students. This immediate feedback is necessary for rapid and efficient learning, as well as for motivation.

Individualized educational experiences are often provided through a game format; indeed, many teachers interpret construction of educational materials to mean solely construction of teaching games. The many advantages of using instructional games for all types of learners warrant the inclusion in this text of a separate chapter (Chapter 13) devoted to this topic. Teacher adaptation and construction of materials involve many areas other than that of the educational game, as is shown by examples in the following section of the chapter.

Modification in Various Dimensions

Once the specific teaching objective has been determined, the teacher should look at the material available. Educational programs, specific materials, and teaching methods can be adapted or modified in many different dimensions. The student's physical handicaps, preferred mode of learning, reading level, achievement level, attention span, and motivating interests are factors to be considered when deciding how to adapt or modify to provide for his specific needs. Changes can be made in many different ways: difficulty of subject matter, level of vocabulary, simplification of directions for use; provision of intermediate steps or subtasks; provision of built-in feedback; change of learning channel; removal of distracting factors; adaptation for easier manipulation of component parts; alteration of format, pictures, etc. for suitability to chronological age, cultural group, or interests; or combining portions of several programs or materials. This is only a partial listing of the many possible areas for adaptation. Examples of modifications in specific areas and of adaptations in use of materials follow.

Provision for Gaps in Skills Learning   At any point in the learning process, the child may have failed to acquire mastery of any skill or concept necessary for success at subsequent levels. It is imperative that the teacher fill in these gaps in the learning sequence. Provision of remediation within textbook levels can be made easier through rearranging or programming the text. The tasks of skill retrieval and remedial prescription are made easier through this procedure. Both arithmetic and language arts textbooks are suitable for this programming.

When assessment of a child has indicated that remediation is needed, and specific deficiencies have been pinpointed through placement and competency tests, tasks at the appropriate level for remediation can be quickly located if prior programming of the text has been done. The steps in carrying out this procedure are:

1. Study the table of contents and identify the skills included in the program.
2. Arrange the identified skills into major task areas and subtasks. A major task can be analyzed into a series of subtasks, which should be arranged sequentially into order of instruction.
3. Tabulate the position in the text of examples of each of the subtasks. These may be used as instructional examples, practice assignments, or test examples.

Table 1 is an example of the rearrangement of a table of contents as described above.

Reading Levels of Materials   Attention should be called to the particularly important area of reading materials written for the slow learner or the educable mentally retarded child. Teachers generally assume that the reading level of materials, as given by the publishers, is correct. Analysis of instructional materials written

Table 1.   Task analysis of the content of a mathematics textbook

Major tasks and subtasks	Instructional examples Page no.	Test examples Page no.
Addition		
addition combinations	5–7	9–13, 462
tens in addition	14	14–15
hundreds in addition	14	16
column addition	16–17	17–27, 56, 454, 458
regrouping in addition	28	28–29
estimating sums	30	31–34, 37, 55–56
mental arithmetic	35	35–36
Subtraction		
subtraction combinations	7–9	9–13, 463
tens in subtraction	14	15, 38
hundreds in subtraction	14	15–16, 38
regrouping in subtraction	40–41	42–47, 56, 455, 459
expanded notation	42	42
subtraction of fractions	48–49	49–51
estimating differences	51	51–52, 53–56
mental subtraction	53	53–55
Multiplication		
multiplication combinations	57–59, 60, 62–63	59, 61, 464
properties of multiplication	66	67
number pairs and graphs	70–71	71
multiplying, using tens	72, 74–75	72–73, 76–77, 456, 460
multiplying, using a machine	78–81	81
mental multiplication	82, 86	82–83, 86–88
estimating products	84	84–85, 88
Division		
division combinations	65	65, 465
properties of division	66	67
division involving remainders	67	68–69, 91, 457, 461
dividing number by single digit	69, 92–93	69, 93, 103, 457, 461
dividing, using tens	72, 92	73, 89, 94–95, 103, 457, 461
trial quotients	95–97	97–98
estimating quotients	96–99	99–100, 102–103
mental arithmetic	101	101–102

specifically for these students shows that this may be a fallacious assumption. Results of one such analysis showed that all the special materials analyzed had mean grade levels different from, usually much higher than, the publishers' mean placements (Lavely, Lowe, and Follman, 1975). Few of the materials tested were progressively sequenced, which made them unsuitable for use in a developmental instructional program. In comparing six books from one publisher, all listed as being second grade reading level, the mean levels as determined by the Spache Readability Formula ranged from 2.9 to 4.4. The range of difficulty within one book spanned six grade levels! Obviously, reading materials of the appropriate level must be provided if the exceptional child is to learn to read at his mental age expectancy. The classroom teacher should ask the reading teacher or reading center for help in determining reading levels of materials, or he should follow the directions for determining reading levels provided by readability formulas, such as the Spache or the Dale-Chagall Formula for Predicting Readability, which can be found in reading methods textbooks.

The teacher must also be aware that the mainstreamed child may be unable to handle the reading requirements of the social studies, science, and language arts texts. Writing or taping simplified versions of the chapters may be necessary. Use of audiovisual materials (see Chapter 11) aids the reading-handicapped child and the child who cannot learn at the abstract level. It is especially important that the child not be penalized by being required to take written tests that he is unable to read. Evaluative devices appropriate to the individual child must be devised. For example, the questions may be taped, and the child marks the appropriate answers on a multiple-choice test. He may tape his answers if the questions call for lengthy responses.

A much-used teaching aid, the dittoed worksheet, often needs modification for use with the exceptional child. Both commercially produced and teacher-made dittoes may have too much material crowded on the page. The teacher's handwriting may be hard to read. The reproduction may be so faint as to be almost unreadable. The child with visual acuity or visual perceptual problems, a short attention span, motor coordination problems, or a reading disability is doubly handicapped. He is "turned off" when such an inappropriate worksheet is given to him. The teacher should also be aware that commercially produced ditto masters for teaching reading-thinking skills, such as inferring from context, predicting outcomes, getting the main idea, etc., are actually at a more difficult reading level than that given by the publisher.

Skills Boxes   Once sequences of skills in arithmetic areas or in phonics have been determined, "skills boxes" are easily correlated with the texts being used. These resource boxes provide the additional practice that may be needed by a child for mastery of a specific skill. To set up the box, arithmetic or phonics workbooks are taken apart and filed according to task area and subtask sequence. In addition to workbooks accompanying textbook series, activity books available in variety shops and drugstores are suitable for adaptation to multilevel, individualized drill activities. Pages of old textbooks can also be neatly mounted and used.

Two copies of each workbook or text are needed, because the task on each side of each page will need to be filed separately. Lamination or use of acetate envelopes or folders, or covering with clear Contact paper, will preserve the pages. The skills box should be easily accessible to the students. A simple method of identification of skill and level should be used, so that the child may easily find his assigned skill activity. The skills might be color coded, for example, with levels within the skill identified by number; a student assignment would then be, "Do Exercise Yellow 13 from the Skills Box." Assignment is made as specific needs are identified. The student gets the sheet, does the work, and checks it, using the answer key (which may be conveniently placed on the back of the sheet). If each child is provided with an acetate sheet taped at one side or the top to a stiff cardboard backing, the activity page may be placed under the acetate and a grease pencil or water-soluble magic marker used to record his answers. Some activities may be more suitable to chalkboard work or to paper and pencil recording.

Uses of Obsolete Textbooks   Sets of discontinued or obsolete textbooks are generally easily secured. School systems often give teachers an opportunity to get without cost those texts no longer in use, before they are destroyed or otherwise disposed of. Teachers should check with the person responsible for management and warehousing of school supplies for information about their availability. Storerooms and unused classrooms in school buildings often contain old texts. Goodwill Industries and similar stores, as well as garage sales, are sources of inexpensive books.

Provision for materials at the student's independent reading level can be accomplished through the use of obsolete readers in teaching reading skills. Individual stories may be removed from readers and bound as books. This disguises the source and reading level. (Color coding may be used to indicate level of difficulty.) Pictures accompanying the story can be removed and those more appropriate to the age level of the student substituted. Such pictures can be taken from magazines, catalogs, other discarded textbooks, or other sources. Snapshots can also be used to illustrate the stories. A word list or glossary, thought questions, or other exercises or activities can be added to each story, and answer cards provided for the student's self checking, as in the Science Research Associates (SRA) Reading Laboratories. Sets of sentences or paragraphs can be combined with questions designed to teach specific reading skills, such as getting the main idea, drawing conclusions, making inferences, locating the answer, and following directions. Important words in a paragraph may be blacked out, and the student may be asked to determine appropriate words through use of the context. Tables of contents can be mounted on cardboard, with specific questions included that will give practice in using the tables.

Paragraphs from old texts are also excellent to use in controlled composition exercises for practice in language skills. Controlled composition is given to students for practice after a grammatical construction has been explained and drilled. It limits the kinds of errors the student can make, and gives an opportunity to use the pattern in context, as well as practice in writing well-organized prose. One kind of controlled composition is the composition frame. The textbook is scanned for a suitable passage—one in which the desired substituted constructions can be made. The following is an example of a composition frame designed for practice in writing the simple past of irregular verbs:

> Directions to student: Copy the whole paragraph. Each time you have a choice between two words in parentheses, copy the correct one and omit the other. Notice that the first sentence is written in the *past* tense.
>
> For three years Daniel lived with the Indian tribe. He (grows, grew) strong and tall during this time. He (is, was) very happy with his new life. The boys of the tribe (become, became) his friends, and they (spent, spend) hours together practicing stalking and shooting skills. Daniel almost (forget, forgot) what had happened to his parents, and (began, begin) to think of himself as a Cherokee. He (feels, felt) very proud when Chief Standing Bear (gave, give) him his Indian name.

There are certain precautions to take when preparing and using the composition frame. Every choice should be one the student has met before. The teacher should begin with two choices, and work cumulatively toward more complicated frames involving several types of choices. There should not be more than three or four choices within the parentheses, and all choices should be internally grammatical: "go, goes, went," but not "goed."

Before the student begins writing, the teacher should remind him of the sentence pattern, read the paragraph slowly aloud, and give needed meanings of words. The work should be checked for correct copying (spelling and punctuation), as well as for correct choices.

Pages from old textbooks may also be used for tracking exercises for improving visual discrimination, left-to-right direction, and skill in following a line of print. The child is to follow the lines of print as if he were reading, circling specific items as indicated—letters of the alphabet in sequence, designated blends or digraphs, words beginning with certain letters, and so forth.

Lower reading level treatment of social science and science topics, again secured from discarded textbooks, can also be bound into books, with pictures and other material added as desired. Maps, charts, graphs, and so forth can be included or mounted separately, with questions and activities for their interpretation and use. Each level of each topic should be bound separately.

Directions for projects or experiments (taken from lower level textbooks, workbooks, children's books, or magazines) that correlate with chapters in the textbooks currently used may be laminated on large cards and filed where easily accessible. The directions may need to be broken down into smaller steps, or the language may need to be simplified.

Newspapers and Other Printed Materials Use of the newspaper as a teaching tool for various subject areas is highly recommended because of its availability, relevance, range of interest, and practical vocational use. However, teachers have been found to generally underestimate the reading level of various sections of the paper (Hirshoren, Hunt, and Davis, 1974). The readability level of those sections of the paper that are to be used by students with reading problems should be determined by application of one of the formulas for such determination.

Information concerning the availability of the Newspaper in the Classroom (NIC) Program in a particular area may be secured from the local school administration, a local university, or from the nearest metropolitan newspaper publishing company. There are approximately 625 metropolitan newspapers throughout the United States that are currently providing training to teachers in appropriate use of the newspaper as a teaching tool for all areas and levels of instruction. These workshops are generally provided through the cooperation of the school system. Credit courses in the appropriate educational use of the newspaper are also given by teacher training colleges and universities.

Mail order catalogs and telephone directories are also motivational, easily available, and usable at many levels and for many objectives, without requiring additional commercial materials. As with the newspaper, these sources may be used for developing and reinforcing reading skills, or may be used for older children for mathematics skills, homemaking skills, budgeting, home furnishing and decorating, and so forth.

The Learning Activity Packet   One teaching tool for individualizing instruction is the learning activity packet (LAP), which provides relevant materials and activities in package form. The style and content of the LAP will be dictated by the subject to be covered, but a LAP intended for class use is typically written to cover a unit of work, and generally consists of an introduction, student objectives, a list of appropriate reading selections from various multilevel texts, listings of available library materials on the subject (books, vertical files, audiovisuals), required and optional activities, and an evaluation section.

The learning activity packet for the exceptional child may need to be written to concentrate on one idea or concept (Faulk, 1974). To be successful with this group of children, the LAP should include achievable tasks, simple directions, manipulative activities, and immediate reinforcement. It should be written on the child's independent reading level; for the nonreader, the directions and other information may be recorded on tape. The packet should include a number of different activities designed to hold the child's interest while providing repeated exposure to the same concept or idea. Activities for the packet are not restricted to worksheets contained in an envelope or folder; the child may be directed to use any learning media or to carry out specific activities even outside the classroom. Immediate reinforcement can be provided through a large variety of approaches. Each LAP should include a posttest or evaluative device to determine whether the concept presented has been learned.

The LAP gives each student a chance to work at his own speed, and a feeling of accomplishment as each activity and packet is completed. Properly planned and prepared learning activity packets can be of great help in meeting the needs of slow learners. Once assembled, the LAP is available for use by any child needing the extra work on the particular concept. The teacher's "LAP library" can be continually expanded.

TEACHER DEVELOPED PROGRAMS

The teacher generally knows more about the educational needs of the handicapped student than does anyone else, and is therefore in a better position to develop appropriate materials for such students.

The two programs described below are examples of teacher adaptation of existing programs to provide for recurring needs. Modifications made by these teachers in available programs to provide for their pupils' individual needs have proved appropriate for other students. Both programs have been successfully used by teachers of special education classes, resource teachers, and teachers in regular classrooms. They demonstrate a desirable flexibility and adaptability, ease of application, and negligible cost factor. Although both programs were originally developed for remedial purposes, they are equally suitable for initial teaching of the skills.

Language in Color

Correct language usage is a primary goal for those children who are deaf or hard of hearing. One teacher of deaf children modified and combined symbols used in other language problems for the deaf, and added teaching procedures she had found effective with this group of children. The sequential program she developed, titled "Language in Color" (Norris, 1969), is strongly visual, incorporating both symbols and color cues to aid the student in identifying the parts of speech and in learning their correct usage. In addition to these visual cues, kinesthetic and rhythmic devices aid in memorization of verb and pronoun groups. Teacher-made wall charts also provide correct models and reinforcement for those students who do not have the spelling and vocabulary skills needed for production of appropriate original sentences.

The program begins with identification of "Who?" and "What?" nouns, followed by pronouns and action verbs. Its sequence carries the capable student into creative and complex sentence writing. Throughout the program, oral as well as written practice of sentence patterns is provided. The need for daily review and practice of language skills is emphasized in the directions for use of the program. Vocabulary used in charts and demonstration sentences is chosen with appropriate regard to student interests. Words from other subject areas are also incorporated into practice sentences.

The simplicity and structure of the program, together with demonstrated student enthusiasm and success, have led to its use with other children who are lacking in oral and/or written language skills, including those for whom English needs to be taught as a second language. The method correlates well with pattern drills, substitution tables, and other activities used for second language learning. A source of further information on the program is given at the end of this chapter.

A Writing-Phonics Program

The writing-phonics program (Anderson, 1970) utilizes visual, auditory, kinesthetic, and tactile channels of learning in coordinated teaching of cursive writing and phonics to learning disabled children. The group for whom the program was originally formulated varied greatly in degree of motor coordination, making it necessary to provide activities for development of prewriting motor skills as well as for development of the correct motor patterns for letter formation. Chalkboard exercises, crayon and paper and pencil and paper tracing, use of directional lines in color and other color cues, and built-in control of distractibility are a few of the adaptations made to accomodate individual differences. Emphasis is placed on the sequential development of eye-motor skills. Modifications of other writing programs include changing the sequence in which the letters are taught and simplification of some letter forms.

Once the child has the necessary eye-motor readiness for letter formation, the most important aspect of the program is that the motor skills are associated with the speech sounds. The child learns and says the sound as he writes the letter or letters. The letters are presented in the sequence used in phonics reading programs. Singular consonants and singular vowels are learned and joined to make words. The child learns blending, or "say-it-fast," and sight words as he writes the letters. Blends, digraphs, and dipthongs are practiced in the same way. This multisensory approach—visual, auditory, kinesthetic, and tactile—capitalizes on the child's learning strengths and strengthens his weaker avenues of learning.

This writing-phonics program has been used extensively by special education teachers in the metropolitan school system where it was developed. A more detailed description of its procedures and sequence can be secured (see resource section of this chapter).

Substitution Tables

A versatile activity, adapted from techniques used in Teaching English as a Second Language (TESL), is the use of the "substitution table" in teaching English grammar. The substitution table can be used both orally and written for constructing a large number of correct sentences. When the student recites or writes a sentence from the table, he concentrates on the content of his sentence. He does not think about the order of the elements of the sentence or about the agreement of the noun/pronoun and verb; the table takes care of these kinds of choices for him. While he thinks about *what* to say he does not worry about *how* to say it, but each time he makes a sentence he practices the pattern correctly. From the display below, the student can make 64 different grammatical sentences that all have the same pattern: NP + is/am/are + V + ing + X, teaching agreement of subject with is/am/are, in the contracted form.

1	2	3
I'm You're He's She's It's We're You're They're	going	to Whitehaven. home. to school. to Frayser. to Dixiemart. to the grocery. downtown. to the Post Office.

The substitution table to be used is written on the chalkboard, or dittoed sheets are prepared. The teacher demonstrates how many different sentences can be made from the combination of words in the table. First choose a word or words from Column 1, for example, "We're"; then from Column 2, "going"; and from Column 3, "to the Post Office." From any column in a simple table like this, the student can choose any group of words, as long as he chooses from each of the columns in order.

After the students have been given the explanation of how the substitution table works, they are called on to make sentences, saying them aloud. After a student gives his sentence, the teacher repeats it, giving the proper pronunciation and intonation. The recitation of sentences should move quickly. The table may then be erased and the students give sentences from memory, with the teacher again reinforcing each response by repeating it, or the students may write three or five sentences, from the board, and then give the sentences from memory.

When the students are familiar with how the table works, the teacher can introduce a more complicated one:

1	2	3	4
I	'm		to Mississippi. to the grocery.
You We They	're	going	home. to bed. to the fair.
He She It	's		to the ball game. to eat lunch. to watch TV.

Attention is called to the double horizontal lines crossing Columns 1 and 2. The student cannot choose just any group of words in Column 1 and match them with any ending in Column 2; for example, "I're" is incorrect. Whenever the student sees the double horizontal line across two columns, the choices from those two columns must be on the same side of the lines. "I" from Column 1 and "'m" from Column 2 can be chosen, making "I'm," because both choices are above the line. "He" from Column 1 and "'re" from Column 2 cannot be chosen, because "He" is below the double line and "'re" is above the double line. The double lines can be drawn with red chalk for added emphasis; also, capitals, periods, apostrophes, and inflected endings can be color cued in this manner to aid in visual perception.

Finally, a testing table like the one shown below is used. From this table, the students again choose words or groups of words from the columns in order, except that in Column 2 they have to make a real choice. One of the words in Column 1 takes "'m," some take "'s", and others "'re." When the student gets to Column 2, he must choose one of the three, making a grammatical choice without the assistance of the table. The testing table can also be used as a pretest.

1	2	3	4
I You He We She They It	'm 's 're	going	to Southhaven. to the dentist. outside. to West Memphis. to be sick. to eat lunch. to go to sleep.

Using the substitution table to cue students to write sentences is a technique to reinforce any pattern that has been drilled orally, and also to teach spelling and punctuation. The writing can come during or at the end of the oral lesson, but never before. Items in the columns can be changed between lessons, but the sentence pattern must remain constant. The teacher should provide an accurate and easily readable copy for the students, and grade on the correctness of the copy as well as the number of sentences produced. It is suggested that only 100s be recorded; no other grades need be considered. A checkmark can indicate the presence of one error; there is no need to make further marks on the paper. Because the format of the substitution table prevents the making of errors other than those resulting from haste or carelessness, this can be a rewarding and positive experience.

When constructing the substitution table, the teacher should be sure that every possible choice results in a grammatically correct sentence. This is very important. The teacher should also make sure that some words are included that the poorest reader will recognize. Words from the week's reading or spelling lessons may be incorporated for reinforcement and extra practice.

ADAPTATION AND
CONSTRUCTION OF MATERIALS AND EQUIPMENT

Any catalog of teaching/learning materials, especially those offered for remediation of educational and perceptual disabilities, will provide ideas for inexpensive construction of similar and satisfactory materials and devices. Teacher-constructed devices, besides being more economical, can have the added advantage of being made more personally relevant to the child. For example, a life-size puzzle for identification of body parts may be made by tracing around the child's body as he lies supine on heavy wrapping paper, with arms and legs straight and slightly extended. Recognition of one's own body and its component parts is exciting!

Even a cursory examination of such a catalog will suggest ideas for construction of materials and equipment. "Rolling blocks," for practice in grammatical construction, can be made by using transparent tape to tape typewritten words to primary counting blocks. The different parts of speech can be color cued by typing the words on colored paper, or by use of colored blocks. (This activity can be coordinated with the "Language in Color" program mentioned above.) Attribute blocks for use in classifying, ordering, discovering equivalence relationships, and other activities involving rational thinking, can be jigsawed from various thicknesses of plywood painted appropriate colors. Giant dominoes are easily made. Variations of materials for visual and auditory memory and perception are numerous.

Ideas such as the above, derived from examination of materials catalogs, are especially valuable for those teachers who have less creative ability than others. Many catalogs include suggested teaching objectives for each item depicted. A file of pictures inspiring ideas for development of similar devices, together with materials development suggestions from other sources, can be useful whenever a child's individualized learning program calls for materials not available.

Industrial arts or vocational classes in the school or school system will often construct materials for the teacher. Students can also participate in creation of their own learning devices. Constructing a balancing scale or a water-drop microscope is a learning experience in itself, as well as a meaningful introduction to the use of such devices.

When reproducing or adapting commercial materials, care must be taken to guard against infringement upon copyrights. The teacher should also be familiar with the rationale, objectives, and methods of specific programs before attempting use of similar materials and methods. Use of materials such as those in the Frostig Program for Development of Visual Perception seems deceptively simple; appropriate use of the program requires more from the teacher than ability to operate the duplicating machine.

Uses of Classroom Furniture

Often the teacher overlooks possibilities for improving instruction through making additional use of classroom furniture and equipment. Lines may be ruled on a chalkboard to aid the child—and teacher—in proper placement and proportion of letters and in organization and neatness of boardwork. A grid for easy presentation of graphs, multiplication charts, latitude and longitude, etc. can also be drawn in faint but permanent lines. Additional chalkboard space is often necessary. Masonite, cut into appropriate sizes and coated with chalkboard paint, provides a portable board for use with small groups. Smaller boards can be provided for each child to use at his desk for work of a temporary nature. One ingenious teacher in an impoverished neighborhood created individual chalkboards by painting all the desktops with the chalkboard paint. (This is an excellent suggestion, but not one to be carried out without permission of the principal.) Turning a kindergarten or study table top into a horizontal chalkboard can also provide "scribble space," or a surface for practice of prewriting motor skills.

The floor can be used as a learning area. For example, number lines painted on the floor (again, only with permission of the principal) add a kinesthetic element to the learning of addition and subtraction. Sides of metal file cabinets are convenient magnetic boards for manipulation of refrigerator door note magnets, thus providing concrete arithmetic experiences. A chair turned upside down on a table top provides a temporary easel for a painting board made by clipping, stapling, or taping newsprint to rigid cardboard cut from large packing cartons. (The board is placed between the legs of the chair, not against its back.) Bookcases and supply cabinets, turned into the room, provide room dividers, study areas, and excellent space on their backs for posters, pictures, and other visual materials that need close study and inspection.

Construction of Large Equipment

The vocational arts department of the school, or parents with home workshops, may need to be called on for help in construction of larger equipment such as puppet stages, walking boards for improvement of motor coordination (simple to reproduce from a catalog picture), and so forth. A giant abacus can be made from an old window frame, wire rods, and painted spools or large wooden beads. Saving money is the most important reason for construction rather than purchase of such items. "Brainstorming" with the fathers of the pupils is an excellent way to get parental interest and involvement with the school, as well as to get suggestions for ways to save on equipment and volunteers to build it. The teacher should be able to present specific needs for the equipment and objectives for its use: this is always a prerequisite to acquisition, adaptation, or use of any material.

An additional example of a motivational and multilevel, multiuse piece of equipment is the electric board, a device for presenting questions and answers to students so that a buzzer sounds or a bulb lights when a correct answer is chosen. One lead wire is placed on a question and another on its correct response. When the two are matched, the circuit is complete and the student is provided with feedback stating that his answer is correct. Pairing of terminals should be changed at intervals so that the student will not be able to memorize the board pattern for correct answers. The board may be used with all levels of instruction, from matching pictures to instruction in geometric figures, areas and volumes, events and dates, chemistry symbols and names, vocabulary, pictures, and maps. Directions for its construction, and suggested uses, are given by Freedman and Berg (1967), and in other easily obtainable books on audiovisual materials and teaching aids.

Suggestions given in Chapter 10 for modification of classroom equipment to provide for the physically handicapped may be found helpful for other students. The poorly coordinated child may need devices for holding paper in place when writing, holding the textbook open, or training appropriate pencil grip.

SUMMARY

Adaptation, modification, or construction of materials by the classroom teacher is economical, educationally desirable, and often the only way in which an individual child's learning needs can be appropriately met. Adaptation or construction of any material must be preceded by identification of the specific learning problem and formulation of the instructional objective. Once the objective is clearly identified, the teacher can proceed with the task of "making the match" between pupil and material, by adaptation or modification of whatever dimensions are indicated by the pupil's preferred mode of learning, reading level, physical or sensory handicaps, or other factors. No program or material, however desirable it seems, should be used in a child's educational program unless there can be a positive answer to the question, "Will this be effective for reaching the specific objective(s) previously identified for this child?"

It is recognized that accumulation of appropriate individualized instructional materials requires much teacher time and effort. This is again a reason for preparing materials only after the need has been identified. Pooling of teacher-made materials in a school is suggested as one way of making appropriate materials more available. Construction of materials that are versatile, multilevel, and adaptable to a variety of tasks or subjects is emphasized.

The classroom teacher faces many problems involved in individualizing instruction for the exceptional child in his room. Skill in adaptation, modification, or construction of appropriate educational materials will make it easier to provide for this child, and all the other children in the room. Pooling of teacher ideas at the local level is a most valuable resource. Properly executed, such an exchange of ideas and/or materials can do much to ease the job of the individual teacher and lessen the financial strain on the school system.

RESOURCES

Listed below are sources of additional information on some of the programs and materials mentioned in this chapter. In addition, a few of the many excellent materials available today are listed. A final word of caution is given: A material is excellent only if it is useful in reaching the specific objective previously identified.

Aids to Developing Instructional Objectives

Gronlund, N. E. 1970. Stating Behavioral Objectives for Classroom Instruction. The Macmillan Company, New York.

Mager, R. F. 1962. Preparing Instructional Objectives. Fearon Publishers, Belmont, Ca.

Collections of Suggested Activities and Materials

Special Education Teacher's Kit: Books and Instructional Materials

This kit contains over 1,000 ideas that have been classroom tested for teachers of exceptional children in special and regular classrooms. Included are strategies for teaching exceptional children, pupil activity sheets, art and science tasks, music based instruction, arithmetic and language learning games, spirit duplicating masters, as well as educational games for physically handicapped children.

Successful Learning Kit: Resource Room and Learning Center Materials

This kit is designed to aid the elementary school teacher in the instruction of reluctant learners. It contains materials for all areas of instruction and may be used by regular and special education teachers. The kit contains hundreds of ideas and permits the teacher to individualize instruction through open-ended activities. Areas included are arithmetic, reading, science, art, language, story writing, physical education, communication, and direction following. Includes 144 spirit masters, laminated reusable cards, learning center projects, books, activity sheets, basic strategies, and a teachers manual.

Both kits are available from:

> Love Publishing Company
> 6635 East Villanova Place
> Denver, Co. 80222

The books and activities contained in these kits are also available separately from the publishing company.

> SPICE Series
> Educational Service, Inc.
> P.O. Box 219
> Stevensville, Mi. 49127
> (also available at local school supply dealers)

Fourteen different titles provide learning games and activities for all elementary academic areas.

> The Continental Press, Inc.
> Elizabethtown, Pa. 17022

Publishers of preprinted masters for liquid duplicators, individual pupil books, transparencies, filmstrips, and boxed instructional material. Non-reading activities and other materials are designed specifically for slow learners. Demonstration catalogs, available upon request, show the contents, in reduced form, of each title in the various programs. These exact reductions of the corresponding full-sized preprinted carbon master allow the teacher to evaluate their suitability for his needs before ordering.

Materials for English Grammar, Composition, and Vocabulary Development

Dixson, R. J. 1971. Modern American English. Rev. Ed. Books 1 and 2. Correlated workbooks and recordings. Available from:

> Regents Publishing Company
> Division of Simon and Schuster
> West 39th St.
> New York City, N.Y. 10018

A functional vocabulary is used in teaching English with second language learning methods.

Dykstra, G., Port, R., and Port, A. 1966. Ananse Tales: A Course in Controlled Composition. Workbook for Ananse Tales. Available from:

> Teachers College Press
> Columbia University
> New York City, N.Y. 10027

Norris, P. 1969. Language in Color. Available from:

> P. Norris
> 855 Yates Road S., No. 3
> Memphis, Tn. 38117

This language development program has been copyrighted, but is not commercially produced. Its originator welcomes correspondence from teachers and others interested in the program.

Anderson, T. 1970. Writing-Phonics Program. Available from:

> T. Anderson
> 32 N. Holmes
> Memphis, Tn. 38111

The developer of this program welcomes inquiries as to details of the scope, sequence, and implementation of the program.

Materials for Mathematics Learning

Laycock, M., and Watson, G. 1975. The Fabric of Mathematics. Rev. Ed. Available from:

> Activity Resources Company
> P.O. Box 4875
> Hayward, Ca. 94540

This resource book includes a scope and sequence of 38 concepts. Each item is defined and supported by objectives and assessments for various levels (K–junior high), and incorporates manipulatives, games, activities, audio-visuals, and children and teacher references that can be used to present a fresh approach to each concept. The book is designed to be used with any good mathematics text.

Manipulatives and Activities Resource Guide. 1974. Fountain Valley Teacher Support System in Mathematics. Available from:

> Richard L. Zweig Associates, Inc.
> 20800 Beach Boulevard
> Huntington Beach, Ca. 92648

Materials for Science Learning

Basal/Supplemental Science. 1974. Available from:

> Webster Division of McGraw-Hill
> 680 Forrest Road N.E.
> Atlanta, Ga. 30312

Units on such topics as "Bulbs and Batteries," "Mystery Powders," and "Primary Balances" provide individualized discovery experiences in science.

Workshops on Materials Production

Project Materials Access and Production

> Project Director: B. J. Willis
> Project Coordinator: S. Willis
> Tennessee Technological University
> Cookeville, Tn. 38501

The director and coordinator of Project MAP provide materials construction inservice workshops for teachers upon request of public or private agencies and school systems in any area of the nation.

> The Education Center
> 1411 Mill St.
> Greensboro, N. C. 27408

Information is given upon request about seminars held across the country on construction of materials for interest centers.

REFERENCES

Anderson, T. 1970. Writing-phonics program. Mimeographed.

Anderson, R. M., Hemenway, R. E., and Anderson, J. W. 1969. Instructional Resources for Teachers of the Culturally Disadvantaged and Exceptional. Charles C. Thomas Publisher, Springfield, Il.

Berman, A. 1977. Learning disability materials: The great rip-off. J. Learn. Dis. 10(5): 261–263.

Bullough, R. U. 1974. Creating Instructional Materials C. E. Merrill Publishing Company, Columbus, Oh.

Coppen, H. 1971. Aids to Teaching and Learning. Pergamon Press, Oxford and N.Y.

Faulk, F. J. 1974. Learning activity packets for slow learners. Slow Learn. Work. 2(4): 1–4.

Freedman, F. B., and Berg, E. L. 1967. Classroom Teachers' Guide to Audio-Visual Materials. Chilton Books, New York.

Garvey, M. 1972. Teaching Displays: Their Purposes, Construction, and Use. Linnet Books, Hamden, Ct.

Hirshoren, A., Hunt, J. T., and Davis, C. 1974. Classified ads as reading material for the retarded. Except. Child. 41(1): 45–47.

Kohfeldt, J. 1976. Blueprints for construction: Teacher-made or teacher-adapted materials. Foc. Except. Child. 8(5): 1–14.

Lavely, C., Lowe, A. J., and Follman, J. 1975. Actual reading levels of EMR materials. Educ. Train. Ment. Ret. 10(4): 271–275.

McCormack, J. E. 1976. Using a task analysis format to develop instructional sequences. Educ. Train. Ment. Ret. 11(4): 318–323.

Minskoff, E. H. 1973. Creating and evaluating remediation for the learning disabled. Foc. Except. Child. 5(5): 1–11.

Norris, P. 1969. Language in Color. Mimeographed.

Thomas, J. I. 1975. Learning Centers: Opening Up the Classroom. Holbrook Press, Boston.

Willis, B., and Willis, S. 1977a. Project materials access and production. Unpublished manuscript, Cookeville, Tn.

Willis, B., and Willis, S. 1977b. The Tennessee Revisions of the System FORE Classroom Management Program. FORE Train, Gainesboro, Tn.

10

Adapting the Learning Environment for Hearing Impaired, Visually Impaired, and Physically Handicapped

Bonnie B. Greer, Ph.D. and Jo Allsop, M.Ed.

Although some of the more severely physically handicapped, deaf, and blind students are still educated in self-contained special classes, many are being mainstreamed with only support personnel to assist the regular classroom teacher. This process, which meets the requirements of educating the handicapped child in the least restrictive environment, as specified in recent federal legislation (Public Law 94-142), is frightening to many regular teachers. With little or no formal training to teach exceptional children, they find themselves ill-equipped to make the necessary curricular and materials adjustments for the specific needs of the child.

Individualizing instruction even for regular students is always more difficult than mass teaching. However, learning gains are greater when a student's educational strengths and weaknesses are assessed and appropriately matched with instructional materials and methods. It is this same process that is required with exceptional students; in fact, it is mandated by law in the form of an Individualized Educational Plan (IEP). The adaptations involved in teaching the exceptional child are merely a part of individualizing for his needs.

This chapter provides some basic suggestions for adapting both the classroom environment and specific media and materials to accommodate the hearing impaired, visually impaired, and physically handicapped students. With some fairly basic modifications by the teacher, each of these exceptionalities can become a secondary rather than a primary consideration in the educational program of the child. Hence, learning becomes the focal point.

ACCOMMODATING THE HEARING IMPAIRED

As has been emphasized throughout this book, it is extremely important that the classroom teacher know the students as individuals before attempting to match their learning needs with adapted materials. This is especially true with the child who has a hearing impairment.

Language, speech, comprehension, and communication are each cornerstones in the learning process. It is precisely these skills that are lacking or impaired in the deaf or hard of hearing, with the result that many of these students fall behind academically, although they are intellectually normal or bright. In fact, the language processes are so crucial that they form the basis of the definition of hard of hearing and deaf. "By definition, the person with a hearing loss which still allows him to hear and understand connected speech is defined as hard of hearing, while the individual who has such a severe or profound hearing loss that he cannot hear and understand connected speech, even with the assistance of amplification, is defined as deaf" (Brill, 1975, p. 378).

To assume that a child can hear what is being said because he wears a hearing aid is a fallacy. Why then does a deaf child wear a hearing aid? Often the aid enables him to pick up residual sounds and noises, and this added to speech reading permits him to understand what is being said. It is very important to know if the child relies primarily on speech reading to learn, because this would affect both the methods and the materials that the teacher uses. Even if the child is hard of hearing, he will use speech reading to some extent.

The Classroom

When a deaf or hard of hearing child becomes a member of a regular classroom, he most likely will have had special training with a therapist in speech and language, and this will continue throughout his educational program, usually on a weekly basis. In addition, an itinerant special education teacher will be assigned to work with the child and to assist the regular teacher in tasks such as adapting materials and presenting outlines or vocabulary lists that will soon be introduced in the regular class.

Seating position in the classroom directly affects the learning potential of the deaf and hard of hearing. It is best to allow the child to choose his own seat, encouraging him to sit in the front to one side.

This will enable him to see the teacher's face for speech reading, to hear at the closest range, and to easily turn around to see the faces of other children when they speak. Some important tips to help the speech reader are:

1. Clearly spoken speech delivered *at a moderate* rate is most easily understood. *Do not exaggerate* your mouth movements.
2. Give explanations of what you have written on the blackboard *after* you turn around and face the students, not while you are writing or walking around the room.
3. Dictated notes, tests, etc. are not possible, because the partially hearing child cannot simultaneously write and listen as the normal child can. He must constantly be looking at the speaker's lips.

By assigning a "Pal" to the hearing impaired child, it is possible for the teacher to use standard verbal explanations and presentations when introducing new material, as opposed to providing a primarily visual media approach with handouts, overhead acetates, blackboard diagrams, etc. The Pal is a student with normal hearing in the classroom who, while he takes his own notes, is also making a carbon copy for the hearing impaired child on a special notebook provided by the itinerant teacher. In addition, the Pal may clarify something the teacher has said by repeating it while facing the child. It is a good idea to choose an average student to be a Pal rather than a bright one, because the average student will take more detailed and complete notes so that he can later review the important points in the discussion. Often the brighter child knows some of the information already or needs fewer notes to prompt his memory. Thus, while another student is taking notes, the hearing impaired child can concentrate on watching the face of the teacher and using his receptive skills to comprehend what is being said.

Giving oral tests to a deaf or hard of hearing child, which necessitates that he both listen and write, is undesirable, and will give an inaccurate accounting of what he has actually learned. For instance, in giving a spelling test or a math facts quiz, the teacher usually calls out information as the students listen and write the correct answer. Obviously, if the hearing impaired student is watching the teacher's lips to find out what is being said, he cannot write the correct answer at the same time. When he does look down to write, he in all probability is missing the next item being called aloud. This situation provides another excellent opportunity for the itinerant teacher to be of assistance by testing the child slowly at his own rate during a mutually scheduled time.

Materials and Media

The use of visual aids cannot be overemphasized in the learning process of hearing impaired children. Indeed, the child with no hearing loss benefits from visual stimuli. Thus, by conscientiously supplementing the traditional verbal explanations with visual clues, the teacher is increasing the potential for comprehension and synthesis in both the hearing and hearing impaired students. This does not necessarily imply a great deal of extra work or time on the part of the regular teacher. For example, providing a list of key vocabulary words on the blackboard that deal with the new material can eliminate confusion and reinforce the concepts discussed, without exacting demands upon the teacher.

Although sporadically used in some classrooms, an overhead projector should become as commonplace as the blackboard when hearing impaired children are involved. This easy to use visual media can actually save time for the teacher in several ways. By retaining the acetates, the teacher can simply continue or review the discussion at a later date without going to the trouble of rewriting the information, which would be necessary if the blackboard were used instead. In addition, many learning kits come with pre-prepared overhead transparencies that can be shared among the teachers. Because the acetate transparencies are durable and reusable, they provide years of service.

Benefits of the overhead projector to the hearing impaired child are equally as impressive. While using an overhead projector, the teacher usually faces the class in normal light and writes, points to, and talks about the material being projected. This allows the hearing impaired student to watch the lips of the teacher while he describes the important points being illustrated, and at the same time the student can look at the images being projected.

Another easily accessible resource is captioned films (words placed at the bottom of pictures). By using captioned films rather than traditional movies, the teacher is able to accommodate all of his students with very little effort. These films, encompassing a wide range of topics, can be ordered through the itinerant teacher or directly from the Captioned Films and Telecommunications Branch of the U.S. Office of Education.

When the use of captioned films is not feasible, and when a videotape, filmstrip, or television program is shown in class, a few simple procedures will assist the hearing impaired student in benefiting from the learning experience. A brief discussion of what will be seen and a summary of key vocabulary and concepts should precede the event. Immediately afterwards, a comprehensive review of the information will help clarify any points missed during the presentation.

It is evident that with only minimal adaptations and the additional assistance of a speech and hearing therapist and an itinerant special education teacher, the hearing impaired child can be accommodated in the regular classroom. A similar situation exists for the visually impaired.

ACCOMMODATING THE VISUALLY IMPAIRED

Visually impaired students have been successfully integrated into regular classrooms for more than half a century. Their needs, and therefore the demands upon the regular teacher, are primarily determined by the amount of residual vision they can use. Thus, if the child can read printed material, whether enlarged or standard, with the use of magnification, he is classified as partially seeing. However, those children whose vision is so severely impaired that they must rely upon nonprint materials such as Braille and tapes are classified as educationally blind (Gearheart and Weishahn, 1976).

As with hearing impaired children, the adaptations in the learning environment of the visually impaired child are designed to allow the student's other intact sensory channels to compensate for the impaired one. Although it is not true that deaf persons are born with extremely good vision and blind persons are born with extraordinary hearing, the disabled individual does train himself to become more keenly aware of his environment through his unimpaired senses. This is why in the previous section continual stress was placed on adapting the hearing impaired child's environment to emphasize visual learning, and this part of the chapter details ways to utilize the visually impaired child's auditory and tactual senses.

The Classroom

A few simple guidelines will contribute much to the orderly progression of learning in the classroom. By allowing the visually impaired child to choose his own seat, he will be able to use his tactual skills and what little, if any, residual vision he may have, as well as be able to hear from the best vantage point for any given lesson. For example, if the teacher is demonstrating the concepts of on, under, and beside, the visually impaired child would benefit from sitting next to the objects being used so that he could actually feel the objects placed in the positions being shown.

Orientation and mobility are of crucial importance to the visually impaired child. Auditory cues and memory of the placement of objects in the class assist the student in moving around the room. When furniture in the classroom has been rearranged, the child should be informed *before* he enters the room. By explaining the new arrangement and allowing a few minutes for exploration, serious injuries can be avoided. Other members of the class should be trained to push in their chairs and pick up books, umbrellas, etc. that might be carelessly left in the aisles. It is very difficult to remember to close doors completely or to leave them wide open, but an attempt should be made. Walking into a partially closed door is commonplace when the student depends on the auditory cues indicating that it is open.

For those visually impaired children who use Braille books, a Braille writer and/or a typewriter, space, and open shelving should be designated for them to keep their equipment and supplies. Braille materials are oversized and bulky and a large quantity of them will be used by the student each day.

Some things that persons with normal vision take for granted must be adapted for the visually impaired. For example, telling a sighted child to get the scissors and construction paper is an ordinary occurrence. This same direction can and should be given to the educationally blind child, provided that the storage areas have been labeled in Braille. The itinerant/resource teacher can prepare these labels for the regular teacher and also label the bulletin boards, children's desks, lockers, etc. This is just one simple modification that allows the handicapped child to conform to the traditional expectations in the class. For the nonreader, varied tactile materials can be used for labeling as well as for indicating the child's belongings. Thus, in a dental health unit, when each child keeps a designated toothbrush at school, a piece of felt may be added to the handle to indicate the blind child's toothbrush.

Materials and Media

By combining tactual, kinesthetic, and auditory learning modalities, a visually impaired student can adequately compensate for his loss of vision and learn at a rate that parallels that of the sighted student. It is this task of converting visual stimuli into material that can be assimilated through other sensory modalities that the regular and itinerant/resource teachers share. Some materials that can be used successfully with the visually impaired are also suitable for the sighted and are already in the classrooms. Others will need to be adapted. A few specialized items that are specifically manufactured for blind persons will have to be purchased.

An abacus, a tape recorder, and manipulative materials such as pegboards, puzzles, coin sets, and geometric forms or templates are all commonly found in the regular elementary classroom. Each of these can be appropriately used with the visually impaired child with virtually no adaptations. The abacus, in fact, is the most appropriate way of presenting math concepts to an educationally blind student. For example, by manipulating the beads in various combinations of ones, tens, and hundreds, the previously abstract concept of place value becomes a concrete reality.

This same concrete learning is essential throughout the curriculum. There are no substitutes for actual oranges, bananas, onions, corn, etc. when teaching classification of objects into fruits and vegetables. By the same reasoning, it is unwise to present a stuffed toy to the blind child to teach the term "dog." This is a concrete object, but it is only a representation of the actual dog, and confusion will develop when the child is introduced to that barking, lively, face-licking entity also known as "dog." When unsure about how to translate an abstract idea into concrete terms, such as teaching colors to the blind, the itinerant/resource teacher should be consulted first. Sometimes an easy method can be found: i.e., teaching colors by relating them to objects, such as "the sky is blue," "the grass is green." If more complicated approaches are called for, the itinerant/resource teacher can construct needed materials or even teach the concepts to the student.

In some of the most basic curriculum areas, adaptations are required for the visually impaired child so that he can learn. Specifically, reading and writing skills are fundamentally affected by the loss of vision. Obviously, these two areas are not self-contained, and they transcend most of the learning in school. Therefore, any modifications will affect the overall educational progress of the child.

Printed Materials   The partially sighted child will need large print materials for reading instruction. In some cases, the reading series used in the regular classroom can be ordered in large print as well. When this is not possible, the itinerant/resource teacher can have the reader, as well as the student's other books and workbooks, enlarged on an ITEK machine. A little preplanning will ensure that there is no lag in the child's instruction, because the enlargement process usually takes a few weeks. For book reports and leisure reading, most public libraries are amply supplied with large print books.

Primary type or large print should be used when preparing handouts. Dittos and worksheets may need to be outlined with a black Magic Marker. The purple ink does not provide enough contrast for the partially sighted.

Handwriting may be more tedious for the partially sighted student, but instruction should be given at the same time that it would be given for sighted students. Color cued primary paper or script guides may be used to help the student develop coordination. The handwriting samples of partially sighted children will probably be consistently larger than normal, but formation of the letters should be similar.

Braille Braille, as previously mentioned with reference to labeling items in the classroom, is the primary method of reading and writing used by educationally blind persons. It is a combination of raised dots that the student "reads" by feeling while moving his fingers along the Brailled page, or "writes" with a stylus and slate or Braille writer. Specialized training in reading and writing Braille is given to the primary level elementary child by an itinerant/resource teacher on a daily basis. As the child gets older, these special training sessions become more infrequent.

The regular classroom teacher is not expected to learn Braille. Worksheets, handouts, and tests can be given to the itinerant/ resource teacher to be Brailled. Many of the readers and textbooks are available in Braille from the American Printing House for the Blind and the Library of Congress. In addition, the blind student's books can be Brailled by the local school system in many areas, although this requires months to accomplish. There are also alternatives to this solution. The talking book program is available to visually impaired and physically handicapped persons through the Library of Congress. These "talking books" come recorded on either records or tapes so that the student can listen to rather than read the information. Recordings for the Blind is an organization that will tape any book that is sent to them. Two copies of the book are required to shorten the length of recording time to a matter of weeks.

Typewriter and Tape Recorder Answer sheets, reports, etc. prepared in Braille by the student are translated by the itinerant/resource teacher until the child is old enough to type. About the middle of the third grade, when the child has a good foundation in spelling, syntax, and grammar, he is taught the touch system of typing. From this point on, information requested by the teacher can be typed, and notes for the student's own use are made in Braille with a stylus or Braille writer.

The typewriter, in combination with a tape recorder, can eliminate many of the complications in learning that result from vision loss. For example, if the teacher does not have time to get a quiz or a handout for an activity Brailled, he can simply put this information on a cassette tape for the blind student. Then the child can either type the answers or, if space is provided on the tape, simply answer verbally. (Earphones are an asset with the tape recorder so that others are not disturbed.) Sometimes the student may record the teacher's explanations of a particularly complicated process, for example, in math, so that he can listen to this information several times rather than relying on Brailled notes. A particularly good reader in the classroom may be designated to read sections of a book, key vocabulary words, or lengthy assignment instructions to the blind student while simultaneously recording these on a tape.

It should be mentioned that the noise level in the classroom affects not only the use of the tape recorder, but all phases of the visually impaired student's learning. Primary dependence on auditory cues and verbal explanations for learning is contingent upon a minimal amount of extraneous noise. If garbage is being collected outside the classroom window, or if students are talking and giggling in the back of the room, few meaningful verbal explanations will be discriminated by the visually impaired student.

Other than the stylus, slate, and Braille writer that were previously mentioned, there are a few adapted instructional materials that should be purchased for use with visually impaired students. Purchasing is recommended, because the construction of these items by the teacher would be impractical, and in some cases impossible.

Adapted Equipment Raised line writing paper, checkbooks, and a signature guide are especially useful in teaching the educationally blind student those minimal handwriting skills that will be required for everyday living. For example, checks, credit cards, and official documents cannot be signed with a typed name. The signature guide or a script guide will prevent the blind student from writing over a word or line that was previously written.

In the area of math, Braille rulers, clockfaces, and a raised line drawing kit are available. The raised line kit contains special "paper" that allows the blind student to draw geometric configurations and feel the lines on top of the surface as they are made. These lines are also visible to the teacher.

Relief globes and maps will enable the blind student to feel the boundaries of states and countries. Because much of the study of geography involves the location of designated land and water, it is imperative that the blind student have some tactual reference to these areas.

There are two relatively sophisticated items that can be of immeasurable assistance to the educationally blind person. Although comparatively more expensive than most adapted equipment, the technological research involved in their designs accounts somewhat for the cost. The Optacon is a portable device that converts the printed word into a tactual sensation, allowing the blind person to "read" virtually anything. A scanner is moved across the printed page while the other hand rests on a unit transmitting tactual signals that the person then translates, much like Braille. The Speech Plus Calculator was designed by the makers of Optacon, Telesensory Systems Incorporated, and incorporates the best features of a fine calculator into a portable unit that also "speaks." Thus, as the blind student depresses the keys to compute a problem, the calculator announces both the entries and the results through its speaker.

This kind of sophisticated, costly adaptation is not necessary to maintain the visually impaired student in the regular class. Rather, a continuous interaction between the regular and itinerant special education teachers, and some basic but consistent adaptations, especially in the areas of reading, writing, and math, will ensure a mutually successful educational environment for both the visually impaired and sighted students.

ACCOMMODATING THE PHYSICALLY HANDICAPPED

The Classroom

When a physically handicapped student is placed in "the least restrictive environment" or in a regular class setting, careful consideration must be given to the selection of an appropriate environment. In organizing a schoolroom to accommodate the physically handicapped student, priority must be given to the inclusion of that student into the group, because social and emotional development cannot take place in isolation.

One asset the nonhandicapped child has in a classroom is the freedom of movement to allow him to see all of the room, to see it from different perspectives, and to change perspectives at will. This encourages and facilitates much incidental learning, and makes a student feel that he is part of his environment. Movement is just as important, perhaps more important, for the handicapped student. In addition to changing the immediate environment, the handicapped child must avoid long periods of immobility to maintain and improve the motor function that he has, and to prevent loss of function (Peterson and Cleveland, 1975). Furniture must be arranged with wide aisles to facilitate free and easy movement, and activities should be planned to provide a vantage point to all areas of the room at some time during the day. Furniture around which a handicapped student must maneuver should have legs that are perpendicular to the floor to prevent falls caused by stumbling over furniture legs that extend out further than the top of the furniture. Straight legs rarely interfere with the mobility of a student in a wheelchair or a student using a walker.

Furniture for the handicapped student should be sturdy, durable, and have a wide base. Often the student does not "sit down" in a chair—he "falls" onto it. Care should be taken to ensure that all furniture (bookcases, room dividers, etc.) is heavy enough that it cannot be turned over by a child falling against it.

Desks, chairs, and tables must be the proper height. Wooden ones are easily adapted by cutting off long legs to shorten them or by putting on new legs to make them higher. When purchasing new tables and desks, it is advantageous to get those with adjustable legs. Wooden tables may need the frame cut out to allow a wheelchair to roll under them. New tables or desks should have nothing under them that would interfere with wheelchairs.

A quiet corner should be provided where any student can go for special interests or for study. The cerebral palsied student who has uncontrolled movements works best from a quiet, relaxed position. A great deal of extraneous noise and confusion often results in increased random motor activity, which prevents optimal learning conditions. Large beanbags or rest mats on which students can recline are useful for specific periods of relaxation.

Provision must be made for the storage of pencils, paper, books, and similar school supplies. For children in wheelchairs, a bag can be made or purchased that can be placed over the back or arm of the chair, or a storage shelf can be provided close at hand, at a height that allows the student easy access to it. For students with muscular weakness of the upper torso and arms, books should always be kept on the desk so that no lifting is necessary. Desks with pencil grooves are helpful, and some desks and tables are available with material storage compartments on the side.

Crutches tend to get in the way when they are not in use. Provision, should be made for crutches, and children should be trained to keep them in their proper place. Crutch holders can be fastened to either the back or side of a child's chair (see Figure 1). This makes the crutches easily accessible to the student and out of the way of others.

The physically handicapped student has less available energy than does a nonhandicapped person. In addition to a lower energy reserve, the student often must use muscles with abnormal tone to

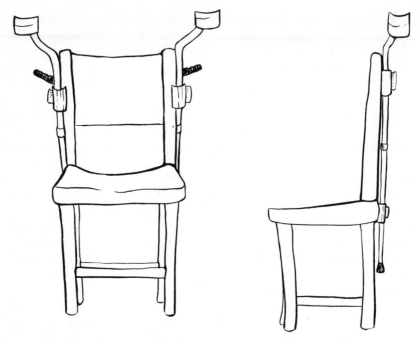

Figure 1.   Crutch holders can be attached to either the side or back of school chairs.

perform necessary tasks. For this reason, all adaptive methods and/ or assistive devices are important from the standpoint of increased independence, educational progress, and resulting self-worth (Hardy and Cull, 1974). For example, if a child must utilize an inordinate amount of energy to keep himself in an upright position, he has little energy left to learn. Therefore, a stable, secure seating posture is mandatory.

Many items that are readily available can be used to achieve an optimal seating position. Desks and chairs with arm rests can be used with the student who has little lateral stability or who is seizure prone. If more stability is needed, lateral trunk supports can be built onto the back of a wooden chair that would support the trunk, particularly around the ribs (see Figure 2). Footrests, built so that the hips, knees, and ankles are placed at 90° angles or less, will often help the student who has some spasticity in the hips and legs, which tends to make him slide forward in his seat. Security and comfort will be enhanced if a wedge seat is used in conjunction with the footrest. It may also be necessary to place firm foam rubber behind his lower back to position him further forward in the chair. Velcro belts at 45° angles to the hip will help hold the child securely in the chair (see Figure 3). The Velcro material is particularly good for strapping purposes because it holds tightly and can be easily and quickly fastened and unfastened. Some other commercially available seating accessories are safety straps, lateral trunk supports, wedge cushions, and knee separators.

Once a practical arrangement has been worked out that accommodates the needs of the handicapped student as well as those of the teacher and other students, it should be maintained. A stable environment provides a feeling of security and enhances the probability of success (Hardy and Cull, 1974). With the student comfortably positioned in an accessible environment, learning can become the primary focus of attention.

Materials and Media

The handicapped child often appears in the classroom before the teacher has time or money available to order special assistive devices and instructional materials. Teachers should not be discouraged. Most materials can be adapted for use, and others can be made or altered using materials that are readily available.

Materials to Adapt and Construct   Paper and pencil tasks will be easier for students with involuntary motor movements if the

Figure 2.   Trunk supports can be attached to school chairs to provide stability for the student, thus lessening the amount of energy required to sit upright.

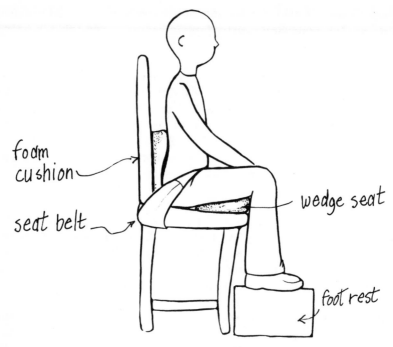

foam
cushion

seat belt

wedge seat

foot rest

Figure 3.   Footrests, foam rubber, seat belts, and wedge seats provide security and comfort for disabled students. Once these are established, learning can become the primary focus.

paper is taped to the writing surface. The use of large paper will help, because their writing will be larger and thus less difficult to read. For those students who need supplemental assistance in fine motor control, color cued control paper that has four red and green control lines (Developmental Learning Materials—DLM, Ideal) or "right line paper" that has raised lines to help the student stay on the lines when writing (Modern Education Corp.—MEC) may be substituted for the large primary paper. The teacher should also realize that large pencils and pens are easier for some handicapped students to grasp. The grip can be built up by using styrofoam hair curlers, small rubber balls, dental acrylic, or foam. In addition to these homemade adaptations, cylindrical foam padding (Sammons) and vinyl triangular pencil grips (DLM, Ideal) can be purchased. Cardboard stencils can be made that will help a child draw horizontal, vertical, and diagonal lines. These lines, when combined with circles and arcs, form the basic strokes necessary for printing and cursive writing (see Figure 4). Several companies offer grooved letters and numerals for tracing (DLM, Ideal). These assistive devices, when combined with plywood templates and double-handed training scissors (DLM), will provide maximum opportunities for the physically handicapped student to develop fine motor control.

Lap trays to fit on wheelchairs can be made from heavy plywood, and greatly aid the wheelchair-bound student. The trays not only provide the best possible work surface for the student, but also contribute to his feeling of security. They can easily be cut so that they do not interfere with propelling the chair (see Figure 5).

Many children in wheelchairs who have braces need an opportunity to stand every day. This necessitates some physical support. A standing table can be constructed that will provide work surface, enabling the child to continue working while he stands (see Figure 6). In fact, many students will work better on paper and pencil tasks because of the added leverage they get when standing. The standing table can also be adapted for chalkboard use by turning it with the gate next to the board. Students with crutches, who are braced but need added stability, would find this useful when working at a chalkboard. If funds are available, these standing tables may be purchased (Childcraft).

The student with a great deal of rigidity of the hips may find doing paper and pencil tasks on a horizontal surface an impossible task. A slant board can be constructed or purchased (DLM) to provide a correctly angled surface for the student and to hold pencils and keep paper in place (see Figure 7). This same slant board could also become a stand on which a more handicapped student's

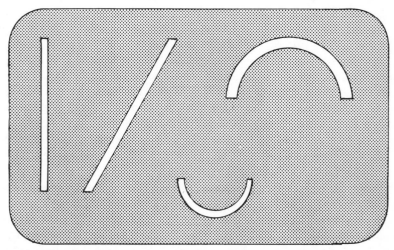

Figure 4.   Cardboard stencils are useful aids in drawing lines, which is a prerequisite for printing.

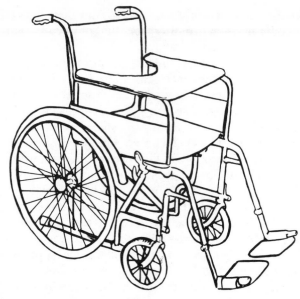

Figure 5. Wheelchairs can be converted into desks by attaching lap trays. They provide the student with security and work space.

typewriter is placed to provide enough angle so that he can see over the keys to read what he has typed.

Typewriters and Special Aids   Those students who have very little manual control for writing should be taught to use an electric typewriter. Some of these students will need a hand pointer with which to strike the keys. Wooden dowels with a rubber tip added to the end can be used for this purpose. Figure 8 shows some diagrams depicting various grasps that can be tried until the best one is found. If the grasp is not dependable, Velcro can be used to strap the device onto the hand. Students who have no useful hand control can be taught to type on an electric typewriter using a head pointer. This is a stationary piece, much like a hand pointer, that is affixed to a cap that is strapped onto the child's head. The head pointer can also be used to point to and move light objects such as answer cards. The Enabler (Adaptive Therapeutic Systems) is an excellent example of a well-constructed head pointer.

Special aids can be purchased to help the students who are using typewriters. Typewriter shields can be purchased that help the child with uncontrolled movements to hit the desired key. If shields are not commercially available for a particular kind of typewriter, they can be made in a metal shop from metal or plastic. Adjustable slant boards and tables can also be made or purchased. They enable the child to reach the keys with a minimum amount of strain.

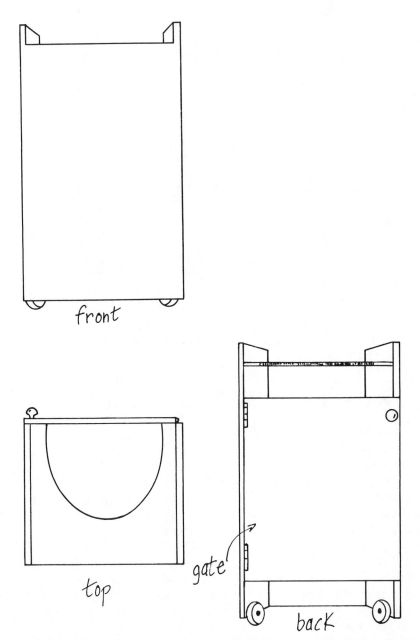

Figure 6.   Standing tables provide work space, and enable many students to more successfully complete writing tasks because of the added leverage.

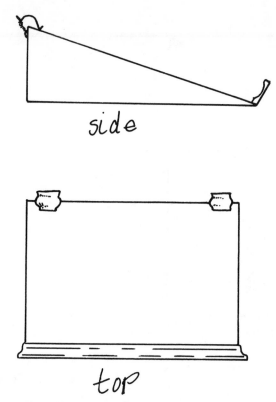

side

top

Figure 7.   If standing tables prove inadequate, students will benefit from the angled surface of a slant board. It can be used for writing or as a typewriter stand.

Alternative Writing Methods   If an electric typewriter is not available, students may be taught to write holding a pencil in their mouth, or by holding it in their hand while bracing it with their cheek for stability. Some have even learned to write with their feet. The important thing to remember is that where there's a will, there's a way. Consultation with an occupational therapist is recommended if assistance is needed for these adaptations.

Adapting Books   The handling of books can also be a very difficult task for the physically handicapped. Books are often cumbersome and heavy, and handling them can consume much energy. The slant board described above can be used to hold books, but this may eliminate a writing surface for those who need it. A book holder can be constructed that can be used in conjunction with the slant board or the typewriter (see Figure 9). Many kinds of book holders are commercially available, and some companies also offer page turners for the severely involved student (Sammons, DLM).

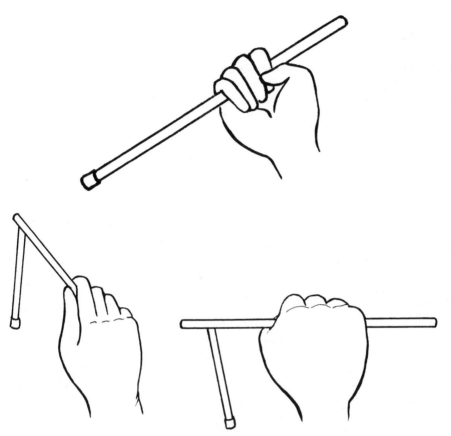

Figure 8.   Students with little manual control should be taught to type. Hand pointers can be used with various grasps to improve typing accuracy.

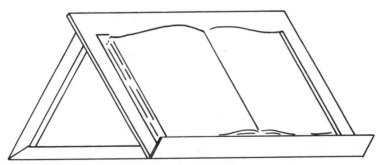

Figure 9.   Book holders, when use in conjunction with slant boards, preserve work space and save children the energy of maneuvering books.

If necessary, books can be taken apart and used a story or chapter at a time to make them less cumbersome. It is well to remember that books and materials are expendable—children are not. If the choice is between the welfare of a book and the welfare of a child, the child must come first.

Talking books can be an aid to the physically handicapped student in that it is an easy way for the student to assimilate knowledge when traditional methods prove slow and physically taxing. Teachers may write to the Library of Congress, Division for Blind and Physically Handicapped, 1291 Taylor N.W., Washington, D.C., 20542, to inquire about how to procure these aids.

Certain adaptations can be made to make workbooks easier for the handicapped student to handle. It is always easier for the student to handle one page than it is to handle a book. Workbooks that the student has purchased may be taken apart and presented one page at a time. This will be necessary for students using typewriters. Sometimes it helps to provide a separate sheet for answering, or to recopy the workbook page to make it usable in the typewriter. If the school provides the workbooks, it may be advantageous to laminate or cover each page with clear Contact paper, so that the answers can be written with grease pencil and erased after they are evaluated and corrected. The workbook would then become a permanent and reusable instructional kit.

Teacher-Made Worksheets   Teacher-made worksheets should have a limited number of activities on each sheet, should be easily readable with large, dark print, and ample space should be provided for the answer. Because many handicapped children have limited interaction with the environment, teacher-made games and other manipulative learning devices are of great benefit to them. Paper and pencil tasks often consume tremendous amounts of energy, and these alternative learning experiences can be used as energy savers as well as good motivators. The materials should be of an appropriate size to be easily manipulated (students with poor manual control will require larger materials), and should be either laminated or covered with clear Contact paper for durability. Many cerebral palsied children drool. This, and their uncontrolled movements, may ruin materials that are not sturdy and durable. Commercially made instructional kits and games will also last longer if they are laminated or covered with clear Contact paper.

Children with erratic head movements often have difficulty keeping their place on a page, which ultimately affects their comprehension. For some students, it is helpful to cover a part of the page to reduce the amount of stimuli and to help the student keep his place. Tagboard or construction paper strips clipped to a page can serve as a place keeper to assist these children, or tachistoscopes can be constructed so that the information is presented in small segments. These simple adaptations can often make the difference between independent learning with books, workbooks, and worksheets, versus time-consuming, one-to-one tutoring with these materials.

Adapting Media Materials   Certain media center materials are also easily adapted to allow independent learning by handicapped children. Even children who must use head pointers can use tape recorders with easily depressed buttons. Individual filmstrip previewers can be useful if the film is advanced by a push button. Storybooks on tape, Language Masters, and calculators may also be useful tools in the instruction of the physically handicapped child, and are time-saving devices for the teacher.

Materials for the Nonoral Child   One of the most challenging problems that may be presented to a teacher is that of the cerebral palsied child who is functionally nonoral. The functionally nonoral child may be completely nonoral, may have some potential for vocalization, or may be partially verbal. In any case, he must have a way of communicating in the classroom. Teachers need not be concerned that a supplemental communication system will completely replace any partial approach a student might have or that it might eliminate any potential for future vocalization. Studies indicate that a communication device tends to increase spontaneous vocalizations in the partially verbal, with the child using his own system when he can, and using the other when his breaks down (Vanderheiden and Grilley, 1975). Because these children are difficult to work with, teachers are encouraged to seek assistance from a speech therapist in the school system or from another agency.

Handwriting is one alternative to oral communication. Although writing is both quick and comprehensive, a prerequisite to the printed word as an alternate means of communication is the student's ability to spell and to express himself in written language. This would greatly limit the use of this means of communication for a child younger than 8 or 10 years of age (Vicker, 1974). Unfortunately, even many older handicapped children have great difficulty writing because of poor fine motor control, and therefore communication through this medium would be slow and laborious. This problem can be partially overcome by the use of a typewriter. As discussed earlier, children who have poor fine motor control can use aids such as hand-held typing sticks, mouth sticks, and head pointers. Using a typewriter would still be a slow means of communication, however, and it would be a nonportable means, restricted to the close proximity of a typewriter.

Another mode of communication for a nonoral student is finger-spelling. Its effectiveness as a communication tool depends on the person's manual dexterity and control, his speed, and his ability to spell. However, his actual communication would be limited to those individuals who know how to read fingerspelling.

Probably the most efficient means of communication for nonoral children is the communication board. This is a piece of plastic, wood, or fiberboard that contains pictures, words, numerals, etc. that the nonoral child recognizes. When some communication is needed, the child indicates the appropriate response on the board. Communication boards can be made to fit on a student's wheelchair tray or they can be made for table use with students using crutches. The first step in the development of a communication board is to select the best means for a student to indicate the words, pictures, etc. that convey the thought he wants to communicate. The technique selected must be the one the student can use most efficiently while expending the least energy (Vanderheiden and Grilley, 1975).

The most commonly used indicating technique is the direct selection approach. This approach is used with the child who has the ability to point to the item he wants or to the exact word or letter on a communication board. When this is not feasible, another method must be selected.

One basic means of indication is called scanning. Scanning, in its simplest form, would be to present words, pictures, or verbal questions to a child one at a time, and to have him indicate *yes* when the desired message is reached. Indication of *yes* could be a smile, a nod, a look up, or some other prearranged signal. A higher level scanning device would present letters one at a time, and the student would indicate the letters that would spell his message. One advantage of this approach is that it can be used with severely physically handicapped students who have useful hand control, as well as with the multiply handicapped whose cognitive capabilities limit them to responding only to spoken words or to pictures of basic objects (Vanderheiden and Grilley, 1975).

A fundamental scanning board can be made using plywood or heavy fiberboard. It would contain the alphabet as well as numerals (see Figure 10). The teacher would point to each letter in turn and the student would indicate when the correct letter has been reached. The teacher would then start over until the second letter was indicated. The procedure would be continued until the entire message had been spelled out. The major disadvantage of this aproach is that

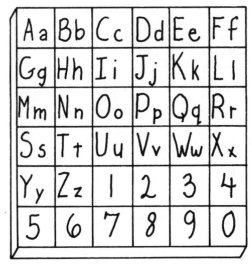

Aa	Bb	Cc	Dd	Ee	Ff
Gg	Hh	Ii	Jj	Kk	Ll
Mm	Nn	Oo	Pp	Qq	Rr
Ss	Tt	Uu	Vv	Ww	Xx
Yy	Zz	1	2	3	4
5	6	7	8	9	0

Figure 10. A fundamental scanning board. This permits severely handicapped children to communicate by spelling out messages.

it is time consuming and therefore not practical for some classroom situations (Vanderheiden and Grilley, 1975).

The encoding approach may be more practical in the classroom, where speed is a consideration. The encoding device pictured in Figure 11 can be easily constructed and, although only slightly quicker than the scanning technique, it would be practical for the child with very little hand control. By pointing to two numbers, the student can indicate a letter any place on the matrix. For example, if he points first to 4 and then to 3, he indicates that the letter is in the fourth row and that it is in the third box.

After a means of indication has been selected, the next step in the development of a communication board is the preparation of the vocabulary itself. A picture chart may be designed for the child who is just beginning to read, but a chart containing letters, numerals, pictures, words, and phrases would be more appropriate for the child who reads and spells. The teacher may find it advantageous to develop several charts. One may be appropriate for communication between the children, another may be more appropriate for communication during special interest sessions (i.e., social studies, math), and still another may be more appropriate for communication at home. In all situations, the chart should be arranged in systematic order so that it can be used efficiently by all. It has been suggested that proper names and pronouns be placed on the left and that these be followed by verbs, modifiers and/or quantifiers, object-nouns,

	1	2	3	4	5	6	7
1	Aa	Bb	Cc	Dd	Ee	Ff	Gg
2	Hh	Ii	Jj	Kk	Ll	Mm	Nn
3	Oo	Pp	Qq	Rr	Ss	Tt	Uu
4	Vv	Ww	Xx	Yy	Zz	yes	no
5		drink					
6	☹	☺			hurt		
7			stop				?

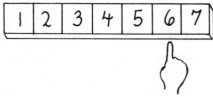

Figure 11. An encoding device with matrix. This means of communication is more practical than the scanning board because it is slightly faster.

prepositions, and words indicating time. Commonly used phrases such as "I don't know," "please," and "thank you" should be included, as well as words needed to communicate a student's special interests, numerals, and the alphabet (Vicker, 1974) (see Figure 12).

Teachers who feel a need for more detail in the development of communication board displays should refer to the Vicker reference in the bibliography at the end of the chapter. It contains a wealth of material, including sample displays.

Communication is the foundation of learning. It is therefore imperative that some type of reliable communications system be established with the physically handicapped child. The nonoral student is undoubtedly the greatest challenge. Typing is often extremely tiring to these children, and the use of communication boards is sometimes impractical because of the length of instructional time involved. This problem can be circumvented by giving the student a choice of responses, from which he selects the correct one. These responses can be presented verbally with a simple *yes/no*

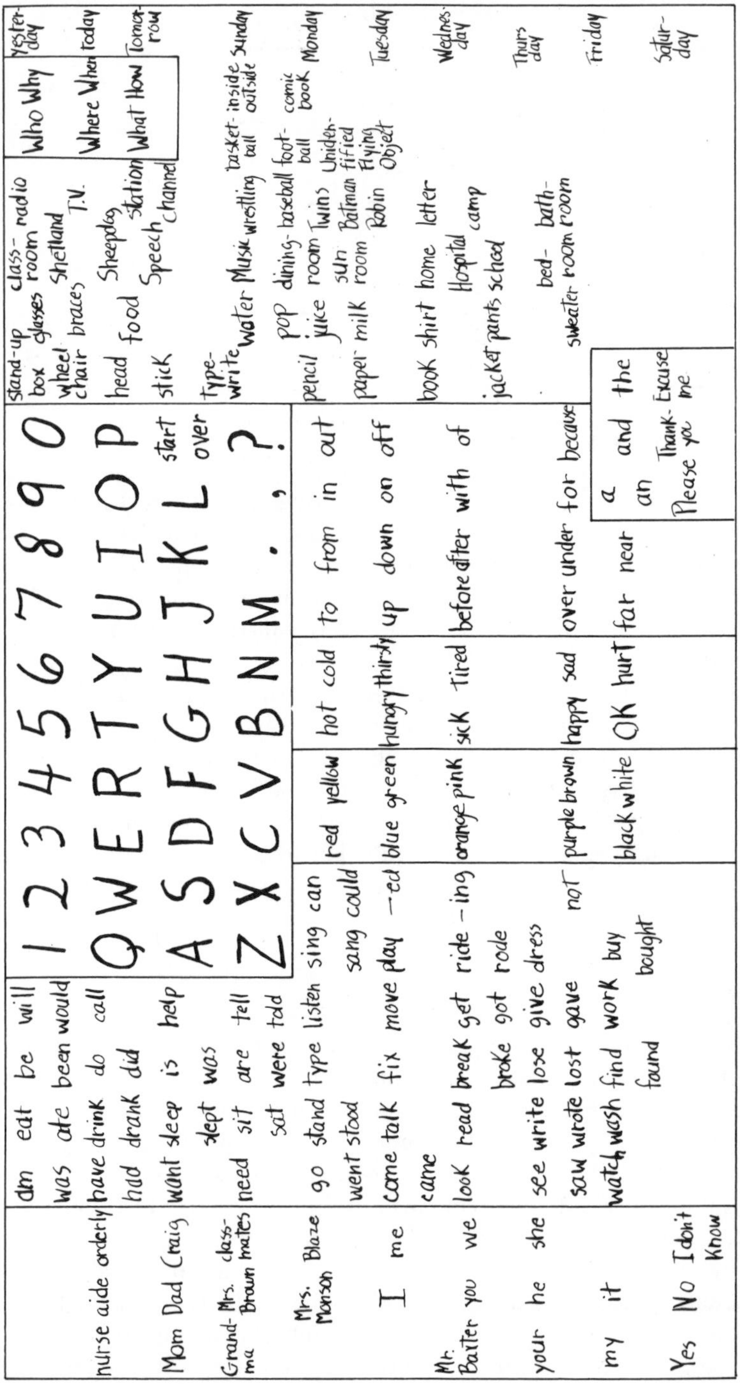

Figure 12. Sample communication display materials, 1964-1967. Reprinted from *Nonoral Communication System Project, 1964-1973*, edited by Beverly Vicker, with permission. Copyright © 1974 by the University of Iowa.

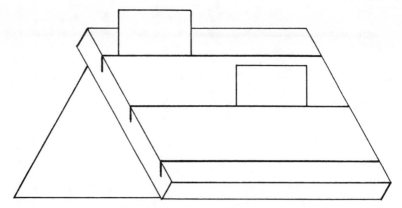

Figure 13.   Card holders help the nonoral student respond to questions. They are easily made from wood or tagboard.

answer, or on cards with the student pointing to the correct response. Picture cards can be used for the nonreader, and cards with written responses should be employed for the student who reads. Card holders can be purchased or simply made. Effective holders similar to those pictured in Figure 13 can be easily constructed from wood or tagboard.

Assuming that the regular classroom teacher has support from the resource and itinerant special education personnel, the previously described adaptations in materials should assist in providing for even the severely physically handicapped child in the class. By making minimal changes in the physical environment, and a few of the modifications to compensate for uncontrolled or inflexible movements and impaired communication, the teacher can smoothly continue the normal teaching/learning process.

SUMMARY

Hearing impaired, visually impaired, and physically handicapped students are being placed in regular classrooms in an effort to provide them with an educational program in the least restrictive environment. With support personnel such as speech and physical therapists, itinerant/resource teachers, and special education consultants, these students can benefit from regular education programs as opposed to being isolated in self-contained units.

The learning environment, as well as media and materials, must be evaluated and sometimes adapted for the students who have hearing, vision, or physical impairments. Seating, the arrangement of the classroom, noise level, and the location of the teacher during instruction are all factors that directly influence the student's learning. These concerns are so integral to the use of instructional materials that the two are inseparable. In most cases, media and materials used in educating impaired students require only minor adaptations, or even just a circumspect attitude when the original selection of materials is made.

This chapter has offered suggestions on the most efficient ways of adapting the environment and instructional materials and media to meet the educational needs of hearing impaired, visually impaired, and physically handicapped students. These ideas are not intended to be comprehensive, but are practical, relatively inexpensive alternatives to common learning barriers. With the cooperative efforts of the regular and special education teachers, the students can easily be accommodated in a regular educational setting.

ASSISTIVE AIDS AND RESOURCES

Adaptive Therapeutic Systems, Inc.
162 Ridge Rd.
Madison, Ct. 06443
203-245-7311

American Foundation for the Blind
15 West 16th St.
New York, N.Y. 10011
212-924-2219

American Printing House for the Blind
1839 Frankfort Ave.
P.O. Box 6085
Louisville, Ky. 40206

Captioned Films & Telecommuni-
cations Branch
Division of Media Services
Bureau of Education for the
Handicapped
U.S. Office of Education
Dept. of HEW
Washington, D.C.

Childcraft Education Corp.
Special Education Division
20 Kilmer Rd., Dept. SCT 6
Edison, N.J. 08817
800-631-5652

Developmental Learning Materials
7440 Natchez Ave.
Niles, Ill. 60648

Dick Blick
P.O. Box 1267
Galesburg, Il. 61401
800-447-8192

Division for the Blind and
Physically Handicapped
The Library of Congress
Washington, D.C. 20542

Educational Teaching Aids
159 W. Kinzie St.
Chicago, Il. 60610
312-644-9438

Fred Sammons, Inc.
Box 32
Brookfield, Il. 60513

Ideal School Supply
11000 South Lavergne Avenue
Oak Lawn, Il. 60453

J. A. Preston Corp.
71 Fifth Ave.
New York, N.Y. 10003
800-221-2425

Kaplan School Supply Corp.
600 Jonestown Rd.
Winston-Salem, N.C. 27103

Modern Education Corp.
P.O. Box 721
Tulsa, Ok. 74101

National Audio Visual Center
National Archives and Records
Service
General Services Administration
Order Section DA
Washington, D.C. 20409
301-763-1896

R. R. Bowker Publishing Co.
Large Type Books
1180 Sixth Ave.
New York, N.Y. 10036

Telesensory Systems, Inc. (Optacon)
1889 Page Mill Rd.
Palo Alto, Ca. 94304

Zaner Bloser
612 North Park St.
Columbus, Oh. 43215
614-221-5851

REFERENCES

Aids and appliances for the Blind and Visually Impaired. 1976–1977. American Foundation for the Blind, New York.

Brill, R. G. 1975. Mainstreaming: Format or quality. Am. Ann. Deaf 120(4): 377–381.

Finney, N. R. 1975. Handling the Young Cerebral Palsied Child at Home. E. P. Dutton Co., New York.

Gearheart, B. R., and Weishahn, M. W. 1976. The Handicapped Child in the Regular Classroom. The C. V. Mosby Company, St. Louis.

Hardy, R. E., and Cull, J. G. 1974. Severe Disabilities: Social and Rehabilitation Approaches. Charles C Thomas Publisher, Springfield, Il.

Kirk, S. A. 1972. Educating Exceptional Children. Houghton Mifflin Company, Boston.

Norwood, M. J. 1976. Captioned films for the deaf. Except. Child. 43(3): 164–166.

Peterson, R. M., and Cleveland, J. O. 1975. Medical Problems in the Classroom: An Educator's Guide. Charles C Thomas Publisher, Springfield, Il.

Rehabilitation Engineering Center. 1974–1976. Activities report. Unpublished manuscript, University of Tennessee, Memphis.

Rose, C. 1965. Helping the hearing impaired child in regular classes. Unpublished manuscript. Vancouver, B. C., Canada.

Vanderheiden, G. C., and Grilley, K. 1975. Non-Vocal Communication Techniques and Aids for the Severely Physically Handicapped. University Park Press, Baltimore.

Vicker, B. 1974. Nonoral Communication System Project, 1964–1973. Campus Stores Publishers, Iowa City.

11

Supplementary Media Resources

Patricia L. Walls, H. Lyndall Rich, Ph.D.,
and Dana P. Quertermous

A review of the literature in both general and special education over the past decade leaves little doubt that increased sophistication in the use of technology and media by teachers will be imperative if we are to meet the needs of special children in mainstream educational programs (Lance, 1977; Norris, 1977; Withrow and Nygren, 1976). Faced with diverse performance levels, learning modalities, and problem areas, the time required to plan and implement appropriate individualized instruction will be quickly exhausted unless teachers exploit available resources—and much is now available. Even a cursory inspection of commercial catalogs can introduce the reader to an amazing array of media materials, ranging from an enormous selection of records, cassettes, films, and videotapes to a variety of sophisticated educational multimedia systems. This is matched by advances in such areas as educational television and the use of computers in instruction.

Despite the need for innovation in the classroom and the proliferation of commercially available media materials, little has actually been done to bring the two together. The field of education has indisputably lagged far behind other professions in embracing modern technology, leaving a wide gap between what we know about and what we actually employ in daily instructional programs.

Why the educational community has been unwilling or unable to insist that modern technology be made available to our teachers and students is not entirely clear. Several reasons, however, are suggested in a cogent article by Lance (1977). First, he points out that education, as an institution, is basically conservative. Very much in the public view, educators shy away from anything new or controversial. When in doubt, traditionally "tried and true" approaches are always favored. Second, Lance believes that educators fear the disruptive effects that proposed technological innovations may have. Although some are concerned over a diminution of the quality of their personal interaction with students, others actually perceive technology as a threat to their job. The third reason noted is the high cost of innovation. Faced with fixed resources and escalating cost, state and local administrators typically spend very little on new materials. Finally, Lance notes that strategies designed to disseminate knowledge of innovations and to encourage their use have got to be adequately developed.

There is obviously much apprehension surrounding the employment of technological innovations in the classroom. At the same time there are major fiscal problems that militate against the maximum use of such instructional tools. Nevertheless, much can and is being done today by teachers all over the country. Emphasizing media materials and systems that are relatively inexpensive and "within bounds" for most teachers, this chapter identifies some of the more common items or programs currently used.

To assist the teacher is using these and any other media materials, the following guidelines are suggested:

1. Early in the school year locate all media (equipment and materials) available in the building or on a loan basis.
2. Examine media and make lists of every possible use for each piece of equipment. Learn how to operate everything.
3. For any teaching objective, use the medium that will most effectively enable the learner to accomplish that objective. Remember, there are times when the chalkboard is better than a technicolor movie!
4. Always give the student a purpose for using any media in a lesson. Direct his attention to the specific objective for listening or looking.
5. Always plan a follow-up to any use of media. Determine how effective the medium was in accomplishing the lesson's objective.
6. Make use of student and adult aides for routinely gathering and setting up media.

PROJECTED VISUAL MEDIA RESOURCES

Visual media resources are materials that stimulate the eye. They may be projected or nonprojected. Examples of nonprojected visual media include charts, graphs, maps, pictures, posters, etc. Projected visual media include transparent, translucent, and even opaque materials magnified onto a screen by means of a motion picture projector, a filmstrip projector, or an opaque projector. Television and videotape recordings are also projected visual media.

These media make use of visual learning, which is a strong learning modality for many students. A picture of a zebra may indeed be worth more to a student than a thousand-word description. Adults acquire 80% of their information visually, and some 30% of children can learn better visually than verbally (Burbank, 1976).

Use of visual resources is consistent with Piaget's sequence of learning (Bigge, 1976). The exceptional child will need many experiences at the pictorial (iconic) level for successful concept learning. Although a "normal" child may quickly grasp concepts presented at the abstract level (he hears two plus two and can mentally "see" or determine four), the special child will need a number of presentations of the concept at both the manipulative and pictorial levels before success can be expected at the abstract level. He needs to see and combine two blocks with two blocks, two toys with two toys, etc. As he progresses to the pictorial level, he needs many visual representations of the concrete objects with which he has worked. Filmstrips, slides, and transparencies are effective additions to the usual workbook page. Many educational television programs also provide vivid, imaginative pictures of the concepts the child is learning.

Television

Television is one of the most widely used visual media in schools today. National Educational Televison (NET) presents series such as *Sesame Street* and *The Electric Company,* as well as many excellent films that supplement all areas and levels of learning. Local educational stations and cable television often present educational series written and produced for and by the local school system. In such cases, teaching guides are provided by the school. Teaching guides and supplemental materials for NET series may be available in the school library. If not, the educational TV channel can be contacted for sources of guides.

Television is also one of the most ill-used media resources, largely because the teacher fails to prepare the students for the viewing experience. He must first familiarize himself with the content of the program in order to prepare the students with a suitable lead-in for what they are about to see. The students should have a reason for watching, and must know in advance what they are to look for. A follow-up discussion or an activity incorporating the program subject matter is also essential to fully benefit from the viewing experience.

By familiarizing himself with the content of a program before it is seen by the students, the teacher not only can give them a purpose for viewing but also might use only those segments of the TV program applicable to his objectives. If videotaping equipment is available, segments of programs may be recorded for later use with individuals or small groups of children. Videotaping may also solve scheduling problems. If a mathematics program is aired only during the middle of language arts, it could be videotaped and shown at a more appropriate time.

Regular television programming may be a stimulus for many activities. Cartoons, plays, newscasts, and even some soap operas may be used as starting points for discussions, lessons on current events, listening activities (listen for all nouns, listen for all commands, etc.), and other assignments. Again, it is important to remember that teachers must be familiar with program content in order to prepare suitable objectives and activities that will give students a purpose for their viewing.

Although usually used in large group instruction, television may be successfully viewed by a small group or even by an individual. By using earphones and arranging the television in a corner of the room, one or more students may view programs without disturbing the rest of the class. Other physical arrangements to consider in television viewing are seating, volume, lighting, and an appropriate work space, such as a desk or table top, if the student will be required to write. The physical environment as well as the quality of the television reception will greatly affect student concentration and resultant learning.

Teachers may also benefit professionally from viewing educational TV programs. Many approaches and materials used on television may be used effectively within the classroom. Even certain aspects of a television teacher's style may be emulated by the classroom teacher for more effective communication.

Videotape Recording (VTR)

Videotape equipment is almost as accessible to public school teachers as television and it provides an infinite variety of uses to the classroom. By being portable and simple to use, it attracts many teachers who otherwise would not use "mechanical" audiovisual media. The equipment consists of a videotape recorder and a television monitor. A camera and microphone are added to this when original tapes are made by the teacher. The videotape recorder can be reel-to-reel or cassette, and all of the equipment is available as a "porta-pak," smaller and lighter weight than the standard unit.

The VTR serves two basic functions: playback of tapes already recorded, and filming and recording tapes for future use. Most teachers enjoy using the playback function because the process is similar to using a tape recorder, with the additional benefit of watching on a televison screen what is being heard from the tape. The tape is placed on the videotape recorder, the television monitor is turned on to a specified channel, and the viewer simply watches what would seem to be a televison program. These tapes are available commercially, through the public schools, at libraries, and by recording them oneself. Topics range from supplemental interest-generating documentaries to comprehensive, sequenced tapes designed to teach basic skills.

The classroom teacher can make videotapes to generate her own instructional materials or to allow for a more creative teaching approach. Events such as guest speakers, student plays, and training in oratory and debate would be natural subjects for filming. With experience, even students can be delegated the responsibilities of filming—the process is a simple one. The camera and microphone are plugged into the videotape recorder, which is turned on to "record," and then the student just focuses the camera. Many teachers have also used the recording feature of the VTR to assist them in critiquing student teachers, and even themselves. By watching a videotape of a teacher presentation, it is sometimes easier to see ways to improve teaching skills and thereby assist the students' learning potential.

If VTR equipment is not available in the school system, it may be borrowed from a Video Access Center at little or no charge. These centers are located at some educational institutions, public libraries, and cable television companies. Harwood (1974) is a source of information on all aspects of videotape recording.

Motion Pictures

A school system usually acquires commercially prepared educational motion picture films as the budget permits. These and other AV materials can then be checked out by the classroom teacher. Because the teachers of any grade in the system will usually all be teaching the same unit at approximately the same time of the school year, a film is seldom available at the appropriate time for its use. Unfortunately, therefore, teachers too often show whatever films are available whenever available. Although the students may welcome this as a break in the daily routine, it is not appropriate use of the teaching medium. As with other AV media, students should be prepared for the learning experience. The film should be used only if it is appropriate for the immediate objectives.

One of the best ways for a teacher to prepare for classroom viewing of a film is to preview it with one or two students. These students might look for new words or difficult concepts. After previewing the film, a follow-up activity should be planned. It might take the form of a project or an experiment suggested in the film, or it might be a spin-off activity based on some idea set forth by the film. A good plan may be to repeat the showing of the film or a portion of the film on later occasions. Students can be instructed to look for new ideas or to compare their first reaction to certain aspects of the film with their current reactions. It is often beneficial to stop a film and review points covered, or set the stage for upcoming ideas. The break in showing the film might serve to redirect students' thoughts and attention to appropriate stimuli.

Films may be used to evaluate students' abilities to apply what they have learned. In viewing a movie of a science experiment, for example, the teacher could turn off the sound at a critical point, and then a student explain what is happening and why it is happening. Similarly, students can be asked to write solutions to a dilemma in a movie dealing with a social problem when the film is stopped before the resolution of the problem. A dramatic film can be stopped short of an ending and students can be asked to create their own conclusions.

It is also possible for students to actually make their own films for classroom use. Without expending a great deal of time or money, students' plays, projects, and special activities can be filmed. Students can then see the result of their cumulative efforts. Making original movies is an excellent way to involve pupils in a whole new creative learning experience.

Another area where motion pictures can be used successfully is for independent study. A student can view a film in a carrel and then complete a worksheet, carry on an experiment or project, or give a report to the class. It is possible for students to view movies just as they would read a book for pleasure. An individual might review a film, previously seen by the entire class, in order to give special attention to the topics covered or skills taught.

Filmstrips

For several reasons, teachers often prefer to use filmstrips rather than movies or videotapes. The equipment used in projection is lighter and easier to use. Filmstrips allow closer control on the part of the teacher or student and are more amenable to individual or small group use. They are relatively inexpensive, and consequently many titles are usually available within a school. Small projectors may be used for individual or small group study, or classroom models may be used to project the filmstrip so that an entire class can view it at one time. Because the frames of a filmstrip are numbered, it is easy to locate and use only those sections appropriate to the teacher's objective. Time spent viewing each frame is under complete control of the teacher or student, and it is easy to review frames if key ideas have been missed. The teacher may provide her own narration for a filmstrip, or narration may be taped if the filmstrip is going to be used a number of times. Many commercially prepared filmstrips are accompanied by cassette recordings.

Possible adaptations for using filmstrips include using a hand manipulated card to provide flash exposures. The sequence of frames may also be varied by covering the lens, counting the appropriate number of clicks forward or backward, and then exposing the next frame to be viewed. Attention can be drawn to specific details on the screen by using a flashlight pointer.

A filmstrip can also be used as a lead-in activity to a movie. The action of a movie is so fast that slow students may have trouble following the concept. If a filmstrip has been used to preteach vocabulary and major concepts, these children may be better prepared to follow the fast-moving motion picture.

Slides

Slides are simply film transparencies made from 35-mm film that have been mounted in 2'' by 2'' holders. A slide projector may be used to show slides individually or to show a slide cartridge containing a number of slides. Some filmstrip projectors are equipped with an adaptor to show slides. Because slides are relatively easy to make and use, teachers find numerous ways to incorporate them into their instruction.

As suggested in the section on motion pictures, all phases of a class project (such as a play) can be photographed using slide film. By viewing a slide presentation of the entire project, students can see the benefits of working in a group and the comprehensive nature of meshing everyone's work into the final production, as well as feel a sense of accomplishment in a job well done.

Other events at school—special displays, bulletin boards, or special projects—may be photographed and viewed at times when the content of the display is being studied by the class. Slides of community or city landmarks provide a personal note for a social studies lesson. Pictures of works of art, famous people and places, and detailed drawings can also be photographed and made into slides. A stand that holds the camera at the appropriate height above the open book for this slide photography can be purchased or constructed.

Slides brought from home by students can provide valuable resources for teaching units about the family, personal health and growth, and even geography and social studies. The vast differences, as well as similarities, of family units can be illustrated with family slides. Slides of one student taken over a number of years, perhaps since birth, give students a meaningful look at personal growth.

One special presentation technique to add variety and interest is the twin-screen slide presentation (Brown, Lewis, and Harcleroad, 1977). A twin-screen slide presentation involves projecting two pictures at a time on a single large screen or on two screens arranged side by side. Examples of uses of this method include presentation of opposites (young person on one screen, old person on the other), medium-range shots and close-up views of certain subjects, and a map on one side and a photographic view of the area on the other side.

Another presentation technique is to show certain slides out of focus. Students look for designs and shapes as they might in a scribble drawing. They can make guesses as to what the slide really will be (Ray, 1971).

To be interesting and enjoyable, slide presentations must be prepared for in advance. Mark slides in the upper right hand corner to show the proper position for inserting the slide into the tray or projector. This will help avoid the common mistake that results in an inverted picture. During the show, slides should generally be changed about every 25 seconds, but this time may vary according to the age of the viewers and the subject matter of the slides. If possible, the teacher should stay by the screen so that the students will not have to shift their attention from picture to speaker. A helper or remote control can be used for changing slides.

Overhead Projector

An overhead projector focuses a bright light source through translucent material to project that material on a nearby screen. The projected image is bright enough for viewing in a lighted room. The transparencies used with the projector are made on clear or tinted acetate or plastic and are usually 8 1/2 by 11″. Commercially prepared transparencies are available on many topics, but teachers can make their own transparencies by writing or drawing with special pencils or Magic Markers on sheets of acetate. It is also possible to use a heat process in making more permanent transparencies. The transparencies may be filed and kept for future use.

One of the advantages of the overhead projector is that the person making a presentation can continue to face the class while using it. Thus, the teacher can be aware of students' needs for more information or further explanation. Another advantage of overhead projection is that pictures, diagrams, outlines, or maps can be prepared on a transparency and enlarged in projection so that even visually impaired students can see the information. The teacher can add action to the projected image by pointing for emphasis or overlaying more information. An overlay is a second or third sheet of acetate that contains extra information and is laid directly on top of the first transparency, therefore complementing material that has already been projected.

Opaque Projector

The opaque projector is one of the easiest pieces of equipment to operate, because it requires only placing the material to be projected into the machine, turning on a bright light, and focusing a lens. It is a large bulky machine, but it will accommodate any flat paper up to 8 1/2 by 11'' as well as slender books or magazines, small three-dimensional objects such as coins, leaves, and seeds, or Petri dishes with cultures. The picture, chart, or three-dimensional object is then instantly accessible to all the students for close observation. This saves a great deal of time that would otherwise be necessary for the duplication of printed materials or making slides or transparencies.

By projecting a student's work (perhaps a poem or a drawing) so that the entire class views it at once, discussions, revisions, and interpretations are facilitated. Any unusual art treasure of which only one copy is available can be projected and discussed by the group before the students individually examine it for predetermined specific points.

AUDIO MEDIA RESOURCES

Audio media make use of the sensory modality of hearing. Research reports that the adult on the average spends 70% of his working time in verbal communication, with 45% of that time in listening (Brown, Lewis, and Harcleroad, 1977). It is certainly advantageous for teachers to make use of media resources that will train students in such a vital skill as listening.

The audio media typically used in a classroom include the radio, phonograph, and tape recorder. Radio has enjoyed only a limited use in classrooms in the past. Currently, however, with the increase in the number of radio stations licensed for educational purposes, radio is becoming a more significant media resource. The phonograph (record player) uses disc recordings (records) and is a popular piece of equipment because of its low cost and ease of use. Records are available on a multitude of topics so that the phonograph is useful for virtually any age or any subject. The tape recorder may use cassette tape recordings or reel-to-reel tape recordings. A special type of tape recorder uses recorded cards, put on a track one at a time.

Audio media are relatively inexpensive and generally easy to use. Many classrooms have their own phonographs and some have their own tape recorders. This eliminates the problem of access to the equipment. The materials (records and tapes) used with this equipment are also relatively inexpensive and are easy to use and store. Tapes may be recorded, erased, and recorded again. Phonographs and tape recorders can be used with headphones so that a number of individual lessons as well as small group instruction may be going on simultaneously in a classroom.

In general, audio resources are well liked by students and are motivating as a means of instruction. Many students are able to operate this equipment and enjoy doing so. They look forward to lessons in which audio equipment will be used. A formerly out-of-print publication, *Auditory Learning Materials for Special Education,* is now available from ERIC Document Reproduction Service (1977), and is an excellent source of information on audio media.

Radio

Use of the radio as an educational tool has returned to popularity in the past few years. School-owned and nonprofit stations make use of program materials distributed through the National Association of Educational Broadcasters (NAEB) and National Public Radio (NPR). Educational radio broadcasting has been especially used by remote, isolated schools. Scheduling has been a problem in the past, but programs aired at inconvenient times are now often tape recorded and replayed at a more appropriate time.

A more effective result of classroom radio is that it promotes the use of imagination by the student (Klasek, 1972). Radio can present the most up-to-date, live happenings, as well as recreating events from other times and places, thus conveying an emotional impact to the student.

Another of the radio's more frequent uses is in music appreciation. Introductory activities, such as a study of the historical era in which the composer lived, the life of the composer, the instruments used, etc. would be lead-ins to listening to a performance of classical music. The same type of activities could be planned around a comparative study of rock music or jazz.

As has been mentioned with visual media, it is most important that students be given purposes for radio listening. The teacher can usually rely on a guide or advance announcement to provide an overview of the program. Special vocabulary or new concepts should be presented in advance. As with all other uses of media, follow-up activities should be planned after the broadcast.

Phonograph

Many classrooms today are equipped with a phonograph, especially at the primary level. The records are inexpensive, easy to store and use, and are available on nearly every subject and at all levels. Teachers have long used phonographs for music, drama (especially at holidays), and for supplementary information in the curricula areas of science and social studies.

A record player and headphones can be placed in a corner of the classroom to provide a listening center for the individual student to do drill work, or for supplementary enrichment activities. Mathematics facts, phonics drills, and specialized activities such as following directions are available on records for use by the child needing extra work on the specific topic.

There are a number of common classroom activities that incorporate records. For instance, it is possible to order records that provide supplementary activities for use after viewing *Sesame Street* and *Mr. Roger's Neighborhood* television programs. Teachers often play records during physical education activities that present background rhythms and cadence counts for calisthenics. Creative dance and movement exploration and mood painting and drawing are artistic activities that depend on recorded music.

Affective education is the subject of many records now available. Situations involving feelings are presented in dialogue form. Students give their reactions to solutions presented on the record or they may give their own solution to the conflict. With this wide variety of functions, it is not surprising that the phonograph is one of the most frequently used pieces of media equipment in the classroom.

Tape Recorder

The tape recorder is a versatile example of audio media. It is simple to operate and tapes are easily cataloged and stored. The tape cartridge and the cassette have added even more simplicity to the use of the tape recorder and have gained substantial popularity. The magnetic tape used with a tape recorder is an acetate or plastic ribbon coated on one side (the shiny side) with iron oxide particles. Tapes vary according to reel size, thickness, number of tracks, and speed. Generally the faster the tape speed, the better the quality of the recording. Tapes may be used again and again and a new recording can even be made over an old one.

AV resources such as the tape recorder are important teacher aids for repetitive activities. These repetitive activities are time-consuming for the teacher, but are necessary for some forms of learning. However, in areas of curriculum with much repetition, about 90% of teacher/pupil interaction has been found to be either negative or neutral (Hofmeister, 1972). By using tapes for mathematics facts drill or other drill work, the teacher not only frees his time for other activities but also eliminates possible negative interactions with the student.

Information that the teacher anticipates having to repeat may be tape recorded and used again and again. Students who are unable to keep up with the class may work at their own pace by using the tape recorder. The teacher can prepare tapes of spelling words, auditory training activities, arithmetic facts, and so forth. A permanent file of mathematics drill tapes is invaluable to the teacher. Weights and measures, the metric system, multiplication tables, and any other aspect of math can be placed on tape, and worksheets can be prepared to provide a sequential drill experience. Similar provision can be made for work in phonics instruction. The student uses the tape, which should include feedback, to practice his words or sounds until he feels he is proficient. After teaching evaluation, he proceeds to the next tape or continues drill at the same level, whichever is indicated.

An important skill that should be taught but is often neglected is that of following directions. Teacher-made tapes are invaluable for providing practice in this area. The directions may involve use of paper and pencil (make an "x" in the bottom right-hand corner of your paper), physical movement (stand up, turn and face the window), or more complicated and lengthy instructions for activities correlated with textbook assignments.

Tapes of chapters for social studies, science, or other texts can be made by the teacher or by students with superior oral reading skills. These tapes can then be used to accompany textbook assignments by students who read poorly. Condensations of chapters can be taped for review purposes. The student may be directed to locate key sentences in the textbook, carry out certain activities using maps and charts, find definitions for words, and so forth.

"Simultaneous oral reading," in which the student reads along with the teacher or others, is a remedial reading technique. The teacher can prepare tapes of stories, at appropriate reading levels, to be used in a variation of this remedial method. Hoskisson and Krohm (1974) described a program that involved "reading by immersion," implemented by using a tape recorder and listening posts. Stories on or just above the students' reading levels were taped. Each child had a copy of the story, and pronounced the words aloud or to himself while listening to the taped story. Teachers involved in the study reported the procedure to be very beneficial. Schneeberg (1977) also suggests that students listen to the tape of a story or play while following in their books, using a paper marker or finger as a pointer to ensure matching of the heard and the printed word. The reader is directed to Sciara and Walter (1973) for additional reading activities involving the use of the tape recorder.

The cassette recorder is probably the most versatile of the audio media. The tapes themselves are easy to handle and the relatively small cost of the tapes and the recorder make them accessible to much of the population. This factor increases the scope of activities that can be planned with cassette tapes. For example, class discussions may be taped and then evaluated by class members. Lessons can be taped for absent students. Directions or narration for filmstrips or slides can be taped and used whenever needed. Students in vocational subjects can tape interviews and analyze the skills used or needed. Tapes can even be made and exchanged with classes in other states or countries. This modern version of "pen pals" is motivating and is also an excellent learning experience. Much thought and planning should go into deciding what information to include on the tape.

COMPLEX MEDIA SYSTEMS

Traditionally, complex media such as teaching machines have presented programmed materials with the purpose of achieving specific educational goals. Information is presented in frames of visual material usually stored on discs, tapes, or cards. In most cases, commercial programs must be used with teaching machines, because writing programs becomes extremely time consuming for the classroom teacher. These programs are designed to allow the student to move at his own pace, respond to individual steps of instruction, and receive immediate feedback with regard to correctness or incorrectness of the response. The threat of stress and strain that usually occurs as he tries to retain the pace established by other students is removed.

Language Master, System 80, Classmate 88, and Programmed Assistance to Learning (PAL) are representative of the complex systems available to today's teacher. Prices are within a range affordable to most school systems. The following descriptions, which summarize each program, have been adapted from brochures published by the individual companies.

The Language Master System, by Bell and Howell, involves the child in the learning process through the senses of sight, speech, touch, and hearing. The system includes compact portable units that are simple to use yet durable, and that provide complete, self-contained dual-track recording and playback capabilities. The units are used with sets of cards containing visual material and a strip of dual-track magnetic recording tape. One of the recording tracks on the tape is prerecorded and serves as an instructor, and the second track is used for recording the student response. To use the Language Master Unit, the student inserts a card in the machine, watches and listens, then records his response and compares his response with the information on the instructor track for immediate feedback.

In addition to the commercially prepared programs, the teacher or even the students can create cards to meet specific needs. An activity booklet, *Mastering Language* (1974), available through any Bell and Howell representative, is designed to help the teacher in preparing programs or individual cards to provide for personalization of instruction.

Borg-Wagner's System 80 is a diagnostic and prescriptive audiovisual learning system developed by Dr. Donald Durrell, Dr. Lola May, and Dr. William LaPlante. The system offers over 800 individual lessons in 15 curricular areas such as letter sounds, structural analysis skills, spelling skills, fractions, decimals, time, and metric measurement. These lessons are programmed on units that are inserted into the System 80 machine. This simultaneously screens the lesson and gives verbal directions to the student, who pushes a button to indicate the correct response at each successive level.

Before a child takes the pretest for a curriculum area, a pressure-sensitive test tab is attached to the answering unit. As the child proceeds through the test lesson, a hole is punched in the paper test tab for each incorrect response. When the machine-scored pretest is placed over the prescription key, the punched holes indicate lessons the child needs in order to remediate deficiencies. The teacher then circles the prescribed teaching and review lessons on the child's record card. The student continues through his individualized lesson at his own pace while the teacher carries on with regular instruction. By placing the machine-scored posttest over the prescription key, the teacher can immediately measure the child's progress. System 80 has been successfully used to teach Vietnamese refugees in Pittsburgh schools and to instruct educationally deprived children in Palm Beach County schools in Florida.

Classmate 88, produced by the Monroe Education Center, is an algebraic calculator that includes over 70 programs for drill and practice in computational skills development. The student sets his own pace as he works toward a mastery of computational skills in addition, subtraction, multiplication, division, fractions, decimals, and number concepts. Immediate reinforcement is given, which promotes a higher retention of learning skills. All programs provide automatic scoring, allowing the teacher to continuously evaluate student progress. The individual student can gain confidence as he experiences success working at his individual level without peer pressures.

Programmed Assistance to Learning (PAL) was designed for the language impaired child by the Bureau of Education for the Handicapped, The National Foundation for the Improvement of Education, the U.S. Office of Education, and the General Electric Company. Systematic, programmed instruction through filmstrips and cassettes is directed toward developing adequate figure-ground relationships, pattern analysis, object memory, color memory, sequencing, and receptive language by gradually introducing the child to language principles, concepts, and basic sentence patterns.

The Combo 8 Controlled Reader was introduced by Educational Developmental Laboratories of McGraw-Hill Book Company. The Combo 8 utilizes tachistoscopic training to foster improved reading. Stories or math materials are projected on a screen one line at a time at precisely-timed speeds of 40–800 words per minute. Students move the rate of projection ahead as their reading rate and comprehension skills improve. Exposures may be repeated as many times as necessary for slower readers. Alternatives to the Combo 8 are the Controlled Reader, Tach-X, Controlled Reader Processing Motor, and the Skill Builder, all available from Educational Developmental Laboratories. The Controlled Reader is recommended for large groups and the Junior model of Controlled Reader is designed for individual work. The machine is teacher directed at speeds of 20–130 lines per minute. The Tach-X is useful for large or small groups of students but requires the presence of the teacher to operate. Words are presented at speeds of 1/100 to 1 1/2 seconds. The Controlled Reader Processing Motor presents words at a rate of 90–900 lines per minute, and the Skill Builder has a slower projection rate of two to 18 lines per minute.

Calculators such as the Abstract Linking Electronic calculator (ABLE), available from Texas Instruments, Inc., are found in many classrooms today and provide supplemental, innovative ideas to otherwise ordinary classroom procedures. The ABLE calculator has six interchangeable snap-on keyboards or "faces" so that its capabilities can be easily adapted to the child's growing skills in mathematics. Other assets are its bright display, colorful keyboard, and color keyed "Keeping Track" charts and ballot pads for monitoring student progress. Four ABLE calculators with accompanying faces are included in each classroom unit.

Uses and Adaptations of Media Computers

Computers are used in virtually every aspect of today's society. Computer Assisted Instruction (CAI) was developed by Suppes and his associates to assist in mathematics and reading programs (Suppes and Ihrke, 1970). CAI is now used for drill and practice and tutorial teaching of new material. Eventually it will be used for dialogue, in which the computer will be able to understand the spoken language. CAI has been used in regular classrooms as well as in schools for the deaf. For instruction with the deaf, visual computer materials have produced advantages not available from more traditional teaching techniques.

In New York City, a program was initiated using CAI Dial-a-Drill arithmetic lessons for 24,000 students in their homes, using the telephone (O'Leary and O'Leary, 1972). The authors report that CAI has the unique advantage of responding to errors by immediately producing materials to remediate the error before the student is allowed to proceed further into the program. Another positive factor is that CAI efficiently uses only one computer center that is joined to many individual units throughout the country by telephone.

Another automatic teaching system, called PLATO, has been developed at the University of Illinois' Coordinated Science Laboratory. Students work at stations with an electronic keyset (similar to a typewriter keyboard), a television screen, an electronic book, and an electric blackboard. Each student may be studying a different subject or topic. In a program called "tutorial logic," the student reads a page of his electronic book—which is a number of slides in an electronic slide selector controlled by the computer. As he finishes a page, he pushes a button and continues to new material or reviews a previous page. When he begins a set of questions, he must answer them all correctly before he can proceed. If he cannot answer all questions correctly, he pushes a "help" button and the machine carries the student through a review of the material called a "help sequence." Short courses in math, computer programming, and electrical engineering have been taught recently with PLATO and the program is currently in use at Florida State University and at the University of Quebec in Canada (Norris, 1977).

It may be several years before computer systems such as PLATO are commonly found in school systems. In 1975, only 27% of schools surveyed by the American Institute for Research used computers to aid in instruction (Cunningham, 1977). It is not likely that the average classroom teacher will soon have access to a computer for classroom instruction, but there are promising possibilities for the not too distant future.

SUMMARY

Media resources are not a panacea for the special or regular classroom teacher. Nevertheless, they have many varied uses that will assist any teacher in more effectively accomplishing her teaching objectives. Teaching equipment and materials must be thoroughly examined, prepared, and used suitably in order to be beneficial to the teacher. A haphazard use of whatever equipment may be stored in the closet will be of little benefit to anyone. The teacher must take time to make supplementary media resources work for him.

Technology perhaps holds the key to the future of educating exceptional children. Computers both for managing and directing instruction, teaching machines, and videodisc technology all make contributions toward individualized education for each student. The approximately 800 special education learning resource centers that exist around the United States are beginning to close the gap between what is known about instructional media and what is being practiced.

A multiplicity of complex systems has been developed in past years; these have the potential of becoming invaluable resources for classroom teachers. Now that many of the systems are available and have proved effective in actual learning situations, monetary support from state and federal governments is critically needed. Also, a shift from emphasizing traditional curricula to stressing more innovative learner-directed systems will be required of teacher-training programs.

The requirements of Public Law 94-142 demand that special educators provide any services necessary to meet the needs of exceptional learners. These needs cannot be met with a few textbooks and a ditto machine. In fact, the requirements of individualizing each pupil's educational program cannot be met without the aid of technology.

PROGRAM REFERENCE LIST

Classmate 88. 1975. Monroe Educational Center, The American Road, Morris Plains, N.J. 07950.

Combo 8 Controlled Reader. Educational Developmental Laboratories, McGraw-Hill Book Company, 1221 Avenue of the Americas, New York, N.Y. 10020.

Language Master System. Developed by P. Lewis. Bell and Howell, Audio Visual Products Division, 7100 N. McCormick Road, Chicago, Il. 60645. Phone: 312-262-1600.

Programmed Assistance to Learning (PAL). Instructional Industries, Inc., Executive Park, Ballstone Lake, N.Y. 12019.

System 80. 1970. Developed by D. D. Durrell, L. J. May, and W. A. La Plante. Borg-Werner Educational Systems, 600 W. University Drive, Arlington Heights, Il. 60004. Phone: 800-323-7577 (toll free).

REFERENCES

Auditory Learning Materials for Special Education. ERIC ED 102 757. ERIC Document Reproduction Service. Arlington, Va.

Bigge, M. L. 1976. Learning Theories for Teachers. Harper and Row, New York.

Brown, J. W., Lewis, R. B., and Harcleroad, F. F. 1977. AV Instruction Technology, Media, and Methods. McGraw-Hill Book Company, New York.

Burbank, L. 1976. Visual Communication in Special Education Using Television and Manipulative Materials. ERIC Ed. 134 156. ERIC Document Reproduction Service.

Cunningham, W. G. 1977. The need for dialogue between educators and technologists. Phi Delta Kappan 58 (6): 451, 456.

Harwood, D. 1974. Everything You Always Wanted to Know About Video-Tape Recording. VTR Publishing Company, Queens, N.Y.

Hofmeister, A. 1972. Audio-Tutorial Programming with Exceptional Children. ERIC ED 114 401. ERIC Document Reproduction Service.

Hoskisson, K., and Krohm, B. 1974. Reading by immersion: Assisted reading. Elem. Eng. 51 (6): 832–836.

Klasek, C. B. 1972. Instructional Media in the Modern School. Professional Educators Publications, Lincoln, Ne.

Lance, W. D. 1977. Technology and media for exceptional learners: Looking ahead. Except. Child. 44 (4): 92–96.

Mastering Language. 1974. Audio Visual Products Division, Bell and Howell, Chicago.

Norris, W. C. 1977. Via technology to a new era in education. Phi Delta Kappan 58 (6): 451–453.

O'Leary, K. D., and O'Leary, S. G. 1972. Classroom Management: The Successful Use of Behavior Modification. Pergamon Press, New York.

Ray, H. W. 1971. Media for the exceptional child. Foc. Except. Child. 3 (6): 1–11.

Schneeberg, H. 1977. Listening while reading: A four-year study. Read. Teach. 30 (6): 629–635.

Sciara, F. J., and Walter, R. B. 1973. Reading Activities with the Tape Recorder. Instructor Handbook Series, Dansville, N.Y.

Suppes, P., and Ihrke, C. 1970. Accelerated program in elementary school mathematics: The fourth year. Psychol. Schools 3: 111–126.

Withrow, F. B., and Nygren, C. J. 1976. Language, Materials, and Curriculum Management for the Handicapped Learner. Charles E. Merrill Books, Columbus, Oh.

12

Affective Concerns in the Utilization of Instructional Materials

H. Lyndall Rich, Ph.D.

Affective education is that phase of the teaching-learning process primarily concerned with the mental health of children. Affective objectives, as opposed to cognitive and psychomotor objectives, "emphasize a feeling tone, an emotion, or a degree of acceptance or rejection" (Krathwohl, Bloom, and Masia, 1956, p. 7). Although affective needs are known to influence student performance, student success in school is generally determined by student performance on cognitive (academic) tasks. Teaching procedures reflect this concern for the development of cognitive skills through the frequent and repetitive use of impersonal, group oriented techniques such as homework, testing, and lecturing. Similarly, innovations in instructional technology, textbook design, curricular patterns, and materials promote more effective methods for learning math, reading, science, and social studies. This singular priority in education has been implemented to the relative exclusion of affective objectives. The discrepancy between cognitive and affective concerns exists because the curriculum is based on the cognitive requirements of subject matter disciplines rather than affective needs (Weinstein and Fantini, 1970).

Teachers have long known that childrens' intellects and academic performance cannot be separated from their feelings, emotions, and degree of acceptance (Wirth, 1977). Nevertheless, many teachers have been reluctant to deal with this "sacred," personal area and have chosen to ignore affective objectives. Instead, educators have assumed that students experience home, school, and community situations that adequately promote positive feelings and emotions. However, for many children, the available evidence indicates that social institutions are not promoting affective development. The increasing frequency of school truancy, classroom disruptions, academic failure, personal isolation, anger, and apathy are visible indicators that the affective component is lacking.

Without a planned, systematic approach for dealing with affective needs, educators have typically provided spontaneous affective experiences. Teachers who praise children, fail them, or express social-moral values are providing affective experiences. Unfortunately, these teaching-learning experiences tend to be a reflection of teachers' preconceived ideals and personal values, which are applied unilaterally—they are rarely used individually in light of the childrens' affective needs.

Educators can no longer assume that appropriate positive affective experiences are being provided in the home, school, and community. This deficiency is particularly relevant for teachers, because the affective domain has been seriously minimized and underrated in education, even though schools could be much more influential (Valett, 1977). The important responsibility of developing the "whole" child, cognitively and affectively, cannot be left to chance. Educators must assume greater responsibility and take a more active and positive role in the creation of educational experiences that will facilitate personal affective growth (Maurer, 1977).

The purpose of this chapter is to discuss teaching-learning factors associated with the use of cognitive materials that will facilitate positive affective development. Although materials and techniques have been developed that focus exclusively on affective objectives, affective concerns can be incorporated within the regular classroom without major changes in the teaching-learning process. Obviously, many special children have such severe intrapersonal problems that well designed affective programs are required. However, these special children are rarely enrolled in the regular classroom. Special children—even "normal" children—with mild mental health problems who are enrolled in the regular class can develop affectively with minimal adjustments in materials and teacher procedures. The combined implementation of affective procedures with cognitive materials thus reduces the need to develop a specific affective curriculum.

In order to provide appropriate affective experiences, it is essential to first recognize that the classroom environment contains a number of factors that interact to produce negative student affect; conversely, the interaction of factors can be modified to produce more positive student affect. The factors considered in this chapter are: 1) student (childrens') affective needs, 2) instructional techniques (teacher procedures and instructional materials, 3) student responses to educational experiences, and 4) cognitive-affective feedback.

The interaction of the four critical factors (Figure 1) may be portrayed by a "cycle" reflecting the sequential and interdependent relationships among the factors. The cycle may represent a positive or negative experience for the children, depending on the degree of appropriate individualization reflected in the instructional plan. In short, instructional materials and teacher techniques, based on individually assessed student affective needs, will potentially produce successful student responses. Successful student responses result in positive feedback, thus enhancing the fulfillment of affective needs. On the other hand, materials and techniques that are inconsistent with the child's affective needs will produce inappropriate or inadequate responses. Incorrect responses typically result in negative feedback, thus increasing the intensity of affective needs.

An example of the negative cycle in operation may include a child who feels inadequate in reading, but who regards himself as competent in math (*affective needs*). The teacher, pursuring a cognitive objective, gives the entire class a series of math reading problems (*inappropriate materials*). Because of a deficit in reading skills, the child does not complete any of the math problems correctly (*inadequate responses*). The child consequently receives a zero or "F" for his math performance (*negative feedback*). This failure cycle reinforces his feelings of inadequacy regarding reading and now causes the child to question his competency in math. Adjustments in the materials by differentiating math and reading skills, each consistent with the child's level of competence, could have produced a success cycle.

In order to explain the cycle more fully, the four distinct factors are discussed separately. A final chapter section is devoted to specific

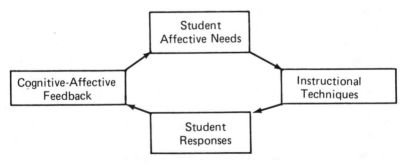

Figure 1.   The affective learning cycle.

affective materials, techniques, and programs that may be routinely used in the classroom and adapted for children with more severe psychological and/or behavioral problems.

STUDENT AFFECTIVE NEEDS

A concise statement of student affective needs is difficult to construct because of the diversity of theories and definitions that currently exist. Concepts such as ego development (Llorens and Rubin, 1967), self-concept (LaBenne and Greene, 1969), and self-control (Fagen, Long and Stevens, 1975) are typical of the affective needs expressed in the literature. Psychosocial factors such as student needs for trust, autonomy, initiative, and identity (Erikson, 1965) have been used to describe mental health crises of childhood and early adolescence. Motivational needs for safety, self-esteem, love, and belongingness (Maslow, 1965) represent affective needs considered important in the development of the human personality. Bloom (1976) regards these as affective entry characteristics that are "a complex compound of interests, attitudes, and self-views" (p.75).

In general, the variety of affective needs may be reduced to two basic concerns: positive feelings about one's self and a degree of control over one's environment. In the case of positive feelings, it is important that the student has a self-concept as a worthy and successful individual who possesses a number of "good" qualities, and who is valued by others. Control is related to exercise of choices over one's own destiny—a degree of power in making decisions that are respected. Both self-concept and self-control have a direct and causal effect on the successful use of materials and the continued affective growth of children.

Self-Concept

LaBenne and Greene (1969) define self-concept as an individual's "total appraisal of his (her) appearance, background and origins, abilities and resources, attitudes and feelings which culminate as a directing force in behavior" (p. 10). The authors additionally cite a number of research studies that report a positive relationship between self-concept and both academic performance and classroom behavior. C. M. Charles (1976) draws a similar conclusion stating that "students who think well of themselves also happen to do better in school" (p. 20). Charles further specifies that good readers have more positive self-concepts than do poor readers.

Even though the relationship between self-concept and classroom performance is well established, whether or not one causes the other is not clear. For individual special children, feelings of inadequacy, low frustration tolerance, and attitudes toward education (including teachers) have resulted in academic failure or disciplinary actions. Children with poor self-concepts, for example, may be unwilling to verbally express themselves or to read aloud for fear of failure or disapproval; they may be unable to sit for long periods, completing numerous academic tasks; and they may be unable to tolerate the constant personal control by an autocratic teacher.

Thus, in individual cases, there is reasonable evidence of a causal relationship between self-concept and academic success. However, for many children both negative self-concept and academic failure arise from a lifelong process of environmental deprivation, parental hostility or apathy, and educational programs without purpose. Even though self-concept development is a lifelong process, "this does not mean that affective needs cannot be more fully attended to throughout the years of school" (Valett, 1977, p. 23).

Materials and techniques that do not attend to self-concept will be ineffective in accomplishing the designated cognitive objectives. Materials that require more information than the child possesses, that require more work space and time than the child is provided, that require more stringent controls and limitations than the child can manage, and that require an environmental background the child has not experienced are inappropriate for the development of self-concept.

It should be understood that one of the primary functions of the human organism is to maintain consistency with one's concept of self. If a child considers himself agile, attractive, or smart, the child will engage in behaviors designed to protect and maintain those self-conceptions. Similarly, if a child feels clumsy, ugly, or dumb, behaviors will be evidenced that perpetuate those negative conceptions. The effort to maintain consistency is evidenced in behaviors that are designed to counter any threat to one's self-concept, even though such behaviors may seem to be counter-productive. Teachers who discipline a child by conveying such messages as "big boys don't act like that" or "ladies would never do such a thing" can expect a child to react in order to defend his self-concept. They may chose to return verbal abuse, become defiant, get into a fight—anything to recover the damage inflicted upon the self-concept. Children who lose peer-group stature because of academic failure may resort to similar counterproductive behaviors in order to achieve self-concept consistency.

The case of negative self-concept is accentuated for special students who do not enter their educational roles with skills or attitudes comparable to regular class students. Bloom (1977) has indicated that the "latent" or unwritten curriculum is one of competitive and personal comparisons among students. This comparative process teaches children how well they function in relation to other children in the classroom and school. If, then, the learning experiences have been relatively negative through the comparative process, the special student is apt to be academically unsuccessful, is apt to regard himself as inadequate, and is apt to develop a negative view toward learning and school. Figure 2 illustrates the systematic deterioration of self-concept as a result of unsuccessful school experiences.

The case for individualizing materials and procedures based on self-concept is an immediate affective need. It may be necessary to

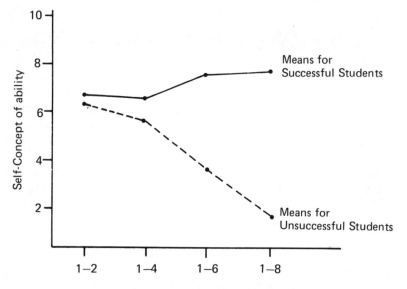

Years of successful or unsuccessful school experiences

Note: Successful students were in the upper fifth on teacher's grades, while unsuccessful students were in the lower fifth on the same criterion.

Source: B. S. Bloom, Human Characteristics and School Learning, New York: McGraw-Hill, 1976.

Figure 2. Self-concept of ability rating over years of schooling. Successful students were in the upper fifth on teacher's grades; unsuccessful students were in the lower fifth on the same criterion. Reprinted by permission from *Human Characteristics and School Learning* by B. S. Bloom. Copyright © 1976, McGraw-Hill Book Company, New York.

sacrifice some of the traditional cognitive objectives in favor of materials and procedures that enhance a student's sense of adequacy, creating a more positive self-concept.

Self-Control

An individual's ability to direct, control, or regulate his own behavior in a way that realistically meets the requirement of a given situation is evidence of self-control. Educators are aware of the great waste of student potential and the enormous amount of teacher resources and energy necessary to deal effectively with disruptive, defiant, and aggressive behaviors. These types of acting-out student behaviors are signals that students do not have the necessary self-control to function effectively in the typical classroom. This conclusion is particularly appropriate for some special children who have sensory and/or neurological impairment and, therefore, may have a distorted perception of reality.

However, there is a second side to self-control; namely, the need to determine or control one's own destiny. Rotter (1966) uses the term "internal control" to describe an individual who perceives that reinforcement is contingent upon his own behavior, and is not the "result of luck, chance, fate, as under the control of powerful others" such as the teacher (p. 2). In short, students with self-control or internal control have developed a degree of personal autonomy, identity, and independence and are not dependent, nor do they desire that others manage their lives. It is in this area that educators and children find themselves in conflict.

Fagen, Long, and Stevens (1975) have identified three "basic educational distortions" that have impeded freedom of choice and have contributed to teacher-student conflicts:

1. Externally controlled academic tasks: This particular distortion is evident when the teacher defines the nature of the task without giving consideration to the learner's needs, interests, and abilities. In effect, the teacher decides what is to be done, when and by whom without significant input from the student. . . .
2. Restrictive competition for grades and recognition: This distortion exists when the number of students receiving positive reinforcement is restricted substantially. That is, praise, acclaim, encouragement or affection are offered on a space available basis. . . .
3. Focus on narrow academic products: American education historically has concentrated on tangible signs of productivity. Thus, the classroom focus has been on the correct answer—the pertinent fact—the material outcome (pp. 31–32).

Adequate individualization of instructional materials and teaching procedures can effectively contribute to the child's needs of self-control and independence. Obviously, continuous teacher control, with specific expectations regarding both behavior and academic performance, has cast the student into a role of dependency, helplessness, and for some, frustration. Unless a child has been "beaten" into a role of submission and/or dependency, children will inevitably "test" their environment—home, school, and community—for limits to their own power and control. For example, a child who "talks back" to a teacher may be attempting to exercise a degree of control or independence over a confining and frustrating educational situation. The exercise of absolute power by the teacher, without the availability of programmatic options, is a basis for conflict.

Teacher procedures and instructional materials must be modified and adapted to accommodate reasonable expectations for self-control. The development of student independence and control can be encouraged through the use of meaningful student input, optional types of materials, and teacher control that is exercised in an amount appropriate for the individual child.

In summary, teacher procedures and instructional materials should be used with a thorough knowledge of the special child's individual affective needs. If procedures and materials are employed unilaterally and inclusively to the classroom group, some children will fail. The children will fail academically, and more importantly, they will fail affectively—feeling less adequate and less independent.

INSTRUCTIONAL TECHNIQUES

Instructional materials and teacher procedures, or instructional techniques, represent the second component of the affective learning cycle. The implication of the cycle is that the instructional techniques must be consistent with student affective needs for the maintenance of the self-concept and development of self-control. Although materials and procedures are interrelated, the separate techniques will be discussed individually in order to identify some critical features of each.

Instructional Materials

Educational or instructional materials are typically selected as a secondary vehicle to the direct instruction provided by the teacher. Consequently, most materials are used to reinforce cognitive objectives through the use of alternative stimuli (input) and/or responses (output). Although materials represent a broad array of functions and designs, the underlying affective rationale is limited to increasing student attention and motivation. Certainly with some students the affective benefits of materials are appropriate; however, the affective function tends to be of secondary concern. Thus, any affective benefits occur by chance, and not through preplanned implementation. If the affective component of materials was as well conceived as the cognitive component, then both objectives could be met simultaneously for the individual student.

Weinstein and Fantini (1970) emphasize the need for educational relevance by using materials that are affectively appropriate. Affectively appropriate educational materials are those that personally involve students in cognitive content by relating to the students' experiences and their feelings about those experiences. Experience and feelings are not synonymous with self-control and self-concept, but they are affective objectives: feelings, emotions, and acceptance.

The failure to incorporate experience and feelings is evidenced in materials about far away lands, when some children do not understand much of their own environment; materials about etiquette and manners, when some children need to survive on a day-to-day basis; and materials on the doctor, dentist, or police, when some children fear pain, darkness, and authority. For many children the materials may have relevance, but for other children the materials are outside their realm of experience, and do not deal with their feelings. This irrelevance is frequently accentuated for special children because of their environmental, physical, and/or psychological handicap or disability.

In recent years, the textbook and commercial materials industry has introduced stories, activities, and illustrations with children representing different races, religions, and socioeconomic backgrounds. Obviously, blacks, Chicanos, and other minority group children had found it difficult to identify with the typically all white case of middle-class life portrayed in the materials. Similarly, physically limited children were psychologically excluded from materials that emphasized physical strength and mobility, such as topics dealing with sports and exploring.

The list of potentially irrelevant material content is endless, but could be highly appropriate if individually utilized. A visit to grandfather's farm, an airplane ride, an adventure in the moutains or at the ocean, the wonderful world of Disneyland, and so on, may be related to the experiences and feelings of some children, but certainly not for every child in the classroom. Another example of potentially irrelevant material includes reading and comprehension stories on such topis as birthdays, including a grand party with presents, cake, and friends. Many students in the class may not have shared that experience. In fact, birthdays may have occurred during the school year with little attention, if any, to the individual student's birthday, yet the materials convey the message of importance. Certainly, doors to life beyond the students' immediate environment must be opened, but to require performance and participation and to be cognitively evaluated on irrelevant content denies the feelings and experiences of the children.

The choice of materials must also consider the input-output modalities in light of both the student's knowledge and feelings and the student's cognitive style. For example, students from lower socioeconomic environments, whose language experience is "restrictive" rather than "expressive," tend to perform poorly on materials that require verbal output. Similarly, deficient reading skills among many exceptional children tend to limit their interest and understanding of materials that rely heavily on written words. Therefore, poor performance may result from the negative affective feelings associated with cognitive materials that emphasize or utilize student weaknesses rather than strengths. The poor performance will be accentuated if the subject of the material is outside the realm of the learner's experience.

The physical requirements of both the classroom and the materials must also be evaluted. Individual students have different skills and require varying degrees of time and space to complete activities. Whereas some children function adequately with their individual desks, other children require larger, less encumbered areas. Whereas some children have excellent motor coordination and can complete physically intricate tasks, other children have extreme difficulty drawing a line, circling an answer, or coloring a figure. Whereas some children can see the chalkboard and hear the teacher, other children need additional visual and verbal information.

In the above examples, children may be able to sort shapes into the appropriate stack, but they continue to get knocked from the desk; children may know that "George" goes with "Washington," but cannot draw the connecting line; and children may know that two plus two equals four, but cannot see the problem on the board. In short, materials may be inappropriate because of environmental limitations. Such limitations create frustration, disinterest, and, ultimately, cognitive failure, resulting in a less adequate self-concept and less self-control.

Teachers are aware of the cognitive objectives of materials, but they are less aware of the affective and environmental effects. Knowledge of the individual student is a prerequisite to the introduction of materials. The choice of materials should consider both affective and cognitive objectives. Affectively the materials should relate to the feelings, experience, and cognitive style of the students by utilizing strengths and interests that are appropriate for the individual.

Teacher Procedures

In addition to the instruction materials themselves, the methods and techniques used by teachers in the employment of materials are of critical importance. "Whether planned or unplanned, the influence of the school or, more specifically, the teachers, has a great deal to do with developing student self-concept (and self-control)" (LaBenne and Greene, 1969, p. 27). This general notion that teachers have the power to establish the emotional atmosphere within the classroom is well documented (Flanders, 1965; Geer, 1968; Withall and Lewis, 1963). The specific teacher procedures most appropriate for developing student affect are influenced by the personal characteristics of the teacher and teaching style.

The personal characteristics of the teacher, rather than knowledge of subject matter, are critical to affective growth in the teaching-learning process (Hamachek, 1969). Teachers, like students, have affective needs that are reflected in their classroom behavior. Although numerous personal or personality characteristics are evident among teachers, a positive self-concept, sensitivity, and flexibility, in particular, contribute significantly to student affective growth.

It has been demonstrated that teachers with positive self-concepts have more positive views of others (students, administrators, parents, and fellow teachers) and are optimistic regarding the success of others. The implications of teacher self-concept are pervasive in terms of classroom interaction and promoting student affective development. Rather than expecting failure and observing inappropriate behavior, teachers with positive self-concepts expect success and observe appropriate behavior. In short, they highlight accomplishments both academically and behaviorally.

Sensitivity, or perceptiveness and empathy, are important for a teacher to accurately identify and predict how a student will feel and what the student will do within the classroom (Smith, 1966). Teachers with high levels of accurate sensitivity are "person oriented," honest with themselves, and are motivated to understand their students. A sensitive teacher can recognize subtle cues, either in terms of body language or verbal communication, to know that a student has positive or negative affect regarding classroom activities, including the use of materials. Kounin (1967) uses the term "withitness" to convey a similar concept: i.e., the teacher's awareness of the total classroom and the ability to identify children who are not responding adequately to the instruction or materials and, consequently, provide appropriate intervention.

The personal freedom, or flexibility, to pursue options and alternatives in the teaching process has direct implications for the use of materials. Many teachers doggedly move through an activity to accomplish specified objectives at the expense of losing the student, cognitively and affectively, along the way. Flexible teachers recognize that more than one activity or set of materials may be appropriate for accomplishing an objective, and provide secondary resources. Flexibility in teaching style is also relevant to student affective development; whereas some students require freedom in the pursuit of objectives, others need direction and structure. However, such flexibility is not spontaneous but planned, based on the affective needs of the student.

Teacher self-concept, sensitivity, and flexibility are personal characteristics that are considered prerequisites to the appropriate use of materials for the accomplishment of both cognitive and affective objectives. Obviously, the list is only partial; however, they are considered priority teacher characteristics for the development of student affective growth. Specifically, the characteristics indicate the capacity and willingness to adapt teaching procedures, including materials, to the cognitive and affective needs of the individual student.

The characteristic manner in which the teacher fulfills the ascribed classroom leadership role in an educational environment is called a teaching style. The construct traditionally used to describe teaching style has been ascribed to a continuum of teacher-centered to child-centered behaviors. In the final analysis, this teaching style dimension can be described as representing an external-internal control continuum. Although the descriptive terms may vary (e.g., authoritarian-democratic, direct-indirect, or controlled-reflective), the critical factor is the exercise of power by the teacher. "In essence, the . . . continuum involves the extent to which the teacher makes decisions for the child" (Kauffman and Lewis, 1974, p. 281). Terms such as "direct," "dominant," and "authoritarian" styles are reported to be characteristic of external control style, in which the interaction and objectives are more inclusively regulated by the teacher. "Indirect," "reflective," and "democratic" styles have been associated with internal control style in which students assume intrapersonal regulation of their own behavior. Thus, internal teaching styles are characterized by a limited exercise of teacher control, which encourages student interaction and the exercise of personal responsibility.

The controversy over the desirability and efficacy of external-internal styles has been the subject of educational research and literature for several decades. For example, Bills (1956) states that the idea of self-discovered learning (internal) is as effective as traditional procedures (external) in the learning of course content, and more effective in achieving personal adjustment. However, George Stern (1962), in a review of studies dealing with learning environments, found that only one research report actually demonstrated that internal oriented style resulted in significantly greater mastery of subject matter. More recently, Bennett (1976) concluded that formal or traditional teacher methods (external style) demonstrated superiority over informal styles (internal) in student acquisition of academic skills.

Flanders (1965), in his analysis of teacher influence, emphasized the differential effects of direct (external) and indirect (internal) teacher styles. Direct styles, characterized by lecturing, directing, and criticizing, are typical of external control behavior; indirect styles, characterized by encouragement, building on student ideas, and responding to feelings, are typical of an internal style orientation. When the educational goals are unclear to students, direct styles tend to increase student dependence and indirect styles stimulate student expression. If educational goals are clear, then the student's positive or negative evaluation of the goals tends to be more influential than teacher style.

Anderson (1959), in "A Resume of the Authoritarian—Democratic Studies," concluded that democratic or internal style is associated with higher morale and affective development, and the authoritarian or external style tends to be more effective with low-level task-oriented objectives. McKeachie (1962) reached a similar conclusion—students achieved higher scores on cognitive examinations when instructed by external style teachers, but internal style teachers were associated with more positive personal adjustment on the part of students.

Obviously, a singular internal-external construct grossly oversimplifies a complex dimension of teacher behavior. Nonetheless, the construct does permit a number of generalizations regarding special children, instructional materials, and affective development. The generalizations assumed from the literature and research include a "match" between educational objectives and teaching style.

The nature of the objectives to be achieved by the student are directly related to both instructional materials and teaching style.

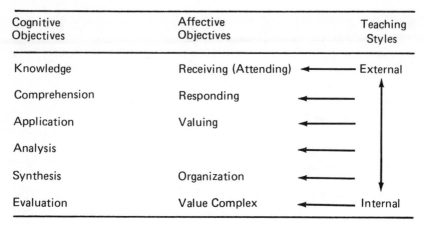

Cognitive Objectives	Affective Objectives	Teaching Styles
Knowledge	Receiving (Attending)	External
Comprehension	Responding	
Application	Valuing	
Analysis		
Synthesis	Organization	
Evaluation	Value Complex	Internal

Figure 3.   Major classes of educational objectives and teaching styles.

Educational objectives, such as those constructed by Bloom (1956) and Krathwohl, Bloom, and Masia (1956), have been presented in the form of taxonomies or a hierarchy of educational outcomes. In the main, the two taxonomies identify major classes of educational outcomes that form a cumulative hierarchy for simple, concrete objectives to complex, abstract objectives (Figure 3). Student affective development is related to the degree of consistency between the materials, objectives, and teaching style.

In terms of "matching," a critical concern is to determine which strategies are the most effective for the achievement of which objectives. Research with both normal and special children, using a variety of methods and strategies, including teaching styles, has yielded some consistent patterns. External methods have demonstrated significantly superior results in student achievement of lower-level cognitive and affective objectives such as attending, knowledge, and comprehension (Salomon and Achenbach, 1974; Wright and Nuthall, 1970). However, children who have achieved the lower-level objective personally prefer and more readily achieve higher-level objectives with internal teaching style methods (Flanders, 1965; Hamachek, 1969; Scheuer, 1971). This objective-style relationship is consistent with the child's feelings and experience.

Thus, it may be stated that the accomplishment of an educational objective, by its nature and hierarchical position, can be facilitated by the use of procedures (both materials and teacher style) that are concrete and specific, and that it tends to be more readily achieved by children when the materials and teaching style are concrete and specific. Advanced, higher-level objectives, which require more elaborate cognitive and affective processing, are achieved more readily by children when the environment encourages interaction and affective exploration to increase self-concept and self-control.

STUDENT RESPONSES TO MATERIALS AND PROCEDURES

Elementary students respond differently to different materials and procedures. Some students seem eager and interested, other students are methodical or emotionally unresponsive, and other students evidence apprehension, even anger. Change the materials and procedures and a new set of affective responses may occur—students formerly unresponsive may evidence greater interest; students who were eager may become unresponsive.

This variety of student responses may result from the differential meeting of student affective needs by the instructional materials and teacher procedures. If both materials and procedures are adequately individualized in terms of student affective needs, specifically self-concept and self-control, then student responses tend to be more appropriate in terms of classroom behavior, achievement, and teacher expectations. Instructional techniques that are consistent with the child's cognitive skills (knowledge and modality), and that capitalize on the child's background and feelings and enhance self-concept and self-control, have a high probability of capturing the child's attention and producing appropriate responses.

If, on the other hand, materials and procedures are employed without regard for individual affective needs, a number of inappropriate feelings and behaviors are likely to result (Table 1).

The hypothesized aspect of the relationship is emphasized, because probable feelings and behaviors are theoretically projected

Table 1. Hypothesized relationship between student affective needs and responses to inappropriate techniques

Student affective needs		Student responses to inappropriate techniques	
Self-concept	Self-control	Feelings	Behavior
Negative	Low	Anxious	Impulsive or hyperactive
Positive	Low	Frustration	Aggressive or disruptive
Negative	High	Inadequacy	Submissive or negativistic
Positive	High	Apathy	Manipulative or unresponsive

and will obviously vary with individual students. The probable feelings and responses are compounded by the degree of self-concept and self-control, the extent to which the techniques comply with the students' knowledge and modality strengths, and the extent to which the content applies to the students' background and experience. It is important to recognize that the inappropriate feelings and behaviors presented are common occurrences in the classroom, many of which are rooted in inappropriate materials and procedures.

The responses of many special children, particularly those listed in Table 1, tend to be a characteristic pattern of feelings and behavior associated with educational environments. All children from time to time respond similarly, but for most children the reaction is only temporary or transient. For many special children, these responses have become so ingrained that they have become an established school reaction pattern. Dramatic or consistent changes cannot be expected within a short period of time. Bloom (1976) maintains that deep-seated affective changes are so slow and subtle, "it is likely that most teachers may not be entirely aware of the small positive or negative changes in affect that take place in the student during the semester or academic year that they are in contact with him" (p. 141).

It is important to understand that many negative feelings and behaviors are a ressult of affective needs that are not being met through the educational program. Typically, when students react in a manner that is inconsistent with teacher expectations, teachers tend to blame the child and manage the behavior, thus increasing the intensity of the feelings and behaviors. Consequently, teacher intervention normally occurs at the point in time when the child is reacting to inappropriate materials and procedures. Teacher energies could be better spent in the individualization of materials and procedures, thus preventing many of the negative feelings and inappropriate behaviors.

Materials and procedures that are inappropriate for the child's affective needs contribute to negative feelings and behavior, resulting in negative feedback. On the other hand, materials and procedures that are appropriate result in success, or positive feedback. The teacher's sensitivity to help children succeed is critical in the development of student self-concept and self-control.

COGNITIVE-AFFECTIVE FEEDBACK

Cognitive and affective feedback are considered inseparable within educational environments. Although individual exceptions to this combination may occur, it is obvious that a child's affect and school performance have a reciprocal influence on each other. "Children who consistently experience difficulty in competing academically . . . will come to believe that they cannot read, write, or do arithmetic, and their inadequate view of self becomes crippling to the individual" (Wirth, 1977, p. 34).

Effects of Instructional Techniques

Bloom's (1976) data, which demonstrate a declining concept of self with cumulative years of unsuccessful school experience, are evidence of the relationship between unmet needs and negative feedback. According to Bloom, there are several constraints in education that perpetuate this model for failure: 1) "school learning . . . is largely group learning," 2) "school learning is subject centered," and 3) "students are expected to learn from a set of materials and a teacher" (pp. 20–21). To overcome these constraints, educators must conceptualize "learning which can be related to group or individual learning, to graded subject-centered as well as non-graded less formal learning situations, and which can reflect the style and characteristics of the instructional materials and the instructor" (p. 21).

The application of predetermined instructional techniques designed to achieve the same cognitive objective for all children in the classroom will result in failure, producing negative feedback for a substantial percentage of the group. The commonplace undifferentiated procedure leads one to believe that all children in a classroom group are the same, they learn in the same way, and they need to know the same thing. Unfortunately, many classroom settings continue to represent external control models in which teachers possess the power to make decisions for students—what they will learn and how they will learn it. Indicative of this pattern is the fact that elementary teachers spend more than 90% of their time evaluating, monitoring, lecturing, directing, and criticizing, but less than 10% of their time is devoted to encouraging, building on student ideas, and accepting student feelings (Rich, 1973). Under such circumstances, many children will not achieve the prescribed cognitive objectives, nor will they develop self-control or a positive self-concept.

Most teachers recognize the waste of human potential and the inefficiency of continuous group instruction. However, economic, time, and physical limitations have reduced teacher motivation and the availability of resources to individually planned materials and procedures based on individual student needs. Students confronted with expedient but irrelevant materials, that are exclusively subject-matter oriented and administered by a controlling teacher, will respond in a way that may not be consistent with teacher expectations—or even their own. Students may psychologically withdraw, become submissive, express aggression, or tenaciously struggle through the lesson without hope for achieving the objective. Regardless of the behavior or feeling, the children will not achieve the cognitive objective desired by the teacher, nor will they achieve their own affective objectives. Both teacher and student will have lost.

If the reaction is flagrant enough (e.g., talking back, hitting, or cursing), the student may be sent to the office, morally devalued, forced to comply, failed, or sent home. Each of these examples represents forms of negative feedback that perpetuate a negative cycle. Negative feedback intensifies affective needs by reducing self-concept and self-control. This intensification causes the standard materials and procedures to be even more irrelevant, resulting in inappropriate feelings and behavior. Again, more negative feedback. Consequently, the child goes around and around the cycle as it spirals to greater irrelevance, and the child becomes more lost in the system called education.

There is a positive cycle! Many teachers recognize individual affective needs and plan the use of materials and procedures according to those needs. Such teachers typically have positive self-concepts, are sensitive to the feeling and behavior of children, and demonstrate flexibility in the use of a variety of techniques to accomplish both cognitive and affective objectives. Above all, successful teachers have successful students.

Success, or positive feedback, is not intended to convey the accomplishment of objectives in comparison to some standardized norm or group performance scale. Instead, success is measured by the feelings and behaviors that are appropriate for the child individually. All children, no matter how severe the problems or behavior, engage in some activities appropriately and respond correctly. To reverse the trend that demonstrates a declining concept of self with cumulative years of unsuccessful school experience, teachers must begin a conscious, systematic effort to provide positive feedback. Teachers cannot continue to expect perfection—school is a place where children should be able to make mistakes and, at the same time, be encouraged for what they attempt and for what they accomplish.

In order to provide meaningful, positive feedback, teachers must be good observers, alert to any possibility for accentuating correct responses, reinforcing appropriate behaviors, responding to feelings, and providing material and procedure options. Positive feedback requires that the teacher build on those feelings and behaviors that exist and begin to shape experiences so that the children feel good about themselves and have some control over their personal destinies.

Accentuating Correct Responses   It is easy enough to find errors, miscalculations, omissions, etc. in the cognitive activities completed by students. However, there will be parts that are correct in any activity. For example, if a student completes 30 of 40 math problems, the teacher could mark the paper +30 or 75% correct, rather than −10, thus emphasizing what the student completed correctly. In a writing activity, if a student does not use the correct format but has expressed some meaningful ideas, the latter should be emphasized. Accentuating correct responses does not mean that incorrect respones are ignored, but that they receive minimal attention in terms of feedback. A more affective and cognitive solution for incorrect responses is the individualization of materials and procedures to enhance the probability of a higher rate of correct responses—thus, more positive feedback.

Reinforcing Appropriate Behavior   This form of positive feedback is not substantially different from accentuating correct responses, except that the emphasis is on personal behavior rather than cognitive responses. To increase positive feedback, teachers could adopt the philosophy of rewarding appropriate behavior first and minimizing the importance of inappropriate behavior. For example, a child may be out of his seat 30 minutes of each hour, but is also seated for 30 minutes of each hour. Calling attention to the sitting behavior rather than continually demand that the child be seated will increase the probability that the child will remain seated, provide positive feedback, and minimize teacher and student nonproductive time. Behaviors such as whispering, hand raising, and talking out could be treated in a similar manner—that is, rewarded when not engaging in inappropriate behavior.

Responding to Feelings   Special children in the elementary school tend to be deficient in the verbal skills necessary to express feelings. This difficulty is compounded by the fact that children tend to view many teachers as insensitive classroom managers who are not interested in their feelings. Consequently, children do not generally share with teachers their frustrations, fears, or feelings about themselves, learning, or school. Their feelings are typically expressed indirectly, through inappropriate behaviors. To eliminate the need for physical expression that results in negative feedback, teachers need to be able to listen sympathetically to children, to help them verbalize feelings, and to build upon the child's ego strengths and

Table 2.   Teacher assumptions behind positive and negative affective learning cycles

Cycle factors	Positive (Success) cycle	Negative (Failure) cycle
	Teacher assumptions	
1. Affective needs	All children have feelings and emotions and desire self-control and a positive conception of self	All children have basically the same needs for cognitive achievement
2. Instructional techniques		
A. Materials	Individualized materials are needed to match personal skills and concerns for each student	All children should achieve a level of competency using standardized materials
B. Teacher procedures	Children differ in the amount of control versus freedom needed to accomplish objectives	All children require the same amount of control, direction, and guidance
3. Children's responses	All children should be expected to function intrapersonally and with others, and it should be recognized that inappropriate behavior may be caused by the learning environment	All children should be expected to conform to a prescribed set of rules and standards
4. Feedback		
A. Cognitive	Children can learn from what they know best	Children should learn from their mistakes
B. Affective	All children need to know that they are important, that feelings and emotions are important, and that they can begin to manage their own lives	All children need to know when their behavior is inappropriate and when they are interfering with others

sense of reality. Responding to feelings, as opposed to behaviors, additionally provides the teacher with information for developing more appropriate instructional techniques.

   Providing Material and Procedure Options   Because children respond differently to different materials and procedures, it is necessary to consider alternative strategies for individual children.

Whereas some children may require a structured, sequential program for achieving lower-level cognitive objectives, others may need considerably more freedom for exploration to achieve higher-level objectives. Similarly, some children function well with abstract materials requiring only passive involvement; others, however, may need concrete, lifelike experiences that are multisensory and action oriented. Providing options increases the probability that the materials and procedures will increase the frequency of success, thus increasing the frequency and meaningfulness of positive feedback. As a result, affective objectives can be achieved by increasing the child's self-control and promoting a more positive self-concept.

In summary, the perpetuation of positive (success) and negative (failure) affective learning cycles is based on different teacher assumptions regarding the role of affective needs in education (Table 2). In the case of the positive (success) cycle, sensitive teachers are aware of student affective needs; this is reflected in the individual and flexible use of materials and procedures. This individualization increases the accuracy of student responses to cognitive materials, as well as increases appropriate classroom behavior. Successful student response, accentuated by teacher reinforcement, develops a pattern of positive feedback, thus enhancing self-concept and self-control.

AFFECTIVE PROGRAMS

This chapter has been devoted to the affective use of cognitive materials for special children in the mainstream of education. Although the focus was on special children, it was noted that the regular class students have affective needs that should also be considered in the use of materials and procedures. Affective education may be implemented through the use of routine materials and procedures if they are adapted or planned for individual students. The suggested use of materials and procedures could, therefore, be introduced without significantly altering the regular classroom operation.

Specific materials for affective objectives were not identified within the context of this chapter. However, there are many affective models, commercial materials, and reference books available that provide specialized procedures, materials, and objectives. Most of these affective models can be adapted to the regular classroom for both special children and the regular student population.

There are also many children who demonstrate such severe emotional and/or behavioral problems that minor teaching-learning changes will not be sufficient to bring about the necessary adjustment. For these children, specific, well-conceived affective programs are required. It is doubtful that such children will be the total or primary responsibility of the regular classroom teacher, but knowledge of more exclusively affective programs can serve as a resource for classroom planning.

The affective programs discussed in this section represent only a small sample of the available programs, materials, and activities. When choosing from this wide variety, teacher selection of partial or total programs should be based on the objectives of the program, the cost, and preparation required. The objectives (or aims) of the program should be consistent with the desired objectives for individual students or the classroom group; the cost should be relatively inexpensive, because many teacher- and student-made materials may serve equally well; and the time and preparation necessary to employ the program must be considered, particularly for educational settings.

Affective Teaching Models

John Miller (1976) has identified a number of affective teaching models, outlined in Table 3. According to Miller, each model

Table 3.   Affective teaching models

	Model	Theorist(s)	Orientation	Aims
1.	Ego development	Erikson	Developmental	Resolution of ego crises
2.	Psychological model	Mosher and Sprinthall	Developmental	Facilitation of ego, cognitive, and moral development
3.	Psychosicial model	Ryan and Hoffman	Developmental	Positive self-concept and independent learning skills
4.	Moral development model	Kohlberg	Developmental	Avoidance of stage retardation
5.	Values clarification	Simon, Raths, Kirschenbaum and Harmin	Self-concept	Incorporation of valuing process
6.	Identity education	Weinstein and Fantini	Self-concept	Positive identity, self-control, and relatedness to others
7.	Classroom meeting model	Glasser	Self-concept	Sense of identity through responsible decision-making

Table 3—*continued*

	Model	Theorist(s)	Orientation	Aims
8.	Role-playing model	Shaftel and Shaftel	Self-concept	Positive self-concept, group cohesiveness, and problem-solving skills
9.	Self-directed model	Rogers	Self-concept	Fully functioning person
10.	Communication model	Carkhuff	Sensitivity and group	Communications skills
11.	Sensitivity-consideration model	McPhail	Sensitivity and group	Awareness of others' needs and feelings
12.	Transactional analysis	Harris, Berne and Ernst	Sensitivity and group	Open communication and personal growth
13.	Human relations training	National Training Laboratory	Sensitivity and group	Interpersonal skills
14.	Meditation	Ornstein	Consciousness expansion	Awareness and centeredness
15.	Synectics	Gordon	Consciousness expansion	Creative and imaginative capacities
16.	Confluent education	Castillo, Brown and Hillman	Consciousness expansion	Integration and holistic perception
17.	Psychosynthesis	Assagioli and Crampton	Consciousness expansion	Integration through centeredness

From *Humanizing the Classroom: Models of Teaching in Affective Education* by John P. Miller. Copyright © 1976 by Praeger Publishers. Reprinted by permission of Praeger Publishers, a division of Holt, Rinehart and Winston.

subscribes to a specific orientation and has individual aims or objectives. The model to be employed, therefore, would depend on the problems evidenced by the individual child or group of children and the expected objectives to be achieved.

The models that have a developmental or self-concept orientation tend to be the most frequently used in the classroom, because they focus on objectives or aims that are consistent with the perceived role of educational systems. However, the models that have a sensitivity and group orientation are equally applicable for education if problems or concerns involve the classroom group. The consciousness expansion models are more clearly an extension of traditional educational programs, enabling individuals to achieve levels of intrapersonal development not normally addressed within education.

The affective teaching models identified by Miller have been used successfully in achieving the specified aims in a variety of teaching-learning settings. However, there are at least two major limitations to the incorporation of total models within the classroom. First, the role of affective education has not been clearly established nor widely accepted as a legitimate function of education within many school systems. Second, most of the models require specialized leadership training and resources if the total model is to be adopted for use in the classroom. These limitations do not preclude the use of selected procedures from the models. The selection of procedures that are reasonably familiar to the teacher, that are consistent with the objectives to be accomplished, and for which there is acceptance within the educational system, could be used in the classroom to develop student affect.

Commercial Programs

There are a number of commercial programs that are appropriate for use in the elementary classroom. Teacher selection of commercial programs should be based on the intended purpose of the program because the programs focus on a variety of objectives, using a variety of materials and procedures. The primary advantages of commercial programs include the prepared materials, specific and sequential instructions, and attractive packaging, which increase student attention and motivation. The primary limitations are the general, nonindividualized nature of the materials and activities and cost of purchasing the programs. For information, field-test reports, and cost, write directly to the publisher.

Developing Understanding of Self and Others (DUSO), by Don Dinkmeyer, published by Americal Guidance Service, Inc., Circle Pines, Mn. 55014

The purposes of the DUSO program are not limited to children with affective problems, but are based on the concept that all children encounter normal developmental problems that require affective attention. The DUSO program consists of two kits: Kit D-1 is designed for children in grades K-2, and Kit D-2 is designed for children in grades 2-4. The basic objectives of DUSO Kit D-1 program consist of learning about feelings, goals, and behavior. Kit D-2 emphasizes understanding of personal uniqueness, interpersonal relations, personal expression, and developing a sense of accomplishment.

The DUSO kits contain posters, storybooks, puppets, audio cassette tapes, and records. Duso, the dolphin puppet, is the primary character throughout the series of activities.

Focus on Self-Development (FSD), no author, published by Science
Research Associates, 259 E. Erie Street, Chicago, Ill. 60611
The basic objectives of the FSD program are to assist children in
understanding themselves, others, and their environment. These
objectives are designed to be accomplished through three stages
of activities: awareness, responding, and involvement. Stage 1,
awareness, for K-2 children, emphasizes awareness of self and
the environment through sensory, social, and problem-solving
activities. Stage 2, responding, for grades 2-4, encourages
children to respond to their life situation: i.e., personally
(interests, concerns, etc.), socially (communication, acceptance,
etc.), emotionally (feelings, emotions, etc.) and intellectually
(abilities, skills, etc.). Stage 3, involvement, encourages intermediate children to examine their involvement with self, others,
and their environment, and to evaluate beliefs and values
associated with their experiences, family, justice, and so on.

The FSD program was designed to correspond with the first
three levels of the Taxonomy of Educational Objectives: Affective Domain (Krathwohl, Bloom, and Masia, 1956). The
program contains filmstrips, records, audiotapes, photoboards,
and activity books. The FSD program can be used with entire
groups or adapted for individual children.

The Human Development Program (HDP), created by Uvaldo
Palomare and Geraldine Ball, published by Human Development Training Institute, 7574 University Avenue, LaMesa, Cal.
92041
The HDP, also known as the "Magic Circle," was created as a
vehicle for developing social skills and emotional health. The
emphasis of the program is on three basic areas: awareness of
feelings; a sense of mastery to develop self-concept; and social
interaction skills. Aside from the general manual, profile, and
story and activity booklet, materials for elementary aged
children are contained in separate grade level guides. Each guide
contains daily lesson plans for ongoing groups, as well as basic
activities for children new to the program. Workshops and
presentation regarding the HDP may be arranged.

The Social Learning Curriculum (SLC), by Herbert Goldstein,
published by Charles E. Merrill Company, 1300 Alum Creek
Drive, Columbus, Oh. 43216
"The emphasis of the SLC is basic to social adaptation.
Activities such as listening, discussion, role playing, motor
involvement, music, art, games, and other teacher-student

interactions are carefully selected to develop the student's potential for critical thought and independence. The SLC activities aid the special student in assuming responsibility, both personally and socially, and in making decisions and acting upon them within the broad limits society describes as social adaptation" (advertisement brochure).

The general objectives of the SLC are achieved through a variety of physical, social, and mental activities that are sequenced over 16 phases. A phase consists of several activities devoted to a specific objective, such as recognition of emotions, communicating with others, and acting out interdependence. Included in the program are "phase books," stimulus pictures, duplicating books, sound cassettes, overhead transparencies, charts, and supplemental books. The SLC is packaged and sold in two separate parts: Primary (Phases 1–10) and Intermediate (Phases 11–16).

Toward Affective Development—I, (TAD—I), by Henry Dupont, Ovitta S. Gardner, and David S. Brody, published by American Guidance Service, Inc., Circle Pines, Mn. 55014

The objectives and activities for the TAD—I program include "looking and listening clues; communicating feelings through body language as well as verbal expression; accepting self and reaching out to new experiences; recognizing the differences and needs of others; brainstorming and developing resourcefulness; resolving interpersonal conflicts; [and] thinking ahead to future aspirations" (advertisement brochure). The sequence of activities was derived from Jean Piaget's developmental research on the affective stages of child behavior.

The TAD—I objectives and activities, designed for children in grades 3–6, are included in 191 sequentially arranged lessons. The individual lessons cover such topics as participation skills, (listening, taking turns, and sharing), peer acceptance, recognizing nonverbal communication (expressions and gesturing), and developing alternatives to conflict situations. The TAD—I program is compactly packaged and includes student activity sheets, audio cassette recordings, career folders, and an assortment of stimuli cards and materials.

Books Containing Affective Activities

The following annotated list of paperback books provides a variety of affective materials, procedures, and activities. The books represent a broad range of objectives dealing with self-concept, self-control, values, feelings, social interaction, and general affective concerns. These paperback books are relatively inexpensive and provide an extensive array of activities, requiring a minimum amount of materials and preparation time. The annotations are intended to provide the reader with the general scope and focus of each book.

Canfield, J., and Wells, H. C. 1976. 100 Ways to Enhance Self-Concept in the Classroom. Prentice-Hall, Englewood Cliffs, N.J.
As the title indicates, this book contains over 100 individual activities for developing the self-control or self-esteem of children in the classroom. The activities are included in seven units on building positive environments, my strengths, who am I, accepting my body, where am I going, the language of self, and relations with others. The book contains activities that are clearly identified, with specific directions, procedures, and materials, including numerous illustrations.

Castillo, G. A. 1974. Left-Handed Teaching: Lessons in Affective Education. Praeger Publishers, New York.
This book is concerned with confluent education, or the teaching of cognitive and affective skills simultaneously. The book contains over 100 lessons, complete with procedures and activities. There are 12 units, including such topics as awareness, imagination, communication, trust, aggression, and nature. The major objective of the book is to present the affective aspects of learning as an integral part of the cognitive experience.

Chase, L. 1975. The Other Side of the Report Card. Goodyear, Santa Monica, Ca.
"This book is a smorgasbord of ways to help children learn some of the survival skills they need today and tomorrow. It was written because of my conviction that a teacher in a classroom can significantly affect the social and emotional growth of students in positive, helpful ways. The activities, directions, and topics described in this book are relevant. They have been used with kids and grownups, and most have worked most of the time" (author's preface). The book does provide several affective units, with activities, on an array of topics: for example, friendship, fear, promises, lying, and taking tests. Overall, the book contains an excellent assortment of affective activities.

Fagen, S., Long N. J., and Stevens, T. 1975. Teaching Children Self-Control. Charles E. Merrill Books, Columbus, Oh.
This book represents a series of curriculum units and activities that are designed to help children achieve freedom and responsi-

bility through self-control. Although the curriculum was designed primarily for disruptive students, the activities can benefit normal children by encouraging responsible decision-making in a democratic society. The curriculum includes activities to develop readiness or cognitive skills (stimuli selection, storage, and sequencing) before introducing self-control skills (anticipating consequences, appreciating feelings, managing frustration, inhibition and delay, and relaxation). Although the curriculum is sequential in nature, activities may be selected that are appropriate for individual students.

Johnson, D. 1972. Reaching Out: Interpersonal Effectiveness and Self-Actualization. Prentice-Hall, Englewood Cliffs, N.J.

The title accurately conveys the objective and emphasis of the book. Interpersonal skills are considered in terms of self-disclosure, trust, communication, expression of feelings, acceptance, and styles of listening and responding. The book provides both theory and experiences, with the latter taking the form of activities and self-evaluation. The significant content of this book is for teachers, rather than children, in understanding and developing positive, helpful communication within the classroom.

Lyon, H. C. 1971. Learning to Feel—Feeling to Learn. Charles E. Merrill Books, Columbus, Oh.

The primary strength of this book is in the rationale and background for humanistic (affective and cognitive) education. Part III, "Applying Humanistic Techniques to Classroom Situations," does provide affective examples and activities that can be employed in the classroom. However, without modification, the activities would be limited to older and verbal elementary students.

Simon, S., Howe, L. W., and Kirschenbaum, H. 1972. Values Clarification. Hart Publishing Company, New York.

This book contains 79 strategies "designed to engage students and teachers in the active formulation and examination of values. . . . The goal is to involve students in practical experiences, making them aware of their own feelings, their own ideas, their own beliefs, so that the choices and decisions they make are conscious and deliberate, based on their own value system" (cover page). Each strategy is presented with a standard format that specifies the purpose and describes the procedure for implementing the activity.

Valett, R. E. 1977. Humanistic Education: Developing the Total Person. The C. V. Mosby Company, St. Louis, Mo.

This book deals with the general topic of affective or humanistic education, including background information, curriculum guides, research studies, learning materials, and so forth. Chapter 10, "Experiential Activities," contains a number of learning experiences with specific objectives, procedures, and activities. This book represents an excellent variety of information regarding the rationale and role of humanistic education.

REFERENCES

Anderson, R. C. 1959. Learning in discussions: A resume of the authoritarian-democratic studies. Harvard Educ. 29: 201–215.

Bennett, N. 1976. Teaching Styles and Pupil Progress. Harvard University Press, Cambridge.

Bills, R. E. 1956. Personality changes during student centered teaching. J. Educ. Res. 50: 121–126.

Bloom, B. S., (ed.). 1956. Taxonomy of Educational Objectives. Handbook I: Cognitive Domain. David McKay Company, New York.

Bloom, B. S. 1976. Human Characteristics and School Learning. McGraw-Hill Book Company, New York.

Bloom, B. S. 1977. Affective outcomes of school learning. Phi Delta Kappan 56: 193–198.

Charles, C. M. 1976. Individualizing Instruction. The C. V. Mosby Company, St. Louis, Mo.

Erikson, E. H. 1965. Youth and the life cycle. In D. E. Hamachek. (ed.), The Self in Growth, Teaching, and Learning. Prentice-Hall, Englewood Cliffs, N.J.

Fagen, S. A., Long, N. J., and Stevens, D. J. 1975. Teaching Children Self-Control: Preventing Emotional and Learning Problems in the Elementary School. Charles E. Merrill Books, Columbus, Oh.

Flanders, N. A. 1965. Teacher Influence, Pupil Attitudes, and Achievement. Cooperative Research Monograph No. 12, U.S. Department of Health, Education and Welfare, Office of Education Publication No. OE-25040. U.S. Government Printing Office, Washington, D.C.

Flanders, N. A. 1967. Teacher influence in the classroom. In E. J. Amidon and J. B. Hough (eds.), Interaction Analysis: Theory, Research and Application. Addison-Wesley Publishing Company, Reading, Ma.

Geer, B. 1968. Teaching. In International Encyclopedia of the Social Sciences. The Macmillan Company, New York.

Hamachek, D. E. 1969. Characteristics of good teachers and implication for teacher education. Phi Delta Kappan 50: 341–345.

Kauffman, J. M., and Lewis, C. D. 1974. Teaching Children with Behavior Disorders: Personal Perspectives. Charles E. Merrill Books, Columbus, Oh.

Kounin, J. S. 1967. An analysis of teachers' managerial techniques. Psychol. Schools 4: 221–227.

Krathwohl, D. R., Bloom, B. S., and Masia, B. B. 1956. Taxonomy of Educational Objectives. Handbook II: Affective Domain. David McKay Company, New York.
LaBenne, W. D., and Greene, B. I. 1969. Educational Implications of Self-Concept Theory. Goodyear Publishing Company, Pacific Palisades, Ca.
Llorens, L. A., and Rubin, E. Z. 1967. Developing Ego Functions in Disturbed Children. Wayne State University Press, Detroit, Mi.
McKeachie, W. J. 1962. Procedures and techniques of teaching: A survey of experimental studies. In N. Sanford (ed.), The American College: A Psychological and Social Interpretation of the Higher Learning. John Wiley and Sons, New York.
Maslow, A. H. 1965. A theory of human motivation. In D. E. Hamachek (ed.), The Self in Growth, Teaching, and Learning. Prentice-Hall, Englewood Cliffs, N.J.
Maurer, C. G. 1977. Of puppets, feelings, and children. Elem. School Guid. Counsel. 12: 26-32.
Miller, J. P. 1976. Humanizing the Classroom. Praeger Publishers, New York.
Rich, H. L. 1973. The effect of teaching styles on student behaviors as related to social-emotional development. Final Report to to the U.S. Office of Education, HEW (OEG-4-72-0020), Washington, D.C.
Rotter, J. B. 1966. Generalized expectancies for internal versus external control of reinforcement. Psychol. Monogr. 80, no. 1.
Salomon, M. K., and Achenbach, T. M. 1974. The effects of four kinds of tutoring experience on associate responding. Am. Educ. Res. J. 11: 395-405.
Scheuer, A. L. 1971. the relationship between personal attributes and effectiveness in teachers of the emotionally disturbed. Except. Child. 37: 723-731.
Smith, H. C. 1966. Sensitivity to People. McGraw-Hill Book Company, New York.
Stern, G. C. 1962. Environments for learning. In N. Sanford (ed.), The American College: A Psychological and Social Interpretation of the Higher Learning. John Wiley and Sons, New York.
Valett, R. E. 1977. Humanistic Education. The C. V. Mosby Company, St. Louis, Mo.
Weinstein, G., and Fantini, M. D. 1970. Toward Humanistic Education: A Curriculum of Affect. Praeger Publishers, New York.
Wirth, S. 1977. Effects of a multifaceted reading program on self-concept. Elem. School Guid. Counsel. 12: 33-40.
Withall, J., and Lewis, W. W. 1963. Social interaction in the classroom. In N. L. Gage (ed.), Handbook of Research on Teaching. Rand McNally and Company, Chicago.
Wright, C. J., and Nuthall, G. 1970. Relationships between teacher behaviors and pupil achievement in three experimental elementary science lessons. Am. Educ. Res. J. 7: 477-491.

13

Instructional Games

John G. Greer, Ph.D., Irise M. Friedman, and Virginia K. Laycock, Ed.D.

One of the most difficult challenges facing the classroom teacher is the motivation of his students. Although the selection and use of relevant and interesting instructional materials will help tremendously, this alone is often not enough. With typically large classes, and little if any outside assistance, it is no easy task to generate enthusiasm and to actively engage children in the process of learning. Passive reception of subject content rather than active examination and exploration of ideas therefore characterizes many educational settings. Although the naturally eager, bright child might learn in spite of such conditions, most of his classmates need more attention and encouragement than is normally offered.

Many techniques have been promulgated to assist teachers in meeting this challenge. Unfortunately, most are difficult or impractical for the average teacher to implement without an aide or a relatively small class. There is, therefore, a critical need for procedures that can be employed easily by regular and special teachers without assistance.

This chapter examines one possible solution—the use of instructional games. It is not a new idea. John Dewey, one of the founders of modern American education, noted decades ago that when such activities are used, "going to school is a joy, management is less of a burden, and learning is easier." Nevertheless, many teachers do not take full advantage of games and physical activities in their teaching. It is hoped that in this chapter the reader will come to recognize the positive and practical alternative that instructional games can provide, and the numerous ways in which they can enhance the effectiveness of other instructional materials.

Parts of this chapter were adapted from material published in *Motivating Learners with Instructional Games* by Greer, Schwartzberg, and Laycock with permission. Copyright © 1977 by Kendall/Hunt Publishing Company, Dubuque, Iowa.

GENERAL PRINCIPLES AND PROCEDURES

Rationale

An instructional game is an activity that utilizes the elements of fun and competition to teach and reinforce educational objectives. Although children probably learn something from every gamelike activity in which they engage, the instructional game is designed specifically to promote the acquisition of fundamental academic and social skills. Ranging from quiet board games to physical activities, a vast array of games has been adapted for use in the classroom. If selected according to the age, ability, and interests of the children, and if used appropriately, they can be very effective teaching tools. Rather than simply a form of amusement or a way to pass the time, such games can be used as an integral part of every educational program.

The reasons for their effectiveness are numerous, and to some experienced teachers, obvious. Those, for example, who teach kindergarten and young, elementary age children know full well the importance of games in the daily routine. Given the typically high levels of energy that such children bring into the classroom, it is unwise if not impossible to impose long, uninterrupted periods of quiet, passive endeavors. Games employed at frequent intervals offer an effective change of pace, and, if coordinated with the overall program, can constructively channel all that childhood energy in educationally meaningful ways. For similar reasons, teachers of slow learning or retarded children have long found games to be an invaluable tool. Faced with the fact that handicapped learners deal more effectively with concrete rather than abstract terms, they have found games to be an effective instructional medium. Moreover, they assist in handling the attention span and motivational problems that are so often a factor with these children.

Although games are probably of special value to teachers of very young children or handicapped learners, they can and should be used by other elementary and even junior high educators. There are four basic reasons for this. First, games are naturally motivating and are enjoyed by all children. At the same time, the use of games for instruction is in harmony with most modern theories of learning. Games are also easy to use and can be adapted in many ways to facilitate the individualization of instruction. Finally, instructional games offer unique opportunities for the affective and social growth of children. Each of these factors is critical to good education, and is examined in detail below.

Games Are Naturally Motivating   Motivation to learn is a vital ingredient in the classroom and, if it is lacking, the effects can be devastating. Teachers quickly recognize this fact, and employ many diverse strategies to encourage high levels of student interest and participation. One of the most popular approaches has been to use a variety of reward incentives. The children are allowed to earn prizes or privileges for progress made in their academic achievement, their social behavior, or in any other areas of performance considered important to their overall development. With the advent of the token economy, teachers needing this type of extrinsic motivation could more easily and effectively distribute rewards to the children. This and other similar techniques have enjoyed widespread success, and have been the subject of innumerable books and articles.

It is abundantly clear that the use of extrinsic forms of motivation in the classroom can be and has been successful. It is also clear that it can be and has been overused. Tangible rewards, such as trinkets and candy, are unnecessary in most classrooms. Similarly, point systems or token economies are not required everywhere. Instead, teachers should examine more carefully the more natural sources of motivation that already exist or can easily be introduced into the educational setting. Instructional games are a perfect example.

All children enjoy games. They are naturally competitive and rarely miss an opportunity to demonstrate their skill or try their luck in any "contest" situation. When participation and success in such activities is made dependent on learning something, like the alphabet or the multiplication tables, then school work can take on a whole new meaning. If knowing the answer to a history question gets the child a "hit" in the baseball game or puts his horse one move ahead in the "Shady Oaks Derby," then studying history lessons can become more relevant and fun for him than ever before. Games can easily be adapted by the classroom teacher to encourage and enforce participation by children who otherwise might find their subjects dry and boring.

Games Reinforce Learning   Among other things, modern learning theory emphasizes the importance of immediate feedback, practice, and review in the educational process. In a natural and enjoyable format, instructional games provide ample opportunity for all three.

As is described later in this chapter, each instructional game is designed so that the player is required to answer questions, solve problems, spell words, or in some other way demonstrate his knowledge frequently during the course of the game. Depending on the particular game format, correct answers or responses might allow the child to take a turn, draw a card, move his piece, or help his team. Incorrect answers, as would be expected, result in the loss of a turn or move, and eventually lead to defeat. In either case, each child knows immediately if his response is appropriate. This is a critical adjunct to learning that must be present if students are to progress quickly and efficiently. Moreover, such feedback provided in the game setting is fun. Most children are elated and excited if they are right, and when playing on a team they receive congratulations from their teammates. Children typically love such challenges, and many times think harder and apply themselves better than they do on final examinations.

In addition to the immediate feedback inherent in most game formats, there is a unique opportunity for practice of newly learned skills and review of past subjects. The more situations in which children are required to use or recall information, the better are the chances that they will remember it later. Children frequently think of practice or review work as boring and uninteresting, and more often than not they are right. An unending series of dittoed exercises would discourage anyone. When, by contrast, such work is incorporated into an instructional game, it ceases to be drudgery altogether. Interest and attention can be maintained for long periods of time, and the needed practice can be completed in a pleasant and meaningful way.

Games Facilitate Individualization of Instruction   There are many imaginative ways in which games can be employed to individualize instruction. It is a relatively easy procedure to adapt them to the various instructional levels and learning styles of the children in a classroom. In fact, the same game can be played and enjoyed by children of different ages and abilities by simply adjusting the difficulty of the questions or problems required for each player. Item pools, which are later described in detail, can be developed for each child according to his current level of performance and his profile of strengths and weaknesses. A collection of questions which are typically printed on index cards, item pools can be used with the child for participation in any one of a number of instructional games.

Games can also be adapted to a variety of instructional settings and grouping arrangements. The effectiveness of learning centers, for example, can be increased by the incorporation of games or gamelike activities along with them. Similarly, the newly emerging concept of peer assisted learning combines very nicely with use of instructional games. Two children quiz each other in a subject area to determine their turns, moves, etc. in the game they are playing. This is a very motivating way to provide practice or drill, on a one-to-one basis, for those students who need it.

Attention and encouragement for problem learners can also be increased at home, if the parents of such children are willing. Teachers can suggest specific games that can be played by the entire family to reinforce the mastery of important skills needed by the child. Programs of this kind enhance the generalization of material learned in school. At the same time, parents who frequently feel helpless in dealing with their child's academic problems are given a concrete method of contributing to his education.

Indirectly, games promote individualization of instruction by allowing greater flexibility in the use of teacher time. If, for example, through the interest and motivation inherent in games, children can be effectively engaged in tutoring each other, this can free teacher time to help those children who have the most difficulty. Likewise, if games of concentration can absorb students in independent work, whether at their seat or in learning centers, the same possibility exists.

Finally, it must be pointed out that games can provide a nonthreatening method of evaluating student performance. Children, especially those with histories of frustration and failure in school, often give up or withdraw when they know they are being tested or observed. Unobtrusive measures of their behavior are therefore more valid indicators of their ability or achievement. When engrossed in a game and eager to win, their responses to questions or attempts to solve problems clearly indicate whether or not they know the material. The teacher, using a checklist of skills, can obtain more reliable information and thereby design instruction better suited to the child's individual needs.

Games Foster Affective and Social Development
Children learn much from each other, especially in terms of their social behavior. It is important, therefore, to provide frequent opportunities for positive interaction among the students in a classroom. Involving them in an active game situation is one of the best ways to accomplish this. Whether in two-person games or team contests, children develop numerous important social skills and attitudes. Waiting their turn, avoiding harsh criticism of teammates, and winning or losing gracefully are only a few of the behaviors typically needing reinforcement from the teacher. A sensitive teacher, watching a child at play with his classmates, can quickly assess his level of maturity and can identify important social skills the child

could be helped to develop. Games and players compatible with attaining these objectives can then be selected. More mature classmates can serve as models for appropriate behavior while the child is gradually involved in more competitive games. Combined with lavish teacher praise for all children acting in socially appropriate ways, this strategy of using games as a medium for growth can be very effective. Benefits in the hard to reach areas of self-concept and self-control easily justify the limited time and effort required of the teacher.

A Case Study The meaning of the above discussion can possibly be enhanced if an example is now provided. Consider the case of Mr. Anderson, a fifth-grade teacher who was hired in the middle of the year of replace a woman on maternity leave. The class that he inherited was apparently uninterested in everything but gym and art class, and was accustomed to doing little more in the class than watching the clock. This was partly because of the unimaginative program of the previous teacher, and partly because of the low value that the class put on academic achievement.

Numerous things had to be done to correct this situation. It was complex and defied any simple solutions. Nevertheless, instructional games played a key role. Anderson, from the beginning, noted a continuing rivalry and competition between the boys and the girls in the class. He decided to exploit this in a game of "History Baseball"— the boys against the girls. He wanted their first experience with an instructional game to be a positive one, and history was their favorite subject.

First he made up a large number of questions based on the history lessons in class over the past several weeks, and the accompanying reading assignments. Each question was printed on an index card. Subsequently, the questions were divided into four piles according to their level of difficulty. The most difficult questions were then put in a box marked "home runs," the next most difficult in the "triples" box, etc. The easiest questions were "singles." With the questions in order, Anderson then made a large feltboard baseball diamond, complete with funny little creatures to run the bases. He was now ready to try out the game.

After a particularly good history lesson the following week, he announced and explained the game. The girls would be allowed to bat first. Each player, when it was her turn, was to choose what "hit" she wanted to try for. If the player wanted to play it safe, she could go for a single or double, or be bold and try for a triple or home run.

Whatever she chose, the teacher would randomly pull out a question from the corresponding box and read it aloud. If she answered it correctly within a minute, she made her hit safely and a runner would be put on the appropriate base. If she was incorrect, however, she would be out. After three outs, the boys were allowed to bat. Score was kept on the blackboard.

After much laughter and even more boasting, the students eagerly decided on their batting lineups. (The boy and girl who knew the most about history batted "cleanup" for their team.) Then the game began. As each youngster asked for a question, everyone listened intently as the teacher read it aloud and waited anxiously for the answer. Teammates encouraged teammates, and cheered when "hits" were made and runs scored. In the end, the girls won, but both sides thoroughly enjoyed the game and immediately demanded a rematch.

By using history baseball with his fifth graders, Mr. Anderson accomplished several important things. First, he raised the level of interest and participation in the class to an all time high. This was true, not only during the game, but also during the history lessons. For one thing, it was now more meaningful to learn and remember the information because it would probably be included in the next game questions. Moreover, having the game at all was contingent upon having a good lesson.

Another benefit was the effective and meaningful practice that the game provided. All of the students listened carefully to each question whether or not it was their own turn, and judging from the immediate cheers from teammates or opponents, most were actively thinking of the answer. The immediate feedback, in the form of cheers and elation of one team or the other, was no doubt more effective in helping the players learn and remember their history than grades probably ever were.

An opportunity for review was yet another advantage. The students realized, from the beginning, that material covered weeks and even months earlier would possibly be covered by the questions. Mastering today's lesson alone, therefore, would not prevent being "out" in the game. They knew that each day Mr. Anderson added new questions, and that these were simply mixed in with all the old questions.

The response of the children to this game was so positive that the teacher soon added "Math Baseball," as well as a variety of other game activities. Using games both broke up the daily routine with

occasional periods of fun and competition, and used the time productively. The children were surprised to discover that learning could be
so much fun.

Guidelines for Game Selection and Use

As with any educational approach, the effectiveness and success of
instructional games depend heavily on careful planning. Only in this
way can such activities be coordinated with the ongoing program to
accomplish important classroom objectives. It is also the only way to
prevent the waste of time and the possible harm in which the haphazard use of instructional games can result. The guidelines listed
below were developed with this in mind. If considered by the teacher
when selecting and employing educational games, his experience with
them should be enjoyable and constructive.

1. The teacher should consider the behavioral objectives he wishes
    to achieve. This is a critical first step and must be done if the
    game is to be truly instructional. The activity ultimately
    selected should clearly reinforce these objectives by providing
    ample opportunity for their practice and review.
2. The teacher should choose games that attract the interest of the
    children in his class. They should be appealing and colorful.
    They should also be relevant to the experiences and back-
    grounds of the students. If the game is teacher-made, it could
    easily incorporate familiar names, pictures, and even
    photographs of the children themselves.
3. The teacher should ensure an appropriate level of complexity—
    keep the games simple. If the games employed are too complex
    for the age or ability of the children involved, they will be self-
    defeating. Instead of stimulating interest and motivating par-
    ticipation, difficulty with learning the game itself can have an
    opposite effect. Complicated games, therefore, could be sim-
    plified for young players or avoided altogether.
4. Directions that are easily understood by every child should be
    used. They should be few in number and should be stated in the
    children's own language. It sometimes helps to have the
    children go through a brief "dry run" of the game, while the
    teacher accompanies each step with any necessary explanation.
5. The teacher should adjust the game so that every child has a
    chance to win. This is an obvious requirement. No one enjoys or
    will continue to play a game that he can never win. Con-

sequently, the teacher must modify the game format and objectives sufficiently to allow even the weakest student occasional victories. As is discussed later, item pools provide a simple yet effective way to accomplish this.

6. Games that provide immediate feedback for every response should be chosen. As discussed earlier, such feedback reinforces learning in a very effective and meaningful way. It makes discrimination between correct and incorrect responses much easier than the guesswork and confusion that characterize learning when the results are delayed.

7. The teacher should consider the degree of social interaction desired. For the withdrawn child, the sudden requirement of participation in a competitive team game may be too threatening. Similarly, for a highly excitable youngster, such a game may also be inappropriate. On the other hand, a less intense game may offer both children an optimum medium for social growth. This important factor should be examined in relation to every child.

8. The teacher should assess the physical requirements for the game. Although most instructional games do not require any special physical arrangements or equipment, it is good to plan ahead. For example, with the more active games, like "Chalkboard Relay," it is important to have a clear, safe area in which to play. By contrast, a game of "Concentration" for two or three children might best be played in a corner of the classroom set aside especially for such activities.

9. The amount of teacher involvement necessary should be estimated. Although large group activities usually require teacher participation, many instructional games do not. If appealing games are wisely employed, they can serve to constructively occupy part of the class while freeing the teacher to work more closely with other students needing help. They must, however, be uncomplicated and self-correcting.

10. The teacher should determine an appropriate pace and duration for the game. For young children, especially, it should be kept short. This allows for frequent replaying and for the involvement of more children. The added redundancy and repeated practice are of benefit to many students. More lengthy games are probably suitable for older children, but can easily bog down and should be used sparingly. Attention is maintained most easily when games are fast-moving and waiting periods between turns are brief.

11. The cost effectiveness of each game should be evaluated. Whether purchased commercially or homemade in the classroom, games can be expensive in terms of both time and money. It is important, therefore, to assess ahead of time the general usability and overall impact that each game will probably have. The most practical games are durable and can easily be adapted for use with various age groups and diverse instructional objectives. Those games that are singular in purpose and suitable only for a narrow age range or for interest groups are probably not worth the price.

12. The teacher should pilot the game with children to assess its practical and instructional utility. This is necessary to identify unexpected difficulties with newly constructed games and to make any necessary modifications in the design before introducing it for general use. Is it too difficult? Is it really as appealing as the teacher considers it to be? Is there a better way to explain it to the children? Such questions are better answered in the beginning than later on.

If each of these guidelines is considered by the teacher employing instructional games, it is probable that they will nicely complement the classroom routine and heighten student interest and motivation. Most, if not all, of the problems sometimes associated with the use of games will be avoided. Nevertheless, it is worthwhile at this point to examine these dangers in some detail. The more aware teachers are of them, the less likely it is that any of them will be allowed to occur in the classroom. Therefore, the teacher should study the following cautions carefully:

1. Beware of overuse. As with anything else, too much of a good thing can be counterproductive. Indeed, children love games, but they will tire of them if they are used too often. To avoid this problem, some teachers limit their use of games to certain periods of the day. Others reserve such activities as rewards for good behavior. Students must earn the privilege of playing the games. Whatever strategy is used, its effectiveness will be enhanced if the games themselves are frequently changed. Old games can be temporarily retired and new ones added to ensure continuing student interest.

2. Use instructional games as a supplement rather than a substitute for good teaching. Nothing can take the place of sound, well-planned instruction and a conscientious and dedicated teacher. Added to this, games can be a wonderfully effective teaching device. On the other hand, in the absence of good teaching, they

will do little more than keep the children busy. An unintegrated, haphazard patchwork of games can in no way be considered instructionally beneficial.

3. Avoid excessive competition or peer pressure. Although there is little danger of this happening with most children, the slow learning or handicapped child could find intense competition extremely frustrating. If, as a team member, his frequent mistakes cost points, or victory itself, he could become the object of peer pressure, criticism, and even scorn. The stimulation of gaming activities can greatly motivate learning, but excessive competition can incapacitate a youngster with anxiety and heighten his sense of failure.

4. Prevent overstimulation. As alluded to earlier, there are children who become very excited in gamelike activities. Although most instructional games are relatively quiet, there are some games that can quickly get out of hand. Care must be taken therefore in the selection of the game as well as the participants for which it is best suited.

Suggestions for Game Construction

There are numerous commercially available games that can be used by a teacher for instructional purposes. With only minor changes they can be employed to accomplish educational goals in a wide variety of academic and social areas of development. Nevertheless, they are expensive. Few teachers have the financial backing that would be required to supply their classrooms with a suitable array of such games. Moreover, even if there is money, there are a multitude of instructional objectives for which commercial games have not yet been produced.

For these reasons, many teachers have learned to construct their own instructional games. Such an endeavor can be time consuming, but it is inexpensive. At the same time, the games produced are often more personally and academically relevant to the children for whom they are intended than anything currently on the market.

The procedures required for the construction of sound instructional games are fairly simple. The guidelines listed above for game selection and use are applicable to construction as well. Beginning with the identification of the specific objectives that the teacher wishes to achieve, each point should be considered carefully in the process. With a little experience, this can become a productive and enjoyable venture. For the novice, however, the following suggestions may make those first efforts a little easier.

1. All sorts of useful game-making materials can typically be obtained for free from nearby retailers. At lumber or building supply companies, for example, all sorts of scrap wood, masonite, and linoleum can usually be found. Likewise, interior decorator shops will often donate old wallpaper books or carpet samples. A few phone calls and a trip or two to such places can result in a bounty of free and effective materials.

2. Games should follow a theme, such as treasure hunting, football, or horse racing. Appropriate illustrations can usually be found in old comic books, workbooks, sports magazines, etc., and should be used whenever possible to make the game more colorful and interesting.

3. Many techniques can be used to ensure that any necessary printing is legible and easy to read. Tracing stencils and press-on letters come in various colors, sizes, and styles. Primary typewriters can also be used. However, the teacher should make sure to employ a style of lettering that is consistent with that familiar to the children.

4. Remembering the guideline on cost effectiveness, do not waste time constructing games that will not last. Make them out of durable materials that will endure normal classroom use for several years.

5. Laminating film or clear Contact paper (with delayed bond) provide an easy and effective way to protect gameboards and other game parts. Remember, however, to use water-based markers underneath to avoid fading or bleeding of colors.

6. If Contact paper or lamination is used, scoreboards can be included right on the gameboard itself. Score is kept with a grease pencil or felt-tipped pen and wiped clean at the conclusion of each game.

7. Kitchen timers can add a great deal of excitement to many games. The challenge of beating the clock can be used not only in group activities, but also as the basis for one-person games. The individual tries each time to better his performance before the allotted time runs out.

8. To save teacher time, the directions to more difficult games can be recorded on cassettes and played for the children as they use the game for the first time.

9. Many times unused metal surfaces, like the sides of file cabinets and book cases, can be converted into unique game "boards." Magnetic tape, available in most hardware stores, can be applied to all kinds of game parts and pieces. They can

then be moved about by the players like magnetic letters on a refrigerator door.

10. A variety of more active games can be devised by using linoleum tiles. Arranged on the classroom floor according to some game design, they can be used to represent the spaces typically contained on a gameboard. Young children often enjoy serving as the "pieces," and stepping off the number of spaces they gain or lose each turn.

11. For young children and other nonreaders, color coding and other visual cues can be used in game construction to enhance understanding. For example, arrows can indicate directionality, and green and red discs may identify where to start and finish. At the same time, each child's item pool can be made of different color cards to avoid confusion with those of another child.

12. Games should be self-contained. All loose pieces should be kept in a clearly marked box or envelope. Directions should actually be attached to the game whenever possible.

Item Pools

Given the diversity of population that typifies most classrooms, it is often difficult to identify two children who are homogeneous in their academic profiles. Even when they are functioning at similar levels of overall achievement, their particular patterns of strengths and weaknesses can be very different. Considering this fact, how can instructional games be designed to serve each child's specific needs? Moreover, if winning is predicated on content knowledge and mastery, what is to prevent the slower child from always losing? These are serious questions that require a satisfactory response. Otherwise, the instructional game would be severely limited as a meaningful educational tool.

One solution lies in the creation and employment of item pools. An item pool is a collection of stimulus cards that can be used in an instructional setting to elicit responses from the learner. Each item pool focuses on some aspect of a subject area. In harmony with the natural developmental sequence of the content, and a careful task analysis of the performance desired, items are formulated so as to include all of the major concepts and ideas, and to ensure optimum educational benefit from their use. They are always based on material that has already been introduced and explained to the children in class. The level of difficulty and range of content covered, however, should be based solely on the needs of the child for whom the item pool is constructed.

The number of item pools ultimately developed by a teacher depends on how extensively he wants to employ instructional games. He may wish to begin by providing each student with an item pool focusing on one of his weaker areas of performance. Later, he may construct additional games if positive and satisfactory progress is made. This initially represents a substantial investment in time. As each child progresses and masters the material covered by the current pool cards, new and more challenging cards must be added. Nevertheless, the original item pools can be filed and again employed when another child needs work in that particular area.

The actual shape and design of the item pool cards vary considerably. Often, the items are printed on 3″ by 5″ index cards. They are readily available, easy to handle, and small enough to stack and shuffle like playing cards. Not unlike flash cards, many item cards typically have questions or problems printed on one side and the correct answer printed on the back. Others do not provide the answer in this way, but allow confirmation of responses either by an answer sheet, through the teacher, or in some other way. For many games, and especially for young children, the item pool cards can be cut into different shapes, like fish, balls, rockets, etc. depending on the theme of the game being played.

Once the item pools are constructed, their incorporation into instructional games is simple. Each child's move or turn is made contingent upon a correct response to an item pool card. These are randomized before each game and presented to the child, one at a time, when it is his turn. If several children can benefit from practicing the same content, and are functioning on equal levels, the same pool of stimulus cards can be used for all of them. If, on the other hand, they are at different levels, or even need practice in different content areas, separate item pools are provided for each. As long as each child's item pool is personally challenging, the actual differences in content difficulty will not adversely affect the game. Each participant will have an equal chance to win, while practicing or reviewing material that is most relevant to his individual academic progress.

The Role of Games in Classroom Assessment

Determining precisely what a child has learned and how he approaches learning is an essential step in the instruction process. Effective planning depends on this up-to-date information. Traditionally, diagnosis and evaluation have become synonymous with testing, and to a certain extent, testing has been removed from the teaching process per se. In most classrooms, specific samples of student performance are collected only at designated intervals. The weekly spelling test, the math quiz, and the social studies unit test are all familiar examples of this approach to evaluation.

Between tests, students are continually interacting with the teacher and with instructional materials. Each time a child makes any response to a task, he is revealing his level of proficiency. The daily performance of the child may provide the richest source of diagnostic data. It is not taken into account in the periodic test, however, because the time interval may be too large to reflect subtle fluctuations in performance. A child who has mastered a concept on Tuesday should not have to wait until Friday to prove that he knows it before going on to new material. Likewise, the child who is having difficulty should not have to fail the unit test in order to receive help. Such problems can be avoided if a teacher can obtain daily information on a child's performance.

A further difficulty with overreliance of testing concerns the anxiety it may produce in students. Children often feel threatened, or perceive a test as their only chance to do well and avoid a bad grade. Many times, performance deteriorates under such pressure. More accurate diagnostic information is available from a child's natural, everyday learning activities.

Instructional games are particularly well suited for use as diagnostic tools. The game format dispels anxiety and encourages more representative performance. Children are motivated to do their best, and they are not threatened by fear of failing grades. Games allow great variety in the types of responses required from students and can, therefore, be structured to promote optimal performance. For example, a child who has handwriting difficulties can demonstrate his spelling skills orally in a baseball game. Games may have particular value for determining the abilities of the very timid or unresponsive child. Games such as bingo and dominoes require no verbal responses, yet tap the student's knowledge of a concept. At the same time, these games may serve as "ice-breakers," helping to establish the rapport necessary for later involvement.

Games afford the teacher a chance to observe a greater range of behaviors that might be apparent in other assessment situations. The first concern in diagnosis is, of course, to exactly determine a child's level of mastery for a particular skill. By using carefully selected item pools and games, a teacher can find out specifically which tasks are passed and failed by a student. As the child is playing the games, the teacher can also observe his approach to problem-solving. In addition, the teacher may be concerned about the child's social skills. How does a child conform to rules, such as taking turns or missing a move? How does he respond to competition and a win-lose situation? The unique ways that an individual copes with frustration are often apparent in games. An observant teacher, therefore, can discover much about a child's cognitive and affective skills as he joins in classroom games.

It is important to keep in mind that assessment and instruction are inseparable in the teaching process. The general guidelines for using games cited earlier continue to apply; however, several points are particularly important in reference to diagnostic games.

Selecting Item Pools   Select and sequence item pools with care. The success of games as assessment and teaching tools hinges upon the content of the item pools. Developmental sequencing is critical, because the major purpose of diagnosis is to determine a child's level in the progression of skills toward a final objective. This corresponds with his entry point into the instructional sequence. Therefore, both assessment and instruction should be based on the same developmental sequence of tasks. For most subject areas, sequences or checklists are available in curriculum guides, in teachers manuals of commercially produced programs, or in reference books in professional education. On occasion, it may be necessary for á teacher to construct an original skill sequence. This is often referred to as a task analysis, because it involves a sequential listing of all subskills contributing to performance of the desired task.

It is recommended that a teacher always consult or construct a developmental sequence before preparing item pools. Item pools should then be made in sets that are graduated in level of difficulty. A teacher using games extensively will want to devise a filing system for storing item pool cards in sequence according to skill area. In this way, the desired cards will be easily accessible for both assessment and instruction.

Game Format   Choose an appropriate game format. When collecting diagnostic information, it is important to select a game that requires the child to respond to the material at the desired level of complexity. The most basic games demand only a matching response; others call for recognition or identification. More difficult games may involve operating on the material in some way, such as performing math calculations or punctuating sentences. Still other games may encourage a child to generate creative solutions. Thus, with minor adaptations, one set of item pool cards might be used to assess skills at several levels of difficulty. Again, it is advisable to check a developmental sequence for the specific tasks appropriate in each instructional area.

As an example, a teacher concerned with assessing and teaching alphabet skills notes that a child must first be able to discriminate likenesses and differences among letters before he will be able to recognize or pick out individual letters. Likewise, letter recognition is a prerequisite for letter identification or naming. Table 1 was constructed to show sample games appropriate for each task involved in alphabet skills. For all of the games listed, the item pool consists of letter cards, yet the child responds to them in different ways at each level. In discrimination games, the child simply matches or makes pairs. At the recognition level, the student must name individual letters as he sees them in print. The response expected of the student becomes slightly more difficult at successive levels.

Some individuals may question the need to be so precise in differentiating the tasks involved in a simple matter of "knowing the alphabet." Yet there is a logical sequence inherent in learning to identify letters of the alphabet that cannot be violated in teaching without jeopardizing a child's chances for success. Moreover, when a student is not able to perform the final task, identifying letters of the alphabet, it is necessary to determine exactly at what level the child is having difficulty. It is for this reason that a sequenced and systematic approach is imperative.

As Table 1 illustrates, a game such as bingo may be used at more than one level with certain variations. In one case, the teacher holds up a stimulus letter for the student to make a visual match by covering the same letter on his card. Later, the child is asked to

Table 1. Example of an index relating games to a particular skill

Task	Game	Response
Discriminating letters	Bingo	Finds a letter like the one the teacher holds up and covers it
	Dominoes	Builds a design with only identical letters touching
	Old Maid	Makes pairs of matching letters
Recognizing letters	Bingo	Finds the letter named and covers it
	Racing Game	Finds the letter named and advances his marker to it
Naming letters	Racing Game	Draws a card and names the letter to move ahead
	Fish in a Bucket	Names the letter on the fish caught
	Hopscotch	Throws a marker, names the letter, and hops to it
	Beat the Clock	Reads a list of letters before the timer buzzes

locate and cover the letter whose name is called orally by the teacher. Racing games are also easily adapted for different task levels.

A chart such as that given in Table 1 would be a valuable reference for a teacher, because it provides a ready index of games available to a particular skill. Each teacher may develop a personalized system for cataloging games. A well-organized item pool and an index of games for different instructional areas will assure a teacher of a nearly inexhaustible supply of assessment and teaching activities.

Cautions   Plan to avoid problems with diagnostic games. Several cautions concerning the use of games are worth repeating in reference to assessment. When a teacher is seeking diagnostic information, it is important that features of the game do not interfere with the child's performance. Avoid overly competitive or distracting games. It is best to stick with simple, straightforward formats. Generic games lend themselves well to diagnostic use because most children are already familiar with playing procedures.

In order to determine the extent of a child's ability, some items will have to be difficult for him. To prevent undue frustration, mix items of varying levels of difficulty. It is desirable always to begin and end on a positive note. Although it is possible to gather diagnostic information on several children simultaneously, it is best to keep groups small in number.

Planning ahead will help to minimize problems involved in using games diagnostically. The teacher who employs basic games with small groups using item pools on the appropriate level of difficulty will find that games provide a rich source of evaluative data.

INVOLVING PEERS AND PARENTS

Peer Assisted Learning With Instructional Games

Once games are recognized as valid instructional media and are systematically incorporated into the curriculum, new teaching-learning possibilities emerge. Conditions surrounding the use of games can be modified in various ways to further individualize instruction. One very effective arrangement is Peer Assisted Learning. This involves the strategic pairing of students to work together in a tutorial relationship. It provides a helpful variation of the gaming approach for those times when a teacher feels that a child needs special individual attention. As a program, Peer Assisted Learning attempts to provide sufficient structure for the tutor to feel comfortable in teaching, while maximizing learning opportunities for the tutee. It also seeks to capitalize on the natural spontaneity of children interacting with each other. This approach to student tutoring can combine the advantages of instructional games with the benefits of one-to-one teaching.

Peer Assisted Learning is founded upon two well-supported observations. First, children learn effectively from other children. Much of what they learn, from riding a tricycle to the facts of life, is usually mediated by their peers. Children naturally tend to model the behavior of other children. Many times they learn more easily from one who shares the same perspective or "speaks the same language." In a well-planned tutorial situation, a child meets encouragement and success. Friendships develop as students work together on a regular basis. Such positive experiences are likely to increase a child's confidence and enhance his feelings about himself. As programs in peer tutoring increase in number, educators are realizing how much a tutee can gain both academically and affectively from the one-to-one attention.

Peer Assisted Learning is also based on the discovery that when one teaches, two learn. In order to work with someone else, the tutor at least reviews the material. More often, he reformulates his knowledge through the processes of analysis, synthesis, and application. The tutor's experiences with learning at higher cognitive levels are often reflected in impressive academic gains. In addition, the realization that one has something to offer and has been entrusted with the responsibility of teaching someone else does much to boost self-concept. Studies investigating effects of peer tutoring have revealed advantages for the tutor that may even outweigh gains of the tutee.

Peer Assisted Learning is an extremely flexible approach that may be adapted to meet differing needs in a variety of settings. A single teacher may successfully use peer tutoring within his own classroom, or several teachers within a school may team to develop a program on a larger scale. Unlike many special programs, Peer Assisted Learning is immediately available, offering teachers a unique means of personalizing instruction without making unrealistic demands upon their time. Principals and other administrators are typically supportive of Peer Assisted Learning because it does not call for the expansion of professional staff or the purchase of additional instructional materials. At a time when educators are struggling to accommodate a wide range of individual differences within the classroom, many are acknowledging the new relevance of the practice made famous in the American one-room schoolhouse—students tutoring other students. Peer Assisted Learning through games may offer one cost-effective option for tailoring an instructional program to individual needs.

Certainly the outcomes of Peer Assisted Learning depend on the quality of the specific program. Careful planning and organization are necessary for it to be successful. Initiating Peer Assisted Learning is not a difficult task for the teacher who is already using games, however, because the basic goals and operating procedures are similar. Peer tutoring is simply an extension of the use of instructional games into a particular one-to-one arrangement. The previously suggested guidelines for using games are, therefore, prerequisites for peer tutoring. In addition, the following steps are essential for implementing Peer Assisted Learning: 1) selecting tutors, 2) training tutors, 3) arranging tutoring sessions, and 4) monitoring progress. Although programs will vary in emphasis as well as size, the basic considerations for Peer Assisted Learning remain the same. Each step in establishing a student tutoring program is now considered in greater detail.

Selecting Participants   Within a single classroom, a teacher may use peer tutoring by having classmates work together. Cross-age tutoring is also possible when older students from higher grades are asked to help younger children. The primary criterion for allowing students to become involved in Peer Assisted Learning is interest. Any child who wants help in learning should be eligible to receive tutoring. Children who crave attention are prime candidates. Caution should be exercised, however, in assigning extremely withdrawn or acting-out children to be tutored. Although in some cases these children do relate better to a peer than to a teacher, in other instances they may be too difficult for another student to manage. If there is a chance that a child will respond to peer tutoring, the teacher may want to include him in the program, but should monitor his progress very carefully.

Desire is the major qualification for tutors as well. Any child who sincerely wants to tutor can contribute to the program, regardless of his level of academic proficiency. Children who are behavior problems in the classroom should not be overlooked. Often students who are unmotivated in their school work or disruptive in class make excellent tutors. In fact, low achievers and children with behavior and adjustment problems not only make effective tutors, but are often those who profit most from the experience. In setting up a Peer Assisted Learning program, it is usually advisable to include a cross-section of students from the school population, ranging from superior or model students to children with learning and behavioral difficulties. Being a tutor should be presented as a prestigious privilege. Students may be accepted into the program upon recommendation by the teacher, or prospective tutors may apply for the position on their own.

Once tutors and tutees have been identified, it is necessary to match them in pairs. Within a single classroom where children know each other, students may pair themselves by simply choosing a partner with whom they would like to work. A teacher may want to have students indicate two or three preferences, in case the first choice is not appropriate or available.

For cross-age tutoring, teachers must determine initial pairings. The general intent is to pair students whose personalities complement each other. Children with similar extreme behavior styles should not be placed together. It is easy to imagine that a tutoring session involving two withdrawn children might become boring or ineffective. At the other extreme, two talkative or aggressive children might get little accomplished working together. When a teacher is uncertain about a particular choice for a partner, it may be helpful to observe what type of individual the student naturally has picked as friends.

Feelings of the children should always be respected when a teacher is attempting to pair students for tutoring. Some children have definite preferences regarding tutor characteristics. A seventh-grade boy may enjoy being tutored by a ninth-grade boy, but he may not tolerate being tutored by an eighth-grade girl. In many instances, factors such as age and sex may not be major considerations. In cross-age arrangements, however, tutors of the same sex and at least two or three years older are typically more easily accepted by reluctant tutees. Tutoring assignments should initially be presented to children as tentative. It is usually advisable to tell students that they will be working together on a trial basis for the next several weeks. In this way, no one is being set up for failure, and children have little trouble accepting new assignments, should a change in partners be necessary.

The length of tutorial assignments varies according to individual needs. Some students may only require tutorial assistance for a short period of time until a particular skill is mastered. Others may continue in the program for several months or even an entire academic year. Once students become accustomed to the helping relationship, they may be phased in and out of the tutoring network as needed. A child who is on the receiving end in one situation may serve as the tutor in another assignment. Such active participation in the teaching-learning process does much to foster cooperation in the classroom and appreciation of individual differences.

Training Tutors   Adequate preparation of tutors is a critical aspect of Peer Assisted Learning. Anyone who has observed children playing school would probably admit that their conception of "teacher" is often less than flattering. Some children become very harsh and authoritarian when they assume the role of teacher. A punitive approach would be inconsistent with the basic purpose of Peer Assisted Learning—to provide a positive learning experience for both children involved. It becomes desirable, therefore, for tutors to acquire some general interaction skills related to teaching. Tutors should know how to present a task enthusiastically and how to encourage tutees to attempt things that may be difficult for them. It is also important that tutors learn to give feedback immediately after a child responds. They should praise or confirm correct answers and deal with errors in a constructive manner. It is often helpful to teach tutors a two-fold procedure for correcting errors that involves telling the tutee the correct response and encouraging him to reattempt the item. If a child makes a mistake in a reading game, for example, a tutor might say, "No, that word is 'forest.' Try it again."

It is not necessary for tutors to master complicated teaching methods in order to help children. Each tutor need only master the particular strategies to assist the child in learning. For instance, a teacher may suggest that Martha trace with her finger each of the words missed from her item pool. In another case, a teacher may instruct a tutor to show all of the steps in doing multidigit multiplication problems with his tutee in the Time Bomb game. Tutors should learn procedures for the games most frequently played, so that they can present them to tutees. A teacher may also explore with tutors ways to make a not-so-evenly-matched game interesting for the learner when they play together. One alternative is to have a tutee play against himself in a board game, pitting one pawn against another by answering for both.

In other games where points are called, a tutor may serve as an opponent who gains one point each time the tutee makes a mistake. In this way, the learner is really playing his number right against his number wrong. No adaptations are necessary with games such as bingo, which involve a large element of chance. Here, even the less skilled player may finish with a victory. When preparing students to tutor, it is a good idea to discuss some of these game variations for helping a tutee to be challenged and involved.

Procedures for training tutors will vary. When there are only a few tutors, training may best be accomplished through individual conferences with the teacher. In addition to explaining and discussing with the tutor, a teacher may also model desired approaches working with the tutee. After the tutor observes the teacher helping the child for several sessions, he may take over his new role. Teacher supervision is phased out as the tutor gains confidence and expertise.

Whenever several tutors need to be trained at once, a group approach becomes more efficient. Training workshops or seminars may be conducted for six to ten students at a time. In these sessions, prospective tutors become involved in many participation activities, such as discussing, brainstorming, and role playing. Although the teacher may initially present or model certain skills, the students should be given ample time to practice and to personalize them. When introducing the notion of encouragement, for example, he may demonstrate encouraging behavior and explain its importance in tutoring. The session might then become more student-centered as tutors brainstorm a list of encouraging comments and role play the use of encouragement in a simulated tutorial setting. Group training is the approach most often used in larger and cross-age tutoring programs, where students from the upper grades will be helping with the younger children.

Arranging Tutoring Sessions   Once tutors have acquired the basic skills for Peer Assisted Learning, the actual tutoring may begin. Because tutoring is viewed as a supplement to, and not a substitute for, teacher-directed instruction, neither tutors or tutees should miss important lessons in their own classrooms. Usually, time alloted for study or independent work is most appropriate for tutoring. Brief lessons, 20 to 30 minutes in length, provided three to five times a week, are typically most effective.

Tutoring may take place in a variety of settings. In open classrooms or rooms with learning centers, students can often tutor inconspicuously in the corner. Actual "tutoring stations" may be designated within a room. In some schools, tutoring is done in the resource room, reading lab, or library. If classroom space is at a premium, students may work in hallways, large closets, or other cubbyholes throughout the school. Portable screens may be set up to reduce distraction in areas where other activities are taking place.

For tutoring to be most beneficial, individual lessons must be carefully planned. Goals and objectives, activities, and materials must be specified for each lesson. Planning for tutorial lessons is vastly simplified by the use of instructional games. Once the teacher has determined the specific skills to be mastered and has provided the appropriate item pools, generic games can become instant lesson activities. In most cases, a student tutor is already familiar with accepted rules for generic games, so that little preparation is required. The tutor can actively contribute to the planning process as he chooses games to correspond to his child's interests. Students often enjoy creating new games to be used in the tutorial setting.

Monitoring Progress Continual communication between tutor and teacher is a vital component of Peer Assisted Learning. Concise yet informative record-keeping provides the basis of this communication. Student tutors may gather and record data on the learner's progress. This is one essential way for the teacher to keep abreast of tutorial effectiveness and the tutee's achievements. In addition, the teacher should periodically observe the children working together. Brief conferences should be held on a regular basis for the tutor and teacher to discuss problems and accomplishments and to revise lesson plans.

Mrs. Conover, a second-grade teacher, asked her friend who taught sixth grade if she had any students who might be interested in helping younger children with their schoolwork. Mrs. Conover explained that she could really use a few tutors to work with her second graders. When Mrs. Tait presented the idea to her class, the response was enthusiastic. She immediately got five volunteers. During several of her planning periods, Mrs. Conover met with her prospective student tutors to prepare them for their new responsibilities. All of the tutors would work individually with a tutee in a Game Center at their scheduled times. Each assignment was slightly different, however. Leslie was to use bingo and several racing games to help Karen learn sight words. Paul was to play bingo in another way to teach addition facts to Mark. Michael and Cindy were working on spelling skills playing Three Minute Eggs. Marianne needed help in verbal expression, so her tutor, Pam, was going to use the Picture This game. John was one second grader who excelled in academics, but needed to develop some social skills for interacting constructively with other children. Chris was asked to play a variety of games with John to help him learn to accept rules and to win and lose more gracefully.

The tutors came to the classroom at different times of the day for 15- to 20-minute lessons. The second graders would have loved to have them stay longer, and Mrs. Conover was extremely pleased with the progress her students were making. Mrs. Tait frequently commented on the new confidence and responsibility exhibited by her student tutors.

Parent Involvement With Instructional Games

Until recently, very few educators ever seriously attempted to involve parents in the formal instruction of their children. Some felt that most parents lacked the willingness, training, or sophistication required to contribute in any meaningful way. Others believed that parents were too close to the problem and would too easily become emotionally involved. Whatever the reason, it was pointed out that any resulting parental frustration or lack of patience in instructional settings would be discouraging to the children and counterproductive to the educational process.

There is some truth to these arguments, but they should not preclude the involvement of parents who are willing and able to participate. Many teachers are now recognizing this and are actively seeking ways to engage these individuals in cooperative school-home programs. When well thought-out, practical, and uncomplicated suggestions can be offered, the resulting parent involvement can benefit all concerned.

The average parent would have little difficulty employing the games in the manner advocated in this chapter. With a minimum of guidance he could use item pools supplied by the teacher to provide important practice and review of classroom objectives at home. Moreover, the positive parent-child interaction promoted by the games can contribute significantly to the child's development of healthy attitudes toward schoolwork and learning. Offered such a simple yet productive method of helping their children learn, many parents would probably respond with an increased spirit of cooperation and enthusiasm.

The actual steps necessary to establish a parent involvement program with instructional games will vary. Some teachers may initially propose the idea to a few of the parents with whom they are best acquainted. With their help, any unforeseen problems with the approach can be quickly ironed out, and the way prepared for wider utilization. Other teachers may decide to introduce the concept for all parents together at a PTA meeting or through a letter sent home. For those indicating an interest in the program, a meeting could be set up for more detailed explanations and demonstrations. Normally scheduled parent-teacher conferences might also be used for this purpose. Whatever the case may be, any teacher undertaking this type of program should consider the following suggestions:

1. Start small. Avoid any possible confusion by introducing only one instructional game and item pool in the beginning. Once suc-

cess is indicated and continued enthusiasm is apparent, then other games and objectives could be provided.

2. Suggest games the child is known to be interested in and familiar with. This helps to guarantee success because the difficulties sometimes encountered in learning a new game are avoided.

3. Emphasize the importance of winning. Children are quick to lose interest in games if they cannot win occasionally. Although most parents are aware of this, they must be prepared to give assistance or make on-the-spot modifications in the game if the child is not succeeding.

4. Provide a continuing supply of appropriate item pools. Allow the children to check out stacks of item cards for the night, the week, etc.

5. Get parents to monitor the progress their child is making. Provide them with the desired standard for mastery in terms of the approximate percentage of responses correct, and encourage them to indicate whenever this is reached. At such time a new, more challenging item pool can be sent home.

6. Caution the parents about any possible problems that might arise. They should, for instance, be warned about the dangers of excessive competition and the anxiety that it can produce in the child. Advice about overuse would also be helpful. Any hints or suggestions that would help them foresee and prevent difficulties should be provided.

7. If their initial experience is a positive one, explore with the parents any other situations in which the effectiveness of the games may be enhanced. For example, the entire family could become involved in some of the activities. Moreover, considering the earlier section on Peer Assisted Learning, older or same age siblings might participate as tutors or learn together in mutually stimulating games.

With relatively little teacher time and effort, parent involvement of the kind discussed above can in many cases be very beneficial. When parents are willing and interested, few if any serious problems will arise. One suggestion, however, is in order. The actual provision of games for use at home can quickly become expensive, as well as difficult to coordinate. A large inventory of games would be required if many parents were participating, and they would probably have to be replaced frequently. The borrowed games would occasionally be damaged. Parts would be lost. Sometimes they would never be returned. Unless operated with only a very few parents, therefore, an alternative procedure should be employed.

In addition to using educational games at home, interested parents might also become involved in other ways. Many times, parents can provide valuable assistance to the classroom teacher in developing a good supply of instructional games. A teacher may solicit help by asking families to contribute old games and game parts. Worn game boards can easily be made over, and spinners, dice, play money, and other pieces put to new use. Children love to donate things from home. Their interest often soars because they have a personal investment in classroom games. PTAs and homeroom parent groups might organize drives to obtain materials for constructing games or to raise funds for purchasing commercial ones.

Parents who are willing and able to give some of their time may help the cause in other important ways. Adults often enjoy getting together to make instructional games for the classroom. If the teacher carefully explains what is needed and provides samples of various types of games, parents can do the actual designing and constructing. Volunteers can also be helpful in printing or typing item pool cards as directed by the teacher. After a few morning sessions or a Saturday "Game Day," an exciting array of new games can be ready for use.

Adults who would like to become involved on a continuous basis may work with teachers to form a parent volunteer program. Some parents may serve as aides in the classroom. Having an extra adult available in the games center is a great help, especially in the lower grades. A parent can introduce new games, answer questions, settle disputes, and generally provide support and encouragement. A capable volunteer can be an invaluable assistant in record keeping as well.

Some parents may also work on a one-to-one basis with students. As stressed in the rationale for peer tutoring, certain children thrive on individual attention, and tutoring can be a powerful instructional arrangement. Parent volunteers can be very effective in this role. By working closely with a child's teacher, the tutor can implement instructional strategies that would be difficult to do in a group situation. Again, games provide motivating and effective activities for tutorial sessions.

PART III

USING EDUCATIONAL MATERIALS
Resources and References

14

Editorial Introduction

This final part of the book includes three chapters that focus on the sources to which educators may turn for assistance in providing individualized instructional approaches for problem learners in mainstream educational settings. Chapter 15 describes the major information resources currently in existence and explains how they can be used. These include the extensive information services of the Council for Exceptional Children, the Educational Resources Information Center, and the National Center of Educational Media and Materials for the Handicapped. The final section of Chapter 15 is a compilation of published professional books and papers related to the systematic utilization of educational media and materials. Organized under seven categories, the bibliography should be useful to teachers, supervisors, and administrators, as well as to college students and instructors.

In Chapter 16, a bibliography of references that can serve as models for mainstreaming is provided. Whereas other chapters in the book have dealt with content directly related to the use of educational materials, this chapter presents sources that describe a wide array of instructional alternatives or innovative programs for children with special needs. There is an obvious relationship between the unique organization of these mainstream programs and the resulting demand for increased sophistication in the utilization of materials by teachers. The content of these publications, therefore, should help to fill a possible "gap" in the professional preparation of teachers who must begin to individualize instruction in an unfamiliar context.

The concluding segment of this book, Chapter 17, presents a historical review of some of the most significant approaches to the development of prototypes of instructional materials for handicapped learners. In this section, landmark contributions are summarized that even now serve as the theoretical and philosophical basis for many of our contemporary instructional materials. The authors hope that this background information will provide teachers with at least a rudimentary theoretical yardstick against which the practical utilization of materials can be measured. Finally, there is included an up-to-date bibliography of materials identified as valuable and effective by teachers who have used them in the classroom.

15

Educational Media and Materials

Selected Resources and References

Janet W. Anderson, M.Ed.,
Robert M. Anderson, Ed.D.,
and Sara J. Odle, Ed.D.

American educators now have access to the most comprehensive information resources on instructional materials for educationally handicapped children ever developed in the United States or elsewhere. Unfortunately, the majority of teachers either are unaware of these resources or for one reason or another do not choose to use them. Chapters 15, 16, and 17, therefore, have been designed to provide teachers with an awareness of the major information resources currently in existence and some understanding of how they can be used to enhance the educational programs of children with diverse needs and problems.

Whereas other chapters have dealt with various procedures and systems for directly retrieving appropriate instructional materials for youngsters with special needs, the chapters in this section focus on a variety of professional resources and references, all closely related to teacher utilization of instructional materials, but not *directly* involved with the retrieval of a prescribed set of materials based on a diagnostic prescriptive profile of a child with specific, identifiable problems.

One such source is the Council for Exceptional Children (CEC) Information Service. It provides excellent bibliographies, abstracts, computer searches, indexes, journals, and miscellaneous publications that are often relevant to the utilization of instructional materials. An understanding of the services provided by the CEC Information

Some of the descriptive material used in this chapter was obtained or adapted from brochures used by organizations such as CEC and NCEMMH to disseminate information about their resources.

Center as described in the section that follows, as well as the other resources included in this section, will enable teachers to tap comprehensive collections of information vital to their work with educationally handicapped learners.

THE CEC INFORMATION CENTER

The Council for Exceptional Children established its Information Center in 1966 as part of the Education Resources Center of the Office of Education. Dr. William C. Geer (1977), Executive Director of CEC, describes the Center as follows:

> It is the CEC-ERIC Center on Handicapped and Gifted Children. Since its beginning, more than 25,000 volumes and references have been abstracted and the abstracts published through Exceptional Child Education Abstracts. Now, we are currently adding more than 3,000 references per year. Effective with the new volume now being prepared, ECEA's name has been changed to Exceptional Child Education Resources, and we are adding a listing of films about exceptional children and abstracts of dissertations (p. 86).

In addition to numerous other activities, the Center prepares topical bibliographies, conducts custom computer searches, and publishes a variety of books and nonprint media. These activities are described in the following sections. For additional information, interested readers should contact:

> The Council for Exceptional Children
> ERIC Clearinghouse on Handicapped and Gifted Children
> 1920 Association Drive
> Reston, Virginia 22091

Exceptional Child Education Resources (ECER)

The ECER reference guide, formerly entitled *Exceptional Child Education Abstracts,* is generally considered to be one of the most comprehensive information resources currently available to practitioners or researchers working or studying in any field involving the education of the handicapped or gifted. This compilation, published quarterly, includes abstracts of current special education publications, as well as doctoral dissertations and professional media materials. The coverage includes research reports, journal articles, curriculum guides, teacher activity manuals, administrative surveys and guidelines, and texts.

Topical Bibliographies

For an overview of a general subject, the Council for Exceptional Children provides over 60 preselected, preprinted bibliographies. The series encompasses a wide variety of subject areas, including several that focus on mainstreaming. These topical bibliographies include citations from earlier volumes of ECER published through Fall, 1976.

CEC has recently initiated a new bibliography series entitled *Exceptional Child Education Resources Bibliography Series—1977*. Seventeen new titles, *selected to meet expressed user needs*, were made available, containing selected abstracts of the most significant references from Volume 8 of *Exceptional Child Education Resources*, described in the preceding section. Each fall, a new set of titles will be taken from the most recent volume of ECER. Each bibliography will average 50–100 citations with publication date, author, title, source, and 200-word summary.

Custom Computer Searches

If none of the topical bibliography titles adequately covers a researcher's topic, a custom computer search can give him access to the most current and comprehensive information on a specialized topic tailored to his specific needs. The *Exceptional Child* data base provides access to references on more than 23,000 documents and articles related specifically to handicapped and gifted children.

For example, one might request "all references you have on educational materials and media for visually handicapped children in the mainstream." At that point, information specialists would analyze the request, formalize the search strategy, and edit a personalized computer printout containing citations with abstracts.

Other CEC Publications

The Council for Exceptional Children publishes a variety of curriculum guides, cassette tapes, surveys, and reports on current concerns. Included among recent publications are five items that are highly relevant to the practical application of instructional materials.

The most elaborate of these publications is a language stimulation and development kit, *Learning Language at Home*. Developed by Merle B. Karnes, this sequenced program for children at the 3–5 year level may be used by parents, paraprofessionals, and teachers. Lesson plans are correlated with 200 sequenced lesson cards that combine 1,000 activities. The lessons are color coded by four skill areas and sequenced in order of difficulty. Each lesson includes reinforcement and extension activities, and suggestions of instructional materials needed.

Another publication by Karnes, *Creative Games for Learning: Parent and Teacher Made Games*, includes 50 games designed to foster the social, motoric, cognitive, and academic learning of young children. According to Karnes, these games were chosen from among hundreds of possibilities because they were the easiest to construct and the most fun to play. The games can be created inexpensively and can be modified to meet the individual needs of the child. In the Introduction, suggestions are made on how to modify the games to meet the needs of handicapped and gifted youngsters. Techniques for ensuring the success of a game and the benefits of using homemade games are listed. The objective of each game is stated, followed by a drawing of what the game looks like, what materials are needed, how to construct the game, and how to play it.

An additional resource, *Teaching Aids and Toys for Handicapped Children* (Barbara Dorward), describes constructional use of pegboards, puzzles for developing size and space perception, color discrimination, and reading and number readiness.

Teaching Exceptional Children, one of CEC's professional journals, explores practical procedures to use in the classroom—preschool through adolescent. It includes creative suggestions on instructional methods and learning material, educational diagnostic techniques, and evaluation of instructional materials. It also includes a Teacher Idea Exchange.

More than 100 teacher tested ideas on instructional materials and techniques have been compiled and reprinted from the popular Teacher Idea Exchange. Published in *Teacher Idea Exchange,* the approaches are presented in convenient card format for easy filing.

The Southwest Educational Development Laboratory has compiled a collection of games, activities, and instructions for making manipulative learning equipment from inexpensive and recycled materials for preschool handicapped and nonhandicapped children. Designed for home use by parents as well as for classroom activities, the material is grouped by modality: visual, auditory, fine motor, gross motor, touch and smell, and language and concept development. Also available in Spanish, the publication is titled, *How to Fill Your Toyshelves Without Emptying Your Pocketbook: 70 Inexpensive Things to Do or Make.*

Audiovisual Resources for Instructional Development contains over 1,000 annotations on audio, films, film loops, filmstrips, multimedia, slide shows, transparencies, and videotapes. The annotations are cross indexed under seven descriptors.

EDUCATIONAL RESOURCES INFORMATION CENTER (ERIC)

The Educational Resources Information Center (ERIC) was established by the U.S. Office of Education. It began operations in

1966 and is managed by the National Institute of Education. ERIC serves as a national information system through a network of decentralized information centers (e.g., college and university libraries, resource centers). ERIC collects, screens, organizes, and disseminates reports of educational interest, and furnishes copies of these reports at a nominal cost. Interpretive summaries, research reviews, and bibliographies on critical topics are also prepared by ERIC.

The ERIC system is comprised of the *Thesaurus of ERIC Descriptors, Resources in Education (RIE)*, and *Current Index to Journals in Education (CIJE)*. The Thesaurus is a listing of subject headings or descriptors. The descriptors are a structured vocabulary of 7,200 terms used in the ERIC indexes. *RIE* is a monthly abstract journal in which recently completed research reports, descriptions of outstanding programs, and documents of educational significance are arranged by subject, author, and institution. Semiannual and annual cumulative indexes are provided. *CIJE* is a monthly guide to more than five hundred major educational and education related publications.

To use ERIC, first use the *Thesaurus* to determine the appropriate major and/or minor descriptors. Then look up the descriptor in the subject index of *RIE*. Relevant articles are listed under the subject heading. An ED number is assigned to each article and corresponds to abstracts in the Document Resumes section. Complete copies of articles may be obtained in microfiche. *CIJE* searches follow a similar format and employ the same descriptors used for *RIE*. EJ numbers are used to identify articles. *CIJE* articles are not available in microfiche and have to be found in their respective journals.

A computer search of the ERIC data base is available for a small fee.

PUBLICATIONS FROM NCEMMH

National Catalog of Films in Special Education

The National Center on Educational Media and Materials for the Handicapped (NCEMMH) has just published the first *National Catalog of Films in Special Education* (1977), an annotated bibliographic list of more than 700 films about teaching children with handicaps. The catalog includes films from about 250 distributors, indexed under approximately 200 descriptors pertinent to handicapping conditions or special education needs. This new reference tool brings together in one source an inclusive listing and description of films that had previously been included in widely scattered sources. Users of the catalog may browse through the entire list of 200 descriptors to become familiar with them before beginning a search for a film on a given subject. Some examples of the descriptors include "Diagnostic Prescriptive," "Handwriting," "Perceptually Handicapped," "Educational Methods," and "Hyperactivity." A Sample Entry—Abstract is shown in Figure 1. This listing, which the National Center plans to update periodically, may be obtained from the Ohio State Press, 2070 Neil Avenue, Columbus, Ohio 43210 (price $3.00). The other publications described in this section may be obtained from the same address.

Publishers Source Directory

The NCEMMH has also just announced the availability of the new and extensively updated third edition of the *Publishers Source Directory*. This directory is designed to provide assistance in locating information about where to buy or rent instructional materials and other educational aids, devices, and media. The directory, which lists nearly 1,700 distributors of 74 kinds of instructional materials (non-print as well as print), will be of interest to teachers responsible for ordering instructional materials, members of materials selection committees in school systems, school administrators, and learning resource center staff and librarians. Although the reference book was compiled primarily as an aid to special education instructors, many of the producers and distributors listed also distribute instructional materials for use in general education.

The instructional materials are listed according to 74 categories—e.g., high interest-low vocabulary, manipulative materials, color keyed materials, puppets, tachistoscopes, etc.

The publishers, producers, and distributors are listed in alphabetical order. Under the name and address of each publisher, producer, and distributor are code numbers that correspond to the type of instructional aids, devices, and media that each publisher produces, distributes, sells, rents, or loans. Figure 2 illustrates one of the entries.

Turn Off the Sound

The *Turn Off the Sound* manual was developed by the former Northeast Regional Media Center for the Deaf in 1974 and revised and reissued by MCEMMH, 1977.

Turning off the sound in filmstrip programs—converting it to visual material—is a valuable way to adapt instructional material for

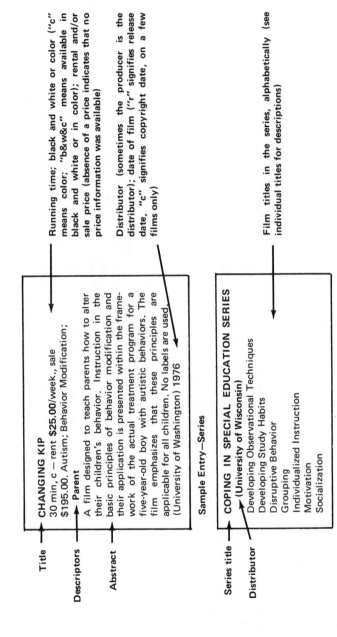

Title → **CHANGING KIP**   → Running time; black and white or color ("c"
30 min, c — rent $25.00/week., sale   means color; "b&w&c" means available in
$195.00. Autism; Behavior Modification;   black and white or in color); rental and/or
Descriptors → **Parent**   sale price (absence of a price indicates that no
A film designed to teach parents how to alter   price information was available)
their children's behavior. Instruction in the
basic principles of behavior modification and
Abstract → their application is presented within the frame-   Distributor (sometimes the producer is the
work of the actual treatment program for a   distributor); date of film ("r" signifies release
five-year-old boy with autistic behaviors. The   date, "c" signifies copyright date, on a few
film emphasizes that these principles are   films only)
applicable for all children. No labels are used.
(University of Washington) 1976

Sample Entry—Series

Series title → **COPING IN SPECIAL EDUCATION SERIES**
Distributor → **(University of Wisconsin)**
Developing Observational Techniques
Developing Study Habits   Film titles in the series, alphabetically (see
Disruptive Behavior   individual titles for descriptions)
Grouping
Individualized Instruction
Motivation
Socialization

Figure 1. Sample entry-abstract from *National Catalog of Films in Special Education*, 1977, p. viii. Reprinted by permission of Information Services, National Center on Educational Media and Materials for the Handicapped.

Example. In the examples given below, the firm produces audiovisual aids (6), captioned film strips (10), filmstrips (24), high interest low vocabulary materials (28), and so on.

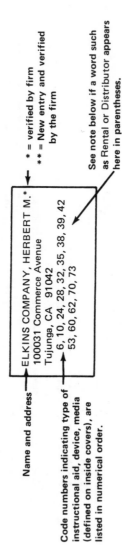

Name and address → ELKINS COMPANY, HERBERT M.*   * = verified by firm
                   100031 Commerce Avenue   ** = New entry and verified
                   Tujunga, CA 91042   by the firm
                   6, 10, 24, 28, 32, 35, 38, 39, 42
                   53, 60, 62, 70, 73

Code numbers indicating type of
instructional aid, device, media
(defined on inside covers), are
listed in numerical order.

See note below if a word such
as Rental or Distributor appears
here in parentheses.

If the word Rental appears after the codes, the firm listed rents films or other materials but does not sell them.

If the word **Distributor** appears after the codes, the firm is a distributor only and does not produce. Such a firm distributes products of many companies. Consult the firm's catalog for a list of such companies.

If the words **Loan only** appear after codes, the firm loans materials but does not sell or rent them.

Figure 2. Sample entry from NCEMMH *Publishers Source Directory*, 1977, p. viii. Reprinted by permission of Information Services, National Center on Educational Media and Materials for the Handicapped.

use with the hearing impaired, according to this compact and comprehensive do-it-yourself manual. It shows special educators or audiovisual coordinators ways to expand educational resources for the handicapped by creating individualized instructional materials from standard materials. The manual gives clear, step-by-step, carefully illustrated procedures for adapting sound filmstrip programs to silent programs for use with the hearing impaired.

The manual describes the entire adaptation process; delineates the steps, materials, and equipment needed for 10 separate adaptations; and provides appendixes that suggest resources and include captioning guidelines from a school for the deaf and from the Caption Center at Boston television station WGBH-TV. Many of the techniques involved in changing either the text or the visual part of a filmstrip are not difficult and require only inexpensive equipment. Cautions are outlined concerning copyrighted material and other material requiring permission.

Until the early 1970s, silent filmstrips were a mainstay in the education of the hearing impaired. However, producers began a new trend of abandoning the silent format because sound filmstrip programs were so popular and successful. This book (originally entitled *Turn Off the Soundtrack*) was written to ensure that educators of the hearing impaired would continue to have a good supply of usable high-quality filmstrips, in spite of their scarcity in the marketplace.

Many sound filmstrip programs are well organized and interesting and have accurate and reliable content that does not depend on sound. Changing them to meet the requirements of hearing impaired learners easily falls within the capabilities of most special educators and media personnel. The approach fits the special educators' long tradition of creating individualized materials from standard materials.

Workshop: Creating
Instructional Materials for Handicapped Learners

The *Workshop: Creating Instructional Materials for Handicapped Learners* kit was created by the former Northwest Special Education Instructional Materials Center, reissued by NCEMMH, and is now available from the National Audiovisual Center, General Services Administration, Washington, D.C. 20409 (order no. 009688).

This product has two main purposes—to show teachers how to create materials for teaching handicapped learners, and to guide teachers in selecting, evaluating, adapting, and using commercial materials for educating handicapped children. It is intended for use in an inservice workshop. The workshop at which the material is presented should take two sessions. Session I, on adapting and improvising instructional materials, requires a day; Session II, on evaluating instructional materials, should follow two weeks later and can be accomplished in an evening.

The coordinator's guide includes master copies of activity sheets to be duplicated and distributed to workshop participants. It also contains the complete scripts for the other components of the kit: "Selecting Instructional Material," 7-minute audio cassette and filmstrip; "Creativity," 13-minute audio cassette; and "Educating Young Handicapped Children: Getting the Most Out of Materials," 15-minute audio cassette and filmstrip.

A SELECTED BIBLIOGRAPHY

The major underlying assumption of this book is that many school administrators, supervisors, and teachers have only a cursory knowledge of "how to use" instructional materials. As stated in Chapter 2, most students completing teacher education programs and, indeed, a surprisingly large number of teacher educators and experienced teachers, need increased knowledge and greater understanding of the rationale and procedures for selecting, retrieving, assessing, and evaluating materials. This book has therefore presented a sequential approach to the acquisition of these competencies. Readers should now be familiar with terms such as "descriptors" and "individual prescription," and should be knowledgeable about matching instructional materials with specialized strategies and teaching units. In addition, it has been shown how the effective use of media and technology, including both equipment and materials, can provide increased individuality of instruction, greater pupil interest and achievement, and flexibility of teaching style.

Although many educators are relatively unfamiliar with the literature on educational media and technology, a substantial number of papers have been published in professional journals in recent years. In completing the research for this book, the authors identified numerous useful articles. However, the literature in which they appear is so widely scattered that few practitioners will have an opportunity to master this body of knowledge. In this section of the book, therefore, a selected bibliography of resources related to the systematic utilization of educational media and materials has been compiled.

The references have been organized under the following categories:

Identifying, Selecting, and Retrieving
Creating, Adapting, and Constructing
Evaluating and Assessing
Technology and Media
Content Areas
Sensorially Handicapped
Severely and Multiply Handicapped

It is hoped that the bibliography that follows will be useful as a guideline for regular and special class teachers, supervisors, and administrators, and as a resource for college students and instructors.

Identifying, Selecting, and Retrieving

Adamson, G., and Van Etten, M. C. 1970. Prescribing via analysis and retrieval of instructional materials in the educational modulation center. Except. Child. 36(7): 531–533.

Anderson, R. M., Zia, B., Springfield, H. L., and Greer, J. G. 1977. Educational media and materials for the handicapped. Educ. Train. Ment. Retard. 12(3): 226–234.

Annotated Bibliography of Multi-Ethnic Curriculum Materials. 3rd suppl. 1975. Midwest Center for Equal Educational Opportunities, Columbia, Mo.

Audiovisual Resources for Instructional Development. 1975. The Council for Exceptional Children, Reston, Va. Department of HEW, Office of Child Development, Washington, D.C.

Belland, J. C. 1973. The national center on educational media and materials for the handicapped. Audiovis. Instruct. 18(2): 7–9.

Boland, S. K. 1974. Managing your instructional material dollar. Teach. Except. Child. 6(3): 134–139.

Carlson, B. L., and Pellant, R. W. 1972. Serving teachers in rural areas through a university associated SEIMC. Except. Child. 39(1): 58.

Carlson, M. A., and Tillman, R. 1967. Selection and evaluation of learning materials. Child. Educ. 43(5): 266–270.

Daily, R. 1971. Thesaurus for Special Education Instructional Materials. The Council for Exceptional Children. Information Center on Exceptional Children, Reston, Va. Department of Health, Education and Welfare, Office of Education, Bureau of Education for the Handicapped, Washington, D.C.

Draper I. L. 1975. A Materials Resource Guide for Teachers of Preschool Children with Special Needs. Detroit Public Schools, Pre-School Technical Assistance Resource and Training Center, Detroit. U.S. Department of HEW, USOE/BEH, December, Washington, D.C.

Driscoll, J. 1968. Educational films and the slow learner. Ment. Retard. 6(1): 32–34.

50 Tactile and Visual Perception Games for Under $10: A Guide to Readiness for Pre-School Teachers, Head Start Teachers and First Grade Teachers. Continuing Education Publications, Corvallis, Or.

Forrester, B., Brooks, G. P., Hardge, B. M., and Outlaw, D. D. 1971. Materials for Infant Development. George Peabody College, Demonstration and Research Center for Early Education (37263), Nashville, Tn. National Program on Early Childhood Education, Department of Health, Education and Welfare, Office Education, Washington, D.C.

Free and Inexpensive Learning Materials. 1974. Division of Surveys and Field Services, George Peabody College for Teachers, Nashville, Tn.

Gross, C., and Werlin, K. 1972. Removing the blinders: A shopper's guide to instructional materials. Educ. Train. Ment. Ret. 7(3): 141–145.

Happ, F. W. 1967. Teaching aids for the mentally retarded child. Ment. Retard. 5(4): 33–35.

Hofmeister, A. M., and Atkinson, C. M. 1976. The TELEPAC Project: A Service Delivery Model for the Severely Handicapped in Rural Areas. Utah State Exceptional Child Center. Logan, Ut. U.S. Department of HEW, USOE/BEH, Washington, D.C.

Instructional Materials: A Selective Bibliography. 1972. Exceptional Child Bibliography Series 637, Council for Exceptional Children, Reston, Va. Information Center on Exceptional Children, Department of Health, Education and Welfare, Office of Education, Bureau of Education for the Handicapped, August, Washington, D.C.

Instructional materials and resource materials available to teachers of exceptional children and youth. Addendum 1972. University of Texas, College of Education, Department of Special Instructional Materials Center, Bureau of Educational Research for the Handicapped, Austin.

Instructional Materials Thesaurus for Special Education. 1973. The Council for Exceptional Children, Information Center on Exceptional Children, Reston, Va.

Lambert, R. H. 1975. A Bibliography of Materials for Handicapped and Special Education. 2nd ed. Center for Studies in Vocational and Technical Education, Wisconsin University, Madison.

Lance, W. D. 1975. Instructional materials for the mentally retarded: A review of selected literature. Educ. Train. Ment. Retard. 10(3): 161–166.

Lange, R. R. 1974. Needs for Instructional Media and Materials Services for Handicapped Learners: A Summary of Extant Information. Ohio State University, Columbus. National Center on Educational Media and Materials for the Handicapped, U.S. Department of HEW, USOE/BEH, Media Services and Captioned Films Branch, Washington, D.C.

Lawhon, D., and Thornton, L. 1975. An Annotated Catalog of Visual Materials Relating to the Identification and Management of Handicapping Conditions of Preschool Children. Appalachia Educational Laboratory, Charleston, W. Va.

Logan, D. A. 1970. Educational materials: Instructional materials resources. Educ. Train. Ment. Retard. 5: 130–132.

McCarthy, J. L. (ed.). 1969. A Guide to Curriculum Materials for Exceptional Children. Lowell Publications, Mt. Pleasant, Mi.

Mainstreaming training systems, materials, and resources: A working list. 3rd ed. 1976. Minnesota University Leadership Training Institute/Special Education, August.

Martin, E. W. 1973. Introducing the national media center for special education. Audiovis. Instruct. 18(2): 5.

Materials for Secondary School Programs for the Educable Mentally Retarded Adolescent. ED 042310. 1970. New England SEIMC, Boston University, Boston.

Media, Methods and Materials for Special Educators. 1972. Michigan State Department of Education, Division of Special Education, Lansing, Mi.

NICEM Indexes. 1973. National Information Center for Educational Media, University of Southern California, Los Angeles, Ca.

Reichard, C. L. 1970. Instructional materials specifically for the retarded. Teach. Except. Child. 2: 187–188.

Resources for effective teaching. 1972. Michigan State Department of Education, Division of Special Education, Lansing, Mi.

Rude, C. 1973. Media analysis and retrieval system. Midwestern Educational Resource Center, Coralville, Ia.

Selected materials for teaching the trainable mentally retarded. 1970. New England SEIMC, Boston University, Boston.

Stile, S. W., and Atkinson, C. 1976. Project TELEPAC: Packaged home instructional materials for parents of the severely handicapped: A concept analysis. Exceptional Child Center, Utah State University, Logan. U.S. Department of HEW, USOE/BEH, Washington, D.C.

Suttles, P. 1972. Elementary Teachers Guide to Free Curriculum Materials. Educators Progress Service, Randolph, Wi.

Swiss, T. 1976. ERIC/RCS: Bicentennial reading sources. J. Read. 19(4): 345, 347, 349.

Thorum, A. R. 1976. Instructional materials for the handicapped: Birth through early childhood. Olympus Research Corporation, Salt Lake City, Ut. Department of Health, Education and Welfare, Office of Education, Bureau of Education for the Handicapped, ED 125 167, Washington, D.C.

Ward, T. 1968. Questions teachers should ask in choosing instructional materials. Teach. Except. Child. 1(1): 21–23.

Weinthaler, J., and Rotberg, J. M. 1970. The systematic selection of instructional materials based on an inventory of learning abilities and skills. Except. Child. 36(8): 615–619.

Wood, R. K., and Stephens, K. G. 1977. An educator's guide to videodisc technology. Phi Delta Kappan 58(6): 466–467.

Zimmerman, L. D., and Calovini, G. 1971. Toys and learning materials for pre-school children. Except. Child. 37(9): 641–654.

Creating, Adapting, and Constructing

Altman, R., Drew, C. J., and Dykes, M. 1973. Acquisition of instructional material information: Manual design and material complexity. Educ. Train. Ment. Retard. 8(3): 150–153.

Belland, J. C., and Rothenberg, S. 1973. Developing instructional materials for the handicapped. Guidelines for preparing materials suitable for wide distribution. National Center on Educational Media and Materials for the Handicapped, Columbus, Oh. Department of Health, Education and Welfare, Office of Education, Bureau of Education, Washington, D.C.

Fincher, J., Chatfield, M. V., and Vergason, A. 1970. Playing cards as instructional aids. Teach. Except. Child. 2(2): 93–94.

Fuchigami, R. Y., and Smith, R. F. 1968. Guidelines for developing and evaluating seatwork materials for handicapped children. Educ. Train. Ment. Retard. 3(3): 141–145.

Gitter, L. L. 1973. Montessori materials and activities, Part II. J. Spec. Educ. Ment. Retard. 9(2): 3–8, 115.

Hollestelle, C. H., and Kelly, R. R. 1972. Bulletin boards: No deposit-no return. Teach. Except. Child. 5(1): 36–39.

Homemade Innovative Equipment. 1973. American Association for Health, Physical Education and Recreation, Northwest Washington, D.C.

Howell, D. 1972. Project 5050. Arith. Teach. 19(1): 29–33.

Huff, R. 1972. Development of an enlarged abacus, Educ. Vis. Hand. 4(3): 88–90.

Jacobson, I. 1969. Stop! Look! Listen! Instructor 148–149.

Keiffer, M. 1968. The development of teaching materials for low achieving pupils in seventh and eighth grade mathematics. Arith. Teach. 15(1): 599-608.

Koehler, N., and Wolinsky, G. F. 1973. A cooperative program in materials development for very young hospitalized children. Rehab. Lit. 34(2): 34-41, 46.

Lambert, R. H. 1975. Modifying regular programs and developing curriculum materials for the vocational education of the handicapped: Progress report. Madison University Center for Studies in Vocational Technical Education. Wisconsin State Board of Vocational, Technical, and Adult Education, Madison.

Latham, G. 1976. Teacher use of instructional materials and other matters related to special education IMC/LRC Collections. Theoretical paper no. 59, Fall, ERIC Document ED 126 663.

McCabe, M. P. 1973. Adaptations of Material and Equipment for Individualizing Remediation in Learning Disabilities Resource Rooms. Escambia County, Division of Instruction, Pensacola, Fl.

Meyen, E. L. 1970. Field Testing: A source of evaluation in developing instructional materials. Educ. Train. Ment. Retard. 5(1): 31-36.

Old, A. 1970. Spelling for educable mentally retarded—It works. Instructor 79(8): 117.

Seitz, S., and Merryman, S. 1970. An investigation of factors influencing learning in the mentally retarded, and their use in the design of instructional materials. Interim report. ED 042 319. Texas Research Institute, Houston.

Wedemeyer, A., and Cejka, J. 1970. Creative Ideas for Teaching Exceptional Children. Love Publishing Company, Denver, Co.

Wilds, T. 1975. Audiovisual resources for instructional development. The Council for Exceptional Children, Reston, Va.

Woodward, H. 1976. A workshop for the development of specialized materials and arrangement of learning environments. J. Spec. Educ. Ment. Retard. 12(3): 201-11.

Evaluating and Assessing

Adamson, G., and Van Etten, M. C. 1970. Prescribing via analysis and retrieval of instructional materials in the Educational Modulation Center. Except. Child. 36(7): 531-533.

Armstrong, J. 1971. A model for materials development and evaluation. Except. Child. 38(4): 327-333.

Bailey, G. G. 1977. Improving classroom instruction with means-referenced objectives. Educ. Technol. 17(7): 13-15.

Baker, R., and Shutz, R. (eds.). 1971. Instructional Product Development. Van Nostrand Reinhold, New York.

Berman, M. L., and Haring, N. G. 1972. Evaluation and specification of the instructional materials and management procedures through use of a pupil performance profile and a predictive model. Washington University, Child Development and Health Retardation Center, Seattle. Department of Health, Education and Welfare, Office Education, Bureau of Education for the Handicapped, Washington, D.C.

Briggs, L. J. 1970. Handbook of Procedures for the Design of Instruction. American Institutes for Research, Pittsburgh, Pa.

Clawson, E. V., and Barnes, B. R. 1972. The effects of organizers on the learning of structured materials in the elementary grades. Education 93(2): 150–157.

Computer based project for the education of media for the handicapped. Second annual report. 1971. Syracuse City School District, Syracuse, N.Y. Department of Health, Education and Welfare, Office of Education, Washington, D.C.

Drew, C. J., and Martinson, M. C. 1971. Educational methodology: An examination of approach. Except. Child. 38(2): 117–120.

Drew, C. J., Altman, R., and Dykes, M. K. 1971. Evaluation of instructional materials as a function of material complexity and teacher manual format. Educ. Train. Ment. Retard. 6(3): 118–121.

Eash, M. 1969. Assessing curriculum materials: A preliminary instrument. Educ. Prod. Rep. 2(5): 18–24.

Ensminger, E. E. 1970. Learning disabilities and instructional materials. Foc. Except. Child. 1(9).

Ensminger, E. E. 1972. A proposed model for selecting, modifying, or developing instructional materials for handicapped children. In E. L. Meyen, G. A. Vergason, and R. J. Whelan (eds.), Strategies for Teaching Exceptional Children. Love Publishing Company, Denver, Co.

Evaluations of kits for early learning, no. 48. EPIE Educational Product Report. Educational Products Information, Exchange Institute, 463 West St., New York, N.Y. 10014.

Johnson, S. R., and Johnson, R. B. 1970. Developing Individualized Instructional Material. Westinghouse Learning Press, Palo Alto, Ca.

Junkala, J. 1970. Teacher evaluation of instructional materials. Teach. Except. Child. 2(2): 73–76.

Klein, M. F., Michael, W. B., and Tyler, L. L. 1971. Recommendations for the Evaluation of Curriculum and Instructional Materials. Tyle Press, Los Angeles.

Kuhfittig, P. K. D. 1973. Learning aids in the classrooms: Experimental evidence of their effectiveness. Education 94(2): 135.

Lucco, R. J. 1976. Conceptualizing evaluation strategy: An evaluation systems framework. Paper presented at the annual meeting of the American Educational Research Association (60th), April 19–23, San Francisco, Ca.

McIntyre, R. B. 1969. Empirical evaluation of instructional materials. Educ. Technol. 9(2): 24–27.

McIntyre, R. B. 1970. Evaluation of instructional materials and programs: Applications of a systems approach. Except. Child. 37(3): 213–225.

Materials Analysis. 1976. J. Learn. Dis. 9(7): 408–416.

Meyen, E. L., Frank, A. R., and Rodee, M. 1970. Field testing: A source of evaluation in developing instructional materials. Educ. Train. Ment. Retard. 5(1): 31–36.

Proger, B., Carfioli, J. C., and Kalapos, R. L. 1973. A neglected area of accountability: The failure of instructional-materials evaluation and a solution. J. Spec. Educ. 7(3): 269–282.

Reichard, C. L. 1970. Instructional materials specifically for the retarded. Teach. Except. Child. 2: 187–189.

Reichard, C. L., Reid, W. R., et al. 1970. Evaluative procedures for instructional materials. Acad. Ther. 6: 171–175.

Rooz, G. E. 1969. Empirical evaluation of instructional materials in affective area. Educ. Technol. 9(4): 53–56.

Splaine, J. E. 1977. Models for making decisions about controversial instructional materials. Educ. Technol. 17(3): 38–41.

Thiagarajan, S. 1977. Interaction individualization: An intermediate instructional technology. Educ. Technol. 17(1): 39–44.

Thompson, D. D. 1973. Evaluation of an individualized instructional program. Elem. School J. 73(4): 213–221.

Ward, T. 1968. Questions teachers should ask in choosing instructional materials. Teach. Except. Child. 1: 21–23.

Weinthaler, J., and Rotberg, J. M. 1970. The systematic selection of instructional materials based on an inventory of learning abilities and skills. Except. Child. 36: 615–619.

Technology and Media

Adams, S. R. 1968. Utilization of educational television for teaching of the handicapped. Proceedings of the Institute on Educational Television for Teaching the Handicapped. State Education Department, State University of New York, Albany.

Aserlind, L. 1966. Audiovisual instruction for the mentally retarded. Audiovis. Instruct. 11(9): 727–730.

Audio visual lending library resource list. Meyer Children's Rehabilitation Institute, Omaha, Ne.

Avance, L. D., and Carr, D. B. 1972. Development of audio and visual media to accompany sequenced instructional programs in physical education for the handicapped. U.S. Department of HEW, Office of Education, Bureau of Research, Washington, D.C.

Bitzer, D. L., Lyman, E. R., and Easley, J. A. Jr. 1966. The uses of PLATO, a computer controlled teacher system. Audiovis. Instruct. 11(1): 16–21.

Blackhurst, A. E. 1965. Technology in special education—Some implications. Except. Child. 31: 449–456.

Brown, J. W., Lewis, R. B., and Harcleroad, F. F. 1977. AV instruction technology, media and methods. McGraw-Hill Book Company, New York.

Brown, L., Huppler, B., Van Deventer, P., Sontag, E., and York, R. 1973. Use of reinforcement principles to increase comprehension of instructional filmstrips. Educ. Train. Ment. Retard. 8(1): 50–56.

Burbank, L. 1976. Visual Communication in Special Education Using Television and Manipulative Materials. Eastern Pennsylvania Regional Resources Center for Special Education, ERIC ED 134 156, King of Prussia, Pa.

Cawley, J. 1970. Teaching arithmetic to mentally handicapped children. Foc. Except. Child. 2(4): 1–8.

Dagnon, C., and Spuck, D. W. 1977. A role for computers in individualizing education—And it's not teaching. Phi Delta Kappan 58(6): 460–462.

Davis, P. A. 1970. Methods and Aids for Teaching the Mentally Retarded. T. S. Dennison and Company, Minneapolis, Mn.

Florida—Developed Products Listing: Education for Exceptional Students. 2nd ed. 1975. Florida State Department of Education, Bureau of Education for Exceptional Students, Tallahassee.

Grossman, B. 1976. The uses of media in early childhood education. Young Child. 31(4): 256–262.

Guidelines for developing computer based resource units. Educational Research and Development Complex, State University of New York, Buffalo.

Haring, N. G. 1970. The new curriculum design in special education. Educ. Technol. 10(5): 24–31.

Hofmeister, A. 1972. Audio-tutorial programming with exceptional children. Kansas State College Teachers Resource Center, ERIC ED 114 401, Emporia, Ks.

Hubalek, F. 1975. The production of audio-visual media in school. Educ. Med. Int. 3: 19–26.

Instrument turns sound of music to sight of music at Aux Chandelles. 1970. Educ. Med. 1(10): 16–17.

Jamison, D., Suppes. P., and Wells, S. 1974. The effectiveness of alternative instructional media: A survey. Rev. Educ. Res. 44(1): 1–67.

Johnson, G. F. 1968. Programmed instruction and the exceptional learner. Except. Child. 34: 453–457.

Lance, W. D. 1977. Technology and media for exceptional learners: Looking ahead. Except. Child. 44(2): 92–96.

Levine, S. J. 1968. Educational uses of cartridge tapes: Dissemination document (11). Michigan State University, RIMC for H. C. & Y, East Lansing. Department of Health, Education and Welfare, Bureau of Education for the Handicapped, Washington, D.C.

Liberman, H. 1968. Use of the overhead as a tachistoscope. Audiovis. Instruct. 13(4): 384.

Littleton, A. C., and McBrayer, J. D. 1971. Hardware with software: Implications for special education. Educ. Technol. 11(8): 55–57.

Mackenzie, L. 1969. Programmed learning for slow learners. Am. Voc. J. May: 55–56.

Mares, C. 1975. Television and radio as resources in special education. Educ. Broadcast. Int. 8(2): 59–62.

Mauk, W. C. 1971. Applied media: The philosophy and technique. Rehab. Rec. 12(5): 1–5.

Meyen, E. L. 1969. The use of overhead projections in classrooms for the mentally retarded. Iowa University, Iowa City. Special Education Curriculum Center, Iowa City. Iowa State Department of Public Education, Des Moines. Department of Health, Education and Welfare, Office of Education, Washington, D.C.

Murphy, L. C. 1971. Video tape as a motivator for non-hearing students. Teach. Except. Child. 3(4): 169–171.

Murphy, H., and Delmonte, O. 1971. Snapping pictures for communication skills. Teach. Except. Child. 3(4): 169–171.

Norwood, M. J. 1975. Instructional technology: Its emerging role in the education of the handicapped. J. Educ. Technol. 4(1): 63–72.

Oldsen, C. F. 1976. The national instructional materials information system. Audiovis. Instruct. 21(10): 48–50.

Opperman, J. J. 1976. An association for special educational technology. Audiovis. Instruct. 21(10): 16.

Ray, H. W. 1972. Media for the exceptional child. In E. L. Meyen, G. A. Vergason, and R. J. Whelan (eds.), Strategies for Teaching Exceptional Children. Love Publishing Company, Denver, Co.

Retzlaff, W. F. 1973. Project worker: Videotaping work stations in industry. Teach. Except. Child. 5(3): 135–137.

Rovet, J. F. 1976. Can audio-visual media teach children mental skills? Paper presented at the American Educational Research Association Annual meeting, San Francisco, Ca.

Schisgall, J. 1973. The creative use of multimedia (or the shape of things to come). Teach. Except. Child. 5(4): 162–169.

Schultz, M. J. 1965. The Teacher and the Overhead Projection. A Treasury of Ideas, Uses and Techniques. Prentice-Hall, Englewood Cliffs, N.J.

Scoggins, R. T., Jr., Sullivan, J. P., Kohn, S., and Batarseh, G. J. 1972. A team approach using cassette tapes. Child. Today 1(4): 16–19.

Selected mental health audiovisuals. National Institute of Mental Health, Rockville, Md.

Sharapan, H. B. 1973. Misteroger's neighborhood: A resource for exceptional children. Audiovis. Instruct. 18(2): 18–20.

SMILE: Special Materials Improve Learning Experiences. 2 vols. 1975 suppl. Central Pennsylvania Special Education Resource Center, Harrisburg, Pa.

Smith, C. M. 1973. Effective use of media in the classroom. Foc. Except. Child. 5(6): 1–11.

Smith, H. R., and Nagel, T. S. 1972. Instructional media in the learning process. Charles E. Merrill Publishing Company, Columbus, Oh.

Striefel, S., and Eberl, D. 1974. Imitation of live and videotaped models. Educ. Train. Ment. Retard. 9(2): 83.

Thiagarajan, S. 1973. Exceptional children, unexceptional grown-ups, and mediated resources. Audiovis. Instruct. 18(2): 21–22.

Viggiani, J. C. 1969. The use of photography to enhance learning in the classroom. Spec. Educ. Canada 44(1): 13–26.

Withrow, F. B. 1976. Educational technology for the handicapped learner: In F. B. Withrow and C. J. Nygren (eds.), Language, Materials, and Curriculum Management for the Handicapped Learner. Charles E. Merrill Books, Columbus, Oh.

Content Areas

Alkema, C. J. 1968. Art and the exceptional child. Part II. Child. House 3(1): 12–15.

Armstrong J. R., and Schmidt, H. 1972. Simple materials for teaching early number concepts to trainable-level mentally retarded pupils. Arith. Teach. 19(2): 149–153.

Avance, L. D., and Carr, D. B. 1973. A sequenced instructional program in physical education for the handicapped Phase III. Producing and disseminating demonstration packages. Final report.

Los Angeles Unified School District, Ca. Department of Health, Education and Welfare, Office of Education, Bureau of Research, September, Washington, D.C.

Bitter, J. A., and Bolanovich, D. J. 1966. Job training of retardates using 8mm film loops. Audiovis. Instruct. 11: 731–732.

Blackhurst, A. 1967. Tachistoscopic training as a supplement to reading instruction for educable mentally retarded children. Educ. Train. Ment. Retard. 2: 121–125.

Bloom, B. 1971. New instructional program teaches personal property concept to trainable children. Teach. Except. Child. 3(4): 195–200.

Brown, V. (ed.). 1975. Programs, materials and techniques: Reading miscue analysis. J. Learn. Dis. 8(10): 605–611.

Burelson, D. L. 1975. Use and abuse of audio-visuals in sex education. J. Spec. Educ. Ment. Retard. 11(1): 122–125.

Callahan, J. J., and Jacobson, R. S. 1967. An experiment with retarded children and Cuisenaire rods. Arith. Teach. 14(1): 10–13.

Cawley, J. F. 1972. Teaching arithmetic to mentally handicapped children. In E. L. Meyen, G. A. Vergason, and R. J. Whelan (eds.), Strategies for Teaching Exceptional Children. Love Publishing Company, Denver, Co.

Cawley, J. F., and Vitello, S. J. 1972. Model for arithmetical programming for handicapped children. Except. Child. 39: 101–110.

Dailey, R. F. 1971. CEC/ERIC's the now way to know: Me Now—Life sciences for the mentally retarded. Educ. Train Ment. Retard 6(3): 127–131.

Davis, C., Hunt, J. T., and Hirshoren, A. 1974. Classified ads as reading material for the educable retarded. Except. Child. 41(1): 45.

Dunn, L. M., Nitzman, M., Pochanart, P., and Bransky, M. 1968. Effectiveness of the Peabody Language Development Kits with educable mentally retarded children: A report after two and one-half years. IMRID papers and reports, Vol. V, no. 15. ED 043 185. Peabody College, Nashville, Tn.

Dunn, L. M., and Smith, J. O. Peabody Language Development Kits. Level #1, 1965; Level #3, 1967; Level #P (with K. B. Horton), 1968. American Guidance Service, Circle Pines, Mn.

Edmonson, B., Leach, E., and Leland, H. 1969. Social Perceptual Training Kit for Community Living. Educational Activities, Freeport, N.Y.

Educator's Guide to Free Science Materials. Educator's Progress Service, Randolph, Wi.

Educators Guide to Free Social Studies Materials, Educator's Progress Service, Randolph, Wi.

Enstrom, E. A. 1975. Homemade handwriting. Education 91(2): 135-137.

Franks, F., and Huff, R. 1973. Educational materials development in primary mathematics: Fractional parts of wholes. Educ. Vis. Handi. 5(2): 46-54.

Higgins, C., and Rusch, R. R. 1967. Development and evaluation of auto-instructional programs in arithmetic for the educable mentally handicapped. Final report. ED 014 190 Albany Public Schools, Albany, N.Y.

Instructional Aids in Mathematics, National Council of Teachers of Mathematics. Yearbook 34. 1973. National Council of Teachers of Math, Washington, D.C.

Koran, J. T., and Wilson, J. T. 1973. Science curriculum materials for special education students. Educ. Train. Ment. Retard. 8(2).

Kramer, T., and Krug, D. A. 1973. A rationale for teaching addition. Educ. Train. Ment. Retard. 8: 140-145.

Lee, R. 1970. Art for retarded children. Instructor 79(6): 108-109.

Lough, E., Rembolt, R. R., and Brown, F. 1968. Industrial arts for handicapped children in a hospital school. Except. Child. 34(5): 357-360.

Materials on creative arts (arts, crafts, dance, drama, and music) for persons with handicapping conditions. American Association for Health, Physical Education, and Recreation, Washington, D.C.

Nist, J. F. 1975. Media for children: Cornucopia for language learning. Elem. Engl. 52(4): 513-514.

Onesto, S., and Inglehart, B. 1975. Multi-media materials on ethnic studies: A selected bibliography. Ill. Schools J. 56(3): 54-78.

Paulston, P. 1972. Language training via videotape. Audiovis. Instruct. 17(4): 30.

Peters, N., and Peters, J. 1973. Better reading materials for the content areas: Criteria for better use and annotated bibliography. Volta Rev. 75(6): 375-87.

Reich, R. 1968. Puppetry—A language tool. Except. Child. 34: 621-623.

Ross, D. 1967. The use of games to facilitate the learning of basic number concepts in pre-school educable m.r. children—final report. Office of Education, Washington, D.C.

Soeffing, M. 1972. Designing a multiple option arithmetic curriculum for the mentally handicapped: An interview with John Cawley. Educ. Train. Ment. Retard. 7(3): 151-156.

Towne, D. C., and Wallace. S. 1972. Vocational instructional materials for students with special needs. Northwest Regional Educational Laboratory, Portland, Or.

Townsend, I. J. 1972. Science for the special child. Part II: Development of some appropriate techniques. School Sci. Rev. 53: 475–496.

Watchman, C. R. 1971. Numbers with the less able child. Forw. Trends. 15(2): 55–60.

Wilson, J. T., and Koran, J. J. 1973. Science curriculum materials for special education students. Educ. Train. Ment. Retard. 8(2): 30–32.

Wolff, S., and Wolff, C. 1974. Games Without Words: Activities for Thinking Teachers and Thinking Children. Charles C Thomas Publisher, Springfield, Il.

Woodcock, R. W. 1970. Using rebuses to teach reading to the mentally retarded. Paper presented at the meeting of The Council for Exceptional Children, April, Chicago.

Sensorially Handicapped

Altschuler, D. 1970. Use of video tape in programs for the deaf. Volta Rev. 72(2): 102–6.

Barnes, D. O., and Finkelstein, A. 1971. The role of computer assisted instruction at the National Technical Institute for the Deaf. Am. Ann. Deaf. 116(5): 446–8.

Boyd, J., and Vader, E. A. Captioned television for the deaf. Am Ann. Deaf. 117(1): 34–37.

Brown, J., and Arkebauer, H. J. 1970. Using the language master with hearing impaired children. Teach. Except. Child. 2(2): 81–5.

Caldwell, D. C. 1973. Use of graded captions with instructional television for deaf learners. Am. Ann. Deaf 118(4): 500–507.

Catalog of Music Publications. 1976. American Printing House for the Blind, Louisville, Ky.

Catalog of Vacuum-Formed Publications. 1977. American Printing House for the Blind, Louisville, Ky.

Clarcq, J., and others. 1973. Career development and media utilization at the National Technical Institute for the Deaf. Am. Ann. Deaf 118(5).

Commercial Aids That May be Used or Adapted for Visually Handicapped. American Printing House for the Blind, Louisville, Ky.

Directory of Agencies Serving the Visually Handicapped in the United States. American Foundation for the Blind, New York.

Educational Aids Catalog. American Printing House for the Blind, Louisville, Ky.

Educational Aids for Visually Handicapped—September, 1971. American Printing House for the Blind, Louisville, Ky.

Fitch, J. L., Sachs, D. A., and Marshall, H. R. 1973. A program to improve visual perception skills of pre-school deaf children. Am. Ann. Deaf 118(3): 429–32.

Fonville, W. 1973. Making and using self-teaching movies in the occupational education classroom. Am. Ann. Deaf 118(5).

Garner, W. L., and Zerrp, C. E., Jr. 1971. Evaluating programmed learning materials. Am. Ann. Deaf 116(5): 456–64.

General Catalog of Braille Publications. 1977. American Printing House for the Blind, Louisville, Ky.

General Catalog of Cassette Tapes. 1976. American Printing House for the Blind, Louisville, Ky.

General Catalog of Large Type Publications Produced by the Short-Run Process. 1977. American Printing House for the Blind, Louisville, Ky.

General Catalog of Large Type Textbooks. 1977. American Printing House for the Blind, Louisville, Ky.

General Catalog of Talking Books. 1976. American Printing House for the Blind, Louisville, Ky.

Gray, G. L. 1972. Instructional Strategies. Media Production Workshop for Teachers for the Deaf. New Mexico State University, Southwest Regional Media Center for the Deaf, Las Cruces, N.M. U.S. Department of HEW, USOE/BEH, Washington, D.C.

Instructional materials appropriate for use in deaf education. 1973. Los Angeles California University Special Education Instructional Materials Center U.S. Department of HEW, USOE/BEH, Washington, D.C.

International Catalog of Aids and Appliances for Blind and Visually Impaired Persons. 1973. American Foundation for the Blind, New York.

Ivey, L. P., and Teel, J. R. 1974. Sensory language stimulation with the TAVF unit. Am. Ann. Deaf 119(3): 318–320.

Krug, R. R., and Hawkins, F. P. 1970. A project to develop and evaluate the effectiveness of instructional materials for the deaf, designed to emphasize the syntactical meaning of words. Final report. Colorado University, Boulder, Co. U.S. Department of HEW/BEH, Washington, D.C.

La Gow, R. 1972. Dialogue films: Discussion and inquiry. Am. Ann. Deaf 117(5): 500–507.

Lloyd, C. 1975. Resources for the educator of severely or multiply handicapped. Educ. Train. Ment. Retard. 10(4): 303–6.

McCarr, J. E. 1971. Programmed instruction in a school curriculum. Am. Ann. Deaf 116(5): 476–9.

Materials for Prescriptive Teaching for Utilization of Low Vision. 1975. Instructional Materials Reference Center for Visually Handicapped Children, American Printing House for the Blind, Louisville, Ky.

Materials Reference List. Instructional Materials Reference Center for Visually Handicapped Children, American Printing House for the Blind, Louisville, Ky.

Murphy, L. C. 1974. Videotape as motivator for non-hearing students, or can you see yourself on TV and still be bored in school. Teach. Except. Child. 7(1): 10–14.

Programmed learning for the deaf student. 1971. Symposium on Research and Utilization of Educational Media for Teaching the Deaf Lincoln Nebraska, March 22–24, Nebraska University, Midwest Regional Media Center for the Deaf, Lincoln, Ne. U.S. Department of HEW, USOE/BEH, Media Services and Captioned Films for the Deaf Branch, Washington, D.C.

Project LIFE—Language improvement to facilitate education: A multimedia instructional system for the deaf child. National Education Association, U.S. Department of HEW, USOE/BEH, Washington, D.C.

Recorded Materials. Instructional Materials Reference Center for Visually Handicapped Children. American Printing House for the Blind, Louisville, Ky.

A Resource Guide for Teachers of Young Hearing Impaired Children. Capitol Region Education Council, West Harford, Ct. U.S. Department of HEW, USOE/Bureau of Elementary and Secondary Education, Washington, D.C.

Reynolds, H. N., and Rosen, R. F. 1973. The effectiveness of textbook, individualized, and pictorial instructional formats for hearing impaired college students. Paper presented at the Annual Meeting of the American Educational Research Association, February 25–March 1, New Orleans, La.

Schmitt, R. 1972. The affective domain: A challenge to ITV. Am. Ann. Deaf 117(5): 493–499.

Sources of Materials for the Partially Sighted. Instructional Materials Reference Center for Visually Handicapped Children, American Printing House for the Blind, Louisville, Ky.

Suppes, P. 1971. Computer assisted instruction for deaf students. Am. Ann. Deaf 116(5): 500–8.

Sylves, D. 1973. Utilization of Sesame Street materials with a deaf population. Final report. State University of New York, Educational Research and Development Complex, Buffalo.

Sylves, D. and Sprickman, A. (eds.). Sesame and You—A Teacher's Helper. State University of New York, Educational Research and Development Complex, Buffalo.

Takemori, W., and Snyder, J. 1972. Materials and techniques used in teaching language to deaf children. Am. Ann. Deaf 117(4): 455-8.

Television for the Hearing Handicapped Learner: Preservice Teacher Handbook. 1974. Southern Regional Media Center for the Deaf, Knoxville, Tn. U.S. Department of HEW, USOE/BEH, Media Services and Captioned Films, Washington, D.C.

Thiagarajan, S. 1973. A new role for teachers: The teacher of the deaf as an instructional designer. Volta Rev. 75(8): 473-9.

Volunteers who produce books: Braille, large type, tape. Division for the Blind and Physically Handicapped, Library of Congress, Washington, D.C.

Wacker, C. H., Jr. 1975. A proposal for the use of tape recorders for corrective feedback in the blind skill training. New Outl. Blind 69(10): 473-475.

Withrow, F. B., and Brown, D. W. 1968. An experimental program of language development using a systematic application of audio-visual aids to reinforce the classroom teacher's program for children with impaired hearing. Final report. Illinois School for the Deaf, Jacksonville, Il. U.S. Department of HEW, Bureau of Research, Washington, D.C.

Wood, T. A. 1976. The development of programmed instruction in orientation and mobility for multiply handicapped blind children. Paper presented at the annual International Convention, the Council for Exceptional Children, Chicago, Il.

Ziff, L. 1974. Utilization of visually-oriented media to motivate and develop language facility in hearing impaired children. Volta Rev. 76(3): 178-181.

Severely and Multiply Handicapped

Bare, C., Boettke, E., and Waggoner, N. Self-help clothing for handicapped children. National Easter Seal Society for Crippled Children and Adults, 2023 West Ogden Avenue, Chicago, Il.

Gold, M. W. Try Another Way. (Series of films showing applications of task analysis to skill training of the retarded.) Film Productions of Indianapolis, Indianapolis, In.

Hoffmann, R. B. 1970. How to Build Special Furniture and Equipment for Handicapped Children. Charles C Thomas Publisher, Springfield, Il.

I CAN Individualized Physical Education Curriculum Materials for the Trainable Mentally Retarded. Module I, Aquatics. Hubbard Press (Division of Hubbard Scientific Company), Northbrook, Il.

I CAN Individualized Physical Education Curriculum Materials for the Trainable Mentally Retarded. Module II, Body Management. Hubbard Press (Division of Hubbard Scientific Company, Northbrook, Il.

I CAN Individualized Physical Education Curriculum Materials for the Trainable Mentally Retarded. Module III, Fundamental skills. Hubbard Press (Division of Hubbard Scientific Company), Northbrook, Il.

I CAN Individualized Physical Education Curriculum Materials for the Trainable Mentally Retarded. Module IV, Health fitness. Hubbard Press (Division of Hubbard Scientific Company), Northbrook, Il.

Lowman, E., and Klinger, J. L. 1969. Aids to Independent Living: Self-Help for the handicapped. McGraw-Hill Book Company, New York.

Macey, P. G. 1974. Mobilizing Multiply Handicapped Children: A Manual for the Design and Construction of Modified Wheelchairs. Division of Continuing Education, University of Kansas, Lawrence, Ks.

Pearson, L. R. 1973. Guide to homemade innovative equipment for activities in physical education and recreation for impaired, disabled, and handicapped participants. Service No. ED 080-524. U.S. Department of HEW, Office of Education, BEH, Washington, D.C.

Project MORE. (Systematic training packages for training the mentally retarded in the area of daily living skills.) George Peabody College, Nashville, Tn.

Robinault, I. P. 1973. Functional Aids for the Multiply Handicapped. Medical Department, Harper and Row, Hagerstown, Md.

Rosenberg, C. 1968. Assistive devices for the handicapped. A-V Publications Office, Sister Kenny Institute, Minneapolis, Mn.

Wehman, P. 1976. Selection of play materials for the severely handicapped: A continuing dilemma. Educ. Train. Ment. Retard. 11(1): 46–50.

Yuker, H. E., Feldman, M. A., Fracchia, J. F., and Younng, J. H. The modification of educational equipment and curriculum for maximum utilization by physically disabled persons. Human resources study #8: Educational and school equipment for physically disabled students. Human Resources Center, Albertson, N.Y.

Yuker, H. E., Revenson, J., and Fracchia, J. F. The modification of educational equipment and curriculum for maximum utilization by physically disabled persons. Human resources study #9: Design of a school for physically disabled students. Human Resources Center, Albertson, N.Y.

Yuker, H. E., Younng, J. H., and Feldman, M. A. The modification of education equipment and curriculum for maximum utilization by physically disabled persons. Human resources study #11: Staffing a school for physically disabled students. Human Resources Center, Albertson, N.Y.

Zimmerman, M. 1965. Self-help Devices for Rehabilitation: Part I. William C. Brown, Dubuque, Ia.

Zimmerman, M. 1965. Self-help Devices for Rehabilitation: Part II. William C. Brown, Dubuque, Ia.

16

Models for Mainstreaming Special Children

**John W. Schifani, Ed.D., Larry Chapman,
and Robert M. Anderson, Ed.D.**

BIBLIOGRAPHY

As discussed earlier, mainstreaming is a relatively recent programmatic development that has been widely implemented in the public
schools only since the early 1970s. It is a radical departure from the
historical pattern of special education in the United States; by its
definition alone it has profound implications for regular as well as
special education. As its name implies, mainstreaming refers to the
re-entry of handicapped children into the regular education system,
into the "mainstream of education." Those children mainstreamed
have come largely from the traditional disability categories of the
educable mentally retarded, the mildly emotionally disturbed and
learning disabled, the hearing impaired, visually impaired, and
physically handicapped.

Many educators have expressed concern that mainstreaming
handicapped children in regular classrooms can result in inadequate
educational programs for both normal and exceptional pupils unless
there is a concerted effort to assist classroom teachers in coping with
children who have special problems. It is obvious that the effects of
mainstreaming will be disastrous if adequate budgets and supportive
services are not provided. Now, as never before, there is a growing
need to individualize instruction through increased sophistication in
the use of instructional materials, better classroom organization, task
analysis, diagnostic prescriptive teaching, utilization of a variety of
supportive personnel, and more systematic use of behavior management techniques.

This chapter assists in the process of dissemination of relevant
information by offering a bibliography of references that can serve as
models for mainstreaming. A substantial number of publications that
describe instructional alternatives or innovative programs for

children with special needs are now available to teachers and administrators. Therefore, the authors have developed a compilation that, although not exhaustive, is representative of programs and approaches now being implemented across the United States. Obviously, the nature of these mainstream programs will dictate that teachers must utilize materials much more systematically and effectively than they have in the past. These publications, when read carefully and related to the content of this book, will fulfill a very special need of teachers who are committed to individualizing instruction for handicapped learners.

The references have been organized under the following categories:

Mainstreaming: Least Restrictive Environment
Due Process, Litigation, and Public Law 94-142
Evaluation
Administrative Considerations
Professional Issues
Teacher Preparation
Traditional Categories
Program Interventions

Mainstreaming: Least Restrictive Environment

Anderson, W. 1971. Who gets a "special education?" In M. C. Reynolds and M. D. Davis (eds.), Exceptional Children in Regular Classrooms. Leadership Training Institute, Department of Audio-Visual Extension, University of Minnesota, Minneapolis, Mn.

Barnes, E. 1975. Children Learn Together: The Integration of Handicapped Children into Schools. Human Policy Press, Syracuse, N.Y.

Berry, E. 1972. Models for Mainstreaming. Dimensions Publishing Company, San Rafael, Ca.

Bertness, H. 1971. Action for handicapped. In M. C. Reynolds and M. D. Davis (eds.), Exceptional Children in Regular Classrooms. Leadership Training Institute, Department of Audio-Visual Extension, University of Minnesota, Minneapolis, Mn.

Birch, J. W. 1971. Special education for exceptional children through regular school personnel and programs. In M. C. Reynolds and M. D. Davis (eds.), Exceptional Children in Regular Classrooms. Leadership Training Institute, Department of Audio-Visual Extension, University of Minnesota, Minneapolis, Mn.

Blatt, B. 1971. Handicapped children in model programs. In M. C. Reynolds and M. D. Davis (eds.), Exceptional Children in Regular Classrooms. Leadership Training Institute, Department of Audio-Visual Extension, University of Minnesota, Minneapolis, Mn.

Caster, J. 1976. What is "mainstreaming"? Except. Child. 42: 174.

Chaffin, D. 1974. Will the real 'mainstreaming' program please stand up—(Or . . . should Dunn have done it?). Foc. Except. Child. 6 (5): 1–18.

Childs, R. E. 1975. A review of the research concerning mainstreaming. J. Spec. Educ. Ment. Retard. 11 (2): 106–112.

Divoky, D. 1976. Mainstreaming: Moving special education out of the basement. Compact 10 (1): 2–3.

Edmonds, M. 1976. Accountability for all children in the regular classroom. Lang. Arts 53 (4): 425–427.

Gearheart, B. R., and Weishahn, M. W. 1976. The Handicapped Child in the Regular Classroom. The C. V. Mosby Company, St. Louis, Mo.

Gickling, E. E., and Theobald, J. J. 1975. Mainstreaming: Affect or effect. J. Spec. Educ. 9 (3): 317–328.

Grosenick, J. 1971. Integration of exceptional children into regular classes: Research and procedure. Foc. Except. Child. 3 (5): 1–8.

Haring, N. G., and Schiefelbusch, R. L. 1976. Teaching Special Children. McGraw-Hill Book Company, New York.

Hewett, F. M. 1971. Handicapped children and the regular classroom. In M. C. Reynolds and M. D. Davis (eds.), Exceptional Children in Regular Classrooms. Leadership Training Institute, Department of Audio-Visual Extension, University of Minnesota, Minneapolis, Mn.

Hewett, F. M. 1974. Education of Exceptional Learners. Allyn and Bacon, Boston.

James, R. L., and Wilderson, F. B. 1976. Mainstreaming and the Minority Child. The Council for Exceptional Children, Reston, Va.

Jordan, J. B. (ed.). 1976. Teacher, Please Don't Close the Door: The Exceptional Child in the Mainstream. The Council for Exceptional Children, Reston, Va.

Keogh, B. K., and Levitt, M. L. 1976. Special education in the mainstream: A confrontation of limitations? Foc. Except. Child. 8 (1): 1–11.

Lance, W. D. 1976. Who are all the children? Except. Child. 43: 66–76.

Lewis, A. J. 1971. Increasing educational services to handicapped children in regular schools. In M. C. Reynolds and M. D. Davis (eds.), Exceptional Children in Regular Classrooms. Leadership

Training Institute, Department of Audio-Visual Extension, University of Minnesota, Minneapolis, Mn.

MacMillan, D. L. 1976. Mainstreaming the mildly retarded: Some questions, cautions and guidelines. Ment. Retard. 14 (1): 3–10.

Maker, C. J. 1977. Providing Programs for the Gifted Handicapped. The Council for Exceptional Children, Reston, Va.

Mann, L. M., and Sabatino, D. A. 1974. The Special Review of Special Education. Grune and Stratton, New York.

Morse, W. C. 1971. Special pupils in regular classes: Problems of accomodation. In M. C. Reynolds and M. D. Davis (eds.), Exceptional Children in Regular Classrooms. Leadership Training Institute, Department of Audio-Visual Extension, University of Minnesota, Minneapolis, Mn.

Principal's Guide to Mainstreaming. 1975. Craft-Mel Publications, Waterford, Ct.

Rauth, M. 1976. Mainstreaming: A river to nowhere or a promising current? Am. Teach. 60 (8): 1–4.

Reynolds, M. C. 1976. Mainstreaming: Origins and Implications. The Council for Exceptional Children, Reston, Va.

Roberts, B. 1975. Making it into the "mainstream." Teacher 93 (4): 37–39

Schifani, J. W., Anderson, R. M., and Dietrich, W. L. 1976. Contemporary Issues in Mainstreaming Handicapped Citizens. Kendall-Hunt Publishing Company, Dubuque, Ia.

Smith, W. L. 1971. Ending the isolation of the handicapped. Am. Educ. 7 (9): 340–345.

Stephens, W. E. 1975. Mainstreaming: Some natural limitations. Ment. Retard. 13 (3): 40–41.

VanEtten, G., and Adamson, G. 1975. The fail-save program: A special education service continuum. In E. N. Deno (ed.), Instructional Alternatives for Exceptional Children. The Council for Exceptional Children, Arlington, Va.

Zufall, D. 1976. The exceptional person: Approaches to integration. J. School Health 46 (3): 142–144.

Due Process, Litigation, and Public Law 94-142

Abeson, A. A. 1973. Legal Change for the Handicapped through Litigation. The Council for Exceptional Children, Reston, Va.

Abeson, A., Bolick, N., and Hass, J. 1975. A Primer on Due Process: Education Decisions for Handicapped Children. The Council for Exceptional Children, Reston Va.

Adamson, G. W. 1972. Upgrading Special Education in the Regular Classroom. University of New Mexico, Albuquerque.

Aiello, B. 1976. Making It Work: Practical Ideas for Integrating Exceptional Children into Regular Classes. The Council for Exceptional Children, Reston, Va.

Ballard, J., Nazzaro, J. N., and Weintraub, F. J. 1976. P.L. 94-142, the Education for All Handicapped Children Act of 1975. The Council for Exceptional Children, Reston, Va.

Ballard, J., and Zettel, J. 1977. Public law 94-142 and section 504: What they say about rights and protections. Except. Child. 44 (3): 155.

Birch, J. W., and Reynolds, M. C. 1977. Teaching Exceptional Children in All America's Schools, A First Course for Teachers and Principals. The Council for Exceptional Children, Reston, Va.

Ceska, J. M., and Needham, F. 1974. Approaches to Mainstreaming: Teaching the Special Child in the Regular Classroom. Teaching Resources Corporation, Boston.

Cole, R. W., and Dunn, R. 1977. A new lease on life for education of the handicapped: Ohio copes with 94-142. Phi Delta Kappan 59 (1): 3-7.

Digest of State and Federal Laws: Education of Handicapped Children. 1975. The Council for Exceptional Children, Reston, Va.

Hedbring, C., and Holmes, C. 1977. Getting together with P.L. 94-142: The IEP in the classroom. Educ. Train. Ment. Retard. 12 (3): 212-224.

Irving, T. 1976. Implementation of Public Law 94-142. Except. Child. 43 (3): 135-137.

P.L. 94-142: Implementing Procedural Safeguards: A Guide for Schools and Parents. 1977. The Council for Exceptional Children, Reston, Va.

Rousseau, M. K., and Parks, A. L. 1976. The Public Law Supporting Mainstreaming: A Guide for Parents and Teachers. Learning Concepts, Austin, Tx.

Schrag, J. 1976. Individualized Educational Programming (I.E.P.): A Child Study Team Process. Learning Concepts, Austin, Tx.

Solomon, E. L. 1977. New York City's prototype school for educating the handicapped. Phi Delta Kappan 59 (1): 7-11.

Weintraub, F. J., Abeson, A. R., Ballard, J., and LaVor, M. L. 1976. Public Policy and the Education of Exceptional Children. The Council for Exceptional Children, Reston, Va.

Evaluation

Escovar, P. L. 1976. Another chance for learning—The assessment class. Teach. Except. Child. 9: 2-3.

Fortna, R. O., and Boston, B. O. 1976. Testing the Gifted Child: An Interpretation in Lay Language. The Council for Exceptional Children, Reston, Va.

Klein, S. D. 1975. Psychological Testing of Children: A Consumer's Guide. The Exceptional Parent Bookstore, Manchester, N.H.

Martinson, R. A. 1975. The Identification of the Gifted and Talented. The Council for Exceptional Children, Reston, Va.

Mauser, A. J. 1977. Assessing the Learning Disabled: Selected Instruments. Special Learning Corporation, Guilford, Ct.

Roswell, F., and Natchez, G. 1976. Reading Disability. The Library of Special Education, Riverside, N.J.

Administrative Considerations

Biklen, D. 1974. Let Our Children Go. Human Policy Press, Syracuse, N.Y.

Cantrell, R., and Cantrell, M. L. 1976. Preventive mainstreaming: Impact of a supportive services program on pupils. Except. Child. 42 (7): 381–386.

Christie, L. S., McKenzie, H. S., and Burdett, C. S. 1972. The consulting teacher approach to special education: In-service training for regular classroom teachers. Foc. Except. Child. Oct.: 1–14.

Connor, R., and Jennenbaum, A. J. 1974. An integrated training program for in-service and pre-service teachers in a systems approach to home instruction. Columbia University Teachers College, New York.

Deno, S., and Gross, J. 1973. The Seward-University project: A cooperative effort to improve school services and university. In E. N. Deno (ed.), Instructional Alternatives for Exceptional Children. The Council for Exceptional Children, Arlington, Va.

Erickson, D., and Blackhurst, A. 1970. Information resources for special educators. Foc. Except. Child. 2 (7): 1–12.

Fromong, T., and Kelleher, D. 1971. A Model for Integrating Special Education into Regular Classrooms. University of Puget Sound, Tacoma, Wa.

Guidelines for Personnel in the Education of Exceptional Children. 1976. The Council for Exceptional Children, Reston, Va.

Kroth, R. L. 1975. Communicating with Parents of Exceptional Children: Improving Parent-Teacher Relationships. Love Publishing Company, Denver, Co.

Lazar, A. L. 1972. The SOME system approach: A paradigm for educational instruction and remediation by the special class teacher. In E. L. Meyen, G. A. Vergason, and R. J. Whelan (eds.),

Strategies for Teaching Exceptional Children. Love Publishing Company, Denver, Co.

Lindsey, R. J. 1973. A building administrator's perspective of individualized instruction. In E. N. Deno (ed.), Instructional Alternatives for Exceptional Children. The Council for Exceptional Children, Arlington, Va.

Meisgeier, C. 1973. The Houston plan: A proactive integrated systems plan for education. In E. N. Deno (ed.), Instructional Alternatives for Exceptional Children. The Council for Exceptional Children, Arlington, Va.

Melcher, J. W. 1971. Handicapped children in regular school settings: Four suggested models using BEPD funding. In M. C. Reynolds and M. D. Davis (eds.), Exceptional Children in Regular Classrooms. Leadership Training Institute, Department of Audio-Visual Extension, University of Minnesota, Minneapolis, Mn.

Practical advice to parents: A guide to finding help for handicapped children and youth. 1976. In Closer Look. The National Information Center for the Handicapped, Washington, D.C.

Smith, W. 1976. Guidelines to Classroom Behavior. Childcraft Education Corporation, Edison, N.J.

Special Education Administrative Policies Manual. 1977. The Council for Exceptional Children, Reston, Va.

Stewart, J. C. Counseling Parents of Exceptional Children. MSS Information Center, New York.

Taylor, F. D., and Soloway, M. M. 1973. The Madison school plan: A functional model for merging the regular and special classrooms. In E. N. Deno (ed.), Instructional Alternatives for Exceptional Children. The Council for Exceptional Children, Arlington, Va.

Working with Parents of Handicapped Children. 1976. The Council for Exceptional Children, Reston, Va.

Professional Issues

Cartwright, G., and Cartwright, C. A. 1971. Computer Assisted Remedial Education: Early Identification of Handicapped Children. The Pennsylvania State University, University Park, Pa.

Charles, C. M. 1976. Individualizing Instruction. The C. V. Mosby Company, St. Louis.

Charles, C. M. 1976. Personalized Instruction. The C. V. Mosby Company, St. Louis.

Child, R. E. 1975. A second look at resource room instruction by a resource teacher. Educ. Train. Ment. Retard. 10 (4): 288–289.

Collins, M., and Collins, D. 1975. Survival Kit for Teachers (& Parents). Childcraft Educational Corporation, Edison, N.J.

Cook, J. J. 1972. Accountability in special education. Foc. Except. Child. 3 (9): 1–15.

Davis, M. D., and Wyatt, K. E. 1971. Handicapped teachers or teachers of the handicapped. In M. C. Reynolds and M. D. Davis (eds.), Exceptional Children in Regular Classrooms. Leadership Training Institute, Department of Audio-Visual Extension, University of Minnesota, Minneapolis, Mn.

Deno, E. N. 1971. Strategies for improvement of educational opportunities for handicapped children: Suggestions for exploitation of EPDA potential. In M. C. Reynolds and M. D. Davis (eds.), Exceptional Children in Regular Classrooms. Leadership Training Institute, Department of Audio-Visual Extension, University of Minnesota, Minneapolis, Mn.

Deno, E. N. 1973. Where do we go from here? In E. N. Deno (ed.), Instructional Alternatives for Exceptional Children. The Council for Exceptional Children, Arlington, Va.

Erickson, D. K. 1971. Formula for change. In M. C. Reynolds and M. D. Davis (eds.), Exceptional Children in Regular Classrooms. Leadership Training Institute, Department of Audio-Visual Extension, University of Minnesota, Minneapolis, Mn.

Fox, W. L., Egner, A. N., Paolucci, P. E., Perelman, P. F., and McKenzie, H. S. 1973. An introduction to a regular classroom approach to special education. In E. N. Deno (ed.), Instructional Alternatives for Exceptional Children. The Council for Exceptional Children, Arlington, Va.

Harvey, J. 1969. To fix or to cope: A dilemma for special education. J. Spec. Educ. 3: 389–392.

Hobbs, N. 1975. The Future of Children: Categories, Labels, and Their Consequence. Jossey-Bass, San Francisco.

How the law will affect you: A guide to the new handicapped act. 1977. NEA Rep. 16 (7): 6–7.

Ingold, J. 1972. Where handicaps are forgotten. Am. Educ. 8 (2): 25–28.

Jenson, B. 1973. Removing the stigma from special education. Child. House 6 (1): 14–16.

Karnes, M. B., and Zehrbach, R. R. 1973. Curriculum and methods in early childhood special education: One approach. Foc. Except. Child. 5 (2): 1–13.

Kaufman, M. J., Gottlieb, J., Agard, J. A., and Kukic, M. B. 1975. Mainstreaming: Toward an explication of the construct. Foc. Except. Child. 7 (3): 1–11.

Kraft, A. 1973. Down with (most) special education classes! Acad. Ther. 8 (2): 207–216.

Lawrence, M. M. 1976. Young Inner City Families: Development of Ego Strength Under Stress. Behavioral Publications, New York.

Lilly, M. S. 1970. Special education: A teapot in a tempest. Except. Child. 37: 43–49.

MacMillan, D. L. 1971. Special education for the mildly retarded: Servant or savant. Foc. Except. Child. 2 (9): 1–14.

Martin, E. W. 1972. Individualism and behaviorisms as future trends in educating handicapped children. Except. Child. 38: 517–527.

Martinson, R. A., and May, V. S. 1967. The Abilities of Young Children. The Council for Exceptional Children, Reston, Va.

Nelson, C., and Schmidt, L. 1971. The question of the efficiency of special classes. Except. Child. 37 (5): 381–384.

New law requires free public education for all disabled children. 1977. NEA Rep. 16 (7): 4–5.

Reger, R. 1966. The questionable role of specialists in special education. J. Spec. Educ. 1: 53–59.

Reynolds, M. 1962. A framework for considering some issues in special education. Except. Child. 28: 367–370.

Reynolds, M. C. 1971. Categories and variables in special education. In M. C. Reynolds and M. D. Davis (eds.), Exceptional Children in Regular Classrooms. Leadership Training Institute, Department of Audio-Visual Extension, University of Minnesota, Minneapolis, Mn.

Reynolds, M. C. 1973. Reflections on a set of innovations. In E. N. Deno (ed.), Instructional Alternatives for Exceptional Children. The Council for Exceptional Children, Arlington, Va.

Rosenberg, M. B. 1968. Diagnostic Teaching. Special Child Publications, Seattle.

Schmio, R. E., Moneypenny, J., and Johnson, R. 1972. Contemporary Issues in Special Education. McGraw-Hill Book Company, New York.

Siegel, E. 1975. The Exceptional Child Grows Up. The Library of Special Education, Riverside, N.J.

Smith, R. M., and Neisworth, J. T. 1975. The Exceptional Child: A Functional Approach. McGraw-Hill Book Company, New York.

Teacher Preparation

Aiello, B. 1976. Places and Spaces: Facility Planning for Handicapped. The Council for Exceptional Children, Reston, Va.

Anderson, D. R., Hodson, G. D., and Jones, W. G. 1975. Instructional Programming for the Handicapped Student. Charles C Thomas, Publisher, Springfield, Ill.

Baker, C. D. 1976. Special education preservice training of general educators. Co. J. Educ. Res. 15 (2): 14–16.

Barnes, E., Eyman, B., and Engolz, M. B. 1975. Teach and Reach: An Alternative Guide to Resources for Teachers. Human Policy Press, Syracuse, N.Y.

Blackhurst, A. E., Cross, D. P., Nelson, C. M., and Tawney, J. W. 1973. Approximating noncategorical teacher education. Except. Child. 39 (1): 284–288.

Burke, P. J., and Saettler, H. 1976. The division of personnel preparation: How funding priorities are established and a personal assessment of the impact of PL 94-142. Educ. Train. Ment. Retard. 11: 361–365.

Foster, C. 1974. Developing Self Control. Behaviordelia, Kalamazoo, Mi.

Gearheart, B. R. (ed.). 1976. Teaching the Learning Disabled: A Combined Task-Process Approach. The C. V. Mosby Company, St. Louis.

Haring, N. G. 1971. A strategy for the training of resource teachers for handicapped children. In M. C. Reynolds and M. D. Davis (eds.), Exceptional Children in Regular Classrooms. Leadership Training Institute, Department of Audio-Visual Extension, University of Minnesota, Minneapolis, Mn.

Haring, N. G., and Miller, D. 1973. Precision teaching in regular junior-high-school classrooms. In E. N. Deno (ed.), Instructional Alternatives for Exceptional Children. The Council for Exceptional Children, Arlington, Va.

Hebeler, J. R., and Reynolds, M. C. 1976. Guidelines for Personnel in the Education of Exceptional Children. The Council for Exceptional Children, Reston, Va.

How To Do More. A Manual of Basic Teaching Strategy. 1974. Edmark Association, Bellevue, Wa.

Johnson, R. A. 1975. Handicapped Youth and the Mainstream Educator; Some Perspectives: Implications for Special Educational Leadership Personnel. Minnesota University, Minneapolis.

Kozloff, M. A. 1975. Educating Children with Learning and Behavior Problems. John Wiley and Sons, Somerset, N.J.

Mann, M., and Carriker, W. 1971. A Performance Based Early Childhood Special Education Teacher Preparation Program. University of Virginia, Charlottesville, Va.

Mann, P. H., and McClumb, R. M. 1973. A learning problems approach to teacher education. In E. N. Deno (ed.), Instructional

Alternatives for Exceptional Children. The Council for Exceptional Children, Arlington, Va.

Neff, H., and Pilch, J. 1975. Teaching Handicapped Children Easily. Charles C Thomas, Publisher, Springfield, Il.

Payne, J. S., Polloway, E. A., Kauffman, J. M., and Scranton, T. R. 1976. Living in the Classroom: The Currency-Based Token Economy. Behavioral Publication, New York.

Schwartz, L. 1967. Preparation of the clinical teacher for special education: 1866-1966. Except. Child. 34: 117-124.

Tarr, J. 1976. The diagnostic prescriptive teaching process. In N. J. Long, W. C. Morse, and R. G. Newman (eds.), Conflict in the Classroom: The Education of Emotionally Disturbed Children. 3rd ed. Wadsworth Publishing Company, Belmont, Ca.

Wiederholt, S. L., Hammill, D. D., and Brown, V. 1978. The Resource Teacher: A Guide to Effective Practices. Allyn and Bacon, Boston.

Traditional Categories

Affleck, J. Q., and Lowenbraun, S. 1976. Teaching Mildly Handicapped Children in Regular Classes. Charles E. Merrill Books, Columbus, Oh.

Birch, J. W. 1974. Mainstreaming: Educable Mentally Retarded Children in Regular Classes. The Council for Exceptional Children, Reston, Va.

Birch, J. W. 1975. Hearing Impaired Children in the Mainstream. The Council for Exceptional Children, Reston, Va.

Boston, B. O. (ed.). 1975. Gifted and Talented: Developing Elementary and Secondary Schools. The Council for Exceptional Children, Reston, Va.

Bothwell, H. 1976. 2.5 Million Children: The Invisible Handicap of Hearing Impairment. The Council for Exceptional Children, Reston, Va.

Bruininks, R. H., and Rynders, J. E. 1971. Alternatives to special class placement for educable mentally retarded children. Foc. Except. Child. 3 (4): 1-12.

Clark, G. M. 1975. Mainstreaming for the secondary educable mentally retarded: Is it defensible? Foc. Except. Child. 7 (2): 1-6.

Cruickshank, W. C. 1977. Learning Disabilities in Home, School and Community. Syracuse University Press, Syracuse, N.Y.

Edgington, D. 1976. The Physically Handicapped Child in Your Classroom: A Handbook for Teachers. Charles C Thomas Publisher, Springfield, Il.

Freeman, S. W. 1974. Does Your Child Have a Learning Disability? Charles C Thomas Publisher, Springfield, Il.

Gallagher, J. J. 1972. The special education contract for mildly handicapped children. Except. Child. 38: 527–535.

Gallagher, J. J., Aschner, M. J., and Jenne, W. 1967. Productive Thinking of Gifted Children in Classroom Interaction. The Council for Exceptional Children, Reston, Va.

Gardner, W. I. 1974. Children with Learning and Behavior Problems. Allyn and Bacon, Boston.

Gearheart, B. R. 1977. Learning Disabilities: Educational Strategies. The C. V. Mosby Company, St. Louis.

Guerin, G. R., and Szatlock, K. 1974. Integration programs for the mildly retarded. Except. Child. 41 (3): 173–179.

Hammond, G. W. 1972. Educating the mildly retarded: A review. Except. Child. 38: 565–574.

Kaplan, S. 1975. Providing Programs for the Gifted and Talented—A Handbook. The Council for Exceptional Children, Reston, Va.

Kaufmann, F. 1977. Your Gifted Child and You. The Council for Exceptional Children, Reston, Va.

Klein, J. W. 1975. Mainstreaming the preschooler. Young Child. 30 (5): 317–326.

Kounin, J. S., and Obradovic, S. 1976. Managing emotionally disturbed children in regular classrooms: A replication and extension. In N. J. Long, W. C. Morse, and R. G. Newman (eds.), Conflict in the Classroom: The Education of Emotionally Disturbed Children. 3rd ed. Wadsworth Publishing Company, Belmont, Ca.

Marks, N. C. 1974. Cerebral Palsied and Learning Disabled Children. Charles C Thomas Publisher, Springfield, Il.

Martin, G. J., and Hoben, M. 1977. Supporting Visually Impaired Students in the Mainstream: The State of the Art. The Council for Exceptional Children, Reston, Va.

McGee, D. I. 1976. Critical variables in the mainstreaming of hearing impaired children. Paper presented at the meeting of The Council for Exceptional Children Convention, April, Chicago.

Nix, G. 1976. Mainstream Education for Hearing Impaired Children and Youth. Grune and Stratton, New York.

Pappanikou, A. J., and Paul, J. L. (eds.). 1977. Mainstreaming Emotionally Disturbed Children. Syracuse University Press, Syracuse, N.Y.

Schultz, J. J. 1973. Integration of emotionally disturbed students: The role of the director of special education. Except. Child. 40 (1): 39–41.

Schwartzberg, J. G. 1976. Mainstreaming the hearing impaired child: A parent's experience, Montessori, and some comparisons. Paper presented at The Council for Exceptional Children Convention, April, Chicago.

Torrance, E. P. 1977. Discovery and Nurturance of Giftedness in the Culturally Different. The Council for Exceptional Children, Reston, Va.

Vacc, N. A. 1976. A study of emotionally disturbed children in regular and special classes. In N. J. Long, W. C. Morse, and R. G. Newman (eds.), Conflict in the Classroom: The Education of Emotionally Disturbed Children. 3rd ed. The Wadsworth Publishing Company, Belmont, Ca.

Program Interventions

Adelman, H. 1974. A Competency-Based Model Training Program. University of California, Riverside, Ca.

Bauer, H. 1975. The resource teacher: A teacher consultant. Acad. Ther. 10 (3): 299-304.

Buffmire, J. A. 1973. The statistician model. In E. N. Deno (ed.), Instructional Alternatives for Exceptional Children. The Council for Exceptional Children, Arlington, Va.

Ensminger, E. E. 1972. A proposed model for selecting, modifying, or developing instructional materials for handicapped children. In E. L. Meyen, G. A. Vergason, and R. J. Whelan (eds.), Strategies for Teaching Exceptional Children. Love Publishing Company, Denver, Co.

Gross, J. C., and Johnson, R. A. 1973. Restructuring special education leadership systems—The Minneapolis plan. In Special Education Leadership Systems: Decategorization and the Courts. Proceedings of the 1st and 2nd Minneapolis Leadership Conferences, University of Minnesota, Minneapolis.

Johnson, R. A., and Grismer, R. M. 1973. The Harrison school center: A public school-university cooperative resource program. In E. N. Deno (ed.), Instructional Alternatives for Exceptional Children. The Council for Exceptional Children, Arlington, Va.

Lilly, M. S. 1971. A training based model for special education. Except. Child. 37: 737-739.

Lord, F. E. 1971. Complete individualization of instruction: An unrealized goal of the past century. In M. C. Reynolds and M. D. Davis (eds.), Exceptional Children in Regular Classrooms. Leadership Training Institute, Department of Audio-Visual Extension, University of Minnesota, Minneapolis, Mn.

Morse, W. C. 1976. The helping teacher/crisis teacher concept. Foc Except. Child. 8 (4): 1–16.

Peter, L. J., and Wisely, F. G. 1971. The prescriptive teaching system: A teacher education program. Foc. Except. Child. 3 (3): 1–14.

Prouty, R. W., and McGarry, F. M. 1973. The diagnostic prescriptive teacher. In E. N. Deno (ed.), Instructional Alternatives for Exceptional Children. The Council for Exceptional Children, Arlington, Va.

Quick, A. D., Little, T. A., and Campbell, A. A. 1973. The Training of Exceptional Foster Children and Their Foster Parents: Enhancing Developmental Progress and Parent Effectiveness. Fearon Publishers, Palo Alto, Ca.

Schwartz, L. 1971. A clinical teacher model for interrelated areas of special education. Except. Child. 37: 565–571.

Shaw, S., and Shaw, W. L. 1973. The in-service experience plan: Changing the bath without losing the baby. In E. N. Deno (ed.), Instructional Alternatives for Exceptional Children. The Council for Exceptional Children, Arlington, Va.

Syphers, D. F. 1972. Gifted and Talented Children: Practical Programming for Teachers and Principals. The Council for Exceptional Children, Reston, Va.

Taylor, F. 1972. A learning center plan for special education. Foc. Except. Child. 4 (3): 1–14.

Walker, J. F., and Shea, T. M. 1976. Behavior Modification: A Practical Approach for Educators. The C. V. Mosby Company, St. Louis.

17

Prototype Materials for Effective Mainstreaming

Robert M. Anderson, Ed.D., John G. Greer, Ph.D.,
Sara J. Odle, Ed.D., and H. Lynn Springfield, Ed.D.

The history of the development of instructional materials for the handicapped during the past several hundred years reveals a variety of theoretical and philosophical approaches that have served as a framework for the utilization of materials. Some of the early materials, for example, had their origin in the hypothesis that learning comes primarily through the senses and all persons, no matter how handicapped, can learn, if given adequate sensory stimulation. Therefore, materials were created that fostered sensory and muscular training, on the premise that such activities would stimulate intellectual development. Indeed, this line of reasoning continues to provide the basis for much of the work with handicapped people today.

Other approaches to the development of instructional materials have been based on various perceptual and visual motor suppositions, linguistic or diagnostic remedial viewpoints, neurophysiological theories, and a variety of social and vocational approaches. With the rapid proliferation of these approaches and materials in recent years, it is not surprising that confusion and guesswork have more often than not characterized the efforts of those who must select and daily employ them with handicapped children. It is all too obvious that most teachers, including special educators, have little knowledge of the philosophical or theoretical yardstick against which the selection, utilization, and assessment of instructional materials can be measured.

In the first part of this chapter, therefore, a representation of the major approaches to the development of prototypes of instructional

A part of this chapter was adapted from an article published in *Education and Training of the Mentally Retarded* (Arlington, Virginia: Division on Mental Retardation, The Council for Exceptional Children) by permission of the authors and publishers. The authors gratefully acknowledge Barbara Zia and Lynn Springfield for their help with the previously published article.

materials that have been used successfully with handicapped learners is synthesized and presented. In a section of this size, it is impossible to report every point of view or contribution to the theoretical and philosophical foundation work on which contemporary instructional materials are based. Nevertheless, what the authors consider to be "landmark" events and contributions, representative of the most significant occurrences of the past several hundred years, are summarized. For the reader who wishes to explore this area in greater depth, a number of excellent resources now document the development and application of materials to specific areas of rehabilitation and education (Kirk, 1972; Kirk and Johnson, 1951; Lerner, 1976; McCarthy and McCarthy, 1969; Telford and Sawrey, 1972; Thiagarajan, Semmel, and Semmel, 1974; Wallin, 1955).

The second section of this chapter includes an up-to-date bibliography of instructional materials recommended by teachers, based on their successful use of the materials in the state of Indiana. These materials are representative of the excellent resources now being used effectively in quality programs across the nation.

THEORETICAL AND PHILOSOPHICAL PROTOTYPES

Historical Perspective

Special Education as a formal teaching area emerged from the benevolent philanthropy characteristic of the first 1,600 years of the Christian era into the development of instructional techniques and materials for the deaf and blind in the modern era. For example, Jacob Rodriguez Pereire, a Portuguese, and Pablo Bonet, a Spaniard, were two initiators of instruction for the hearing impaired (Wallin, 1955). Bonet developed a manual alphabet in 1620, and Pereire, about the middle of the eighteenth century, extended it.

Subsequently, programs for the blind were developed in France in the eighteenth century and then spread throughout Europe and America. Valentine Hauy, who made the first organized attempt to educate the blind at his school in Paris, trained his students to read raised or embossed letters by finger exploration. The Braille system, or point alphabet, was proposed by Charles Barbier in 1825 and modified by Charles Braille soon after (Wallin, 1955).

The sensory training techniques of these early educators stimulated the work of two other pioneers of early special education, Jean Itard and Edouard Seguin. These two nineteenth century physicians developed similar special education training programs that incorporated perceptual motor training and development of social and academic readiness skills for severely handicapped children. Itard, in his training procedures with Victor, adhered to a philosophy of sensationalism, which maintained that intellectual deficits and learning disabilities were caused or greatly influenced by environmental factors (Itard, 1932). Seguin, a student of Itard, considered the causes of these handicapping conditions to be neurological defects in the peripheral and/or central nervous systems. Both men developed sensorimotor training programs and utilized such training materials as bells, organs, woodwind instruments, the human voice, form boards, cardboard color shapes, and wooden and metal alphabet letters. They also used such common objects as keys, scissors, books, and eating utensils in discrimination and matching activities. Seguin (1846) shared Pereire's view that touch was the primitive sense, and recommended a program that progressed through the stages of motor training and sensorimotor training to abstract thought. He believed that specific sensorimotor training would strengthen neurological receptors and provide greater stimulation of cortex cells. Many of the methods and materials that he employed are the same as those recommended by developers of more recent perceptual motor approaches to remediating learning problems.

Although these efforts were important and, for the most part, effective, they were limited in scope and sequence as total educational programs for handicapped children. Decroly, and his student Descoeudres (1928), made one of the first attempts in this direction by establishing a comprehensive program for handicapped children in 1901 at Polytechnic Hospital in Brussels. Their major contribution to special education materials was the development of the innovated game for instructional purposes. They extensively utilized the lotto game format in teaching perceptual, reading, and number skills. Many of the games were designed to develop sensory discrimination and to train the observation of likes and differences (Kirk and Johnson, 1951). Manipulative materials such as modeling clay, jigsaw puzzles, and beads were also used for instructional purposes.

At the beginning of the twentieth century, Montessori (1912), another physician-educator, employed perceptual-motor training similar to that of Itard and Seguin. However, she perceived learning deficits to be related to pedagogical rather than medical problems. She believed that it was Seguin's materials, and not his theory, that accounted for his success in educating handicapped children. Consequently, she developed a science of didactic auto-teaching materials for use with young retarded children. The uniqueness of these materials was that they were self correcting: it was possible for the child to have immediate feedback concerning the correctness of his response. This enabled children to learn individually, at their own rates. Examples of materials often associated with Montessori's program are wooden cylinders, shapes, weights, cubes and colors, sandpaper letters and numerals, toys, household furnishings, cloth, and colored pencils.

Since these early beginnings, the development of compulsory education laws and the movement from a rural to an urban society in the United States have focused universal attention on the instructional needs of the handicapped. With an ever growing acceptance of the proposition that intelligence is remediable, and the optimism that this engendered, a wide variety of attempts were made to identify those methods and materials most effective with the retarded. Grouped according to theory or area of emphasis, and summarized below, these diverse efforts represent the trial and error process out of which our current instructional technology has evolved.

Perceptual Motor Approaches

In the late 1940s, Alfred Strauss, a neurophysiologist, working with Lavra Lehtinen, a teacher, and Heinz Werner, a child psychologist, conducted research and organized programs for brain injured children. Strauss and Lehtinen (1947) published a book on the education of these children that emphasized special clinical procedures for remediating the learning disabilities found in such children. Many of the current educational strategies for children with learning disabilities are either derived or extrapolated from Strauss and Lehtinen. Drawing on the works of Itard and Seguin, and borrowing from the work of Kurt Goldstein with brain injured adults, they designed educational materials to remediate behaviors presumed to be caused by neurological impairment. According to Strauss, organic impairment resulted in defects of the neuromotor system and, consequently, the child would manifest disturbances in perception, thinking, and emotional behavior. Principles of Gestalt psychology were used to facilitate learning. Commercial instructional materials were considered too complex and closely spaced, with too much detail, and with a rate of progress that was inappropriate (McCarthy and McCarthy, 1969). Therefore, existing materials had to be extensively adapted to accommodate individual discrepancies in attention span, perceptual and conceptual disorders, perseverative and dissociative tendencies, and motor abilities. For example, for children with figure-ground perceptual difficulties, heavy outlining or contrasting colors were used to increase the stimulus value of the material. To minimize the "distracting effects of extraneous stimuli, masking screens which exposed only one line of print at a time were prescribed, and instead of giving the child a single page with ten arithmetic problems, he is provided ten pages, one at a time, with one problem on each page" (Telford and Sawrey, 1972, p. 285).

The Strauss-Lehtinen work stimulated the development of several other perceptual motor approaches. One of these is the work of Cruickshank, Bentzen, Ratzeburg, and Tannhauser (1961), who advocated the use of a nonstimulating classroom and provision of a highly structured program in which there would be a reduction in the number of choices the child would have to make. Barsch (1965), emphasizing ocular mechanisms, developed a physiologic curriculum based on movigenics, the study of the origin and development of movement patterns leading to learning efficiency. Educational materials consisted of walking and balancing rails, scooter and teeter boards, and tracing templates. Kephart, a one-time associate of Strauss, likewise considered learning problems of children to be perceptual motor in nature and recommended an instructional program that provided remediation of these skills (1960). Kephart developed a variety of educational materials that are designed to enhance ocular control, form perception, space and form discrimination, and general sensorimotor integration. The influence of Strauss is reflected in the use of educational materials that focus on railwalking, balancing, chalkboard training, tracing templates, and music.

Simply stated, the advocates of sensorimotor theories base their approaches on the premise that a significant relationship exists between motor development and learning, and this tenet is reflected in the characteristics of the educational materials that they espouse.

Visual Perception Approaches

Frostig hypothesized that children with disabilities in visual perception will have difficulty in school and that remediation of these disabilities will prevent school failures (Kirk, 1972). This orientation derives largely from the developmental theories of Werner and Piaget, as well as from learning theory and psychoanalysis. She developed the Developmental Test of Visual Perception (1964) to measure a child's ability at tasks in five areas of visual perception: eye-hand coordination, figure-ground discrimination, constancy of shape, position in space, and spatial relations. Frostig and Horne's remedial program (1964) is designed to develop skills in these five areas and is often used to develop readiness before entering school. Included are worksheets for the children, a sequence of gross motor exercises and three-dimensional activities.

The Fitzhughs (1966) developed *The Fitzhugh Plus Program* to remediate visual perception problems in the learning areas of: 1) spatial organization, and 2) language and number. The program consists of self-teaching exercises in workbooks. The spatial organization exercises are designed to improve the child's ability to perceive and manipulate objects and shapes in time and space. The language and number workbooks are intended to develop skills in identifying letters, numbers, words, and pictures, as well as to improve understanding of language symbols and arithmetic operations.

Getman (1965), an optometrist, and his associates (Getman, Kane, Halgren, and McKee, 1968), focusing primarily on visual perception and the ocular mechanism, have developed exercises that utilize the tachistoscope, templates to facilitate form recognition, balance beams, and a variety of worksheets to expedite the acquisition of motor and perceptual skills.

Linguistic Approaches

Orton (1928) theorized that learning and motor problems exhibited by children are caused by lack of cerebral dominance, that is, neither of the two cerebral hemispheres is dominant over the other. This condition can result in reading disability (dyslexia), writing disability (agraphia), delayed speech (motor aphasia), stuttering, motor discoordination (developmental apraxia), word deafness, and combinations of these syndromes. He referred to "strephosymbolia" (twisted symbols) as being the common trait found in all these problems (1937). By this term he meant a difficulty in sequencing or repicturing the proper order of letters, sounds, or other linguistic symbols. These conditions, he believed, could be remediated by early intervention and proper training measures; remediation programs were recommended that were individualized and that involved breaking down faulty motor patterns into the smallest possible units—sounds, letters, movements—and combining them in proper sequence.

Some of Orton's associates have developed diagnostic and phonic-remediation programs to treat children with linguistic, behavior, and cognitive problems (Gillingham and Stillman, 1966; Monroe, 1932).

Kirk and Kirk (1971) developed a test-related approach to remediate learning deficits. The diagnostic instrument that they developed, the Illinois Test of Psycholinguistic Abilities (ITPA), provides information concerning "intraindividual differences," the relationship of abilities and disabilities within the same child (p. 55). When the areas of disability have been pinpointed, intensive training is applied in these areas. Numerous materials have been designed for use in remediating specific deficit areas as indicated by the ITPA. Among these are *Aids to Psycholinguistic Teaching* (Bush and Giles, 1969), *MWM Program* (Minskoff, Wiseman, and Minskoff, 1973), and *Goal Program Language Development Games* (Karnes, 1972).

Bateman (1965) has recommended procedures for the diagnosis and remediation of language problems that involve five stages: 1) determine whether discrepancies exist between what the child is actually learning and what he should be learning, 2) measure the child's present achievement, 3) analyze how the child learns, 4) prepare a diagnostic hypothesis with recommendations for remediation, and 5) develop and implement a strategy for teaching.

Curricular plans have been developed that utilize this skills-sequence approach. Among the most widely used of these are the Distar programs for reading, language, and arithmetic (Engelmann et al., 1969).

The *Peabody Language Development Kits* (Dunn and Smith, 1966) consist of a series of four sets of materials and lessons that are intended to stimulate oral language development in young children. Originally designed for use with retarded children and children from lower socioeconomic backgrounds, the Kits have been extensively utilized with all categories of children having language problems. Although the program's basic goal is to enhance linguistic skills, the improvement of verbal intelligence and enhancement of school achievement are secondary goals (Smith and Mueller, 1969). Lessons are aimed at the stimulation of divergent, convergent, and associative thinking. The children participate actively in the lessons and positive reinforcement of participation is recommended. The Kits consist of stimulus cards, story cards, puppets, phonograph records, and teachers manuals presenting sequenced lessons—all appropriate to the particular levels of the Kits.

Diagnostic-Remedial Approaches

Fernald, a psychologist working in the Clinic School of UCLA, developed a kinesthetic method for working with children who were having difficulty learning to read or spell (Fernald and Keller, 1921). Her techniques have been used widely since then and have withstood the test of time. The method involves four developmental stages (Fernald, 1943). In Stage One, the child traces the form of a known word printed on a word card while saying it, then writes it from memory; this process is repeated until the word is written correctly. In Stage Two, the child looks at the word while saying it, then writes it. In Stage Three, the word card is no longer used; the child looks at the printed word, says it, and writes it. At this stage the child may read anything and as much as he wishes. In the fourth stage the child is taught to read new words on the basis of their similarity to words or word parts already known.

The Fernald method incorporates the belief that children should begin reading their own stories first to provide motivation, and that providing children with sucessful experiences in reading and writing helps condition them favorably to school.

Friedus (1964) has provided a remediation program that can be applied to learning problems as well as to the teaching of subject areas such as arithmetic. She stresses that the child must have a firm foundation of the prerequisite skills before developing more advanced ones, and that the methods and materials used should provide feedback to allow the child to monitor his responses.

Social Learning Materials

The Social Learing Curriculum (SLC) (1974), developed by Gold-stein and his associates at Yeshiva University, is a current example of an effort to provide meaningful curriculum materials for educable mentally retarded children. It is a departure from earlier efforts at curriculum development for the retarded in that it relies on a theoretical construct formulated from research findings, which facilitates the ordering of concepts and content. The individual's needs have been reduced to 14 areas; his environment is seen as expanding through maturity to include the self and reciprocal relationships. The SLC approach also differs from other approaches in that it makes specific attempts to present social reality to the student and is founded on specific considerations of the learning characteristics of the retarded. Goldstein (1976) recommends that teaching of abstractions be done inductively, and states that rote teaching is most efficacious for the learning of facts.

An educational program is considered to consist of three dimensions—social behavior contexts, or the environments in which the child operates; curriculum activity areas, which are easily identifiable subject areas; and psychoeducational processes, or the child's modes of learning through which curriculum materials are presented. The SLC framework is designed as a superstructure within which the skills developed in traditional curriculum areas can be applied to the solution of life's problems (Heiss and Mischio, 1972). Materials that have been developed and field tested include 10 books presenting sequenced activities in the need areas, stimulus pictures, and supplements in the areas of math, physical education, and science.

CURRENT PROTOTYPES FOR MAINSTREAMING

Despite the strong concerted efforts of the various instructional materials and resource centers and scholars in the field, there are still problems related to the delivery of materials to classroom teachers. For example, Project PRIME, funded by the Bureau for

Education of the Handicapped (BEH), sought to study the question: For whom and under what conditions is mainstreaming a viable educational alternative? As part of the study, the researchers evaluated the accessibility of instructional media and materials, and the assistance in their selection and utilization provided for regular teachers who have handicapped children in their classrooms. In their interim report for 1971–1972, they disclosed that 45% of the teachers in the sampling reported that they never had enough instructional materials for their exceptional children, and that only half reported receiving assistance in selection and utilization (Kaufman, Semmel, and Agard, 1973). Based on these data, it would seem that even though a large variety and amount of media and materials had been produced during the late 1960s and early 1970s, an insufficient supply had been made available to practitioners in educational settings in which instructional services to the handicapped were being delivered.

Lance (1975), in a recent comprehensive review of the literature on instructional materials for the mentally retarded, provided information on the status of materials on socialization, prevocational and vocational education, science instruction, number and arithmetic instruction, language and reading instruction, and the creative arts. His concluding statement seems to summarize the "state of the art":

> A coordinated effort among commercial producers, instructional technologists, and special educators awaits the completion of a national needs assessment capable of pinpointing and prioritizing needs followed by systematic development, field testing and delivery. Hopefully, the efforts of the ALRC/NCEMMH/SO Network will bring this to pass in the latter half of the 1970's (pp. 164–165).

To date, efforts of the magnitude suggested by Lance have not been completed. Several significant projects, however, have been attempted at the state level. One of the best and most practical statewide projects, recently completed by the Indiana Department of Public Instruction, is described as follows.

Teacher Initiated Materials Evaluation (TIME) Project

Project TIME was designed to determine the effectiveness of instructional materials as judged by the teachers who used them. The 1977 *TIME Project Report* (Indiana Department of Public Instruction) is a compilation of the instructional materials that the teachers considered to be the most effective materials they were presently using or had used in the past. This project can serve as a prototype for the selection of materials in other states or school systems. The following preface to the bibliography explains the rationale and describes the procedures for the project. The complete listing of materials as well as a listing of publishers is also included.

WHAT IS THE TIME PROJECT?[1]

Which special materials are effective special materials? Which materials are worthy of further investigation? What materials are effective in classes similar to mine? These are questions which the *TIME Project Report* hopefully answers.

The TIME Project is an attempt to identify effective materials for use with exceptional learners. The procedure used was as follows:

TIME reporting forms were developed and disseminated to directors of special education programs.

Directors disseminated the forms to teachers who, in turn, completed the forms and returned them to our office.

The Instructional Materials and Resource Center staff processed the raw data into various exceptionality areas, levels, curricular areas, etc.

TIME Report was prepared, printed and disseminated back to directors for use by teachers and staff.

The reporting forms asked teachers to list the two most effective materials they were presently using or had used in the past. Teachers were asked to list only the title, publisher, subject area and comments concerning these materials. In addition, space was provided for describing the type and level of class the materials were used with and other information so that reporting teachers could be contacted should others want first-hand information. The reporting form was in postcard format to facilitate rapid completion and return to our office.

The materials listed in the *TIME Report* represent the collective efforts of hundreds of teachers and thousands of years of classroom teaching experience. For this reason, the *TIME Report* should be consulted by all special educators involved in the process of selecting special materials.

WHEN SHOULD THE TIME REPORT BE CONSULTED?

The *TIME Report* can serve as an effective aid in the selection of special materials whenever materials are being considered for

---

[1] Reprinted from *1977 TIME (Teacher initiated materials evaluation) project report: An aid in the selection of special education materials.* Indianapolis: Indiana Dept. of Public Instruction, 1977, by permission of the publisher.

purchase. It would be appropriate to consult the *TIME Report* whenever programs are being initiated or expanded or obsolete materials are being replaced.

HOW TO USE THE TIME PROJECT REPORT

The contents of the *TIME Report* are separated into various exceptionality areas (EMR, TMR, LD, etc.) and, where appropriate by level (primary, intermediate, etc.) and curricular area (math, reading, etc.). Thus, to determine which materials have been reported as being effective for the teaching of reading to primary EMR students, one would locate the EMR Primary section and then locate Reading/ Reading Readiness section of this category.

Materials are listed by title and publisher. A directory of selected publishers is also included as part of this project report.

Many materials will have a number in parenthesis following the title. This is a frequency count of how many times the material was reported. Materials reported one time have no number following the title.

Teachers and administrators are encouraged to contact our office if further information is desired concerning any material listed. We also have the capability to quickly identify and locate the person who reported on a given material should others want first-hand information on how material was used, class size, etc. Feel free to contact us if you wish to communicate with the person who reported on any listed program.

SPECIAL FEATURES OF THE 1977 TIME REPORT

The *TIME Project Report* provides a unique method of evaluating special materials in that:

Teachers are reporting on materials they have purchased and use on a daily basis;

Teachers may report on any materials they feel are effective;

The possibility of "loaded" sampling techniques is reduced;

TIME reporting forms are brief and concise to facilitate rapid completion by large numbers of teachers;

TIME results are compiled and reported to all local administrators for use by teaching staffs, and

IMRC staff can put teachers requesting information about a certain program in contact with teachers actually using the program.

FINAL COMMENT

Project sponsors wish to thank the hundreds of teachers and administrators who contributed to the success of the project. The *1977 TIME Project Report* is a result of the input from teachers and administrators, and is, therefore, their publication. Thanks for the participation.

Comments concerning the effectiveness, utility or desired changes of the TIME Project are most welcome. Correspondence should be addressed to:

Instructional Materials and Resource Center
Division of Special Education
Indiana Department of Public Instruction
Box 100, Butler University
Indianapolis, IN 46208
Phone: [317] 633-5259

Persons wishing to contact the actual user/evaluator of specific materials should also direct correspondence to the above address.

Gilbert Bliton, Director
Division of Special Education

Paul Ash, Coordinator
Instructional Materials Center

PRESCHOOL

Title	Publisher
Professional and Reference	
Action Symbols	Developmental Learning Materials
Alpern-Boll Developmental Profile	Psychological Development Publications
Assessment Programming Guide (6)	United Developmental Services
The Baby Exercise Book	Pantheon Books-Random House
Building Effective Home-School Relationships	Allyn and Bacon, Inc.
Curriculum Cards for Preschool Children	Adapt Press, Inc.

The Exceptional Parent	Psy-Ed Corporation
Fay's First Fifty and Fay's Second Fifty	Edmark Associates
The First Twelve Months of Life	Grosset and Dunlop, Inc.
Follett LAT Materials	Follett Publishing Co.
Guide to Early Developmental Training (6)	Wabash Center
LAP—A Planning Guide to Pre-School	Kaplan Press
Learning Accomplishment Profile (2)	Chapel Hill Training—Outreach Project
The Learning Book	The Easter Seal Society
The New Nursery	General Learning Corporation
A Planning Guide—The Preschool Curriculum (2)	Chapel Hill Training—Outreach Project
Portage Guide to Early Education (15)	Cooperative Educational Service Agency 12
Project Memphis (2)	Fearon Publishers
Project MORE	Edmark Associates
Resources for Creative Preschool Teaching	Kansas Association for the Education of Young Children
Sensorimotor Evaluation and Treatment Procedures	IUPUI
Sharing Our Caring	Western Media Printing
Step-by-Step Learning Guide for Retarded Infants and Children (5)	Syracuse University Press
Teaching Children with Developmental Problems	C. V. Mosby Co.
Teaching the Retarded Child to Talk	John Day Company, Inc.
202 Things to Do	G/L Publications
Vance Hall's Series	H & H Enterprises, Inc.

Language Development

Alpha Time	New Dimensions in Education
Audio Flashcards	Educational Development Corporation
GOAL	Milton Bradley Co.
Language Master	Bell & Howell
Max, the Nosey Bear	Golden Fragrance Books

Peabody Language Development   American Guidance Services
  Kits (20)
Perceive and Respond   Modern Education Corporation
Receptive-Expressive Language   None Given
  Emergent Scale
Talking Time   Webster Publishing Co.

Perceptual and Motor

Bristle Blocks   Playskool
Big Cardboard Box
Crawl Box—Patterning Table   Domain-Delacato
Creative Playthings   Creative Playthings
Developmental Learning   Developmental Learning
  Materials   Materials
Dubnoff School Program,   Teaching Resources Corporation
  Level 1
Early Childhood Enrichment   Milton Bradley Co.
  Series (2)
Fisher-Price (especially those   Fisher-Price Toys
  with noise)
Frostig Program for the Develop-   Follett Publishing Co.
  ment of Visual Perception
Hap Palmer Records (2)   Educational Activities
The Learning Well—Basic Early   Educational Activities
  Learning Concepts
Nesting Nuts and Bolts   Playskool
Peabody Early Experience Kit   American Guidance Service
Playskool Materials   Playskool
Postal Station   Playskool
Project Me Filmstrips   Bowmar
Rythmic Exercises Records   Stallman Educational Systems
Shave Cream
Sorting and Matching Sets   Developmental Learning
                             Materials
Starite, O'Hare   Allied Education Council
Young Learners Puzzles   Teaching Resources

Pre-Reading

AIMS   Continental Press
Distar Math and Reading   Science Research Associates
Peabody Rebus Program   American Guidance Service
Playskills Kit   Reader's Digest Services
Readiness Material   Continental Press

Social Development

DUSO Kits	American Guidance Service
Step Text	Follett Publishing Co.
Teaching Moral Values	Interstate Printers and Publishers

Number Concepts

Pacemaker Readiness Program	Fearon Publishers

EDUCABLE MENTALLY RETARDED—PRIMARY

Title	**Publisher**

Reading, Reading Readiness, and Language Arts

Alpha-Time Readiness Program (2)	New Dimensions in Education
Alpha Special	New Dimensions in Education
Animal Stories	Garrard Publishing Co.
Bank Street Readers	MacMillan Co.
Basic Word Sets	Barnell Loft, Ltd.
Cursive Letter Formation Worksets	Education House
Functional Basic Reading Series (2)	Stanwix House, Inc.
Landon Phonics Program	Chandler Publishing Co.
Look, Listen and Learn	Milliken Publishing Co.
MacMillan Basal Reading Series (2)	MacMillan Co.
Merrill Linguistic Readers (2)	Charles E. Merrill Publishing Co.
The New Phonics We Use	Lyons and Carnahan Educational Publishers
The New Open Highways (5)	Scott, Foresman and Co.
Phonetic Sound and Symbol Series	ESP, Inc.
Phonics Workbooks (2)	Modern Curriculum Press
Readalongs from Walt Disney	Walt Disney Educational Materials Co.
Reading Step-by-Step	Continental Press
Reading 360 Ginn	Ginn and Co.
Rebus Reading Program	American Guidance Services

Sequential Picture Cards	Developmental Learning Materials
Skill Packets	Educational Programmers, Inc.
A Sound Approach To Reading	None Given
Special Reading and Language Arts	Hayes School Publishing Co.
Stanwix Reading Series (2)	Stanwix House, Inc.
Sullivan Programmed Reading	Webster/McGraw-Hill
Tutorgram	Enrichment Reading Corporation of America

Arithmetic

Arithmetic Step-by-Step	Continental Press
Author Cards	Kelso, Inc.
Heath Elementary Mathematics	D. C. Heath
Math	Steck-Vaughn Co.
Math Books	Education House
The Modern Mastery Drills	Hayes School Publishing Co., Inc.
Moving Up in Numbers	Developmental Learning Materials
Pacemaker Arithmetic Program	Fearon Publishers
Stern's Structural Arithmetic	Houghton Mifflin

Language Development

Auditory Perception Tapes (2)	Developmental Learning Materials
Basic Word Making Cards	Word Making Productions
Listen and Do Tapes	Houghton-Mifflin
Peabody Language Development Kits (6)	American Guidance Service
Vox-Com (2)	A.V.C. Corporation
Sounds and Symbols	American Guidance Service

Perceptual and Motor

Dubnoff Perceptual Program	Teaching Resources Corporation
Erie Perceptual Program	Teaching Resources Corporation
Fitzhugh Plus	Allied Education Council
Paths, Patterns, and Letters	Continental Press
Pattern Recognition Skills Inventory	Hubbard Scientific Co.
Pegboard and Pegs	Developmental Learning Materials

Social and Affective
Development
DUSO Kits (2)   American Guidance Services

Science
Understanding Your Environ-   Silver Burdett
ment

EDUCABLE MENTALLY RETARDED—INTERMEDIATE

Title   **Publisher**

Reading and Language Arts
Audio-theque 100   Audio Visual Communications
Classmate Series   Lyons and Carnahan Educa-
                                         tional Publications
Ears   The Economy Co.
Edmark Reading Kit   Edmark Associates
Fun and Phonics   St. Regis Instructional Materials
Keys to Good Language   The Economy Co.
Continuous Progress Laboratory   Educational Progress Co.
Language Skills Kit A   Continental Press
Merrill Linguistic Reading   Charles E. Merrill Publishing
   Program (2)   Co.
Mott Language Skills Program   Allied Education Council
My Puzzle Book   Garrard Publishing Co.
The Palo Alto Reading Program   Harcourt-Brace-Jovanovich, Inc.
Phonics and Word Power   Xerox Educational Publications
Phonics Games   Sha Kean Publishers, Inc.
Phonics Workbook   Modern Curriculum Press
Popper Words   Garrard Publishing Co.
Primary Phonics   Educators Publishing Co.
Reading, Thinking, and Reason-   Steck-Vaughn Co.
   ing Skills Program
Sound Foundation Program   Developmental Learning
   I & II   Materials
Specific Skill Series   Barnell Loft, Ltd.
Spelling Pro   Silver Burdett Co.
Sprint Libraries   Scholastic Book Services
Stanwix Readers, Workbooks   Stanwix House, Inc.
Super Books   J. B. Lippincott Co.

Arithmetic

Arithmetic Step-by-Step (2)	Continental Press
Classmate 88	Monroe Education Center
Fundamath Board	Ideal Toy Corporation
Learning Centers	Frank Shaffer
Lennes Essentials of Arithmetic	Laidlaw Brothers
Mathematics Around Us	Scott, Foresman and Co.
Money Game	Developmental Learning Materials
Pacemaker Arithmetic Program (2)	Fearon Publishers, Inc.
Singing Multiplication Facts	Educational Activities
Taskmaster Addition Cards	Taskmaster, Ltd.
Ten-tens Counting Frame	Milton Bradley
Using Money Series	Frank E. Richards Publishing Co.
Ye Old Math	Frank Schaffer

Perceptual and Motor

Auditory Perception-Imagery (2)	Developmental Learning Materials
Design Cards for Small Parquetry and Cubes	Developmental Learning Materials
Parquetry, Blocks, Beads, Stencils	Developmental Learning Materials
Forward Pass	Developmental Learning Materials
Individual Order Tasks	Love Publishing Co.
Primary Perceptual Training Program	Mafex Associates, Inc.

Science

Me Now	Hubbard Scientific Co.
Seasonal Kindergarten Units	Fearon Publishers
Understanding Your Environment	Silver Burdett Co.

Language Development

Peabody Language Development Kits (2)	American Guidance Service
Written Language Cards	Developmental Learning Materials

Social and Affective Development

DUSO Kits	American Guidance Service

Pre-Vocational
How to Hold Your Job   John Day Co.

History
Target American History   Mafex Associates, Inc.

EDUCABLE MENTALLY RETARDED—JUNIOR HIGH

Title   **Publisher**

Reading and Language Arts
All in a Day's Work   Globe Book Co.
Catching On   Open Court Publishing Co.
Checkerboard   Addision-Wesley Publishing Co.
Comic Reading Library   King Comics
Continuous Progress in Spelling   The Economy Co.
Deep-Sea Adventure Series   Addison-Wesley Publishing Co.
Detect Visual and Tactile   Science Research Associates
Distar Reading Program   Science Research Associates
Double Action Reading Series   Scholastic Book Services
English for Everyday Living   Ideal Publications
Eye, Ear, Hand Phonics   Educational Activities
January Productions   David Cook, Publisher
Language Skills   Continental Press
The New Phonics We Use Learn-   Rand McNally School Depart-
  ing Games   ment
Phonics We Use   Lyons and Carnahan Educa-
                                          tional Publishers

Point 31   Reader's Digest Services
Psycholinguistic Learning   University of Illinois Press
  Disabilities Diagnosis and
  Remediation
Racing and Car Series   Bowmar
REACH, Book and Tape   The Economy Co.
Headway, Workbooks and   Open Court Publishing Co.
  Readers
Reading Skill Practice Pad   Reader's Digest Services
Scholastic Action Library   Scholastic Book Services
Specific Skill Series   Barnell Loft, Ltd.
Spell/Write   Noble and Noble, Publishing Co.
Stranger Than Fiction   Globe Book Co.
Super Books   J. B. Lippincott Co.
The Ungame   The Ungame Co.

Weekly Reader, Know Your World	Xerox Educational Publications
You and Your World Newspaper	Xerox Educational Publications

Arithmetic

Activity Books, Cards, Game-boards	Frank Schaffer
Continental Press Mathematics	Continental Press
Growing Up With Arithmetic	McCormick-Mathers Publishing Co.
Learning Skills Series: Arithmetic (3)	Webster Div./McGraw Hill
Money Makes Sense	Fearon Publishers
Pacemaker Arithmetic Program	Fearon Publishers
Sequential Mathematics	Harcourt, Brace, Jovanovich, Inc.
Steck-Vaughn Math Workbooks	Steck-Vaughn Co.

Social Studies and Vocational

Target American History	Mafex Associates, Inc.
The U.S.A.: Its People and Leaders	Globe Book Co.
The Young American Series	Fearon Publishers, Inc.
You and Your World and Know Your World	Xerox Educational Publications

Social Development and Affective Education

Living Skill Techniques	Media Materials, Inc.
Toward Affective Development	American Guidance Service

Science

Concepts and Challenges in Science	CEBCO/Standard Publishing

EDUCABLE MENTALLY RETARDED—SENIOR HIGH

Title	Publisher

Reading and Language Arts

Action Kit	Scholastic Book Services
Action Libraries	Scholastic Book Services
Direction II—Phonic Analysis Learning Center	Steck-Vaughn Co.
Ditto Books	Hayes School Publishing Co.

Dr. Spello	McGraw-Hill Book Co.
Easy Eye Paperbacks	Magnum Books
English on the Job	Globe Book Co., Inc.
Everyday Reading and Writing	New Reader's Press
Functional Basic Reading Skills Series	Stanwix House, Inc.
Language Master	Bell and Howell
New Practice Readers	Webster/McGraw-Hill
Perceptual Material Kits	Developmental Learning Materials
Point 31 (2)	Reader's Digest Services
REACH	The Economy Co.
Scope Skills (3)	Scholastic Book Services
The Sound Way	Hayes School Publishing Co.
Supportive Reading Skills	Dexter and Westbrook, Ltd.
The Getting Along Series	Frank E. Richards Publishing Co.
Word Wheels	Webster/McGraw-Hill
World of Vocabulary	Learning Trends-Globe Book
You	Frank E. Richards Publishing Co.

Pre-Vocational

Building Safe Driving Skills	Fearon Publishers
Career Education	Allied Education Council
Everyday Business Workbooks	Gary Lewson
The Getting Along Series of Skills (2)	Frank E. Richards Publishing Co.
Guide to the Community	Elwyn Institute
Preparing for the World of Work	F. R. Publications
Planning Your Career	Globe Book Co.
Vocational English	Globe Book Co.
World of Work	R. E. H. Publishing Co.

Social Studies

Be Informed Series (2)	New Reader's Press
Focus of Self-Development	Science Research Associates
Foundation of Citizenship	Frank E. Richards Publishing Co.
News for You	New Reader's Press
Study Lessons in Civics	Follett Publishing Co.
The United States Yesterday and Today	Ginn and Company
Workbooks	Fearon Publishers

Science and Health

Basic First Aid Books	Red Cross
Can You Give First Aid	New Reader's Press
Elementary Science—Learning By Investigating Series	Rand McNally School Department
Me Now	Hubbard Scientific Co.

Arithmetic

Learning About Measurements	Frank E. Richards Publishing Co.
The Modern Mastery Drills in Arithmetic	Hayes School Publishing Co.
Spectrum Math Series	Laidlaw Brothers
Steck-Vaughn Math	Steck-Vaughn Co.

TRAINABLE MENTALLY RETARDED—PRIMARY AND INTERMEDIATE

Title	Publisher

Perceptual and Motor

Auditory—Familiar Sounds	Developmental Learning Materials
Colorama	Ravensburg (West Germany)
Developmental Learning Materials (3)	Developmental Learning Materials
Dubnoff School Program	Teaching Resources Corporation
Feel and Match	Lauri Enterprises, Manufacturers
Frostig Worksheets (2)	Follett Publishing Co.
Large Parquetry	Developmental Learning Materials
Learning Games	Milliken Publishing Co.
Listening Tapes	Developmental Learning Materials
Matching Cards	Developmental Learning Materials
Missing Match-Ups	Milton Bradley Co.
Multivariant Sequencing Beads and Patterns	Developmental Learning Materials
Pegboard Designs and Pegs	Developmental Learning Materials
Perceptual Skills Curriculum	Walker Educational Book Corporation

Pictures and Patterns (Frostig) (2) — Follett Publishing Co.

Rhythm Record—Physical Fitness for Primary Children — LeCrone Rhythm Record Co.

Visual Perception — Follett Publishing Co.

Language Development

Bliss Symbols — Blissymbolics Communication Foundation

GOAL Language Development — Milton Bradley

Language Concepts — Educational Programmers, Inc.

Launch — Educational Service, Inc.

Peabody Language Development Kits (2) — American Guidance Service

PEEK (2) — American Guidance Service

Phonetics Factory — Ideal School Supply Co.

Picture/Word Concepts Series — Instructor Curriculum Materials

Spice — Educational Service, Inc.

TALK — University Park Press

Reading and Reading Readiness

Alphabet, Number and Color, Shape Bingo — Trend Enterprises

Beginning Readiness Kit — J. B. Lippincott Co.

Beginning to Learn Fine Motor Skills — Science Research Associates

Functional Basic Reading Series — Stanwix House, Inc.

Groovy Letters — Ideal Toy Co.

The New Phonics We Use — Rand McNally

Rebus Reading Program — American Guidance Service

Arithmetic and Number Concepts

Arithmetic for Beginners Filmstrips — Encyclopedia Britannica Educational Corporation

Coin Stamps — Developmental Learning Materials

Continental Press Materials — Continental Press

Developmental Learning Materials — Developmental Learning Materials

Pacemaker Arithmetic Program — Fearon Publishers

Pupil Pack (Flannel Boards and Cut-outs) — Instructo Corporation

Social Development

DUSO Kits	American Guidance Service
I Can Read Signs Filmstrips	Urban Media Materials, Inc.
Peabody Kit	American Guidance Service
Portage Project	C.E.S.A. 12
You and Safety	Eye Gate House

Music and Art

Ella Jenkins—Play Your Instruments and Make a Pretty Sound	Folkways Records
Ella Jenkins—Early Childhood Songs	Scholastic Records
Hap Palmer Records	Educational Activities
Learning Through Art	Teaching Resources Corporation
Music Activities for Retarded Children	Abingden Press

Professional and Reference

Launch	Educational Service, Inc.
Portage Project and LAP	C.E.S.A. 12

TRAINABLE MENTALLY RETARDED—JUNIOR AND SENIOR HIGH

Title	Publisher

Arithmetic and Number Concepts

The Change Maker	The Teech-Um Co.
Coin Stamps—Money Boxes	Developmental Learning Materials
Duorama	Educational Teaching Aids
Easy Grip Pegs and Jumbo Pegboard	Ideal Toy Co.
Fit-A-Group	Lauri Enterprises, Manufacturers
Money Makes Sense	Charles H. Kanhn-J. B. Hanna
Pacemaker Arithmetic Program (2)	Fearon Publishers
Telling Time, Money Handling	Interpretive Education
Using Dollars and Sense	Fearon Publishers

Reading

Ball-Stick-Bird	Ball-Stick-Bird Publications
Group Word Teaching	Garrard Publishing Co.

The Mott Basic Language Skills
Program

Allied Educational Council

News for You

Lanback Literacy

Stanwix Basic Reading Series

Stanwix House, Inc.

Vowel Sounds, Consonant
Sounds Self Instructional Programs

Milton-Bradley Co.

Professional and Reference

PAC

Aux Chandelle/District Center

Project MORE

Edmark Associates

Wabash Center ADL Cur-
riculum Guide

Wabash Center

Language and Language
Development

Dubnoff Program

Teaching Resources Corporation

Peabody Language Development
Kit (2)

American Guidance Service

Workjobs

Addison-Wesley Publishing Co.

Social and Affective
Development

DUSO Kits

American Guidance Service

Individual Differences Curriculum—An Experience in
Human Relations for Children

Madison Public Schools

Nutrition Set

Instructo

Project MORE

Edmark Associates

Social Perceptual Training Kit

Activity Records, Inc.

Toward Affective Development

American Guidance Service

Perceptual and Motor

Daily Sensorimotor Training
Activities

Educational Activities, Inc.

Design Cards in Perspective and
Colored Inch Cubes

Developmental Learning
Materials

Movement Experiences with MR
and ED Children

None Given

Vocational

Electronic Circuit Boards,
Automobile Subassembly
Parts, Cardboard Partitions,
Packing Materials, and Wiring
Devices

SEVERELY AND PROFOUNDLY RETARDED

Title	Publisher

Perceptual and Motor

Creative Playthings	Creative Playthings
Discrimination Picture and Shape Cards	Philograph Publications
Early Childhood Enrichment	Milton-Bradley Co.
Fisher Price Materials	Fisher Price Toys
Frostig Materials	Follett Publishing Co.
Ideal Jumbo Easy Grip Pegs	Ideal Toy Corporation
Knobbed Puzzles	Childcraft Educational Corporation
Lauri Puzzles	Lauri Enterprises, Manufacturers
Nerf Balls	Nerf
Shapes and Colors	Developmental Learning Materials
Pegboards and Patterns, Formboards, Beads and Patterns	Developmental Learning Materials
Playskool Materials	Playskool
Shift-Shapes	Little Kenny Publications
Tutorgram	Enrichment Reading Corporation of America

Professional and Reference

A Guide for the Activities Coordinator in a Skilled Nursing Facility	California Department of Health
Guide to Early Developmental Training (2)	Wabash Center
Managing Behavior	H and H Enterprises, Inc.
My Everything Book	Mafex Associates, Inc.
Portage Guide to Early Education (2)	C.E.S.A. 12
The RADEA Program	Melton Book Co.
The Right-to-Education Child	Charles C Thomas Publisher
Schoolhouse in a Fun Box	Edu-Cards Corporation
A Step-by-Step Learning Guide for Retarded Infants and Children (2)	Syracuse University Press

Language Development

Learn the Alphabet	Milton Bradley Co.
Peabody Language Development Kits (4)	American Guidance Services
Zygo Communication Board	Zygo Industries, Inc.

Social Development and Self-Help

Fastening Vests	None Given
Portage Guide to Early Education	C.E.S.A. 12
Steps to Independence	Research Press
Toilet Training in Less Than a Day	Simon and Schuster, Inc.
We Dress for the Weather	Instructo Corporation

SPEECH, HEARING AND LANGUAGE

Title   **Publisher**

Language Therapy

Boehm Test of Language Concepts	Psychological Corporation
Auditory Memory Tapes	Developmental Learning Materials
Carrow Developmental Syntax Program (3)	Learning Concepts
Distar Language I	Science Research Associates
Developmental Learning Materials Language Materials (3)	Developmental Learning Materials
Early Childhood Enrichment	Milton Bradley Co.
Emerging Language	The Learning Business
Fokes Sentence Builder (6)	Teaching Resources
GOAL Language Development (3)	Milton Bradley Co.
Language Making Action Cards and Stickers	Word Making Productions
Language Master and Cards	Bell and Howell
Language of Directions	Alexander Graham Bell Association of the Deaf, Inc.
Louie and Company	Evansville-Vanderburgh School Corporation

Newby Visual Language (3)	Newby Visual Language, Inc.
Peabody Language Development Kits (10)	American Guidance Service
Sequential Picture Cards	Developmental Learning Materials
Suggestions for Teaching Language Skills (2)	Word Making Productions, Inc.
Target on Language	Christ Church Child Center
Voxcom Card and Cassette/ Record Player	Tapecon, Inc.

Speech and Hearing, General

English as a Second Language	Bell and Howell
Flowes-Costello Tests of Central Auditory Abilities	Perceptual Learning Systems
Game 1	Pollywog Publications, Inc.
Go-Mo Cards	Go-Mo
My Sound Workbooks	Interstate Printers and Publishers
The Pape Series	Oddo Publishing
Peabody Language Development Kits	American Guidance Service
Sounds and Symbols Development Kit	American Guidance Service
Goldman-Lynch Sounds and Symbols Development Kit (4)	American Guidance Service
A Speech Clinician Talks to Teachers and a Speech Clinician Talks to Parents	Pictograph
Speechlore	Interstate Printers and Publishers
Speech Master Workbooks	Go-Mo
Teaching Resources—Parts of Speech	Teaching Resources
Vox-Com	AVC Corporation

Auditory Training

Auditory Discrimination in Depth (2)	Teaching Resources
DLM Auditory Perceptual Tapes (2)	Developmental Learning Materials
Carrow Test of Auditory Comprehension and Carrow Test of Elicited Language	Learning Concepts, Inc.

Goldman, Fristoe, Woodcock   American Guidance Service
  Auditory SKills Test
Sound Order Sense (2)   Follett Publishing Co.

Articulation
Pendergast Program for Lateral   Kathleen Pendergast
  "S"
Programmed Articulation   Prat Enterprises
  Therapy
More Games Kids Like   Communication Skill Builders
Word Making Cards   Word Making Productions, Inc.

Stuttering
Manual for Stuttering Therapy   Stanwix House
Reduction of Stuttering Behavior   Arizona State University

Tongue Thrust
Tongue Thrust Therapy   Learning Concepts

LEARNING DISABLED

Title   **Publisher**

Reading and Language Arts
Aims   Elsie C. Earlley
Alpha Time and Alpha One   New Dimensions in Education
And So the Story Goes Radio   Psychotechnics, Inc.
  Reading Series
Distar Reading Program   Science Research Associates
Edmark Reading Program   Edmark Associates
Frostig Program for Develop-   Follett Publishing Co.
  ment of Visual Perception
Goldman-Lynch Sounds and   American Guidance Service
  Symbols Development Kit
Language Master   Bell and Howell
Merrill Linguistic Readers (2)   Charles E. Merrill Publishing
    Co.

Monster Series   Bowmar
The Mott Basic Language Skills   Allied Education Council
  Program
The Palo Alto Reading Program   Harcourt, Brace, Jovanovich,
    Inc.

Phonetic Readers   Educators Publishing Service
Phonics Workbook   Modern Curriculum Press
Phonovisual Method   Phonovisual Products, Inc.

Rx Psychotechnics	Psychotechnics, Inc.
Primary Phonics Workbooks	Educators Publishing Service
Reading Booster	Webster/McGraw-Hill
Reading Comprehension and Vocabulary	Frank Shaffer
Slingerland Multisensory Approach to Language Arts for Specific Language Disability	Educators Publishing Service
Specific Skills Series (2)	Barnell Loft Ltd.
Speech to Print Phonics	Harcourt, Brace, Jovanovich, Inc.
Sprint Library	Scholastic Book Services
SRA Reading Lab	Science Research Associates
Sullivan Programmed Reading Series (4)	McGraw-Hill
There's a Monster	Bowmar
Webster New Practice Readers	McGraw-Hill
Word Book Spellers	Rand McNally
Workbooks and Chemritepens	Ann Arbor Publishers
You and Your World	Xerox Educational Publications

Perceptual and Motor

Developmental Learning Materials	Developmental Learning Materials
Developmental Test of Visual Motor Integrations	Follett Publishing Co.
Dubnoff School Program	Teaching Resources
GOAL Program	Milton Bradley Co.
Learning to Think Books	Science Research Associates
Look Alikes Perceptual Skills	Developmental Learning Materials
Missing Match Ups	Developmental Learning Materials
Perceptual Activities	Ann Arbor Publishers
Vanguard School Program	Teaching Resources

Arithmetic

Arithmetic Step-by-Step	Continental Press
Hoffman Math System	Hoffman Information Systems
Language Master	Bell and Howell
Mathematics for Individual Achievement	Houghton Mifflin
Pacemaker Arithmetic Program	Fearon Publishing Co.
SRA Computational Skills Kit	Science Research Associates

| Sullivan Programmed Math Series | McGraw-Hill |

Social Studies

Dittos and Masters	Cebco/Standard Publishing Co.
A Modified History of the U.S.	Ardelle Manning Publishers
New Rochester Occupational Reading	Science Research Associates
Preparing for the World of Work	F. R. Publications

Auditory Skills

Auditory Perception Training (5)	Developmental Learning Materials
Developmental Learning Materials	Developmental Learning Materials
Listening with Understanding	Developmental Learning Materials

Language

Language Master (3)	Bell and Howell
Peabody Language Development Kits	American Guidance Services
Target on Language	Christ Church Child Center

Professional and Reference

| Kid's Stuff | Incentive Publications |

EMOTIONALLY DISTURBED

Title   **Publisher**

Social and Affective Development

Developmental Therapy	University Park Press
Essence I & II	Addison Wesley Publishing Co.
Everybody Cries Sometimes	Educational Activities, Inc.
Magic Circle	Human Development Training Institute
Making Sense of Our Lives	Argus Communications
OBIS	University of California, Berkeley
Toward Affective Development	American Guidance Service
Won't You Be My Friend	Educational Activities, Inc.

Reading, Reading Readiness, and Language Arts

Fitzhugh PLUS Program	Allied Education Council
Learning to Think Series	Science Research Associates
Pal Paperbacks	Xerox Educational Publications
Peabody Language Development Kits	American Guidance Service
Scholastic Reading Collections and Sprint Libraries	Scholastic Book Services
Singer Reader Mate	L. W. Singer Co., Inc.

Arithmetic

Enrich-Telor Programmed Learning Aid	Enrich
Skill Modes In Mathematics	Science Research Associates

Perceptual and Motor

Auditory Perception Training	Developmental Learning Materials
Sight-Sound Skills	Educational Activities, Inc.

DEAF—PRESCHOOL, PRIMARY, INTERMEDIATE

Title	Publisher

Language and Reading

Apple Tree Workbooks (2)	Dormac, Inc.
Continental Press Masters	Continental Press, Inc.
Fokes Sentence Builder	Teaching Resources Corporation
Julie and Jack Reading Series (2)	St. John's School for the Deaf
Kids Stuff—Reading and Language Experiences	Incentive Publications
Know Now Work Text	Jenn Publications
The Language and Thinking Program	Follett Publishing Co.
The Language Curriculum	Rhode Island Schoool for the Deaf
Missing Match Ups	Developmental Learning Materials
Newby Visual Language Series	Newby Visual Language, Inc.
Parts of Speech Complete	Teaching Resources Corporation
Peabody Language Development Kit	American Guidance Service

Project Life (2)   General Electric Co.
Rhode Island Language   Rhode Island School for the
   Curriculum   Deaf
Sight Word Fun—Reading   Frank Schaffer Publications
   Activities
Steps in Language Development   Volta Bureau
   for the Deaf
Structural English—Level 1   Indiana School for the Deaf
Structural Tasks for English   The Center for Continuing
   Practice   Education at Gallaudet
                                                    College
Try Task   Noble and Noble
Who, What, When, Where, Why   Frank Schaffer Publications
   (2)

General—Professional and Reference

Comprehension Joy and Reading   Joy, Inc.
   Joy
Gameboards   Frank Shaffer Publications
Kids Stuff for Nooks, Crannies   Incentive Publications
   and Corners
Language Curriculum   Rhode Island School for the
                                                    Deaf
Frank Shaffer   Frank Schaffer Publications
Systems ONE   Audio Reprint, Inc.

Arithmetic

Cuisenaire Rods   Cuisenaire Company of America,
                                                    Inc.
I Can Count; A Workbook for   Indiana School for the Deaf
   Young Deaf Children
Kentucky Time Program   University of Kentucky, RIMC

Social Studies

Rack-O   Milton Bradley Co.
Captioned Films   Indiana School for the Deaf
Indiana School for the Deaf   Indiana School for the Deaf
   Textbooks and Workbooks

Writing

Tracing Book   Indiana School for the Deaf

Affective Development

Help!   Center for Early Learning

DEAF—JUNIOR AND SENIOR HIGH

Title	Publisher
Mathematics	
A New Look at Common Fractions	Continental Press, Inc.
Pro-Football and Pro-Baseball Math	Learning Center
Refresher Mathematics	Allyn and Bacon, Inc.
Spectrum Mathematics Series	Laidlaw Brothers
Business Education and Vocational	
How to Get and Hold a Job	Relevant Productions, Inc.
The Work Series	Hopewell Books, Inc.
Steps in Home Living	Charles A. Bennett Co.
Social Studies	
Forms—In Your Future	Learning Trends-Globe Book Co.
The Work Series	Hopewell Books, Inc.
World History Study Lessons	Follett Publishing Co.
Language, Reading, Writing	
Controlled Reading	Educational Developmental Labs, Inc.
Language Stories and Drills	Vermont Printing Co.
Laboratory Science	Indiana School for the Deaf
Understanding Yourself	Indiana School for the Deaf
Arts and Crafts	
Art for Teachers of Exceptional Children	William C. Brown Co.
Donna Z. Melilach Books	Crown Publishers, Inc.

BLIND

Title	Publisher
Reading, Language Development and Language Arts	
ABC Jumbo Alpha Numbers	Lauri Enterprises Manufacturers
Ginn 360 Reading Series (2)	Ginn and Co.
Hap Palmer Activity Records	Educational Activities Inc.
Listen and Think (2)	Educational Developmental Lab

Listening Skills for Pre-Readers	Classroom Materials Co.
Listening with Mr. Bunny Big Ears	Educational Activities, Inc.
Manuscript and Cursive Wipe-Off Cards	Zaner-Bloser Co.
Modern Methods of Teaching Braille	American Printing House for the Blind
Scrabble Game	American Foundation for the Blind
Specific Skills Series	Barnell Loft, Ltd.
SRA Listening Laboratory	Science Research Associates
Stearns Structural Reading Series	L. W. Singer/Random House
TAR	American Printing House for the Blind

Perceptual and Braille Readiness

Cylinder Peg Puzzles	Montessori Advisory Committee
Developmental Learning Materials	Developmental Learning Materials
Large Parquetry	Developmental Learning Materials
Optacon	None Given
Tactilmat Pegboards and Pegs	Ideal Toy Co.
Touch and Tell	American Printing House for the Blind

Vocational/Skills

General Theories of Operations	Briggs and Stratton Corporation
Grand Spinet Piano	American Printing House for the Blind
Industrial Arts—Woodworking	Charles A. Bennett Co.
Piano Tuning and Allied Arts	American Printing House for the Blind
Power Technology and Lab Experiences	Delmar Publishers
Typewriting for Elementary School Children	American Printing House for the Blind
Typewriting for Partially Seeing and Blind Pupils	American Printing House for the Blind
Understanding America's Industries	American Printing House for the Blind

Mathematics

Algebra	Addison-Wesley Publishing Co.
Exploring the Metric System	Laidlaw Brothers
Refresher Arithmetic	Allyn and Bacon, Inc.

Social Development

DUSO Kits	American Guidance Service

MULTIPLY HANDICAPPED

Title   **Publisher**

Language Development and
   Reading

Bank Street Readers	The MacMillan Co.
DLM Sound Foundations Program	Developmental Learning Materials
GOAL	Milton Bradley Co.
Language Concepts	Teaching Resources Corporation
Peabody Language Development Kits (2)	American Guidance Service
Peabody Rebus Reading Program	American Guidance Service
Portage Project Checklist	C.E.S.A. 12
Reading Lab	Science Research Associates
Reading Program (Ginn 360)	Ginn and Co.

Mathematics

Count and See	Collier-MacMillan Library
Mathematics Around Us	Scott, Foresman and Co.
Moving Up in Numbers (3)	Developmental Learning Materials
Pacemaker Arithmetic	Fearon Publishers
The Random House Mathematics Program	Random House/Singer School Division
Sorting Box	Developmental Learning Materials

Perceptual and Motor

Auditory-Perception Training-Motor	Developmental Learning Materials
Colored Inch Cubes and Design Cards	Developmental Learning Materials
Hap Palmer Records	Activity Records
Mark-On Wipe-Off	Ideal Toy Corporation

Performance Objectives for Pre-School Children   Delta-Schoolcraft Intermediate School District

Standing Table (or Kneeling Table)   None Given

Triangular and Cylindrical Wedges   None Given

Workjobs   Addison-Wesley Publishing Co.

Professional and Reference

Assessment Manual for Deaf-Blind Multiply Handicapped Children   Midwest Regional Center for Deaf-Blind

Circles, Triangles, and Squares   Collier-MacMillan Library Services

Progress Assessment Chart   Aux Chandelles

Portage Guide to Early Education   Cooperative Educational Service Agency

Affective Development

DUSO Kit   American Guidance Service

PHYSICALLY HANDICAPPED

Title   **Publisher**

Professional and Reference

The Baby Exercise Book   Pantheon Books-Random House

Mothers Can Help   El Paso Rehabilitation Center

Handling the Young Cerebral Palsied at Home   E. P. Dutton and Co., Inc.

Movement and Spatial Awareness in Blind Children and Youth   Charles C Thomas Publisher

Physically Handicapped Children—A Medical Atlas for Teachers   Grune and Stratton, Inc.

Sensorimotor Evaluation and Treatment Procedures   Indiana University Foundation

Sensory Integration and Learning Disorders   Western Psychological Services

Reading

Phonetic Sequence Readers   Modern Curriculum Press

Reader's Digest (2)   Reader's Digest Services

Sullivan Program	McGraw-Hill Book Co.
Tutorgram	Enrichment Reading Corporation of America

Perceptual and Motor

Developmental Learning Materials	Developmental Learning Materials
Perceptual Ditto Masters	Continental Press
Pictures and Patterns	Follett Publishing Co.

Pre-Vocational

Eddie in School	Fearon Publishers
Going Places with Your Personality	Fearon Publishers

Language Development

Peabody Language Development Kits	American Guidance Service

Mathematics

Modern Curriculum Press Math	Modern Curriculum Press

SELECTED PUBLISHERS

AVC Corporation, 2702 Applegate St., Indianapolis, IN 46203

Abingdon Press, 201 Eighth Ave. S., Nashville, TN 37203

ADAPT Press, Inc., 808 W. Avenue North, Sioux Falls, SD 57104

Addison-Wesley Publishing Co., South St., Reading, MA 01867

Allied Education Council, P.O. Box 78, Galien, MI 49113

Allyn and Bacon, Inc., 470 Atlantic Ave., Boston, MA 02210

American Foundation for the Blind, 15 W. 16th St., New York, NY 10011

American Guidance Service, Inc., Publisher's Building, Circle Pines, MN 55014

American Printing House for the Blind, Inc., 1839 Frankfort Ave., Louisville, KY 40206

Ann Arbor Publishers, 611 Church St., Ann Arbor, MI 48104

Ardelle Manning Publications, P.O. Box 125, Palo Alto, CA 94302

Argus Communications, 7440 Natchez, Niles, IL 60648

Au-Vid, Inc., P.O. Box 964, Garden Grove, CA 92642

Audio Visual Communications, 2702 Applegate, Indianapolis, IN 46203

Barnell Loft, Ltd., 958 Church St., Baldwin, NY 11510

Bell and Howell, Audio Visual Products Division, 7100 McCormick Road, Chicago, IL 60645

Charles A. Bennett Co., Inc., 809 W. Detweiler Dr., Peoria, IL 61614

Blissymbolics, 862 Eglinton Ave. E., Toronto, Ontario, Canada M4G 2L1

Bowmar, 622 Rodier Drive, Glendale, CA 91201

William C. Brown Co., 2460 Kerper Boulevard, Dubuque, IA 52001

CEBCO/Standard Publishing, 104 Fifth Ave., New York, NY 10011

CESA No. 12 (See Cooperative Educational Service, Agency 12)

Chandler Publishing Co., Division of Intext Educational Publishers, 124 Spear St., San Francisco, CA 94105

Chapel Hill Training Outreach Project (See Kaplan School Supply)

Christ Church Child Center, 8011 Georgetown Road, Bethesda, MD 20014

Classroom Material Company, 93 Myrtle Drive, Great Neck, NY 11021

Collier-MacMillan (See MacMillan Co.)

Communication Skill Builders, Inc., 21 N. Tyndall Ave., Tucson, AZ 85733

Continental Press, Elizabethtown, PA 17022

David C. Cook, Publisher, School Products Division, Elgin, IL 60120

Cooperative Educational Service, Agency 12, 412 E. Slifer St., Portage, WI 53901

Creative Playthings, P.O. Box 1100, Princeton, NJ 08540

Crown Publishers, Inc., 419 Park Ave. S., New York, NY 10016

John Day Co., Inc., 257 Park Ave. S., New York, NY 10016

Modern Education Publishers, Box 651, San Jose, CA 95106

Delmar Publishers, Inc., Mountainview Ave., Albany, NY 12205

Developmental Learning Materials, 7440 N. Natchez Ave., Niles, IL 60648

Dexter and Westbrook, Ltd., 958 Church St., Baldwin, NY 11510

Dormac, Inc., Box 1622, Lake Oswego, OR 97034

E. P. Dutton and Co., Inc., 201 Park Ave. S., New York, NY 10003

The Economy Co., 5811 West Minnesota, Drawer A, Indianapolis, IN 46241

Edmark Associates, 13249 Northrup Way, Bellevue, WA 98005

Educational Activities, Box 392, Freeport, NY 11520

Educational Development Labs, Inc., Division of McGraw-Hill, New York, NY 10020

Educational Programmers, Inc., P.O. Box 332, Roseburg, OR 97470

Education House, 2619 Ryan Drive, Indianapolis, IN 46220

Educator's Publishing Service, Inc., 75 Moulton St., Cambridge, MA 02138

Elwyn Institute, Elwyn, PA 19603

Encyclopedia Britannica Educational Corporation, 425 N. Michigan Ave., Chicago, IL 60611

ESP, Inc., 2304 E. Johnson, Jonesboro, AR 72401

Evansville-Vanderburgh Schools, 1 Southeast 9th St., Evansville, IN 47708

F. R. Publishing (See Frank Richards Publishing)

Fearon Publishers, Lear Siegler, Inc., Education Division, 6 Davis Drive, Belmont, CA 94002

Fisher Price Toys, East Aurora, NY 14052

Folkways/Scholastic Records, 701 Seventh Ave., New York, NY 10036

Follett Publishing Co., 1010 W. Washington Boulevard, Chicago, IL 60607

Gallaudet College, Kendall Green, Washington, D.C. 20002

Garrard Publishing Co., 1607 N. Market St., Champaign, IL 61820

General Electric Co., Semi-Conductor Products Department, Promotion and Communication, Electronics Park, Building 7, Room 201, Syracuse, NY 13201

General Learning Corporation, Early Learning Division, 250 James St., Morristown, NJ 07960

Ginn and Co., 191 Spring St., Lexington, MA 02173

Go-Mo Products, Inc., 1906 Main St., Cedar Falls, IA 50613

Grosset and Dunlap, Inc., Subsidiary of National General Corporation, 51 Madison Ave., New York, NY 10010

Grune and Stratton, Inc., 111 Fifth Ave., New York, NY 10003

H and H Enterprises, Inc., P.O. Box 3342, Lawrence, KS 66044

Harcourt, Brace, Jovanovich, Inc., 757 Third Ave., New York, NY 10017

Hayes School Publishing Co., 321 Penwood Ave., Wilkinsburg, PA 15221

D. C. Heath Co., 125 Spring St., Lexington, MA 02173

Hoffman Information Systems, 4323 Arden Drive, El Monte, CA 91743

Hubbard Scientific Co., 2855 Shermer Road., Northbrook, IL 60062

Human Developmental Training Institute, 4455 Twain Ave., Suite H, San Diego, CA 92120

Ideal Toy Corporation, 200 Fifth Ave. N., New York, NY 10010

Indiana School for the Deaf, 1200 E. 42nd St., Indianapolis, IN 46205

Indiana University Press, 10th and Morton Streets, Bloomington, IN 47401

Instructo Corporation, Paoli, PA 19301

Interstate Printers and Publishers, 19-27 N. Jackson St., Danville, IL 61832

Jenn Publications, 815-825 E. Market St., Louisville, KY 40201

Kaplan School Supply, 600 Jonestown Road, Winston-Salem, NC 27103

King Features, Education Division, Department 1214, 235 E. 45th St., New York, NY 10017

Laidlaw Brothers, Thacher and Madison, River Forest, IL 60305

Laubach Literacy (See Reader's Press)

Lauri Enterprises Mfgrs., Phillips-Avon, ME 04966

Gary D. Lawson, 9488 Sara St., Elk Grove, CA 95624

The Learning Business, 30961 Agoura Road, Suite 325, Westlake Village, CA 91361

Learning Trends, Division of Globe Book Co., Inc., 115 Fifth Ave., New York, NY 10003

LeCrone Rhythm Record Co., 819 N.W. 92nd St., Oklahoma City, OK 73114

J. B. Lippincott Co., Education Publishing Division, East Washington Square, Philadelphia, PA 19105

Love Publishing Co., 6635 E. Villanova Place, Denver, CO 80222

Lyons and Carnahan Educational Publishers, 407 E. 25th St., Chicago, IL 60616

McCormick-Mathers Publishing Co., 300 Pike St., Cincinnati, OH 45202

McGraw-Hill Book Co., 330 W. 42nd St., New York, NY 10036

The MacMillan Co., 866 Third Ave., New York, NY 10022

Mafex Associates, Inc., 111 Barron Ave., Johnstown, PA 15906

Charles E. Merrill Publishing Co., 1300 Alum Creek Drive, Columbus, OH 43216

Media Materials, Box 168, Riverwood, MD 21139

Melton Book Co., 111 Leslie St., Dallas, TX 75217

Milton Bradley Co., Springfield, MA 01101

Modern Curriculum Press, 13900 Prospest Road, Cleveland, OH 44136

Modern Education Corporation, P.O. Box 721, Tulsa, OK 74101

Monroe Education Center, The American Road, Morris Plains, NJ 07950

The C. V. Mosby Co., Subsidiary of the Times Mirror Co., 11830 Westline Industrial Drive, St. Louis, MI 63141

New Dimensions in Education, 160 Dupont St., Plainview, NY 11803

New Reader's Press, Box 131, Syracuse, NY 13210

Newby Visualanguage, Inc., Box 121-L, Eagleville, PA 19408

Noble and Noble, Publishers, Inc., 1 Dag Hammarskjold Plaza, 245 E. 47th St., New York, NY 10017

Oddo Publishing, Inc., Storybook Acres, Beauregard Boulevard, Fayettville, GA 30214

Open Court Publishing Co., Box 599, La Salle, IL 61301

Pantheon Books, Division of Random House, 201 E. 50th St., New York, NY 10022

Phonovisual Products, Inc., 12216 Parklawn Drive, Rockville, MD 20852

Play 'n Talk, P.O. Box 18804, Oklahoma City, OK 73118

Pictograph Corporation, P.O. Box 2099, Boulder, CO 80302

Playskool (See Milton Bradley Co.)

Pollywog Publications, Inc., 1656 N. Normandy Ave., Chicago, IL 60635

Portage Project (See Cooperative Educational Service, Agency 12)

Psy-Ed Corporation, 635 Madison Ave., New York, NY 10022

Psychological Corporation, 757 Third Ave., New York, NY 10017

Psychotechnics, Inc., 1900 Pickwick Ave., Glenview, IL 60025

Psychological Corporation, 757 Third Ave., New York, NY 10017

Random House, Singer School Division, 201 E. 50th St., New York, NY 10022

Reader's Digest Services, Educational Division, Pleasantville, NY 10578

Research Press, Box 31779, Champaign, IL 61820

Saint John's School for the Deaf, 3680 S. Kinnickinnic Ave., Milwaukee, WI 53207

Frank Schaffer, 26616 Indian Peak Road, Palos Verdes Peninsula, CA 90275

Scholastic Book Services, 904 Sylvan Ave., Englewood Cliffs, NJ 07632

Science Research Associates, Inc., 259 E. Erie St., Chicago, IL 60611

Scott, Foresman and Co., 200 E. Lake Ave., Glenview, IL 60025

Silver-Burdett (See General Learning Corporation)

Simon and Schuster, Inc., 630 Fifth Ave., New York, NY 10020

Singer Society for Visual Education, Education Division, 1345 Diversey Parkway, Chicago, IL 60614

Stanwix House, Inc., 3020 Chartiers Ave., Pittsburgh, PA 15204

Steck-Vaughn Co., P.O. Box 2028, Austin, TX 78767

Syracuse University Press, Box 8, University Station, Syracuse, NY 13201

Teaching Resources Corporation, 100 Boylston St., Boston, MA 02116

Charles C. Thomas Publisher, 301-327 E. Lawrence Ave., Springfield, IL 62703

Trend Enterprises, P.O. Box 8623, White Bear Lake, MN 55110

The Ungame Co., 1440 S. State College Boulevard, Building 2D, Anaheim, CA 92806

United Developmental Service, 1541 Hutchins Ave., Columbus, OH 47201

University of California Press, 2223 Fulton St., Los Angeles, CA 90024

University of Kentucky RIMC-SEIMC, 730 S. Limestone St., Lexington, KY 40506

University Park Press, 233 East Redwood St., Baltimore, MD 21202

Wabash Center, 2000 Greenbush St., Lafayette, IN 47905

Walker Educational Book Co., 720 Fifth Ave., New York, NY 10019

Webster Division, McGraw-Hill Book Co., 1221 Avenue of the Americas, New York, NY 10020

Western Psychological Services, Division of Manson Western Corporation, 12031 Wilshire Boulevard, Los Angeles, CA 90025

Word Making Productions, 60 W. 400 South St., Salt Lake City, UT 84101

Xerox Learning Systems, 600 Madison Ave., New York, NY 10022

Zaner-Bloser Co., 612 N. Park St., Columbus, OH 43215

Zygo Industries, Box 1008, Portland, OR 97207

CONCLUSION

It is now widely recognized at all levels of educational policy-making that instructional materials, media, and educational technology are important in providing quality services for handicapped learners. In order to provide educators with technical assistance, counsel, and materials, the federal government alone has invested millions of dollars since 1966 to support a nationwide system of media and materials support services. Through approaches such as those described in this book, various federal, state, and local agencies and systems hope to meet its challenge of extending appropriate educational opportunities to every handicapped child (Aid for Education of the Handicapped, 1974). We now have at our disposal delivery systems that have the potential to provide all teachers with the capability of selecting, retrieving, adapting, constructing, and evaluating educational materials. The technology for utilization of instructional materials currently exists. If handicapped children are expected to survive in the mainstream, it is essential that their teachers become an integral part of this delivery system.

REFERENCES

Aid for education of the handicapped. 1974. Am. Educ. 10: 29–32.

Barsch, R. 1965. A Movigenic Curriculum. Wisconsin State Department of Education, Madison, Wi.

Bateman, B. 1965. An educator's view of a diagnostic approach to learning disorders. In J. Hellmuth (ed.), Learning Disorders. Vol. I. Special Child Publications of the Seattle Sequin School, Seattle.

Bush, W. J., and Giles, M. T. 1969. Aids to Psycholinguistic Teaching. Charles E. Merrill Books, Columbus, Oh.

Cruickshank, W., Bentzen, F. A., Ratzeburg, F. H., and Tannhauser, M. 1961. A Teaching Method for Brain-Injured and Hyperactive Children. Syracuse University Press, Syracuse, N.Y.

Descoeudres, A. 1928. The Education of Mentally Defective Children. Transl. for the 2nd French ed. by E. F. Row. D. C. Heath and Company, Boston.

Dunn, L. M., and Smith, J. O. 1966. Peabody Language Development Kits. American Guidance Services, Circle Pines, Mn.

Engelmann, S., and Bruner, E. C., 1969. Distar Reading I & II: An Instructional System. Science Research Associates, Chicago.

Engelmann, S., and Carnine, D. 1969. Distar Arithmetic: An Instructional System. Science Research Associates, Chicago.

Engelmann, S., Osborn, L., and Engelmann, T. 1969. Distar Language I: An Instructional System. Science Research Associates, Chicago.

Engelmann, S., and Osborn, J. 1969. Distar Language II: An Instructional System. Science Research Associates, Chicago.

Fernald, G. M. 1943. Remedial Techniques in Basic School Subjects. McGraw-Hill Book Company, New York.

Fernald, G. M., and Keller, H. 1921. The effect of kinesthetic factors in the development of word recognition in the case of non-readers. J. Educ. Res. 4(5): 355–377.

Fitzhugh, K. D., and Fitzhugh, L. 1966. The Fitzhugh Plus Program. Allied Education Council, Galien, Mi.

Friedus, E. 1964. Methodology for the classroom teacher. In J. Hellmuth (ed.), The Special Child in Century 21. Special Child Publications, Seattle.

Frostig, M., and Horne, D. 1964. The Frostig Program for the Development of Visual Perception. Follett Publishing Company, Chicago.

Frostig, M., Lefever, W., and Whittlesey, J. R. B. 1964. The Marianne Frostig Developmental Test of Visual Perception. 1963 Standardization. Consulting Psychologists Press, Palo Alto, Ca.

Getman, G. H. 1965. The visuomotor complex in the acquisition of learning skills. In B. Straub and J. Hellmuth (eds.), Learning Disorders. Vol. I. Special Child Publications, Seattle.

Getman, G. H., Kane, E. R., Halgren, M., and McKee, G. W. 1968. Developing Learning Readiness. Webster Division, McGraw-Hill Book Company, Manchester, Mo.

Gillingham, A., and Stillman, B. 1966. Remedial Training for Children with Specific Disability in Reading, Spelling, and Penmanship. 7th ed., Educators Publishing Service, Cambridge, Ma.

Goldstein, H. 1974. Social Learning Curriculum. Charles E. Merrill Books, Columbus, Oh.

Goldstein, H. 1976. Curriculum design for handicapped students. High School J. LIX: 290–301.

Heiss, W. E., and Mischio, G. S. 1972. Designing curriculum for the educable mentally retarded. In E. L. Meyen, G. A. Vergason, and R. J. Whelan (eds.), Strategies for Teaching Exceptional Children. Love Publishing Company, Denver.

Itard, J. M. 1932. The Wild Boy of Aveyron. Transl. by George and Muriel Humphrey. Appleton-Century-Crofts, New York.

Karnes, M. 1972. Goal Program Language Development Games. Milton Bradley, Springfield, Ma.

Kaufman, M. J., Semmel, M. I., and Agard, J. A. 1973. Project PRIME: Interim Report—Year I, 1971–1972 (purpose and procedures). Unpublished manuscript, U.S. Office of Education, Bureau for Intramural Research Program.

Kephart, N. C. 1960. The Slow Learner in the Classroom. Charles E. Merrill, Books, Columbus, Oh.

Kirk, S. A. 1972. Educating Exceptional Children. 2nd ed., Houghton Mifflin Company, Boston.

Kirk, S. A., and Johnson, G. O. 1951. Educating the Retarded Child. The Riverside Press, Cambridge.

Kirk, S., and Kirk, W. 1971. Psycholinguistic Learning Disabilities: Diagnosis and Remediation. University of Illinois Press, Urbana.

Lance, W. D. 1975. Instructional materials for the mentally retarded: A review of selected literature. Educ. Train. Ment. Retard. 10: 161–166.

Lerner, J. W. 1976. Theories, Diagnosis, Teaching Strategies: Children with Learning Disabilities. Houghton Mifflin Company, Boston.

McCarthy, J. J., and McCarthy, J. F. 1969. Learning Disabilities. Allyn and Bacon, Boston.

Minskoff, E. H., Wiseman, D. E., and Minskoff, J. C. 1973. The MWM Program of Developing Language Abilities. Educational Performance Associates, Ridgefield, N.J.

Monroe, M. 1932. Children Who Cannot Read. University of Chicago Press. Chicago.

Montessori, M. 1912. Montessori Method. Transl. by A. E. George. Frederick A. Stodes Company, New York.

Orton, S. T. 1928. Specific reading disability—Strephosymbolia. J. Am. Med. Assoc. 90.

Orton, S. T. 1937. Reading, Writing, and Speech Problems in Children. Chapman and Hall Ltd., London.

Seguin, E. 1846. Traitement Moral, Hygiene, et Education des Idiots et des Autres Enfants Arrieres. J. B. Balliere, Paris.

Smith, J. O., and Mueller, W. 1969. Research and development of the Peabody Language Development Kits. In J. Hellmuth (ed.), Educational Therapy. Vol. 2. Special Child Publications, Seattle.

Strauss, A. A., and Lehtinen, L. 1947. Psychopathology of the Brain-Injured Child. Grune and Stratton, New York.

Telford, C. W., and Sawrey, J. M. 1972. The Exceptional Individual. 2nd ed. Prentice-Hall, Englewood Cliffs, N.J.

Thiagarajan, S., Semmel, D. S., and Semmel, M. I. 1974. Instructional Development for Training Teachers of Exceptional Children: A Sourcebook. The Council for Exceptional Children, Reston, Va.

TIME (Teacher Initiated Materials Evaluation). Project report: An aid in the selection of special education materials 1977. Indiana Department of Public Instruction, Indianapolis.

Wallin, J. E. 1955. Education of Mentally Handicapped Children. Harper and Row, New York.

Index